Second Roxbury Edition

MAX WEBER

The Protestant Ethic and the Spirit of Capitalism

Translated by Talcott Parsons

Revised Introduction by
Randall Collins
University of Pennsylvania

Includes Weber's Essay
The Protestant Sects and the Sprit of Capitalism

Roxbury Publishing Company

Library of Congress Cataloging-in-Publication Data

Weber, Max, 1864-1920.
[Die Protestantische Ethik und der Geist des Kapitalismus. English]
The Protestant ethic and the spirit of capitalism/Max Weber;
translated by Talcott Parsons; new introduction by Randall Collins.
—2nd ed.
p. cm.
Includes bibliographical references and index.
ISBN 0-935732-90-X
1. Capitalism—Religious aspects—Christianity. 2. Sociology, Christian.
3. Christian ethics. 4. Protestant work ethic.
I. Title.
BR115.C3W413 1998   97-34399
306.6—dc31   CIP

Publisher and Editor: Claude Teweles
Production Editor: Dawn VanDercreek
Production Assistant: David Massengill
Typography: Synergistic Data Systems
Cover Design: Marnie Deacon Kenney

Printed on acid-free paper in the United States of America. This paper meets the standards for recycling of the Environmental Protection Agency.

ISBN: 0-935732-90-X

ROXBURY PUBLISHING COMPANY
P.O. Box 491044
Los Angeles, California 90049-9044
Tel: (213) 653-1068 • Fax: (213) 653-4140
Email: roxbury@crl.com

CONTENTS

Translator's Preface v
Introduction by Randall Collins vii
Essay: *The Protestant Sects and the Spirit
   of Capitalism* by Max Weber xlii
Max Weber's Introduction to the Sociology of Religion . . . 13*

THE PROTESTANT ETHIC
AND THE SPIRIT OF CAPITALISM

Part I:
The Problem
Chapter I.

Religious Affiliation and Social Stratification 35

Chapter II.

The Spirit of Capitalism 47

Chapter III.

Luther's Conception of the Calling
   Task of the Investigation 79

Part II:
The Practical Ethics of the
Ascetic Branches of Protestantism
Chapter IV.

The Religious Foundations of Worldly Asceticism 95
   A. Calvinism 98
   B. Pietism 128
   C. Methodism 139
   D. The Baptist Sects 144

Chapter V.

Asceticism and the Spirit of Capitalism 155

Notes 185
Index 285

---

*In order to consistently reproduce the translator's original pagination, the text of the translation begins on page 13.

TRANSLATOR'S PREFACE

Talcott Parsons (1930)

Max Weber's essay, *Die protestantische Ethik und der Geist des Kapitalismus*, which is here translated, was first published in the *Archiv für Sozialwissenschaft und Sozialpolitik*, Volumes XX and XXI, for 1904-5. It was reprinted in 1920 as the first study in the ambitious series *Gesammelte Aufsätze zur Religionssoziologie*, which was left unfinished by Weber's untimely death in that same year. For the new printing he made considerable changes, and appended both new material and replies to criticism in footnotes. The translation has, however, been made directly from this last edition. Though the volume of footnotes is excessively large, so as to form a serious detriment to the reader's enjoyment, it has not seemed advisable either to omit any of them or attempt to incorporate them into the text. As it stands it shows most plainly how the problem has grown in Weber's own mind, and it would be a pity to destroy that for the sake of artistic perfection. A careful perusal of his notes is, however, especially recommended to the reader, since a great deal of important material is contained in them. The fact that they are printed separately from the main text should not be allowed to hinder their use. The translation is, as far as possible, faithful to the text, rather than attempting to achieve any more than ordinary, clear English style. Nothing has been altered, and only a few comments to clarify obscure points and to refer the reader to related parts of Weber's work have been added.

The Introduction, which is placed before the main essay, was written by Weber in 1920 for the whole series on the Sociology of Religion. It has been included in this translation because it gives some of the general background of ideas and problems into which Weber himself meant this particular study to fit. That has seemed particularly desirable since, in the voluminous discussion which has grown up in Germany around Weber's essay, a great deal of misplaced criticism has been due to the failure properly to appreciate the scope and limitations of the study. While it is impossible to appreciate that fully without a thorough study of Weber's sociological work as a whole, this brief introduction should suffice to prevent a great deal of misunderstanding.

The series of which this essay forms a part was, as has been said, left unfinished at Weber's death. The first volume only had been prepared for the press by his own hand. Besides the parts translated here, it contains a short, closely related study, *Die protestantischen Sekten und der Geist des Kapitalismus*; a general introduction to the further studies of particular religions which as a whole he called *Die Wirtschaftsethik der Weltreligionen*; and a long study of Confucianism and Taoism. The second and third volumes, which were published after his death, without the thorough revision which he had contemplated, contain studies of Hinduism and Buddhism and Ancient Judaism. In addition he had done work on other studies, notably of Islam, Early Christianity, and Talmudic Judaism, which were not yet in a condition fit for publication in any form. Nevertheless, enough of the whole series has been preserved to show something of the extraordinary breadth and depth of Weber's grasp of cultural problems. What is here presented to English-speaking readers is only a fragment, but it is a fragment which is in many ways of central significance for Weber's philosophy of history, as well as being of very great and very general interest for the thesis it advances to explain some of the most important aspects of modern culture.

Talcott Parsons
Cambridge, Mass., U.S.A.
January 1930

INTRODUCTION

by Randall Collins

A classic is a book one can read over and over without becoming bored. A classic has depth, echoes that resonate, such that each reading gives something new. *The Protestant Ethic and the Spirit of Capitalism* is not as dense with ideas as some of Weber's other works, such as his encyclopedic *Economy and Society*, parts of which I have read at least ten times but always with the question "Have I actually read this before?" *The Protestant Ethic* is Weber's best-written and most accessible book, which is one reason for its popularity. Another reason is its layers of significance. It has something to appeal to the introductory sociology student and also to sophisticates sifting the most refined theoretical and meta-theoretical issues. Here one finds Weber as a modernist, or postmodernist if you like; as a conflict theorist or functionalist; as a cultural interpreter but also an analyst of rationality.

The Protestant Ethic reaches the ultimate mark of success: people who have never read it know about it. In the world of educated people, everyone knows (or thinks he or she knows) "the Weber thesis." Such success depends, at one level, upon crystalizing the argument into a few key phrases. Every word in the title conveys what Weber wanted to get across: the Protestant has an "ethic," and "capitalism" has a "spirit"; and the second pair flows from the first pair. The phrases epitomize the intellectual struggle that helped make the argument famous: that Weber turned Marx on his head, making "materialism" depend upon ideas and culture, i.e. on "ethic" and "spirit." The words have acquired a life of their own; now one hears sportscasters talk about an athlete having "the work ethic," probably without ever knowing who Max Weber was.

Very few works of social science reach this outermost popular level. (The nearest example in the late twentieth century is probably Thomas Kuhn's terms "paradigm" and "paradigm revolution," which circulate among people who may never have read his book, *The Structure of Scientific Revolutions*.) In a great classic, the outer layers lead to the inner layers. Weber's "spirit of capitalism" reminds a sociologist of his famous distinction between "traditional" and "rational" capitalism, the latter summed up in his memorable line about the "iron cage" in which modern people live. If one has an eye for it, one can find Weber's craftsmanship throughout the writing, such as the deft way he pays deference to

vii

historical specialists while going on to assert his right to make general statements, as an outsider, which cut across the turf-lines of their fields. One could take *The Protestant Ethic* as a writing manual for a scholarly bestseller.

The Argument of the Protestant Ethic

Weber sets up his argument by noting that in modern times Protestants are more likely to be businessmen, as well as skilled workers, than are Catholics. (The sexist language is intentional; Weber was writing about an historical time when societies were male-dominated.) His evidence comes from Germany around 1900, which raises the question: why should effects linger this long from an historical event, the Protestant Reformation, which began around 1520? In fact, the effects have lingered and spread well beyond Weber's Germany. The United States of America, which began as a Puritan settlement, was, even in Weber's day, the most capitalist society in the world. Research since then has shown a similar pattern, up to a point: American Protestants dominated business and the skilled working-class trades until about 1960. After that, however, Catholics caught up with American Protestants and even overtook them in the higher occupations.

Does this mean that the effects of Protestantism on capitalist business were mistaken, or does it mean that the Protestant Ethic has finally dissipated in modern or, as some say, "postmodern" America? Before jumping to either conclusion, we might note that Protestantism has been spreading rapidly in recent decades in Latin America, as traditional Catholics have been converting to Protestant sects. This religious movement has coincided with the expansion of capitalism in Latin America, and it is just those converts to Protestantism who are leading the drive to expand small business. It looks as if the Protestant Ethic and the growth of capitalism are being played out yet again on another terrain.

Assuming there is a connection between Protestantism and capitalism, how can it be explained? Weber takes issue with a long-standing interpretation of the Protestant Reformation, which regards it as a decline in the religiousness of the Middle Ages. Protestantism was not a move to secularization, but exactly the opposite, an increase in religious intensity. Protestantism did not cause a shift toward worldly enjoyment, which was already quite well advanced in the Catholic societies of the Renaissance. The importance of the Reformation, instead, was the impetus Protestantism gave to the combination of piety with business.

Weber introduces a crucial distinction. Capitalism was not invented by the Reformation; it existed in many societies throughout medieval and ancient history. There were merchants in ancient Greece, slave markets in Rome, all manner of business enterprise in China and India, merchant caravans in the Islamic world, and merchant guilds which dominated the cities of Italy, Germany, and the Low Countries in the Middle Ages. Capitalism was not lacking; what was lacking was a spirit of capitalism, and an organization of capitalism, distinctive to modern capitalism. Weber refers to the two kinds of capitalism as, on the one hand, "traditional" capitalism, and, on the other hand, modern or "rational" capitalism.

Traditional capitalists were certainly interested in making profits; but there was nothing about this that could be regarded as a social "ethic." The ideal was to acquire social position and, of course, the money to support it, but not to become bogged down in the struggle to make money. A comfortable aristocratic lifestyle was the goal, and business was carried out with an attitude of getting it over with as easily as possible. The most lucrative form of capitalist enterprise consisted of long-distance trade, preferably in luxury items on which a large profit could be made: spices from the Indies, silk from China, gold and jewels from the fabled mines the Spanish conquistadors sought in the Americas. Weber calls one version of this "politically oriented adventurers' capitalism" or "booty capitalism," a form of investment combining military and political expeditions with the expectation of making a business profit. Greek, Roman, and Islamic armies made money by capturing slaves; other armies established plantations or conquered trade routes. In the civilian version of "political adventurers' capitalism," prominent during the early modern period in France and other European states, an entrepreneur would buy up government offices in return for a split of their revenue; for instance, one could become a "tax farmer," buying the right to collect taxes in return for a cut of the take.

Weber regards all these forms of "traditional" capitalism as sharp contrasts to "rationalized" modern capitalism. Rational capitalism is based not on luxury trades but on mass production of the commodities of everyday life. The medieval merchant sought to make a fortune out of a single cargo of jewels; the modern capitalist makes a far bigger fortune out of mass marketing humble commodities such as tires or toilet paper. Hence the traditional attitude, the greedy maximization of profit in a one-shot enterprise, has been overcome by a new attitude which relies upon the accumulation of many small gains. Instead of high prices and windfall profits, moderate prices and high, steady sales are the driving force of modern capitalism. It is for this reason, incidentally, that Weber in his later works notes that modern capitalism is not driven by the industrial revolution and the invention of new technologies, but the other way around: mass-production technologies are of no use until there is a mass market for everyday goods. Such technology is pointless in the luxury trades. Modern machinery is the result of a prior revolution in the spirit of capitalism.

Weber finds evidence of the existence of this rational capitalist spirit in the writings of Benjamin Franklin during the 1730s and 40s. Franklin is famous in American folklore as an inventor, patriotic politician, writer, and printer. He was also a successful businessman, and his maxims exemplify the new attitude for doing business: "time is money," "a penny saved is a penny earned," "waste not want not," and so forth. The attitude is that hard work and saving one's money are not only a way of making more money, but an ethical obligation. Wasting time and frivolously spending money are wrong; although Franklin no longer put it in religious language, the carryover is unmistakable: it is a sin.

The religious impetus to rational capitalism emerged in several stages. The most extreme form was Calvinism, a doctrine which spread from Geneva, to the Netherlands, to England, and then traveled with the Puritans who settled New England in the 1620s. John Calvin, who led a religious uprising to take over the city of Geneva during the 1540s, formulated the extreme version with his doctrine of predestination. Calvinism is a branch of so-called "radical" Protestantism; there is also a milder form which began with Martin Luther, who started the original Protestant revolt against the Roman Catholic papacy in 1517. Weber's book thus traces several levels of the development of Protestantism: first Luther's conception of a calling; then Calvinism; finally, he cleans up the loose ends by dealing with some of the other "radical" Protestant sects, what he calls the "ascetic branches of Protestantism," such as the Pietists, Quakers, Methodists, and Baptists.

Luther's crucial contribution was to formulate the idea that work is a "calling." The term is familiar today among Protestant ministers. If a preacher receives a job offer to go to another church, it is referred to as "receiving a call," with the sense of "a call from Above." Luther originated the doctrine that every kind of work, every activity in the ordinary world, is a religiously sanctioned activity. A person is "called" to work in business, or as a laborer, or a farmer. Weber regards this as a key step in turning religious motivations in the direction of ordinary work, which would ultimately lead to the new spirit of capitalism. However, Luther was only the first, half-way step. Luther emphasized traditional social activities, including obedience to traditionally constituted state authority. Luther preached adjustment to the world. He was a social conservative. It was the ascetic sects, going beyond Luther, which harnessed religious motivation to change the world and thereby carried through the revolution in social attitudes.

The ascetic Protestants, in turn, divided into two branches. On one side were the Calvinists, whose key doctrinal point was predestination; on the other were the radical sects (Quakers, Baptists, etc.) who rejected life in the ordinary world entirely and tried to live like the community of early Christian Apostles. Weber regards these radical sects as somewhat tangential to his main argument, although he notes they had important social effects in their own right, including their influence upon American democracy. But his key interest focuses on the Calvinists, for they led the Puritan revolution in England during the 1640s, and it was an offshoot of this group which settled New England and imparted its spirit to American capitalism.

The Calvinist doctrine of predestination holds that God has already picked out who will be saved for Heaven and who will be punished in Hell. Weber argued that this belief must have given rise to a very strong anxiety, as believers wondered whether they were in the category of the saved or the damned. The doctrine holds that we are all sinners, all equally worthy of damnation; our sins are so great that nothing we can do can make us worthy of salvation. Only God, of His own will, mercifully picks out the few who are elected to be saved. Hence doing good works, "praying, going to church, repenting, giving to charity," count as nothing toward one's salvation. But there is one pathway which is psychologically comforting: to live a godly life in every respect, every moment of the day. If one does this, turning one's work into a calling, restricting any impulse to frivolous pleasure, one comes to experience a feeling of assurance that indeed one is a member of the Elect. The Puritan, ascetic lifestyle thus emerges as a response to the doctrine of predestination. Its effects, in turn, are to bring worldly economic activity under religious control and to harness religious motivation to a new spirit of capitalism.

The doctrine of predestination is a set of ideas, and here Weber seems to be giving a very forceful example of how ideas can influence social history, rather than vice versa. It is possible for us to develop other interpretations of what Weber is showing. Weber is dealing with a time when religion was an omnipresent part of daily life. Preachers were the main source of news, education, and even entertainment; the church was the center of village life, and religious ceremonies marked the activities of urban guilds and of aristocratic households. In short, religion comprised not just ideas; it was *social practice*.

The political upheavals which took place during the Reformation broke apart the routine of daily living. Clergy allied with the aristocracy or with the state were replaced by a new type of privately ordained minister; cities became independent under new religious leaders; wars were fought; disbelievers were expelled or killed. The Reformation and the religious wars and revolutions, which continued through the 1500s and into the late 1600s, caused an upheaval in everyday life. Theological beliefs were not just an esoteric concern of church intellectuals, but matters widely discussed among ordinary people. Ideas became symbols of contrasting ways of life. Weber notes that ideas were so important at this time in history because they were closely connected with action; he avoids the question of which came first, ideas or action, insofar as both made up a coherent whole. (Robert Wuthnow's book, cited in this volume's "Suggested Further Reading," gives a brilliant analysis of this complex of ideas and social practices at the time of the Reformation.)

The Calvinistic Puritans, above all, were leaders in the breakthrough to a new lifestyle. The significance of this breakthrough can be seen by contrasting it with the lifestyle and mode of belief that preceded it. Medieval Catholicism was by no means a lax religious system. Weber points out that it channeled religious energies into practices which flowed in a direction away from any possibility of changing worldly economic life. Catholicism emphasized the pursuit of salvation by "good works"; this meant all the things a good Christian could do in order to attain salvation. These included praying, confession, taking part in church ritual, giving charitable contributions to the poor and sick, making pilgrimages to holy places, and worshiping holy relics. Weber comments that the doctrine and practice of "good works" meant that a good Catholic had a kind of spiritual bank account: one acquired sins, but against these one could set off one's repentances and good works. Weber argues that this led to a cycle of sin and repentance, rather than a continuous motivation to make the world into a perfect godly place; it siphoned off the anxiety and the religious motivation, which the Calvinists managed to harness.

There is a second way in which medieval Catholicism siphoned off religious motivation. Christians were divided into two classes: a religious elite of monks and nuns, as compared to ordinary laity. The full-scale pressure to live a godly life was reserved for the monks and nuns, who withdrew from the world into monasteries, and applied themselves to the powerful asceticism of continuous prayer, bodily mortification, and spiritual discipline. Monks displaced the religious energy in a direction away from changing the world; hence it was crucial that Protestantism should eliminate monasteries. Martin Luther, who began as a Catholic monk, returned to the world and married. He became a Protestant minister, living among ordinary laity. By eliminating the monkhood, the level of religious motivation was spread from an elite to the entire population of believers. Without monasteries, henceforward every Protestant Christian had to live the disciplined life of a monk, but applied now to the daily activities of the ordinary world.

Weber has been sketching a causal chain across several links. First, medieval Catholic Christianity harnessed religious energy, but only for the monks and nuns. Second, Luther's Reformation, which abolished the monasteries, made ordinary occupations into religious "callings." Third, radical Calvinism, which turned up the pressure with the doctrine of predestination, made everyday life a constant drive for moral perfection. The economic effects of Calvinism were to set loose the spirit of rationalized capitalism: honest dealings in business, rather than greedy search for a maximal profit; reliable, steady production and sales, turning into a system of mass production; and continuous savings and reinvestment into further business growth.

This led to a fourth stage: the Puritan capitalists began to grow rich. Continuous hard work, combined with ploughing back profits into business expansion, brought about business success. The earlier religious doctrines began to die out. Ben Franklin was no longer a Puritan or a Calvinist. The Americans of his day were turning to Deism, or to other rationalized doctrines which downplayed the supernatural. But the spirit lived on in a secularized form, in the utilitarianism and individualism which comes out in Franklin's worldly maxims, and continued to give an impetus to work, to save, to reinvest, to maintain self-control, and to keep striving for economic success. Modern capitalism took off; it no longer needed the religious motivation which had inspired it.

Was there a fifth stage? Weber implies that by his day, around 1900, even the echoes of religious belief had become superfluous. "The Puritan wanted to work in a calling; we are forced to do so." Like it or not, the momentum of capitalism carries us along with it; to keep from falling to the bottom of the class structure, we need to scramble for success. "Since asceticism undertook to remodel the world and to work out its ideals in the world, material goods have gained an increasing and finally an inexorable power over the lives of men as at no previous period in history." Victorious capitalism no longer needs a religious impetus. Weber even comments that "In the field of its highest development, in the United States, the pursuit of wealth, stripped of its religious and ethical meaning, tends to become associated with purely mundane passions, which often actually give it the character of sport" (quotations from pages 181-2).

Is Weber right about this? Have we outgrown religious capitalism entirely? The spread of capitalism around the world is far from dead. Recall the comment at the outset of this summary, that ascetic Protestant sects have been spreading in Latin America and elsewhere in the very places where the new round of capitalism has been growing. In America, the homeground of the most extreme forms both of the Protestant Ethic and of modern capitalism, religious revivals have taken place periodically, including the most recent round, from the 1970s to the 90s, which coincides with another upsurge in the popularity of capitalism.

Weber wrote about a limited segment of history and expressed himself cautiously about what might happen in the future. He is now part of the generation of our great-grandparents. Nevertheless, in many respects, especially for Americans, his vision is fresher now than he himself would have ever expected it to be.

The Sources of Weber's Argument

It is always possible to construct a list of antecedent authors and present them as "influences" on any particular thinker. We could of course do this for Weber, but the result would be less to clarify than to muddy the originality of his argument and to obscure the passion and immediacy of Weber's vision on this topic. The Protestant Ethic and its ramifications became something of an obsession with Weber. The reasons that his first writings on the subject are so powerful, and why they pulled him onward into one ramification after another, can be seen much more clearly if we approach the question of "sources" from the point of view of Weber's personal

xiv

experience. Two personal conditions are the key: the conflicting "spirits" which Weber felt in his parents, and his visit to America in 1904.

Weber's life is a kind of Freudian melodrama, complete with family conflict, neurotic breakdown, and therapeutic recovery. He grew up in the privileged elite of German political and academic life. His father was the leader of a political party in the *Reichstag* in Berlin. During his youth Max had already met, in gatherings at home, the most famous professors in Germany; by the time he finished his university studies, he was being groomed as their successor, as the scholar who would carry social science to a new level. His only problem was to decide whether to become a leading politician or a famous academic, or perhaps both. Suddenly, at age 33, he had a severe attack of what can only be described as psychosomatic illness. He could no longer lecture or make political speeches and had to retire from his profession. He spent his time visiting psychiatrists, taking rest cures, going on long trips where he whiled away the hours looking idly out of hotel windows, scarcely able to work or sometimes even to think. Gradually his condition improved. In 1904, after seven years of his psychoneurotic incapacitation, he traveled to the United States. Something about America jolted him out of his illness. Returning to Germany, the first thing he published was *The Protestant Ethic and the Spirit of Capitalism*. From then on, his enormous capacity for work-his own work ethic-was unleashed, resulting in thousands of pages by the end of his life.

The Protestant Ethic and the Spirit of Capitalism was the turning point in Weber's life. It was as if the argument had been bottled up inside him, while he brooded on it unconsciously for seven years.[*] When he turned his attention to America, the argument came spilling out. Thus, cured of his neurosis, he went on to become a great sociologist, some say the greatest of all time. What was it about America that was so consequential? Generalizing from his own observations of America, where he visited German-American rela-

---

[*] More precisely, one should say that Weber was working through the neurotic conflict during a period of time when he was gradually coming to formulate his Protestant Ethic thesis. He himself declared he had inklings of the idea in the 1890s, and he began to work on writing it in the summer just before starting on his American journey. Since his family had many American relatives, and American capitalism was already part of his awareness, circumstances probably enabled him to gain some insight into his own personal conflicts even before his visit. It is clear, however, that his actual visit to America was an exhilarating experience and marked the transition to a new intellectual as well as personal stage in his life.

tives, Weber noted that America was both the most capitalist country in the world and the most religious. And he saw the connection between the two: America was so successful at capitalism because it was so Christian. Everything fell into place; the American colonies had originated with a group of radical Protestants, the Puritans, who escaped from Holland and then England in the 1600s to find a land where Protestantism would truly be put into practice. It was, and capitalist America was the result.

From here it is clear how Weber constructed the Protestant Ethic: reading Ben Franklin to find the American spirit of capitalism, then reading John Bunyan's *Pilgrim's Progress* (an extremely popular book in America in the 1700s and early 1800s) to immerse himself in the ethic of the radical Protestants at the time of the English Civil War, and then recalling the connections to Calvin's doctrine of predestination, Martin Luther's concept of the calling, and the rest of the chain as Weber sought ever further back into the causes of Protestantism and modern capitalism. Here we are tracing the intellectual roots of Weber's idea. But let us stick to the personal side, for we have not yet answered a crucial question: why did his encounter with America cure him of his neurosis? His flash of insight into understanding the connection between Protestantism and capitalism set him free to work again; he must have been emotionally paralyzed over something which related to this question. Why should it make such a personal difference? *The Protestant Ethic and the Spirit of Capitalism* is a passionately written book; all the impacted energies of Weber's life came out in it. It is a veritable Freudian catharsis, a releasing of the floods of inner conflict which had incapacitated him for seven years.

Weber never visited Sigmund Freud. In fact, Freud was just developing his own theory of neurosis during the years when Weber was undergoing his travails. A few years later, when both Weber and Freud were becoming famous, Weber became interested in the Freudian movement and even took some of its younger followers under his protection when they fell into legal troubles over their sexual radicalism. Though there was a sexual element in Weber's neurosis, that is not the main point. (The curious may pursue it by referring to Chapter 1 of my book *Max Weber: a Skeleton Key*, cited in "Suggested Further Reading" at the end of this Introduction.) Some of Freud's more general principles regarding the sources of psychological conflicts point us to the key to Weber's problem.

Weber's neurosis clearly derived from a conflict between his parents. They were opposite personality types. His father was domineering, authoritarian, self-indulgent; he was proud of his own success and social position and indulged in a hedonistic lifestyle. In this era of Victorian hypocrisy, he must have clashed deeply with his wife who was sexually very puritanical. Max's mother believed piously that religion should guide one's daily life. Anything but self-indulgent, she believed that worldly goods were in trust from God, and she scrimped at home so that she could give charity to the poor. The parents clashed in politics as well: Max's father was a leader of the political party of the center-right, representing the interests of the big capitalist manufacturers; his mother favored the Christian socialists.

The conflict came to a head in the summer of 1897 when Max's mother, struggling to get away from the dominance of her husband, came to visit Max in Heidelberg. The father showed up in Heidelberg soon after, and a long-standing family quarrel burst out in the open. Max took his mother's side and threw his father out of the house. Max never saw his father again. Before they could reconcile, the father died of a hemorrhage.

Max now sank into his illness: at first insomnia and inability to work; then he could not face a public audience and had to give up his academic and political activities. By the next year, he was stricken by physical symptoms; his arms became paralyzed when he tried to reach up to trim the Christmas tree. In clinical terms, this is a classic example of the psychosomatic illness technically called "hysteria," when conflicting psychological impulses freeze up the muscles so that one cannot move a limb. I would suggest that the gesture of reaching up over his head was part of the complex that kept him from speaking in public; Max had embarked on a political career and was known as a powerful, even fiery orator, probably complete with dramatic hand gestures to emphasize his points. Max's neurosis meant that he could not follow in his father's footsteps and become a leading politician. All this fits the rather obvious Freudian interpretation that Max was angry at his father, that he felt guilt about having rebelled against him, and even that he felt he had killed him. And since Max had identified with his father, his rebellion was also a revolt against a part of himself.

The most valid point of Freudian theory (and I am by no means suggesting that we accept unconditionally everything in the Freudian system) is that repression takes place because there are things that one cannot bear to think about. Repression leads to depression and depletion of emotional energy, when two unconscious forces block one another. Max Weber obviously felt hatred toward and guilt about his father, and he probably came to recognize this. What made his neurosis more severe was something deeper, which he could not stand to have enter his consciousness in any form: that he also hated his mother, with her puritanism, her attempts (highly successful, in fact) to control his sex life, and her interfering in his political career by pressing him toward Christian-socialist causes. His mother constituted a second, rival form of control that had seized Max from within. Later he was to write about the period when the neurosis was ebbing away that he felt "an icy hand has released me." The icy hand could not have been his father; it was the puritanical spirit of his mother.

Weber's father and mother struggled inside him for control of his spirit. Finding a way to depict each of them by an historical emblem allowed him suddenly to see a way clear from his neurosis, by writing his way out of it. His father and mother provided recognition of the several ingredients of the Protestant Ethic. I say several ingredients because what Weber describes in *The Protestant Ethic and the Spirit of Capitalism* is a conflict. He saw, on the one hand, the traditional way of doing business. Then the Protestant Ethic came in, bringing about the transformation of capitalism. Finally the wheel turned again, and the unintended consequence was to make capitalists rich—and the Protestant Ethic faded into the self-absorbed luxury of the wealthy.

Revealingly, when Weber wants to bring out the contrast, he gives a description of how things were "until about the middle of the past century . . . in the Continental textile industry" (pages 66–68). He is not referring to any scholarly study; his picture is something that he knows personally. For Weber's own family had made its fortune in the textile business, and his relatives still operated the factories. The name "Weber" itself means "weaver," indicating that the family had been identified with this occupation for centuries. His picture of the old days depicts a comfortable routine: the linen merchant receives cloth from the local peasants, pays them the customary price, and ships it off to his usual customers. Most of the year hours are short and competition is lax. The businessman has plenty of time to play the leading citizen of some picturesque little German city, drinking in the tavern, smoking a pipe, like a character in the opera *Die Meistersinger von Nürnberg*. One day (Weber goes on), a new character appears on the scene: a young man who no longer sits around and waits for the traditional routines to unfold, but who goes out aggressively into the countryside, reorganizing the cloth weavers, bringing them under control in a factory. With any time he has to spare, he goes on business trips, soliciting customers, luring them with lower prices and higher turnover. The old leisurely pace is disrupted; the old easygoing merchants who cannot keep up are driven out of business, and hard-driving capitalist competition and growth take its place.

It was these two sides of capitalism and their ethical counterparts that Weber saw in his parents, and through them, in his whole family background. Since they were living in a later generation, the religious and economic themes were mingled in them in complex ways and were passed on into Weber's own personality in an even more complex mix. When he spoke of the "ghost of dead religious beliefs" which "prowls about in our lives" (page 182), he was probably speaking first and foremost about himself.

The fact that we can perform a quasi-Freudian analysis does not imply that the Protestant Ethic was nothing but a projection of Weber's neurosis. On the contrary, the conflict between his father and mother may have been a particularly dramatic way for him to become aware of the Protestant Ethic. My recounting of his personal history is intended to show that the Protestant Ethic is a conflict between different ways of life. These forces behind Weber's realization of this conflict were real enough. His family embodied every aspect of the history of capitalism and religious ethics; thus Max Weber was in the best spot to discover it for sociology. Another personal circumstance comes into play: because he had relatives in America, and because he visited them (or even to some degree in planning such a visit), he got the insight which unraveled and corroborated the pattern. That the insight came out of his personal experience is not a criticism of the validity of his theory, although, of course, it is not a proof of it either. The validity of his scholarship has to be judged in the usual way, in its own terms.

Two Versions of Weber's Argument:
Early and Late

The Protestant Ethic and the Spirit of Capitalism, in its English-language version, is really two books in one. Weber wrote about the connection between religion and capitalism at two different times in his life: first in 1904, which is the original Protestant Ethic argument; later (for the most part during 1916–19) he came back to the question, broadening the argument to compare Christianity and Judaism with the other major world religions, regarding their effects upon economic development. To put it a little too simply, one could say early Weber deals with the Protestant Ethic, and late Weber deals with "the Judeo-Christian Ethic" and its effect upon capitalism. Of course, there is a connection between the two arguments, since radical Protestantism is rooted in the Judeo-Christian tradition, and early Protestants (especially during the English Civil War and during the founding of Puritan New England) thought they were returning to early Christianity and even to the Judaism of the Old Testament.

In the process of expanding his argument, Weber researched and wrote many more volumes on the religions of China, India, and ancient Judaism; he intended to write further volumes on Islam, ancient Greece, and early Christianity, and on medieval Catholicism, but he died in 1920 before he could do so. He did manage to complete a lengthy treatise on the sociology of religion and an entire encyclopedia, *Economy and Society*, which treats every major social institution, ranging from the family to politics, from the point of view of its effects upon the rise of modern capitalism. In *The Protestant Ethic*, Weber said he did not intend to put forward a one-sided spiritual explanation of the rise of capitalism, to contrast with the one-sided Marxist materialist explanation; he was only accentuating one process by subjecting it to closer examination. Most of the rest of his life work was devoted to making good on that promise; in his later works he shows all the material and structural conditions which mingle with religious ethics and capitalist spirit. The whole thing amounts to about 20 times the length of his original work on the Protestant Ethic. *The Protestant Ethic and the Spirit of Capitalism* turned out to be a mere drop in what eventually became an ocean, a sociology of world history.

I have said that the English-language version of *The Protestant Ethic*, the book you hold in your hands, is two books in one. It contains the original essay which Weber published in 1904–5; this comprises the main body of the text on pages 35–183. It also contains a piece Weber wrote later which reflects his later theory of capitalism and his responses to critics of the original Protestant Ethic thesis. These parts are printed here in the section headed "Max Weber's Introduction to the Sociology of Religion" (pages 13–31) and in the "Notes," which take up pages 185–284. How these two versions, early and late Weber, became part of the same book can be explained as follows.

In 1920, as Weber was preparing an edition of his comparative writings on the world religions (*Gesammelte Aufsätze zur Religionssoziologie*), the first writing he included was, of course, *The Protestant Ethic*. He added another short paper which he wrote at about the same time, "The Protestant Sects and the Spirit of Capitalism," which consists of observations from his 1904 visit concerning Protestantism in everyday life in America. After this are reprinted his works on the religions of China, India, and ancient Judaism. To string it all together, Weber wrote some of his most important essays, printed between the major monographs, which give overall comparative reflections. Talcott Parsons, the first translator of *The Protestant Ethic* into English, took Weber's introductory essay to the whole collection and printed it as the first section of *The Protestant Ethic*, under the heading "Author's Introduction." Unfortunately, since Parsons did not put a heading in the text to mark where *The Protestant Ethic and the Spirit of Capitalism* actually began, and because of the peculiar way the pages of the first edition were numbered, generations of readers have gotten the impression that the whole thing is one text, instead of a juxtaposition of Weber's earliest and latest writings.

For this edition, I have put back the title of the original German text (at page xxxiii) and clearly marked Weber's 1920 Introduction to his *Collected Essays on the Sociology of Religion* by a heading which leaves no confusion that it is from a separate work. I would advise the reader—especially the student who is reading *The Protestant Ethic* for the first time—to begin where *The Protestant Ethic* actually begins, on page 35, and then come back, at the end, to read "Max Weber's Introduction to the Sociology of Religion" to see where he later took the argument.

Weber's Later Theory

Weber's later work becomes quite complex, and it would be an overload to attempt to untangle it here. To see how the various conditions mesh into his complete causal chain of the conditions for capitalism, one needs a diagram in the form of a flow chart. (The interested reader is referred to my *Weberian Sociological Theory* or to the comprehensive overviews by Kalberg or Käsler, listed in the "Suggested Further Reading.") Here I will only sketch how Weber developed his theory in two main directions.

First, the religious basis of rational capitalism is not just radical Protestantism but the historical phenomenon of Christianity, indeed the entire Judeo-Christian tradition. Recall that the starting point of the whole argument was Weber's contrast between traditional and rational capitalism, which led to the search for the religious roots of traditionalism and rationalism. Weber takes Catholicism as the emblem of religious traditionalism. He focuses especially upon the medieval Catholic emphasis on rituals, penances, pilgrimages, relics of the saints, and the like, all of which Weber regards as examples of magical religion. Magic, for Weber, is the epitome of the traditional and the non-rational, which had to be eliminated before the world could be subjected to the forces of social rationality, and thus to rational capitalism.

In his later works, Weber widened his view to compare the Western religions with the Asian ones. Now he places more emphasis on the entire Judeo-Christian heritage as the religions which most sharply suppressed the magical element from religion. Judaism and Christianity are the religions with the strongest emphasis upon ethical demands, upon living a righteous religious life while in the world. In contrast, Weber tries to show that the other major world religions—Confucianism and Taoism in China, Buddhism and Hinduism in India, Islam throughout North Africa and the Middle East—retained too many elements of magic, and thereby obstructed the pathway toward social rationalization. The differences among the world religions, however, turn out to be more complicated than a contrast between the amount of magic they contain, and Weber went on to develop a typology of the several different versions of religion that are found, mixed in various proportions, in different parts of the world. Besides magical and ritualistic religions, Weber discusses both asceticism and mysticism. Then he presents further subtypes within each of the latter pair, which either directed these religious practices in an other-worldly direction or harnessed them to life within the world. At this point in the development of the theory, the key category, instead of the Protestant Ethic or Calvinistic predestination, is "inner-worldly asceticism," living an ascetic life in the world. This is what brings about the great social transformation of rational capitalism.

Weber's comparative studies of the world religions were a huge project which he never finished. There is still controversy as to whether his model would have worked for Islam, and indeed whether it works the way Weber said it did for China. There is the even bigger question of Japan, which I will take up below.

Second, another side of the explanation which Weber greatly expanded was to consider not just religion, but all the other sociological ingredients for rational capitalism. To simplify it greatly,

Weber in his later works sketched two components or pathways, both of which need to be present if rational capitalism is to emerge. (For Weber's own summary, see Weber's *General Economic History*, Part IV, cited in the "Suggested Further Reading.")

These two component pathways are (a) the religious pathway toward a religious ethic of inner-worldly asceticism, which I have just sketched above, and (b) a political pathway. This latter encompasses the rise of the *bureaucratic state*, counterbalanced by *democratic citizenship* as the basis for a *legal system of private property*. As we can see, Weber tends to view the world as combinations of different ingredients, each of which can be divided into further sub-ingredients. We cannot afford to go too far into detail here, but let me comment briefly on the key ingredients, the rise of bureaucracy and the combination of citizenship plus a legal system.

The essence of bureaucracy is organization by rules and regulations, which is to say by formal paperwork. Bureaucracy has a bad image in our own times, precisely because of our dislike of formal rules and paperwork, and Weber shares some of these misgivings. Nevertheless, Weber points out that bureaucracy is one of the crucial social inventions in the history of the world. Bureaucracy is impersonal; therefore, it rises above individuals, above favoritism and family connections. Bureaucracy separates the person from the job, and treats individuals as interchangeable with respect to the application of general rules. This is one of the things we dislike about bureaucracy, but it also makes possible the calculating, predictable social order within which mass-production capitalism can flourish.

The point comes home to us if we compare bureaucracy to the social forms which existed before bureaucracy was created: this was a world of feudal lords and family lineages, of hereditary aristocracies and robber barons, of states which lived on patronage and conquest and had no legal restrictions on confiscating the property of merchants or of anyone else who lacked military power. In this milieu, mass-production capitalism could not flourish. Business was limited to the versions of traditional capitalism that we have reviewed above: the long-distance luxury traders, trying to squeak through natural and political dangers in order to make one big profit which would allow them to retire from business and enter the socially dominant sector of aristocratic politics; or alternatively political-booty capitalism, making business into a search for plunder.

Weber had the same ambivalent attitude about bureaucracy that we have today. He saw it as part of the "iron cage" in which we are trapped. But Weber was above all trying to be realistic. Without the impersonal bureaucratic cage, modern life based on the rationalized, mass-production economy would be impossible.

Weber added that bureaucracy by itself would crush all private initiative. Bureaucracy is one of the ingredients leading to rational capitalism, but standing alone it acted more as a negative factor. Hence bureaucracy had to be counterbalanced by yet another factor: there needed to be a certain degree of democracy, an institution of the rights of citizens, and this had to be manifested in a legal system that protected private property. Only through this balance could government bureaucracy be turned into a support for rational capitalism. When all these conditions came together, including the appropriate religious ethic, rational capitalism could take off. In Weber's view, all this happened in Europe by around the seventeenth century. Modern capitalism was the result.

I have barely mentioned these several lines of causality, each of which opens out into a theory in its own right. Weber started off with the Protestant Ethic; as he went deeper and deeper into the issues that it raised, he spun off one sociological theory after another. This is how Weber became the great sociologist we look back upon: the founder of the theory of bureaucracy as well as the comparative sociology of religion, the sociology of law, political sociology, theory of democracy, and many other things. We cannot pursue these matters here. These leads can be followed up in Weber's later works and then into the lines of sociological research and theory which have come after them.

Criticism and Further Developments

The Protestant Ethic and the Spirit of Capitalism made Weber famous. It has been controversial since it first appeared. Some of the criticisms have been fairly low-level: for example, the argument that capitalism existed before Protestantism or that Catholics also had capitalism. Such arguments ignore Weber's key distinctions: that he was talking about rational capitalism, not just traditional capitalism, and that his concern was not Protestantism in general, but the way in which the Calvinists harnessed religious asceticism to worldly action. Once we broaden our attention from early to late Weber, we can steer clear of a narrower Catholic-vs.-Protestant polemic by seeking out points in world history where this kind of inner-worldly asceticism has had economic effects. The most famous study along this line was Robert Bellah's *Tokugawa Religion*, which tried to show that there was an equivalent to the Protestant Ethic in Japan during the 1700s, derived from a mixture of Buddhism and Confucianism. Thus the tremendous economic success of Japanese society is not a contradiction to Weber's theory but can be seen as an extension of it, on a more abstract plane.

It is possible to go still further. As we have seen, Weber's full theory involves not only a religious ethic but a whole complex of institutions: the development of bureaucracy, a legal system, and citizenship rights. These can be found in world history in other than strictly Protestant, modern-European form. Weber himself gave some hints when he noted that Catholic monks siphoned off religious energy by confining the life of ascetic discipline to the monastery instead of releasing the energy in the world. Weber commented that this was why it was important that Luther abolished the monasteries: henceforward everyone had to live the life of a monk in daily life.

Following this lead, I have researched the economic importance of the Catholic monasteries themselves. (See the chapters in my *Weberian Sociological Theory*, entitled "Weber's Last Theory of Capitalism" and "The Weberian Revolution of the High Middle Ages," cited in the "Suggested Further Reading.") In the monasteries, on a smaller scale, we find all the elements Weber listed as necessary ingredients for rational capitalism; the key difference was that these factors operated within a religious economy, rather than in the surrounding medieval society in general. As we now know—something of which scholars of Weber's generation were not yet fully aware—there was an economic boom in the Christian Middle Ages around 1100–1300 A.D. The basis for this economic expansion was laid by the growth of the monastic orders, above all the Cistercian order led by St. Bernard. These spread through Europe during this time, expanding agricultural land, growing cash crops, establishing forges, mills, and other early forms of industry. The monks were harnessing religious energy, not just for prayer and ritual, but for making monasteries grow materially.

As I have pointed out, the same set of factors which Weber saw as generating modern capitalism in the era of the Protestant Ethic also existed 300 years earlier within the monastic economy. A religious ethic emphasizing asceticism and hard work, instead of a life of ritualism, was just what the Catholic reformers of the Middle Ages demanded. They reformed the older monasteries so that monks should no longer engage primarily in ritual and otherworldly prayer but in ceaseless efforts and rigorous control of life.

Calvinist predestination, it turns out, is not the only religious doctrine compatible with this kind of religious activity. There was a Catholic ethic too, although it applied only to monks.

The other sides of Weber's model fit here too. We find the Catholic church was a pioneer in the development of bureaucracy, the form of organization centered on codified rules and regulations, record-keeping, and impersonality, exalting abstract and impersonal obligations over the power of individuals and traditions. The first bureaucracy in the Western world, in fact, was the medieval Papacy, and its courts of canon law, established to hear property disputes coming from the prosperous monasteries, became the basis for the modern law of corporate property.

A key point which I cannot fully treat here is that the monasteries broke away from the social structure dominated by families and family connections. Monks could not be married. The point of this was not just a puritanical denial of sex but of a social connection: in a society in which everything was done by the family (hereditary aristocrats at the top, peasant families at the bottom), the monks broke the connection to the family. A monk does not inherit, nor does he have children (at least not legitimate ones), and therefore he cannot leave an inheritance. Whatever a monk accumulates by his work during his lifetime belongs to the monastery. The monastery thus transformed property law. The religious order became a new kind of organization, a corporate unit in which the products of monks' labor were accumulated, not by individuals or families, but by the organization. In effect, the medieval monastery was the first business corporation.

Here the ironic dialectic of Weber's Protestant Ethic comes into play as well. Weber noted that Calvinistic businessmen, by their hard work and frugality, ploughing back their profits into business, ended up becoming rich. The same thing happened to the Catholic monasteries: their asceticism, with the accumulation of gains ploughed back into monastic property, made them rich. The rest of the dialectic also took place. With riches came laxness and corruption. After a few hundred years, the original spirit of the medieval Catholic ethic was lost. By the early 1500s, the church, as Martin Luther viewed it, was fat and greedy, without redeeming religious merit. It was time to abolish the monasteries. When this happened, a new wave of religious motivation was set off, followed by the expansion of full-scale, mass-production capitalism.

Weber only scratched the surface of his historical theme. What he saw was the second wave of takeoff from ascetic religion to capitalism; behind it was a first wave, the "Catholic ethic" of the monastic movements, and the takeoff of the medieval economy. Without the first wave, the second wave would not have been possible.

We could go on to speculate about the future. Perhaps there will be yet a third wave of religion and capitalism, sometime in the generations ahead of us; for that matter, perhaps future historians looking back will say that it had already started in the late twentieth century. Certainly we now live in a time when evangelical Protestant religion—which is to say, the same kind of inner—worldly ascetic religious activism Weber wrote about-has again become a powerful force around the world. This is also a time when capitalism seems especially powerful, including both its change-producing and its harsh, competitive aspects.

I will forego this point in order to mention one more recent development of neo-Weberian theory. Weber was quite Euro-centric (more precisely, one should say Euro-American-centric); his project was to see how the West came to develop rational capitalism, whereas the East did not. This viewpoint ties into the familiar scenario that outside the West, capitalist development came about only by means of Western expansion, whether imitation, colonialism, or imperialism. This is the model of world modernization starting in the West and spreading around the globe as an external influence.

Weber explicitly saw this as a consequence of the Western religions. Western rational capitalism is the end-result of the Judeo-Christian pathway. But time has moved on since Weber wrote during 1905–20. Things are visible now which Weber did not know. One of these is the tremendous economic growth of Japan in the twentieth century, to the point of becoming virtually the world's leading capitalist society. In fact, Weber could have seen signs of this movement in his own day (it happens this was one of the few topics that Weber did *not* pay attention to). Japan after the Meiji Restoration (1868) was already beginning its incredibly rapid surge onto the world economic scene, the only non-Western society to do so without going through a phase of Western colonialism. Current scholarship is now showing, in more and more detail, that Japan was not simply a wonderful "copy-cat": Japan did not merely imitate Western industrialization. Already during the Tokugawa period (1600–1860), Japan was a highly commercial society, on a level with most contemporary European societies. Big capitalist businesses, like Sumitomo and Mitsui, which have become famous in the late twentieth century, were already prominent in the eighteenth century. Now we are finding that in the pre-Tokugawa period, when Japan was in its so-called "feudal" period of domestic warfare (ca. 1460–1600), it was full of virtually independent city-states, monastic orders, and lords' private estates, which built up a solid basis for the later economic growth.

As I have argued elsewhere (see references in "Suggested Further Reading"), this was yet another case where something like the Weberian model applies but without the specific doctrines of the Protestant Ethic. For the key economic developments in the pre-Tokugawa period are connected with the expansion of the Buddhist monastic orders around Japan, spreading a commercial market economy and bringing economic growth. The various features listed earlier as comprising the ingredients of Weber's full-scale model of the causes of rational capitalism can also be found in the Buddhist sector of medieval Japan. Behind this, if we want to trace it further, is the influence of Chinese Buddhism, since Japanese Buddhism was imported from China.

If that was so, we might ask, why wasn't there a capitalist economic takeoff in medieval China? The answer is that indeed there was. During the Sung Dynasty (960–1200), China had the most thriving market economy in the world, complete with many of the features that we associate with rationalized capitalism. And the capitalism of Sung China built up slowly in the previous period, out of the accumulation of economic gains in the Buddhist monasteries which dominated medieval China. (To mention just one instance that has a little familiarity in the West: one of the first markets for a mass-consumption product, namely tea, was pioneered in China and then in Japan by the wave of expansion of the Zen Buddhist monasteries in the countryside.) The Sung dynasty even resembles the period of the Protestant Reformation, in the sense that this was a time just after the Buddhist monasteries had been confiscated and their property taken over into secular hands. I mention these points only as a sketch and a subject which bears further investigation on many points. One of the crucial unanswered questions is how the economy of Sung China went into a crisis, so that instead of further economic development taking place in China, it shifted over to Japan.

It appears now there has been an independent East-Asian pathway toward modern capitalism. The West is not as unique as Weber—and most of the rest of us—have thought it was. This does not diminish Weber's stature as a great pioneer of comparative sociology. He uncovered first the Protestant Ethic, and then the other social structures tied to the pathway of Judaism and Christianity, which led toward modern capitalism in Europe and America. With greater historical knowledge and a further widening of the sociological concepts which Weber pioneered, we can see that there were other breakthroughs: not only a Protestant Ethic but also a "Catholic Ethic," and even a "Buddhist ethic" starting in China and coming to greatest fruition in Japan. This expansion of our understanding, I would suggest, is also an expansion of our universal viewpoint on the underlying similarity of all humanity. Beneath the distinctive doctrines, we are all the same kind of people, responding to the same kinds of conditions for social change.

The Protestant Ethic and American Sociology

The United States has played a special role in making Max Weber famous. When Talcott Parsons first translated *The Protestant Ethic and the Spirit of Capitalism* in 1930, Weber was moderately well known among scholarly specialists in Germany; but sociology in that country was a tiny, struggling field, soon to be snuffed out by the Nazis coming to power in 1933. In England and France, Weber was scarcely regarded at all. Parsons proceeded to make Weber into a truly major figure, taking *The Protestant Ethic* as the exemplar of how sociology should be done: showing the role of ideas and values rather than materialist reduction of the Marxian or even the Durkheimian sort; and showing the importance of *verstehen*, the methodology of understanding subjective orientations to social action. A few years later, in 1937, when Parsons published *The Structure of Social Action*, he elevated Weber to the pantheon of the great sociologists, along with Durkheim and Pareto. Pareto has since fallen out of the list, while Marx and George Herbert Mead have been added, but Weber has remained constant ever since as the greatest star, claimed by everybody as a supporter of at least some aspect of his or her own theoretical position. Ironically, it was via American influence that, after 1950, Weber's reputation began to slowly rise in Germany as well.

There is a more intimate connection between Weber and America. As we have seen, Weber developed much of his insight into the Protestant Ethic while on a visit to the U.S. in 1904. American society is his great example of the connection between radical Protestantism and the most dynamic form of capitalism. When he wants to epitomize the spirit of capitalism, he quotes Ben Franklin; when he sums up in his last pages about the "iron cage" of "care for external goods," he refers to the United States as "the field of its highest development." If one reads through Weber's footnotes, one will find that he did much of his research on the Protestant sects in the libraries of religious colleges in the United States. Especially revealing of the impression American religion made upon him is a companion essay to *The Protestant Ethic* which he published upon returning to Germany, "The Protestant Sects and the Spirit of Capitalism," based on his visits to German-American relatives in Ohio and North Carolina. This essay has been reprinted for this edition; it is discussed in the following section of this Introduction.

In Weber's later works, the Protestant Ethic thesis became watered down, or one might say, abstracted to a new level. In these writings, the focus of attention is no longer radical Protestantism in the narrow sense, but more broadly the "inner-worldly asceticism" of Christianity as it has developed ever since its antecedents in ancient Judaism. From this level of abstraction, we have seen that there can be equivalents of the Protestant Ethic, even a version of a "Catholic ethic" or a Japanese "Buddhist ethic." And structurally, Weber points to the mix of conditions bringing about rationalized capitalism, not only a religious ethic but also bureaucracy, citizenship, and law. Since Weber himself moved away from the Protestant Ethic *per se*, one might wonder why we should still be reading it, instead of concentrating on his later writings.

One answer, of course, is that *The Protestant Ethic* is the best place to begin as a well-written starting point for entering a more complex problem. But there is another answer, which is especially important for American sociologists and American students. Even if the Protestant Ethic is not so central a cause of modern capitalism as we once believed, it remains extremely important for something else: the way of life or social "ethic" of the United States. Drop into the background, if you like, the notion that this is a book about the Protestant Ethic and the rise of modern capitalism in general; what takes the foreground is that this is a book about "the Protestant Ethic and the American way of life."

Many things have changed, of course, between the Puritan settlers of New England in the 1600s and the consumer-oriented society at the turn of the twenty-first century. Nevertheless, the Puritan ethic has had an enormous effect upon our development, and it remains one theme among the many which are contending for control even today. Moreover, it was not just the Calvinists who settled here; all the Protestant sects which Weber describes in Chapter

5—Quakers, Methodists, Baptists—have flourished in the United States more than anywhere else in the world, and they have left their distinctive marks upon our lifestyle. Weber points out, for instance, that the doctrine of the separation of church and state came from these sects, and he refers to the way in which they fostered a decentralized democracy and a distrust of central government. Weber comments on the Puritan tendency to dislike art but to admire science, as well as the Puritan rationale for rejecting charity to the poor as incompatible with predestined salvation or damnation. When one looks at *The Protestant Ethic and the Spirit of Capitalism* closely (including the "Notes"), one sees time after time Weber pointing out themes which are major public issues today and no doubt will continue to be so in the future. Contemporary conservative movements in America appear to be struggling to continue the earlier social tendencies of the Protestant Ethic.

Modern sociologists recognize that any complex society is made up of many, often conflicting, lifestyles and beliefs. There are plenty of values and activities contrary to the Protestant Ethic today: consumerism and the accumulation of credit-card debt instead of saving and reinvestment; a leisure orientation instead of emphasis on the value of hard work; movements for social altruism instead of the individualistic pursuit of spiritual or material success; even a return of "political booty" capitalism in the form of stock-market manipulation and speculation on international money markets, instead of the slow accumulation of small gains through expansion of mass production. Weber himself understood this kind of thing in principle; this is why he took as his methodology the analysis of ideal types, one-sided constructions which accentuate just one of the many forms found mixed together in real life. What makes *The Protestant Ethic* relevant is that it describes a key ingredient which still struggles with all the contrary tendencies of American life. Understanding the outcome of that struggle is one of the key problems for sociologists today.

Weber's Companion Piece to *The Protestant Ethic*: 'The Protestant Sects and the Spirit of Capitalism'

For this edition, we have reprinted along with *The Protestant Ethic and the Spirit of Capitalism* an essay which Weber wrote shortly afterward. As we have seen, Weber's trip to America in 1904 was a turning point in his life. He had begun writing *The Protestant Ethic* as his thoughts had turned to America, his great example of the connection between religion and capitalism. "The

Protestant Sects and the Spirit of Capitalism" was originally a set of newspaper articles which Weber published in Germany after he returned from his trip. They were later expanded for scholarly publication in his collected works. "The Protestant Sects" is more immediate and vivid than *The Protestant Ethic* because it describes Weber's own observations of how American capitalism and religion actually worked. Whereas *The Protestant Ethic* moves on the level of abstract ideas, "The Protestant Sects" deals with how religion affects everyday life, placing special emphasis on why both business and religion make Americans so eager to join organizations.

Weber begins by questioning why the United States is more religious than the Protestant parts of Europe, theorizing that it is because church membership in America serves as a kind of credit rating. Church members can get business loans and will be patronized by other members of the same church. The most important point, however, is that the church gives a rating of one's moral character in the eyes of the whole community.

This moral rating is especially strong in the kind of religious organization that Weber calls a "sect," which he defines as "a voluntary association of religiously qualified persons." In a sect, joining is a deliberate act of faith; correspondingly, one's moral reliability is checked by the group before one is accepted by one's peers. In contrast to "sect" is the concept of a "church," in a specific meaning given to the term by sociologists of religions; Weber defines a "church" as "a compulsory association for the administration of grace." [These definitions are given on page liv.] In other words, a "church" is an officially established organization, like the Catholic church in some European states or the Anglican church in England; one becomes a member simply by being born into it, and one can't escape being a member of a church. A sect is much better at assessing the moral standing of its members, because it only takes in people who actively seek it out.

Weber then launches into an historical analysis of the trajectory of American society. By the early 1900s, he comments, church-mindedness in America began to weaken as the society became secularized. Nevertheless, the influence of the Protestant sects had set America on a pathway toward a certain kind of structure. Religious membership was weakening as the predominant way that Americans assessed each other's moral character, but other kinds of organizational membership had sprung up in its place. College fraternities were exceptionally important in America; in contrast to the situation of European university students, Weber says, in Amer-

ica a student who was not admitted to any club was usually a sort
of pariah [p. il]. Among American adults, athletic and social clubs
(such as the Rotary, Elks, or Junior Chamber of Commerce which
exist today) were equally important. All these clubs, Weber commented, acted as a kind of credential of social acceptability. They
were crucial for a business or professional career, not merely because they were places where one made contacts, but because they
gave a stamp of moral approval to one's character. It was not so
important precisely which club one belonged to, as it was to demonstrate that one was a member of something. In Weber's terminology, belonging to a club made one a member of a *status group*.

How did this American emphasis on the moral standing of belonging to a voluntary association come about? Weber traces it
back to the colonies, where the religious elite were the only full
citizens. This pattern was especially strong among the Puritans in
Massachusetts, and through them it spread throughout New England, and in later generations to the settlers of the West. Another
example was the Quakers in Pennsylvania. These early colonies
were attempts to establish theocracies, places where only the godly
people, those who met the strict standards of the church, would
rule. But the importance of belonging to a sect went beyond the
old connection of membership with political eliteness, which after
all lasted for only a few generations in the colonies. More basi-
cally, members of Protestant sects very early acquired a reputation
for uprightness in business. In the sixteenth and seventeenth centuries Baptists, Quakers, and other sects were often disliked by nonmembers because of their religious extremism, but even their
enemies trusted them in business dealings. The sect members were
known to be honest and reliable. They were preferred by customers
because they sold by fixed prices, instead of haggling. Protestants'
business was more impersonal, but also had less of the tone of
greediness and trickery that characterized buying and selling when
one had to bargain over the price of every purchase.

Weber reviews the origins of the Protestant sects, such as the
Baptists in Zürich, Switzerland, in 1525. The early issue which
made their organization distinctive was the question of whether to
accept members merely by heredity (i.e. to baptize infants because
their parents were members), or whether each individual must be
tested in his own religious faith before he could be admitted to the
sacrament of communion with the rest of the group. Baptist ministers gave out certificates of qualification for travelers, something
like letters of recommendation; these operated just like the letters

which are used so widely today for getting admitted to college or for getting a job. The Protestant sects were run along democratic lines, so that the whole congregation was jointly responsible for accepting new members; this also meant keeping unqualified persons out, so that they would not spoil the purity of the group's communion with God. The sects struggled against falling back into becoming a "church," in the sense that they refused to accept members just by their family status; instead everyone had to come in as the result of their own decision and by passing the judgment of the group.

Now Weber takes up a sociological difficulty. The Protestant sects acted as judges and guarantors of the moral standing of their members; but these were not the only organizations to act that way. In modern secular times, as Protestantism began to weaken in America, fraternities and clubs took over their function. But in Europe, too, there were clubs, such as the duelling fraternities in the German universities, which also judged the qualifications of persons who wanted to be members. The duelling fraternities patterned themselves on the medieval knights, and engaged not only in sword fighting, but in upholding a whole set of manners, clothes, and amusements that added up to what was considered an "honorable" lifestyle. Belonging to the duelling fraternity and upholding its culture gave one a certain "status honor"; it is a typical way that exclusive membership creates a cultural rank in society as a "status group." There are other examples of such status groups: the medieval guilds, members of a particular trade who only admitted those who lived up to the standards of their craft; the aristocracy, whose lifestyle looked down on the vulgar occupations of earning a living, and expressed the cultivated, leisure pursuits of being a "gentleman." The sociological problem, as Weber saw it, was to explain what was different about the Protestant sects in the way they regulated the life conduct of their members. After all, in the medieval church, a Bishop who didn't pay his debts could be disciplined by the church hierarchy; hence Bishops had very good credit ratings, better than kings. In the same way, military officers could be ordered by their superior officers to pay their debts, or lose standing as "an officer and a gentleman." But why, then, didn't bishops and military officers become the basis for modern capitalism? For that matter, why were medieval guilds an obstacle to modern capitalism, if they had the same kind of group structure that Protestant sects did and could provide equal moral regulation of economic dealings?

The difference, Weber answered, lay in the fact that the Protestant sects vested authority in a community of lay persons, and not in a hierarchy. The medieval church or the army officers had a socially-enforced discipline, but it was handed down from above and it was confined mainly to controlling transgressions, such as failure to pay one's debts. The Protestant sects, however, were constantly assessing their members' general moral character, not just their flagrant violations, and the sects kept up the pressure by repeatedly requiring the individual to prove his worthiness. Moreover, the ethos of the Protestant sects was different; whereas aristocratic groups, such as duelling clubs, were generally anti-business and exalted a leisure lifestyle, the Protestant sects were the epitome of middle-class ethical righteousness and methodical discipline. The atmosphere of the Protestant sects was that of a religious community, living in the world but with their eyes on otherworldly things, not on the ostentation of riches and social standing. Weber comments that the distinctive contribution of Protestant sects was to a specifically middle-class version of capitalism. Ruthless acquisition of property is found throughout history, and still exists among the "robber barons" and financial speculators of the upper class; but this was not what made modern capitalism work. Upper-class social clubs and their lifestyle were not the source of capitalist ethic. It came instead from the middle-class sects with their righteousness and work discipline.

Finally, Weber contrasts the Protestant sects with the medieval guilds. The guilds also controlled the business behavior of their members, but their effects on economic conduct were very different. The guilds united people who were competitors in the same occupation (e.g. all the goldsmiths would belong to the same guild); hence their strongest common interest was in monopolizing business and keeping prices high. The Protestant sects, on the other hand, were not based on a specific occupation, but drew together people who worked in different occupations. Their effect on business conduct was not via greed for profit, through monopoly or price-fixing, but via their emphasis on righteousness of character. Hence the central paradox of the Protestant sects: they exerted very strong group controls, but they assessed their members as individuals. The Protestant sects were a key source of modern individualism. Only the sects, Weber concluded, could legitimate individualistic capitalism. In the same way, the aftereffect of the Protestant sects was to make Americans both extremely sensitive to belonging to groups, but also extremely concerned with their own individuality.

"The Protestant Sects and the Spirit of Capitalism" is an important supplement to *The Protestant Ethic and the Spirit of Capitalism* because it brings out this social causality. Notice a change in theoretical tone by the time Weber came to write "The Protestant Sects." Weber emphasizes that social organization and life conduct are the key, rather than religious doctrine. The sects downplayed the importance of doctrine; Weber even goes so far as to say that the sects struggled against being dominated by theologians [pp. liii, lvii]. The Protestant sects were the radicals of the Reformation, who wanted to replace the authority of the minister from above with the horizontal authority of the congregation as a whole. The most extreme version of this church democracy was the Quakers, who had no ministers and simply waited for someone in the congregation to feel moved to speak. The congregation itself reserved the right to accept new members and would boycott any person the whole grouped rejected. "It is not the ethical *doctrine* of a religion, but that form of ethical conduct upon which *premiums* are placed that matters," Weber summed up [p. lxi]. He went on to underline in a footnote: "Again we should like to stress emphatically this absolutely decisive point in the first of these two essays (*The Protestant Ethic and the Spirit of Capitalism*). It has been the fundamental mistake of my critics not to have taken notice of this very fact." [Footnote 35, p. lxxiii] The "Protestant Ethic" is a way of behaving, more than a way of believing; and it is rooted in the distinctive organization of the group. This is Weber's most sociological message.

Practical Advice for Instructors
and Students on
How to Read *The Protestant Ethic*

Many portions of *The Protestant Ethic* are very well written and even have a memorable literary flair. There are also places where Weber goes into detail in discussing theological texts and in pointing out the differences among the various kinds of Protestantism; here the new reader is in danger of losing track of the main argument. The main points can be captured by reading:

Part I (Chapters 1–3), and above all the crucial Chapter 2, "The Spirit of Capitalism."

In Part II, Section A of Chapter 4, headed "Calvinism."

Chapter 5, which brings together the pieces of Weber's argument, leads off with some further textual analysis of the writings of an English Puritan, Richard Baxter. The key summary begins at page 166, with the words "Let us now try to clarify the points in which the Puritan idea of the calling . . . was bound directly to influence the development of a capitalist way of life," and continues to the end (page 183) with Weber's famous image of living in the iron cage.

Max Weber's "Introduction to the Sociology of Religion," which is traditionally printed at the beginning of *The Protestant Ethic* (and without an explanatory title), was written 15 years later and gives a much more complex line of theory. I would suggest that the student read this section *after* reading the main body of the text (or save it for a more advanced course).

The "Notes" which follow the end of the text were for the most part written later, as Weber answered his critics. The introductory student is not likely to find the detail here very worthwhile. Nevertheless, Weber raises some significant points here and there in the "Notes," which I list in case someone wishes to follow up particular topics and ideas:

Weber's "Introduction," footnote 6, page 186: the difference between "rational" capitalism and "political adventurers" or "booty" capitalism, and instances where they blend together.

Chapter 1, footnote 9, pages 193–4: the complexity of what it means to call something "rational" or "irrational."

Chapter 1, footnote 12, pages 194–8: compares the difference in "economic ethics" between an Italian Renaissance aristocrat, whom Weber regards as exemplifying the pre-modern attitude toward capitalism, and Franklin, who exemplifies the modern rationalized spirit.

Chapter 4, footnote 30, pages 223–5: American individualism and resistance to political authority. See also footnote 178, pages 255–6, on Puritanism as a source of American democracy.

Chapter 4, footnote 34, pages 225–6: the impersonality of Puritan "brotherly love" (a tone which Weber obviously disliked).

Chapter 4, footnote 36, pages 226–7: the popularity of the idea of predestination among Christians and its difference from the Muslim idea of belief in predetermination (which applies to the worldly life and not to the afterlife).

Chapter 4, footnote 66, pages 232–3: psychological and logical aspects of religion, with a comparison to William James' analysis of religious experience.

Chapter 4, footnote 73, page 234: Protestantism, avoiding even a single sin, as compared to Catholicism, treating the balance of sins and good works as a kind of bank account.

Chapter 4, footnote 79, page 235: Protestantism took Catholic monasticism and moved it into the world.

Chapter 4, footnote 81, page 235: Protestantism's effects upon military discipline, visible in Cromwell's army of Roundheads, as compared to the knightly passion of the Cavaliers.

Chapter 4, footnote 110, pages 242–3: radical Puritanism as the origin of political toleration of religious freedom and of the separation of church and state.

Chapter 4, footnote 145, page 249: the source of the famous "Merton thesis" that Protestantism gave rise to modern science. See also Chapter 5, footnote 73, page 275.

Chapter 5, footnote 22, pages 263–4: sexual puritanism and the emancipation of women.

Chapter 5, footnote 31, page 265: the Hindu religious ethic in regard to worldly duties.

Chapter 5, footnote 37, page 266: the Puritan belief was not to "love thy neighbour *more than* thyself," but only at the same amount; i.e. self-regard is a duty.

Chapter 5, footnote 45, page 268: Puritan opposition to charity for the poor (a theme which echoes again in the conservative American politics of welfare reform in the 1990s).

Chapter 5, footnote 47, page 268: the American emphasis upon the individual's self-made success, compared to the medieval attitude that only an inherited position is honorable.

Chapter 5, footnote 58, pages 270–1: medieval Jewish business ethics as traditional, compared to the Puritan organization of labor.

Chapter 5, footnote 64, page 272, and footnote 68, page 274: the Puritan attitude led to the decline of English and American music (with the exception of Negro church choirs); and the Puritan attitude toward art generally (relevant for conservative attacks on American museums in the 1980s and 90s).

Chapter 5, footnote 67, pages 273–4: why the Dutch were less influenced by Puritanism than the English.

Chapter 5, footnote 70, page 274: Puritans as the source of modern haircuts and clothing styles.

Chapter 5, footnotes 84–5, page 277, and footnote 107, page 282: Marxist materialist interpretation is partly correct, but only partly, especially in regard to the development of Puritan New England compared to the Southern colonies.

Chapter 5, footnote 108, page 282: the joylessness of modern work as an ascetic duty.

Chapter 5, footnote 115, page 283: a quotation from Weber's visit to German-American families in Ohio, illustrating the difference between the work ethic in the two societies.

Chapter 5, footnotes 118–19, pages 283–4: Weber's concluding comments on the relation between the Protestant Ethic and his wider work on the sociology of religion.

Suggested Further Reading

The Protestant Ethic Thesis:

Gordon Marshall, *In Search of the Spirit of Capitalism. An Essay on Max Weber's Protestant Ethic Thesis*. New York: Columbia University Press, 1982. A thorough discussion of the controversies that have followed the "Weber thesis."

Hartmut Lehmann and Guenther Roth (eds). Weber's *'Protestant Ethic': Origins, Evidence, Contexts*. New York: Cambridge University Press, 1993. Recent Scholarship on how *The Protestant Ethic* thesis was formulated.

Harvey Goldman, *Politics, Death and the Devil: Self and Power in Max Weber and Thomas Mann*. Berkeley: University of California Press, 1992. Emphasizes the importance of strong personalities, such as persons imbued with the Protestant Ethic, as the driving force in Weber's theory of social change.

Contemporary Sociology of Religion:

Robert Wuthnow, *Communites of Discourse. Ideology and Social Structure in the Reformation, the Enlightenment, and European Socialism*. Cambridge, Mass.: Harvard University Press, 1989. Part I shows how Catholic and Protestant doctrines meshed with their opposing modes of daily life, during the historical period Weber was concerned with in *The Protestant Ethic*.

Rodney Stark and William Sims Bainbridge, *The Future of Religion*. Berkeley: University of California Press, 1985.

Roger Finke and Rodney Stark, *The Churching of America, 1776–1990*. New Brunswick: Rutgers University Press, 1992. These last two books show the long-term pattern of religion in the growth of American society, and explain some of the conditions behind the periodic revival of what they call "high-tension" religiousness similar to the Protestant Ethic.

Weber's Life and Work:

Dirk Käsler, *Max Weber: An Introduction to His Life and Work.* Chicago: University of Chicago Press, 1988.

Reinhard Bendix, *Max Weber: An Intellectual Portrait.* Berkeley: University of California Press, 1977.

Stephen Kalberg, *Max Weber's Comparative-Historical Sociology.* Chicago: University of Chicago Press, 1994. Käsler, Bendix, and Kalberg give comprehensive overviews of Weber's life and ideas, written by the leading German and American experts.

Randall Collins, *Max Weber: A Skeleton Key.* Beverly Hills: Sage, 1986. A brief overview; read Chapter 1 for a psycho-biographical interpretation of Weber's breakdown as a key to the conflicting strands of his sociology.

Alan Sica, *Weber, Irrationality and Social Order.* Berkeley: University of California Press, 1988.

Jeffrey Alexander, *Theoretical Logic in Sociology. Vol. 3. The Classical Attempt at Theoretical Synthesis: Max Weber.* Berkeley: University of California Press, 1983. Sica and Alexander stand out by arguing, in their different ways, that the various parts of Weber's multi-sided intellectual personality are inconsistent: i.e., that there is more than one Weber.

Further Writings by Weber:

Max Weber, *Economy and Society.* New York: Bedminster Press, 1968. (Originally published 1922). Weber's most comprehensive statement; one could spend a lifetime studying it.

Max Weber, *General Economic History.* New Brunswick: Transaction Books, 1981. These lectures which Weber delivered at the end of his life give his most comprehensive overview of the development of capitalism; for the overall model, read Part IV, "The Origin of Modern Capitalism."

Max Weber, *The Religion of China.* New York: Free Press, 1951; *Ancient Judaism.* New York: Free Press, 1952; *The Religion of India.* New York: Free Press, 1958. Originally published 1916–19, these three books are all that Weber completed of his comparative studies of the world religions, designed to show how the Judeo-Christian pathway led to rationalized capitalism in the West.

Hans H. Gerth and C. Wright Mills (eds.), *From Max Weber: Essays in Sociology*. New York: Oxford University Press, 1946. Contains an essay very much worth reading in conjunction with *The Protestant Ethic*: "Religious Rejections of the World and Their Directions" was written at the time of Weber's later comparative studies of the world religions. It contains some stunningly accurate anticipations of what modern life would be like later in the twentieth century, especially the tendency for people to become alienated from rationalized institutions and to withdraw their value-commitments into the private enjoyment of entertainment and erotic life.

Later Developments of Weberian Theory of Capitalism:

Talcott Parsons, *Societies: Comparative and Evolutionary Perspectives*. Englewood Cliffs: Prentice-Hall, 1966. Follows up Weber's line of argument by showing that the evolution of world societies was set off along different pathways by their religions.

Robert Bellah, *Tokugawa Religion: The Values of Preindustrial Japan*. New York: Free Press, 1957. Argues that Japan's rapid modernization was impelled by its own indigenous religious equivalent of the Protestant Ethic.

Randall Collins, *Weberian Sociological Theory*. Cambridge: Cambridge University Press 1986. The chapters "Weber's Last Theory of Capitalism" and "The Weberian Revolution of the High Middle Ages" contain the argument that Weber's full-scale theory leads us to find prior take-offs of rational capitalism in the religious economies of the Christian Middle Ages in Europe and in the Buddhist-dominated dynasties of medieval China. The point that medieval Chinese capitalism was transmitted to Japan through the Buddhist monasteries, giving rise to an independent East-Asian path to modernization, is developed in Randall Collins, "An Asian Route to Capitalism: Religious Economy and the Origins of Self-Transforming Growth in Japan," *American Sociological Review,* vol 62, December 1997. Good sources on early Japanese economic development are Chie Nakane and Shinzaburo Oishi, *Tokugawa Japan: Social and Economic Antecedents of Modern Japan*. Tokyo: University of Tokyo Press, 1990; and Neil McMullin, *Buddhism and the State in Sixteenth Century Japan*. Princeton: Princeton University Press, 1984.

THE PROTESTANT SECTS AND THE SPIRIT OF CAPITALISM[1]

Max Weber

For some time in the United States a principled 'separation of state and church' has existed. This separation is carried through so strictly that there is not even an official census of denominations, for it would be considered against the law for the state even to ask the citizen for his denomination. We shall not here discuss the practical importance of this principle of the relation between religious organizations and the state.* We are interested, rather, in the fact that scarcely two and a half decades ago the number of 'persons without church affiliation' in the U.S.A. was estimated to be only about 6 per cent;[2] and this despite the absence of all those highly effective premiums which most of the European states then placed upon affiliation with certain privileged churches and despite the immense immigration to the U.S.A.

It should be realized, in addition, that church affiliation in the U.S.A. brings with it incomparably higher financial burdens, especially for the poor, than anywhere in Germany. Published family budgets prove this, and I have personally known of many burdened cases in a congregation in a city on Lake Erie, which was almost entirely composed of German immigrant lumberjacks. Their regular contributions for religious purposes amounted to almost $80 annually, being paid out of an average annual income of about $1,000. Everyone knows that even a small fraction of this financial burden in Germany would lead to a mass exodus from the church. But quite apart from that, nobody who visited the United States fifteen or twenty years ago, that is, before the recent Europeanization of the country began, could overlook the very intense church-mindedness which then prevailed in all regions not yet flooded by European immigrants.** Every old travel book reveals that formerly church-mindedness in America went unquestioned, as compared with recent decades, and was even far stronger. Here we are especially interested in one aspect of this situation.

---

* The principle is often only theoretical; note the importance of the Catholic vote, as well as subsidies to confessional schools.

** The opening by prayer of not only every session of the U. S. Supreme Court but also of every Party Convention has been an annoying ceremonial for quite some time.

Hardly a generation ago when businessmen were establishing themselves and making new social contacts, they encountered the question: 'To what church do you belong?' This was asked unobtrusively and in a manner that seemed to be apropos, but evidently it was never asked accidentally. Even in Brooklyn, New York's twin city, this older tradition was retained to a strong degree, and the more so in communities less exposed to the influence of immigration. This question reminds one of the typical Scotch *table d'hôte*, where a quarter of a century ago the continental European on Sundays almost always had to face the situation of a lady's asking, 'What service did you attend today?' Or, if the Continental, as the oldest guest, should happen to be seated at the head of the table, the waiter when serving the soup would ask him: 'Sir, the prayer, please.' In Portree (Skye) on one beautiful Sunday I faced this typical question and did not know any better way out than to remark: 'I am a member of the *Badische Landeskirche* and could not find a chapel of my church in Portree. The ladies were pleased and satisfied with the answer. 'Oh, he doesn't attend any service except that of his own denomination!'

If one looked more closely at the matter in the United States, one could easily see that the question of religious affiliation was almost always posed in social life and in business life which depended on permanent and credit relations. However, as mentioned above, the American authorities never posed the question. Why?

First, a few personal observations [from 1904] may serve as illustrations. On a long railroad journey through what was then Indian territory, the author, sitting next to a traveling salesman of 'undertaker's hardware' (iron letters for tombstones), casually mentioned the still impressively strong church-mindedness. Thereupon the salesman remarked, 'Sir, for my part everybody may believe or not believe as he pleases; but if I saw a farmer or a businessman not belonging to any church at all, I wouldn't trust him with fifty cents. Why pay me, if he doesn't believe in anything?' Now that was a somewhat vague motivation.

The matter became somewhat clearer from the story of a German-born nose-and-throat specialist, who had established himself in a large city on the Ohio River and who told me of the visit of his first patient. Upon the doctor's request, he lay down upon the couch to be examined with the [aid of a] nose reflector. The patient sat up once and remarked with dignity and emphasis, 'Sir, I am a member of the — Baptist Church in — Street.' Puzzled about what meaning this circumstance might have for the disease of the nose and its treatment, the doctor discreetly inquired about the matter from an American colleague. The colleague smilingly informed him that the patient's statement of his church membership was merely to say: 'Don't worry about the fees.' But why should it mean precisely that? Perhaps this will become still clearer from a third happening.

On a beautiful clear Sunday afternoon early in October I attended a baptism ceremony of a Baptist congregation. I was in the company of some relatives who were farmers in the backwoods some miles out of M. [a county seat] in North Carolina. The baptism was to take place in a pool fed by a brook which descended from the Blue Ridge Mountains, visible in the distance. It was cold and it had been freezing during the night. Masses of farmers' families were standing all around the slopes of the hills; they had come, some from great distances, some from the neighborhood, in their light two-wheeled buggies.

The preacher in a black suit stood waist deep in the pond. After preparations of various sorts, about ten persons of both sexes in their Sunday-best stepped into the pond, one after another. They avowed their faith and then were immersed completely—the women in the preacher's arms. They came up, shaking and shivering in their wet clothes, stepped out of the pond, and everybody 'congratulated' them. They were quickly wrapped in thick blankets and then they drove home. One of my relatives commented that 'faith' provides unfailing protection against sneezes. Another relative stood beside me and, being unchurchly in accordance with German traditions, he looked on, spitting disdainfully over his shoulder. He spoke to one of those baptised, 'Hello, Bill, wasn't the water pretty cool?' and received the very earnest reply, 'Jeff, I thought of some pretty hot place (Hell!), and so I didn't mind the cool water.' During the immersion of one of the young men, my relative was startled.

'Look at him,' he said. 'I told you so!'

When I asked him after the ceremony, 'Why did you anticipate the baptism of that man?' he answered, 'Because he wants to open a bank in M.'

'Are there so many Baptists around that he can make a living?'

'Not at all, but once being baptised he will get the patronage of the whole region and he will outcompete everybody.'

Further questions of 'why' and 'by what means' led to the following conclusion: Admission to the local Baptist congregation follows only upon the most careful 'probation' and after closest inquiries into conduct going back to early childhood. (Disorderly conduct? Frequenting taverns? Dance? Theatre? Card Playing? Untimely meeting of liability? Other Frivolities?) The congregation still adhered strictly to the religious tradition.

Admission to the congregation is recognized as an absolute guarantee of the moral qualities of a gentleman, especially of those qualities required in business matters. Baptism secures to the individual the deposits of the whole region and unlimited credit without any competition. He is a 'made man.' Further observation confirmed that these, or at least very similar phenomena, recur in the most varied regions. In general, *only* those men had success in business who belonged to Methodist or Baptist or other *sects* or sectlike conventicles. When a sect member moved to a different place, or if he was a traveling salesman, he carried the certificate of his congregation with him; and thereby he found not only easy contact with sect members but, above all, he found credit everywhere. If he got into economic straits through no fault of his own, the sect arranged his affairs, gave guarantees to the creditors, and helped him in every way, often according to the Biblical principle, *mutuum date nihil inde sperantes*. (Luke VI:35)

The expectation of the creditors that his sect, for the sake of their prestige, would not allow creditors to suffer losses on behalf of a sect member was not, however, decisive for his opportunities. What was decisive was the fact that a fairly reputable sect would only accept for membership one whose 'conduct' made him appear to be morally qualified beyond doubt.

It is crucial that sect membership meant a certificate of moral qualification and especially of business morals for the individual. This stands in contrast to membership in a 'church' into which one is 'born' and which lets grace shine over the righteous and the unrighteous alike. Indeed, a church is a corporation which organizes grace and administers religious gifts of grace, like an endowed foundation. Affiliation with the church is, in principle, obligatory and hence proves nothing with regard to the member's qualities. A sect, however, is a voluntary association of only those who, according to the principle, are religiously and morally qualified. If one finds voluntary reception of his membership, by virtue of religious *probation*, he joins the sect voluntarily. It is, of course, an established fact that this selection has often been very strongly counteracted, precisely in America, through the proselyting of souls by competing sects, which, in part, was strongly determined by the material interests of the preachers. Hence, cartels for the restriction of proselyting have frequently existed among the competing denominations. Such cartels were formed, for instance, in order to exclude the easy wedding of a person who had been divorced for reasons which, from a religious point of view, were considered insufficient. Religious organizations that facilitated remarriage had great attraction. Some Baptist communities are said at times to have been lax in this respect, whereas the Catholic as well as the Lutheran churches were praised for their strict correctness. This correctness, however, allegedly reduced the membership of both churches.

Expulsion from one's sect for moral offenses has meant, economically, loss of credit and, socially, being declassed.

Numerous observations during the following months confirmed not only that church-mindedness *per se*, although still (1904) rather important, was rapidly dying out; but the particularly important trait, mentioned above, was definitely confirmed. In metropolitan areas I was spontaneously told, in several cases, that a speculator in undeveloped real estate would regularly erect a church building, often an extremely modest one; then he would hire a candidate from one of the various theological seminaries, pay him $500 to $600, and hold out to him a splendid position as a preacher for life if he would gather a congregation and thus preach the building terrain 'full.' Deteriorated churchlike structures which marked failures were shown to me. For the most part, however, the preachers were said to be successful. Neighborly contact, Sunday School, and so on, were said to be indispensable to the newcomer, but above all association with 'morally' reliable neighbors.

Competition among sects is strong, among other things, through the kind of material and spiritual offerings at evening teas of the congregations. Among genteel churches also, musical presentations contribute to this competition. (A tenor in Trinity Church, Boston, who allegedly had to sing on Sundays *only*, at that time received $8,000.) Despite this sharp competition, the sects often maintained fairly good mutual relations. For instance, in the service of the Methodist church which I attended, the Baptist ceremony of the baptism, which I mentioned above, was recommended as a spectacle to edify everybody. In the main, the congregations refused entirely to listen to the preaching of 'dogma' and to confessional distinctions. 'Ethics' alone could be offered. In those instances where I listened to sermons for the middle classes, the typical bourgeois morality, respectable and solid, to be sure, and of the most homely and sober kind, was preached. But the sermons were delivered with obvious inner conviction; the preacher was often moved.

Today the kind of denomination [to which one belongs] is rather irrelevant. It does not matter whether one be Freemason,* Christian Scientist, Adventist, Quaker, or what not. What is decisive is that one be admitted to membership by 'ballot,' after an *examination* and an ethical *probation* in the sense of the virtues which are at a premium for the inner-worldly asceticism of Protestantism and hence, for the ancient puritan tradition. Then, the same effect could be observed.

Closer scrutiny revealed the steady progress of the characteristic process of 'secularization,' to which in modern times all phenomena that originated in religious conceptions succumb. Not only religious associations, hence sects, have this effect on American life. Sects exercised this influence, rather, in a steadily decreasing proportion. If one paid some attention it was striking to observe (even fifteen years ago) that surprisingly many men among the American middle classes (always outside of the quite modern metropolitan areas and the immigration centers) were wearing a little badge (of varying color) in the buttonhole, which reminded one very closely of the rosette of the French Legion of Honor.

When asked what it meant, people regularly mentioned an association with a sometimes adventurous and fantastic name. And it became obvious that its significance and purpose consisted in the following: Almost always the association functioned as a burial insurance, besides offering greatly varied services. But often, and especially in those areas least touched by modern disintegration, the association offered the member the (ethical) claim for brotherly help on the part of every brother who had the means. If he faced an economic emergency for which he himself was not to be blamed, he could make this claim. And in several instances that came to my notice at the time, this claim again followed the very principle, *mutuum date nihil inde sperantes*, or at least a very low rate of interest prevailed. Apparently, such claims were willingly recognized by the members of the brotherhood. Furthermore—and this is the main point in this instance—membership was again acquired through balloting after investigation and a determination of moral worth. And hence the badge in the buttonhole meant, 'I am

---

* An assistant of Semitic languages in an eastern university told me that he regretted not having become 'master of the chair,' for then he would go back into business. When asked what good that would do the answer was: As a traveling salesman or seller he could present himself in a role famous for respectability. He could beat any competition and would be worth his weight in gold.

a gentleman patented after investigation and probation and guaranteed by my membership.' Again, this meant in business life above all, tested *credit worthiness*. One could observe that business opportunities were often decisively influenced by such legitimation.

All these phenomena, which seemed to be rather rapidly disintegrating—at least the religious organizations—were essentially confined to the middle classes. Some cultured Americans often dismissed these facts briefly and with a certain angry disdain as 'humbug' or backwardness, or they even denied them; many of them actually did not know anything about them, as was affirmed to me by William James. Yet these survivals were still alive in many different fields, and sometimes in forms which appeared to be grotesque.

These associations were especially the typical vehicles of social ascent into the circle of the entrepreneurial middle class. They served to diffuse and to maintain the bourgeois capitalist business ethos among the broad strata of the middle classes (the farmers included).

As is well known, not a few (one may well say the majority of the older generation) of the American 'promoters,' 'captains of industry,' of the multi-millionaires and trust magnates belonged formally to sects, especially to the Baptists. However, in the nature of the case, these persons were often affiliated for merely conventional reasons, as in Germany, and only in order to legitimate themselves in personal and social life—not in order to legitimate themselves as businessmen; during the age of the Puritans, such 'economic supermen' did not require such a crutch, and their 'religiosity' was, of course, often of a more than dubious sincerity. The middle classes, above all the strata ascending with and out of the middle classes, were the bearers of that specific religious orientation which one must, indeed, beware viewing among them as only opportunistically determined.*

Yet one must never overlook that without the universal diffusion of these qualities and principles of a methodical way of life, qualities which were maintained through these religious communities,

---

*'Hypocrisy' and conventional opportunism in these matters were hardly stronger developed in America than in Germany where, after all, an officer or civil servant 'without religious affiliation or preference' was also an impossibility. And a Berlin ('Aryan!') Lord Mayor was not confirmed officially because he failed to have one of his children baptised. Only the direction in which conventional 'hypocrisy' moved differed: official careers in Germany, business opportunities in the United States.

capitalism today, even in America, would not be what it is. In the history of any economic area on earth there is no epoch, [except] those quite rigid in feudalism or patrimonialism, in which capitalist figures of the kind of Pierpont Morgan, Rockefeller, Jay Gould, et al. were absent. Only the technical *means* which they used for the acquisition of wealth have changed (of course!). *They* stood and they stand 'beyond good and evil.' But, however high one may otherwise evaluate their importance for economic transformation, they have never been decisive in determining what economic mentality was to dominate a given epoch and a given area. Above all, they were not the creators and they were not to become the bearers of the specifically Occidental bourgeois mentality.

This is not the place to discuss in detail the political and social importance of the religious sects and the numerous similarly exclusive associations and clubs in America which are based upon recruitment by ballot. The entire life of a typical Yankee of the last generation led through a series of such exclusive associations, beginning with the Boys' Club in school, proceeding to the Athletic Club or the Greek Letter Society or to another student club of some nature, then onward to one of the numerous notable clubs of businessmen and the bourgeoisie or finally to the clubs of the metropolitan plutocracy. To gain admission was identical to a ticket of ascent, especially with a certificate before the forum of one's self-feeling; to gain admission meant to have 'proved' oneself. A student in college who was not admitted to any club (or quasi-society) whatsoever was usually a sort of pariah. (Suicides because of failure to be admitted have come to my notice.) A businessman, clerk, technician, or doctor who had the same fate usually was of questionable ability to serve. Today, numerous clubs of this sort are bearers of those tendencies leading toward aristocratic status groups which characterize contemporary American development. These status groups develop alongside of and, what has to be well noted, partly in contrast to the naked plutocracy.

In America mere 'money' in itself also purchases power, but not social honor. Of course, it is a means of acquiring social prestige. It is the same in Germany and everywhere else; except in Germany the appropriate avenue to social honor led from the purchase of a feudal estate to the foundation of an entailed estate, and acquisition of titular nobility, which in turn facilitated the reception of the grandchildren in aristocratic 'society.' In America, the old tradition respected the self-made man more than the heir, and the avenue to social honor consisted in affiliation with a genteel fraternity in a distinguished college, formerly with a distinguished sect (for instance, Presbyterian, in whose churches in New York one could find soft cushions and fans in the pews). At the present time, affiliation with a distinguished club is essential above all else. In addition, the kind of home is important (in 'the street' which in middle-sized cities is almost never lacking) and the kind of dress and sport. Only recently descent from the Pilgrim fathers, from Pocahontas and other Indian ladies, et cetera has become important. This is not the place for a more detailed treatment. There are masses of translating bureaus and agencies of all sorts concerned with reconstructing the pedigrees of the plutocracy. All these phenomena, often highly grotesque, belong in the broad field of the Europeanization of American 'society.'

In the past and up to the very present, it has been a characteristic precisely of the specifically American democracy that it did *not* constitute a formless sand heap of individuals, but rather a buzzing complex of strictly exclusive, yet voluntary associations. Not so long ago these associations still did not recognize the prestige of birth and *inherited* wealth, of the office and educational diploma; at least they recognized these things to such a low degree as has only very rarely been the case in the rest of the world. Yet, even so, these associations were far from accepting anybody with open arms as an equal. To be sure, fifteen years ago an American farmer would not have led his guest past a plowing farmhand (American born!) in the field without making his guest 'shake hands' with the worker after formally introducing them.

Formerly, in a typical American club nobody would remember that the two members, for instance, who play billiards once stood in the relation of boss and clerk. Here equality of gentlemen prevailed absolutely. This was not always the case in the German-American clubs. When asking young German merchants in New York (with the best Hanseatic names) why they all strove to be admitted to an American club instead of the very nicely furnished German one, they answered that their (German-American) bosses would play billiards with them occasionally, however not without making them realize that they (the bosses) thought themselves to be 'very nice' in doing so. To be sure, the American worker's wife accompanying the trade unionist to lunch had completely accommodated herself in dress and behavior, in a somewhat plainer and more awkward fashion, to the bourgeois lady's model.

He who wished to be fully recognized in this democracy, in whatever position, had not only to conform to the conventions of bourgeois society, the very strict men's fashions included, but as a rule he had to be able to show that he had succeeded in gaining admission by ballot to one of the sects, clubs, or fraternal societies, no matter what kind, were it only recognized as sufficiently legitimate. And he had to maintain himself in the society by proving himself to be a gentleman. The parallel in Germany consists in the importance of the *Couleur** and the commission of an officer of the reserve for *commercium* and *connubium*, and the great status significance of qualifying to give satisfaction by duel. The thing is the same, but the direction and material consequence characteristically differ.

He who did not succeed in joining was no gentleman; he who despised doing so, as was usual among Germans,** had to take the hard road, and especially so in business life.

However, as mentioned above, we shall not here analyze the social significance of these conditions, which are undergoing a profound transformation. First, we are interested in the fact that the modern position of the secular clubs and societies with recruitment by ballot is largely the product of a process of *secularization*. Their position is derived from the far more exclusive importance of the prototype of these voluntary associations, to wit, the sects. They stem, indeed, from the sects in the homeland of genuine Yankeedom, the North Atlantic states. Let us recall, first, that the universal and equal franchise within American democracy (of the Whites! for Negroes and all mixtures have, even today, no de facto franchise) and likewise the 'separation of state and church' are only achievements of the recent past, beginning essentially with the nineteenth century. Let us remember that during the colonial period in the central areas of New England, especially in Massachusetts, full citizenship status in the church congregation was the precondition for full citizenship in the state (besides some other prerequisites). The religious congregation indeed determined admission or non-admission to political citizenship status.[3]

The decision was made according to whether or not the person had *proved* his religious qualification through conduct, in the broadest meaning of the word, as was the case among all Puritan sects. The Quakers in Pennsylvania were not in any lesser way

---

* Student fraternity, comparable to a 'Greek letter society.'

** But note above. Entry into an American club (in school or later) is always the decisive moment for the loss of German nationality.

masters of that state until some time before the War of Independence. This was actually the case, though *formally* they were not the only full political citizens. They were political masters only by virtue of extensive gerrymandering.

The tremendous social significance of admission to full enjoyment of the rights of the sectarian congregation, especially the privilege of being admitted to the *Lord's Supper*, worked among the sects in the direction of breeding that ascetist professional ethic which was adequate to modern capitalism during the period of its origin. It can be demonstrated that everywhere, including Europe, the religiosity of the ascetist sects has for several centuries worked in the same way as has been illustrated by the personal experiences mentioned above for [the case of] America.

When focusing on the religious background[4] of these Protestant sects, we find in their literary documents, especially among those of the Quakers and Baptists up to and throughout the seventeenth century, again and again jubilation over the fact that the sinful 'children of the world' distrust one another in business but that they have confidence in the religiously determined righteousness of the pious.[5]

Hence, they give credit and deposit their money only with the pious, and they make purchases in their stores because there, and there alone, they are given honest and *fixed prices*. As is known, the Baptists have always claimed to have first raised this price policy to a principle. In addition to the Baptists, the Quakers raise the claim, as the following quotation shows, to which Mr. Eduard Bernstein drew my attention at the time:

> But it was not only in matters which related to the law of the land where the primitive members held their words and engagements sacred. This trait was remarked to be true of them in their concerns of trade. On their first appearance as a society, they suffered as tradesmen because others, displeased with the peculiarity of their manners, withdrew their custom from their shops. But in a little time the great outcry against them was that they got the trade of the country into their hands. This outcry arose in part from a strict exemption of all commercial agreements between them and others and *because they never asked two prices for the commodities they sold.*[6]

The view that the gods bless with riches the man who pleases them, through sacrifice or through his kind of conduct, was indeed diffused all over the world. However, the Protestant sects consciously brought this idea into connection with this kind of religious conduct, according to the principle of early capitalism: 'Honesty is the best policy.' This connection is found, although not quite exclusively, among these Protestant sects, but with characteristic continuity and consistency it is found *only* among them.

The whole typically bourgeois ethic was from the beginning common to all aceticist sects and conventicles and it is identical with the ethic practiced by the sects in America up to the very present. The Methodists, for example, held to be forbidden:

(1) to make words when buying and selling ('haggling')

(2) to trade with commodities before the custom tariff has been paid on them

(3) to charge rates of interest higher than the law of the country permits

(4) 'to gather treasures on earth' (meaning the transformation of investment capital into 'funded wealth')

(5) to borrow without being sure of one's ability to pay back the debt

(6) luxuries of all sorts

But it is not only this ethic, already discussed in detail,[*] which goes back to the early beginnings of asceticist sects. Above all, the social premiums, the means of discipline, and, in general, the whole organizational basis of Protestant sectarianism with all its ramifications reach back to those beginnings. The survivals in contemporary America are the derivatives of a religious regulation of life which once worked with penetrating efficiency. Let us, in a brief survey, clarify the nature of these sects and the mode and direction of their operation.

Within Protestantism the principle of the 'believer's church' first emerged distinctly among the Baptists in Zürich in 1523–4.[7] This principle restricted the congregation to 'true' Christians; hence, it meant a voluntary association of really sanctified people segregated from the world. Thomas Münzer had rejected infant baptism; but he did not take the next step, which demanded repeated baptism of adults baptized as children (anabaptism). Following Thomas Münzer, the Zürich Baptists in 1525 introduced adult baptism (possibly including anabaptism). Migrant journeymen-artisans were the main bearers of

---

[*] In *The Protestant Ethic and the Spirit of Capitalism.*

the Baptist movement. After each suppression they carried it to new areas. Here we shall not discuss in detail the individual forms of this voluntarist inner-worldly asceticism of the Old Baptists, the Mennonites, the Baptists, the Quakers, nor shall we again describe how every asceticist denomination, Calvinism[8] and Methodism included, were again and again constrained into the same path.

This resulted either in the conventicle of the exemplary Christians *within* the church (Pietism), or else the community of religious 'full citizens,' legitimated as faultless, became masters *over* the church. The rest of the members merely belonged as a passive status group, as minor Christians subject to discipline (Independents).

In Protestantism the external and internal conflict of the two structural principles—of the 'church' as a compulsory association for the administration of grace, and of the 'sect' as a voluntary association of religiously qualified persons—runs through the centuries from Zwingli to Kuyper and Stöcker. Here we merely wish to consider those consequences of the voluntarist principle which are practically important in their influence upon conduct. In addition, we recall merely that the decisive idea of keeping the Lord's Supper pure, and therefore excluding unsanctified persons, led also to a way of treating church discipline among those denominations which failed to form sects. It was especially the predestinarian Puritans who, in effect, approached the discipline of the sects.[9]

The central social significance of the Lord's Supper for the Christian communities is evidenced in this. For the sects themselves, the idea of the purity of the sacramental communion was decisive at the very time of their origin.[10] Immediately the first consistent voluntarist, Browne, in his 'Treatise of Reformation without tarying for anie' (presumably 1582), emphasized the compulsion to hold communion at the Lord's Supper with 'wicked men' as the main reason for rejecting Episcopalianism and Presbyterianism.[11] The Presbyterian church struggled in vain to settle the problem. Already under Elizabeth (Wandworth Conference) this was the decisive point.*

The question of *who* might exclude a person from the Lord's Supper played an ever-recurrent role in the Parliament of the English Revolution. At first (1645) ministers and elders, that is, laymen, were to decide these matters freely. Parliament attempted to

---

* The English Presbyterians under Elizabeth wished to recognize the 39 articles of the Church of England (with reservations concerning articles 34 to 36, which are here of no interest).

determine those cases in which exclusion should be permissible. All other cases were to be made dependent on the consent of Parliament. This meant 'Erastianism,' against which the Westminster Assembly protested sharply.

The Independent party excelled in that it admitted only persons with tickets to communion, besides the local residents recognized to be in good standing. Members from outside congregations received tickets only upon recommendation by qualified members. The certificates of qualification (letters of recommendation), which were issued in case of removal to another place or in case of travel, also occur in the seventeenth century.[12] *Within* the official church, Baxter's conventicles (associations), which in 1657 were introduced in sixteen counties, were to be established as a kind of voluntary censorship bureau. These would assist the minister in determining the qualification and exclusion of scandalous persons from the Lord's Supper.[13] The 'five dissenting brethren' of the Westminster Assembly—upper-class refugees who had lived in Holland—had already aimed at similar ends when they proposed to permit voluntaristic congregations to exist *beside* the parish and also to grant them the right to vote for delegates to the synod. The entire church history of New England is filled with struggles over such questions: who was to be admitted to the sacraments (or, for instance, as a godfather), whether the children of non-admitted persons could be baptized,* under what clauses the latter could be admitted, and similar questions. The difficulty was that not only was the worthy person allowed to receive the Lord's Supper, but he *had* to receive it.[14] Hence, if the believer doubted his own worth and decided to stay away from the Lord's Supper, the decision did not remove his sin.[15] The congregation, on the other hand, was jointly responsible to the Lord for keeping unworthy and especially reprobated persons[16] away from communion, for purity's sake. Thus the congregation was jointly and especially responsible for the administration of the sacrament by a worthy minister in a state of grace. Therewith, the primordial problems of church constitution were resurrected. In vain Baxter's compromise proposal attempted to mediate by suggesting that at least in case of an emergency the sacrament should be received from an unworthy minister, thus from one whose conduct was questionable.[17]

---

* Even the Brownist petition to King James of 1603 protested against this.

The ancient Donatist principle of personal charisma stood in hard and unmitigated opposition to the principle of the church as an institution administering grace,[18] as in the time of early Christianity. The principle of instituted grace was radically established in the Catholic Church through the priest's *character indelebilis*, but it also dominated the official churches of the Reformation. The uncompromising radicalism of the Independentist world of ideas rested upon the religious responsibility of the congregation as a whole. This held for the worthiness of the ministers as well as for the brethren admitted to communion. And that is how things still stand in principle.

As is known, the Kuyper schism in Holland during recent decades had far-reaching political ramifications. It originated in the following manner: Against the claims of the Synodal church government of the Herformde Kerk der Nederlanden, the elders of a church in Amsterdam, hence *laymen*, with the later prime minister Kuyper (who was also a plain lay elder) at the helm, refused to acknowledge the confirmation certificates of preachers of outside congregations as sufficient for admission to communion if from their standpoint such outside preachers were unworthy or unbelieving.[19] In substance, this was precisely the antagonism between Presbyterians and Independents during the sixteenth century; for consequences of the greatest importance emerged from the joint responsibility of the congregation. Next to the voluntarist principle, that is, free admission of the qualified, and of the qualified alone, as members of the congregation, we find the principle of the sovereignty of the local sacramental community. Only the local religious community, by virtue of personal acquaintance and investigation, could judge whether a member were qualified. But a church government of an inter-local association could not do so, however freely elected such church government might be. The local congregation could discriminate only if the number of members were restricted. Hence, in principle, only relatively small congregations were appropriate.[20]

Where the communities were too large for this, either conventicles were formed, as in Pietism or the members were organized in groups, which, in turn, were the bearers of church discipline, as in Methodism.[21] The extraordinarily strict moral discipline[22] of the self-governing congregation constituted the third principle. This was unavoidable because of the interest in the purity of the sacramental community (or, as among the Quakers, the interest in the purity of the community of prayer). The discipline of the asceticist sect was, in fact, far more rigorous than the discipline of any church. In this respect, the sect resembles the monastic order. The sect discipline is also analogous to monastic discipline in that it established the principle of the novitiate.* In contrast to the principles of the official Protestant churches, persons expelled because of moral offenses were often denied all intercourse with the members of the congregation. The sect thus invoked an absolute boycott against them, which included business life. Occasionally the sect avoided any relation with non-brethren except in cases of absolute necessity.[23] And the sect placed disciplinary power predominantly into the hands of laymen. No spiritual authority could assume the community's joint responsibility before God. The weight of the lay elders was very great even among the Presbyterians. However, the Independents, and even more, the Baptists signified a struggle against the domination or the conurecration by theologians.[24] In exact correspondence this struggle led naturally to the clericalization of the lay members, who now took over the functions of moral control through self-government, admonition, and possible excommunication.[25] The domination of laymen in the church found its expression, in part, in the quest for freedom of the layman to preach (liberty of prophesying).[26] In legitimizing this demand, reference was made to the conditions of the early Christian community. This demand was not only very shocking to the Lutheran idea of the pastoral office but also to the Presbyterian idea of God's order. The domination of laymen, in part, found its expression in an opposition to any professional theologian and preacher. Only charisma, neither training nor office, should be recognized.**

The Quakers have adhered to the principle that in the religious assembly anyone could speak, but he alone should speak who was moved by the spirit. Hence no professional minister exists at all. To be sure, today this is, in all probability, nowhere radically effected. The official 'legend' is that members who, in the experience of the congregation, are especially accessible to the spirit during service are seated upon a special bench opposite the congregation. In profound silence the people wait for the spirit to take possession of one of them (or of some other member of the congregation). But during service in a Pennsylvania college, unfortunately and against my hopes, the spirit

---

* In all probability among all sects there existed a period of probation. Among the Methodists, for example, it lasted for six months.

** Already Smyth in Amsterdam demanded that when preaching the regenerate must not even have the Bible in front of him.

did not take hold of the plainly and beautifully costumed old lady who was seated on the bench and whose charisma was so highly praised. Instead, undoubtedly by agreement, the spirit took hold of a brave college librarian who gave a very learned lecture on the concept of the 'saint.'

To be sure, other sects have not drawn such radical conclusions, or at least not for good. However, either the minister is not active principally as a 'hireling,'[27] holding only honorific position, or else he serves for voluntary honorific donations.[*] Again his ministerial service may be a secondary occupation and only for the refunding of his expenses;[**] or he can be dismissed at any time; or a sort of missionary organization prevails with itinerant preachers[28] working only once in a while in the same 'circuit,' as is the case with Methodism.[29] Where the office (in the traditional sense) and hence the theological qualification were maintained,[30] such skill was considered as a mere technical and specialist prerequisite. However, the really decisive quality was the charisma of the state of grace, and the authorities were geared to discern it.

Authorities, like Cromwell's triers (local bodies for the handling of certificates of religious qualification) and the ejectors (ministerial disciplinary office),[***] had to examine the fitness of the ministers to serve. The charismatic character of authority is seen to have been preserved in the same way in which the charismatic character of the membership in the community itself was preserved, just as Cromwell's army of Saints allowed only religiously qualified persons to pass the Lord's Supper to them, so Cromwell's soldiers refused to go into battle under an officer who did not belong to his sacramental community of the religiously qualified.[31]

Internally, among the sect members, the spirit of early Christian brotherliness prevailed, at least among the early Baptists and derived denominations; or at least brotherliness was demanded.[32] Among some sects it was considered taboo to call on the law courts.[****] In case of need, mutual aid was obligatory.[33] Naturally, *business* dealings

---

[*] The latter was demanded for all preachers in the Agreement of the People of 1 May 1649.

[**] Thus the local preachers of the Methodists.

[***] Thus, in accordance with the proposal of 1652 and essentially also in accordance with the church constitution of 1654.

[****] The Methodists have often attempted to sanction the appeal to the secular judge by expulsion. On the other hand, in several cases, they have established authorities upon which one could call if debtors did not pay promptly.

with nonmembers were not interdicted (except occasionally among wholly radical communities).

Yet it was self-understood that one preferred the brethren.* From the very beginning, one finds the system of certificates (concerning membership and conduct),[34] which were given to members who moved to another place. The charities of the Quakers were so highly developed that in consequence of the burdens incurred their inclination to propagandize was finally crippled. The cohesiveness of the congregations was so great that, with good reason, it is said to be one of the factors determining New England settlements. In contrast to the South, New England settlements were generally ompact and, from the beginning, strongly urban in character.**

It is obvious that in all these points the modern functions of American sects and sectlike associations, as described in the beginning of this essay, are revealed as straight derivatives, rudiments, and survivals of those conditions which once prevailed in all asceticist sects and conventicles. Today they are decaying. Testimony for the sectarian's immensely exclusive 'pride in caste' has existed from the very beginning.***

Now, what part of this whole development was and is actually decisive for our problem? Excommunication in the Middle Ages also had political and civic consequences. Formally this was even harsher than where sect freedom existed. Moreover, in the Middle Ages only Christians could be full citizens. During the Middle Ages it was also possible to proceed through the disciplinary powers of the church against a bishop who would not pay his debts, and, as Aloys Schulte has beautifully shown, this possibility gave the bishop a credit rating over and above a secular prince. Likewise, the fact that a Prussian Lieutenant was subject to discharge if he was incapable of paying off debts provided a higher credit rating for him. And the same held for the German fraternity student. Oral confession and the disciplinary power of the church during the Middle Ages also provided the means to enforce church discipline effectively. Finally, to secure a legal claim, the opportunity

---

* With the Methodists this is expressly prescribed.

** Doyle in his work which we have repeatedly cited ascribes the industrial character of New England, in contrast to the agrarian colonies, to this factor.

*** Cf., for example, Doyle's comments about the status conditions in New England, where the families bearing old religious literary tradition, not the 'propertied classes,' formed the aristocracy.

provided by the oath was exploited to secure excommunication of the debtor.

In all these cases, however, the forms of behavior that were favored or tabooed through such conditions and means differed totally from those which Protestant asceticism bred or suppressed. With the lieutenant, for instance, or the fraternity student, and proably with the bishop as well, the enhanced credit rating certainly did not rest upon the breeding of personal qualities suitable for business; and following up this remark directly: even though the effects in all three cases were intended to have the same direction, they were worked out in quite different ways. The medieval, like the Lutheran church discipline, first, was vested in the hands of the ministerial officeholder; secondly, this discipline worked—as far as it was effective at all—through authoritarian means; and, thirdly, it punished and placed premiums upon concrete individual acts.

The church discipline of the Puritans and of the sects was vested, first, at least in part and often wholly, in the hands of laymen. Secondly, it worked through the necessity of one's having to hold one's own; and, thirdly, it bred or, if one wishes, selected qualities. The last point is the most important one.

The member of the sect (or conventicle) had to have qualities of a certain kind in order to enter the community circle. Being endowed with these qualities was important for the development of rational modern capitalism, as has been shown in the first essay.* In order to hold his own in this circle the member had to *prove* repeatedly that he was endowed with these qualities. They were constantly and continuously bred in him. For, like his bliss in the beyond, his whole social existence in the here and now depended upon his 'proving' himself. The Catholic confession of sins was, to repeat, by comparison a means of *relieving* the person from the tremendous internal pressure under which the sect member in his conduct was constantly held. How certain orthodox and heterodox religious communities of the Middle Ages have been forerunners of the ascetic denominations of Protestantism shall not here and now be discussed.

According to all experience there is no stronger means of breeding traits than through the necessity of holding one's own in the circle of one's associates. The continuous and unobtrusive ethical discipline of the sects was, therefore, related to authoritarian

---

* *The Protestant Ethic and the Spirit of Capitalism.*

lx

church discipline as rational breeding and selection are related to ordering and forbidding.

In this as in almost every other respect, the Puritan sects are the most specific bearers of the inner-worldly form of asceticism. Moreover, they are the most consistent and, in a certain sense, the only consistent antithesis to the universalist Catholic Church—a compulsory organization for the administration of grace. The Puritan sects put the most powerful individual interest of social self-esteem in the service of this breeding of traits. Hence *individual* motives and personal self-interests were also placed in the service of maintaining and propagating the 'bourgeois' Puritan ethic, with all its ramifications. This is absolutely decisive for its penetrating and for its powerful effect.

To repeat, it is not the ethical *doctrine* of a religion, but that form of ethical conduct upon which *premiums* are placed that matters.[35] Such premiums operate through the form and the condition of the respective goods of salvation. And such conduct constitutes 'one's' specific 'ethos' in the sociological sense of the word. For Puritanism, that conduct was a certain methodical, rational way of life which—given certain conditions—paved the way for the 'spirit' of modern capitalism. The premiums were placed upon 'proving' oneself before God in the sense of attaining salvation—which is found in *all* Puritan denominations—and 'proving' oneself before men in the sense of socially holding one's own within the Puritan sects. Both aspects were mutually supplementary and operated in the same direction: they helped to deliver the 'spirit' of modern capitalism, its specific *ethos*: the ethos of the modern *bourgeois middle classes*.

The ascetic conventicles and sects formed one of the most important historical foundations of modern 'individualism.' Their radical break away from patriarchal and authoritarian bondage,[36] as well as their way of interpreting the statement that one owes more obedience to God than to man, was especially important.

Finally, in order to understand the nature of these ethical effects, a comparative remark is required. In the *guilds* of the Middle Ages there was frequently a control of the general ethical standard of the members similar to that exercised by the discipline of the ascetic Protestant sects.[37] But the unavoidable difference in the effects of guild and of sect upon the economic conduct of the individual is obvious.

The guild united members of the same occupation; hence it united *competitors*. It did so in order to limit competition as well as the rational striving for profit which operated through competition. The guild trained for 'civic' virtues and, in a certain sense, was the bearer of bourgeois 'rationalism' (a point which will not be discussed here in detail). The guild accomplished this through a 'subsistence policy' and through traditionalism. In so far as guild regulation of the economy gained effectiveness, its practical reIsults are well known.

The sects, on the other hand, united men through the selection and the breeding of ethically qualified *fellow believers*. Their membership was not based upon apprenticeship or upon the family relations of technically qualified members of an occupation. The sect controlled and regulated the members' conduct *exclusively* in the sense of formal *righteousness* and methodical asceticism. It was devoid of the purpose of a material subsistence policy which handicapped an expansion of the rational striving for profit. The capitalist success of a guild member undermined the spirit of the guild—as happened in England and France—and hence capitalist success was shunned. But the capitalist success of a sect brother, if legally attained, was proof of his worth and of his state of grace, and it raised the prestige and the propaganda chances of the sect. Such success was therefore welcome, as the several statements quoted above show. The organization of free labor in guilds, in their Occidental medieval form, has certainly—very much against their intention—not only been a handicap but also a precondition for the capitalist organization of labor, which was, perhaps, indispensable.[38] But the guild, of course, could not give birth to the modern bourgeois capitalist *ethos*. Only the methodical way of life of the ascetic sects could legitimate and put a halo around the economic 'individualist' impulses of the modern capitalist ethos.

Endnotes

Note: Certain footnotes in this chapter have been placed in the text.

1. This is a new and greatly enlarged draft of an article published in the *Frankfurter Zeitung*, Eastern 1906, then somewhat enlarged in the *Christliche Welt*, 1906, pp. 558 ff., 577 ff., under the title, 'Churches and Sects.' I have repeatedly referred to this article as supplementing *The Protestant Ethic and the Spirit of Capitalism*. The present rewriting is motivated by the fact that the concept of sect as worked out by myself (as a contrasting conception to 'church') has, in the meanwhile and to my joy, been taken over and treated thoroughly by Troeltsch in his *Soziallehren der christlichen Kirchen* [*The Social Teachings of the Christian Churches*, trans. by 0. Wyon, 2 vols., London, 1931]. Hence, conceptual discussions can the more easily be omitted as what is necessary has been said already in *The Protestant Ethic and the Spirit of*

Capitalism, pp. 254 f., note 173. This essay contains only the barest data supplementing that essay.

2. Details are of no interest here. Reference should be made to respective volumes of the 'American Church History Series'—a work of uneven value.

3. The organization of the religious congregation during the immigration to New England often preceded the political societalization (in the fashion of the well-known pact of the Pilgrim Fathers). Thus, the Dorchester Immigrants of 1619 first bound themselves together by organizing a church congregation *before* emigrating, and they elected a parson and a teacher. In the colony of Massachusetts the church was formally a completely autonomous corporation, which admitted, however, only citizens for membership, and affiliation with which, on the other hand, was a prerequisite of citizenship. Likewise, at first, church membership and good conduct (meaning admission to the Lord's Supper) were prerequisites of citizenship in New Haven (before it was incorporated in Connecticut township was obliged to maintain the church) (a defection from the strict principles of Independentism to Presbyterianism).

This at once meant a somewhat laxer practice, for after the incorporation of New Haven the church there was restricted to giving out certificates stating that the respective person was religiously inoffensive and of sufficient means. Even during the seventeenth century, on the occasion of the incorporation of Maine and New Hampshire, Massachusetts had to depart from the full strictness of the religious qualification of political rights. On the question of church membership compromises had also to be made, the most famous of which is the Half-way Covenant of 1657. In addition, those who could not prove themselves to be regenerate were nevertheless admitted to membership. But, until the beginning of the eighteenth century, they were not admitted to communion.

4. Some references from the older literature which is not very well known in Germany may be listed. A sketch of Baptist history is present in: Vedder, *A Short History of the Baptists* (Second ed. London, 1897). Concerning Hanserd Knollys: Culross, *Hanserd Knollys*, vol. II of the Baptist Manuals edited by P. Gould (London, 1891).

For the history of Anabaptism: E. B. Bax, *Rise and Fall of the Anabaptists (New York, 1902). Concerning Smyth: Henry M. Dexter, The True Story of John Smyth, the Se-Baptist*, as told by himself and his contemporaries (Boston, 1881). The important publications of the Hanserd Knollys Society (printed for the Society by J. Hadden, Castle Street, Finsbury, 1846–54) have been cited already. Further official documents in *The Baptist Church Manual* by J. Newton Brown, D.D. (Philadelphia, American Baptist Publishing Society, 30 S. Arch Street). Concerning the Quakers, besides the cited work of Sharpless: A. C. Applegarth, *The Quakers in Pennsylvania*, ser. X, vol. VIII, IX of the

Johns Hopkins University Studies in History and Political Science. G. Lorimer, *Baptists in History* (New York, 1902), J. A. Seiss, *Baptist System Examined* (Lutheran Publication Society, 1902).

Concerning New England (besides Doyle): The Massachusetts Historical Collections; furthermore, Weeden, *Economic and Social History of New England*, 1620–1789, 2 vols. Daniel W. Howe, *The Puritan Republic* (Indianapolis, Bobbs-Merrill Co.).

Concerning the development of the 'Covenant' idea in older Presbyterianism, its church discipline, and its relation to the official church, on the one hand, and to Congregationalists and sectarians on the other hand, see: Burrage, *The Church Covenant Idea* (1904), and *The Early English Dissenters* (1912). Furthermore, W. M. Macphail, *The Presbyterian Church* (1918). J. Brown, *The English Puritans* (1910). Important documents in Usher, *The Presbyterian Movement*, 1584–89 (Com. Soc., 1905). We give here only an extremely provisional list of what is relevant for us.

5. During the seventeenth century this was so much taken for granted that Bunyan, as mentioned previously, makes 'Mr. Money-Love' argue that one may even become pious *in order* to get rich, especially in order to add to one's patronage; for it should be irrelevant for what reason one had become pious. (*Pilgrims' Progress*, Tauchnitz ed., p.114.)

6. Thomas Clarkson, *Portraiture of the Christian Profession and Practice of the Society of Friends*. Third edition (London, 1867), p. 276. (The first edition appeared around 1830.)

7. Sources are Zwingli's statements, Füssli I, p. 228, cf. also pp. 243, 253, 263, and his *Elenchus contra catabaptistas,' Werke III*, pp. 357, 362. In his own congregation, Zwingli characteristically had much trouble with Antipedobaptists [opposed to infant baptism]. The Antipedobaptists, in turn, viewed the Baptist 'separation,' hence voluntarism, as objectionable according to the Scriptures. A Brownist petition of 1603 to King James I demanded the exclusion of all 'wicked liars' from the church and only the admission of the 'faithful' and their children. But the (Presbyterian) Directory of Church Government of (probably) 1584 (published from the original for the first time in the Heidelberg Ph.D. thesis of A. F. Scott Pearson, 1912) demanded in article 37 that only people who had submitted to the disciplinary code, or *literas testimoniales idoneas aliunde attuleriut* [had furnished testimonial letters from elsewhere] be admitted to communion.

8. The problematic nature of the sectarian voluntarist principle follows logically from the demand for the *ecclesia pira* by the reformed (Calvinist) church. This dogmatic principle, as opposed to the sect principle, is strikingly evident in modern times in A. Kuyper (the well-known later Premier minister). The dogmatic position in his final programmatic essay is especially obvious: *Separatie en doleantie* (Amsterdam, 1890). He sees the problem as due to the absence of the infallible doctrinal office among non-Catholic Christianity. This doctrine asserts that

the *Corpus* of the visible church cannot be the *Corpus Christi* of the old Reformed Church, but that it must rather remain divided in time and space, and the shortcomings of human nature must remain peculiar to it. A visible church originates solely through *an act of will* on the part of the believers and by virtue of the authority given them by Christ. Hence the *potestas ecclesiastica* may be vested neither in Christ himself, nor in the *ministri*, but only in the believing congregation. (In this Kuyper follows Voët.) The greater community originates through the legal and voluntary association of the congregations. This association, however, must be a religious obligation. The Roman principle, according to which a church member is *eo ipso* a member of the parish of his local community, is to be rejected. Baptism makes him a mere passive *membrum incompletum* and grants no rights. Not baptism, but only *belijdenis en stipulatie* (confession of faith and profession of good will) gives membership in the congregation, in the legal sense. Membership alone is identical with subordination to the *disciplina ecclesiae* (again following Voët). Church law is believed to deal with the manmade rules of the visible church, which, though bound to God's order, do not represent God's order itself. (Cf. Voët *Pol. Eccles.* vol. I, pp. I and II.) All these ideas are Independentist variants of the genuine constitutional law of the reformed churches and imply an active participation of the *congregation*, hence of the laity, in the admission of new members. (Von Rieker has described this law especially well.) The cooperative participation of the whole congregation also constituted the program of the Brownist Independents in New England. They adhered to it in constant struggle against the successfully advancing 'Johnson ist' faction which advocated church government by the 'ruling elders.' It goes without saying that only 'Regenerates' were to be admitted (according to Baillie 'only one out of forty'). During the nineteenth century the church theory of the Scotch Independents similarly demanded that admission be granted only by special resolution (Sack, loc. cit.). However, Kuyper's church theory *per se* is, of course, *not* 'congregationalist' in character.

According to Kuyper, individual congregations are religiously obliged to affiliate with and to belong to the church as a whole. There can be only one legitimate church in one place. This obligation to affiliate is only dropped, and the obligation of *separatie* emerges only when *doleantie* has failed; that is, an attempt must have been made to improve the wicked church as a whole through active protest and passive obstruction (*doleeren*, meaning to protest, occurs as a technical term in the seventeenth century). And finally, if all means have been exhausted and if the attempt has proved to be in vain, and force has prevailed, then separation is obligatory. In that case, of course, an independent constitution is obligatory, since there are no 'subjects' in the church and since the believers *per se* hold a God-given office. Revolution can be a duty to God. (Kuyper, *De conflict gekomen*, pp. 30–31).

Kuyper (like Voët) takes the old independent view that only those who participate in the *communion of the Lord's Supper* by admission are full members of the church. And only

the latter are able to assume the trusteeship of their children during baptism. A believer, in the *theological* sense, is one who is inwardly converted; in the legal sense a believer is only one who is *admitted* to the Lord's Supper.

9. The fundamental prerequisite for Kuyper is that it is a sin not to purge the sacramental communion of non-believers. (*Dreigend Conflict*, 1886, p. 41; reference is made to Cor. I, II, 26, 27, 29; Tim. I, 5, 22; Apoc. 18, 4.) Yet according to him the church never has judged the state of grace 'before God'—in contrast to the 'Labadists' (radical Pietists). But for admission to the Lord's Supper *only belief* and *conduct* are decisive. The transactions of the Netherland Synods of the sixteenth and seventeenth centuries are filled with discussions of the prerequisites of admission to the Lord's Supper. For example, the Southern Dutch Synod of 1574 agreed that the Lord's Supper should not be given if no organized congregation existed. The elders and deacons were to be careful that no unworthy person be admitted. The Synod of Rotterdam of 1575 resolved that all those who led an obviously offensive life should not be admitted. (The elders of the congregation, not the preachers alone, decided admissions, and it is almost always the congregation which raises such objections—often against the more lax policy of the preachers. Cf. for instance, the case cited by Reitsma [vol. II, p. 231].) The question of admission to the Lord's Supper included the following cases: whether the husband of an Anabaptist could be admitted to the Lord's Supper was decided at the Synod at Leyden in 1619, article 114; whether a Lombard's servant should be admitted, Provincial Synod at Deventer, 1595, article 24; whether men who declared their bankruptcy, Synod of Alkmaar, 1599, article II, similarly of 1605, article 28, and men who had settled an accord, Northern Holland Synod of Enkhuizen of 1618, Grav. Class. Amstel. No. 16, should be admitted. The latter question is answered in the affirmative in case the *consistorium* finds the list of properties sufficient and judges the reservations for food and clothing made therein adequate for the debtor and his family. But the decision is especially affirmative when the creditors state themselves to be satisfied by the accord and when the failing debtor makes a confession of guilt. Concerning non-admission of Lombards, see above. Exclusion of spouses in case of quarrelsomeness, Reitsma III, p. 91. The reconciliation of parties to a legal dispute is a prerequisite for admission. For the duration of the dispute they must stay away from communion. There is conditional admission of a person who has lost a libel suit and has appealed the case. Ibid. III, p. 176.

Calvin may well have been the first to have forced through in the Strassborg congregation of French emigrants the exclusion of the person from the Lord's Supper whose outcome in the examination of worthiness was unsatisfactory. (But then the minister, not the congregation, made the decision.) According to Calvin's genuine doctrine (Inst. Chr. Rel. IV, chap. 12, p. 4) excommunications should legitimately apply only to reprobates. (At the quoted place excommunication is called the promulgation of the *divine* sentence.) But in the same place (cf. p. 5) it is also treated as a means of 'improvement.'

In America, nowadays, among the Baptists formal excommunication, at least in metropolitan areas, is very rare. In practice it is replaced by 'dropping,' in which case the name of the person is simply and discreetly stricken from the record. Among the sects and Independents, laymen have always been the typical bearers of discipline; whereas the original Calvinist-Presbyterian church discipline expressly and systematically strove for domination over state and church. However, even the 'Directory' of the English Presbyterians of 1584 (p. 14, note 2) summoned an equal number of lay elders and ministers to the classes and to the higher offices of the church government.

The mutual relation of the elders and the congregation has been occasionally ordered in different ways. Just as the (Presbyterian) Long Parliament placed the decision of exclusion from the Lord's Supper into the hands of the (lay) elders, so the Cambridge Platform did likewise about 1647 in New England. Up to the middle of the nineteenth century the Scotch Independents, however, used to transmit notice of misconduct to a commission. After the commission's report the whole congregation decided about the exclusion, in correspondence with the stricter view of the joint responsibility of all individuals. This absolutely corresponded with the Brownist confession quoted above, which was submitted to King James I in 1603 (Dexter, loc. Cit. P. 303) whereas the 'Johnsonists' considered the sovereignty of the (elected) elders to be Biblical. The elders should be able to excommunicate even against the decision of the congregation (occasion for Ainsworth's secession). Concerning the corresponding conditions among the early English Presbyterians, see the literature quoted in note 4, above, and the Ph.D. thesis of Pearson quoted in note 7, above.

10. The Dutch Pietists, by the way, believed in the same principle. Lodensteijn, for instance, held to the point of view that one must not commune with non-regenerates; and the latter are for him expressly those who do not bear the *signs* of regeneration. He even went so far as to advise against saying the Lord's Prayer with children since they had not as yet become 'children of the Lord.' In the Netherlands, Köhler still occasionally found the view that the regenerate does not sin at all. Calvinist orthodoxy and an astonishing knowledge of the Bible was found precisely among the petty bourgeois masses. Also here it was the very orthodox who, distrusting theological education and faced with the church regulation of 1852, complained of the insufficient representation of laymen in the Synod (besides the lack of a sufficiently

strict *'censura morum'*). Certainly no orthodox Lutheran church party in Germany would have thought of that at the time.

11. Quoted in Dexter, *Congregationalism of the Last Three Hundred Years as Seen in its Literature* (New York, 1880), p. 97.

12. During the seventeenth century, letters of recommendation from non-resident Baptists of the local congregations were a prerequisite for admission to the Lord's Supper. Non-Baptists could only be admitted after having been examined and approved by the congregation. (Appendix to the edition of the Hanserd Knollys Confession of 1689, West Church, Pa., 1817). Participation in the Lord's Supper was *compulsory* for the qualified member. Failure to affiliate with the legitimately constituted congregation of one's place of residence was viewed as schism. With regard to the obligatory community with other congregations, the Baptist point of view resembled that of Kuyper (cf. above, note 8). However *all* jurisdictional authority *higher* than that of the individual church was rejected. Concerning the *litterae testimoniales* [testimonial letters] among the Covenanters and early English presbyterians, see note 7 and the literature quoted in note 4.

13. Shaw, *Church History under the Commonwealth*, vol. II, pp. 152–65; Gardiner, *Commonwealth*, vol. III, p. 231.

14. This principle was expressed, for instance, in resolutions like the one of the Synod of Edam, 1585 (in the Collection of Reitsma, p. 139).

15. Baxter, *Eccles. Dir.*, vol. II, p. 108, discusses in detail the shying away of doubtful members from the Lord's Supper at the congregation (because of article 25 of the Church of England).

16. The doctrine of Predestination also represents here the purest type. Its relevance and great practical importance is evidenced in nothing so clearly as the bitter struggle over the question whether children of reprobates should be admitted to baptism after having proved themselves to be worthy. The practical significance of the doctrine of Predestination has been, however, again and again unjustly doubted. Three of the four Amsterdam Refugee congregations were in favor of admitting the children (at the beginning of the seventeenth century); but in New England only the 'Half-way Covenant' of 1657 brought a relaxation of this point. For Holland see also note 9.

17. Loc. cit. vol. II, p. 110.

18. Already at the beginning of the seventeenth century the prohibition of the conventicles (*Slijkgeuzen*) caused a general *Kulturkampf* in Holland. Elizabeth proceeded against the conventicles with frightful harshness (in 1593 with threat of capital punishment). The reason behind this was the anti-authoritarian character of asceticist religiosity or, better in this case, the competitive relationship between the religious and secular authority (Cartwright had expressly demanded that excommunication of princes also be permitted). As a matter of fact the example

of Scotland, the classic soil of Presbyterian church discipline and clerical domination against the king, had to have a deterrent effect.

19. In order to escape the religious pressure of orthodox preachers, liberal Amsterdam citizens had sent their children to neighboring congregations for their confirmation lessons. The Kerkraad [church council] of the Amsterdam congregation refused (in 1886) to acknowledge certificates of the moral conduct of the communicants made out by such ministers. The communicants were excluded from the Lord's Supper because the communion had to remain pure and because the Lord, rather than man, must be obeyed. When the synodal commission approved of the objection against this deviation, the church council refused to obey and adopted new rules. In accordance with the latter, suspension of the church council gave the council exclusive disposition over the church. It rejected community with the synod and the now suspended (lay) elders, T. Rutgers and Kuyper, seized by the ruse the Nieuwe Kerk [New Church] in spite of the watchmen who had been hired. (Cf. Hogerfeil, *De kerkelijke strijd te Amsterdam*, 1886, and Kuyper's publications mentioned above.) During the 1820's the predestinarian movement had already begun under the leadership of Bilderdijk and his disciples, Isaac da Costa and Abraham Capadose (two baptized Jews). (*Because* of the doctrine of predestination it rejected, for example, the abolition of Negro slavery as 'an interference with Providence' just as it rejected vaccination!) They zealously fought the laxity of church discipline and the imparting of sacraments to unworthy persons. The movement led to separations. The synod of the 'Afgeschiedenen gereformeerten Geemeeente' [Separated reformed congregation] of Amsterdam in 1840 accepted the Dordrecht Canouns and rejected any kind of domination (*gezag*) 'within or above the church.' Groen van Prinsterer was one of Bilderdijk's disciples.

20. Classical formulations are found in the 'Amsterdam Confession' of 1611 (Publ. Of the Hanserd Knollys Society, vol. X). Thus, article 16 states: 'That the members of every church and congregation *ought to know one another*. . .therefore a church ought not to consist of such a multitude as cannot have practical knowledge one of another. Hence any synodal rule and any establishment of central church authorities were considered in the last instance as principled apostasy. This happened in Massachusetts and likewise in England under Cromwell. The rules, at that time, established by Parliament in 1641, allowed every congregation to provide itself with an orthodox minister and to organize lectures. This measure was the signal for the influx of Baptists and radical Independents. The early Presbyterian Dedham Protocols, published by Usher, also presuppose the individual congregation (actually, at that time, in all probability, the individual minister) to be the bearer of church discipline. Admission by ballot, as evidenced by the protocol of 22 October 1582, states: 'That none be brought in as one of this company without the general consent of the whole.' But as early as

1586 these Puritans declared their opposition to the Brownists, who went in the direction of Congregationalism.

21. The 'classes' of the Methodists, as the foundation of the co-operative cure of soul, were the very backbone of the whole organization. Every twelve persons were to be organized into a 'class.' The leader of the class was to visit each member weekly, either at home or at the class meeting, during which there was usually a general confession of sins. The leader was to keep a record of the member's conduct. Among other things, this book-keeping was the basis for the writing of certificates for members who went away from the local community. By now, and for a long time, this organization has been disintegrating everywhere, including the U.S.A. The manner in which church discipline functioned in early Puritanism may be judged from the above-quoted Dedham Protocol, according to which 'admonition' was to be given in the conventicle 'if any things have been observed *or espied* by the brethren.'

22. In the Lutheran territories, especially those of Germany, either church discipline was notoriously undeveloped or else church discipline completely decayed at an early date. Church discipline was also of little influence in the reformed churches of Germany, except in Julich-Cleve and other Rhenish areas. This was due to the influence of the Luterhan surroundings *and* to the jealousy between the state power and the competing and autonomous hierocratic forces. This jealousy had existed everywhere, but the state had remained overpowering in Germany. (Traces of church discipline are nevertheless found up to the nineteenth century. The last excommunication in the palatinate took place in 1855. However, the church rules of 1563 were there handled in an actually Erastian way from an early date.) Only the Mennonites, and later the Pietists, created effective means of discipline and disciplinary organizations. (For Menno a 'visible church' existed *only* where church discipline existed. And excommunication because of misconduct or mixed marriage was a self-understood element of such discipline. The Rynsburg Collegiants had no dogmas whatever and recognized 'conduct' alone.) Among the Huguenots, church discipline *per se* was very strict, but again and again it was relaxed through unavoidable considerations of the nobility which were politically indispensable. The adherents of Puritan church discipline in England were found especially among the bourgeois capitalist middle class, thus, for instance, in the City of London. The city was not afraid of the domination of the clergy, but intended to use church discipline as a means of mass domestication. The strata of artisan craftsmen also adhered firmly to church discipline. The political authorities were the opponents to church discipline. Hence, in England the opponents included Parliament. Not 'class interests' but, as every glimpse into the documents shows, *primarily* religious, and, in addition, political interests and convictions played their part in these questions. The harshness not only of New England but also of the genuinely Puritan church discipline in

Europe is known. Among Cromwell's major-generals and commissioners, his agents for enforcing church discipline, the proposal to exile all 'idle, debauched, and profane persons,' emerges repeatedly.

Among the Methodists the dropping of novices during the periods of probation was permissable without further ado. Full members were to be dropped after an investigation by a commission. The church discipline of the *Huguenots* (who for a long time actually existed as a 'sect') is evidenced in synodal protocols. These indicate, among other things, censure of adulteration of commodities and of dishonesty in business. Sixth Synod (Avert. Gen. XIV). Thus sumptuary laws are frequently found, and slave ownership and slave trading are *permitted*, Twenty-Seventh Synod; a rather lax practice toward fiscal demands prevails (the fiscus is a tyrant), Sixth Synod, cas de conc. dec, XIV; usury, ibid. XV (cf. Second Synod, Gen. 17; Eleventh Synod, Gen. 42). Toward the end of the sixteenth century, the English Presbyterians were designated as 'disciplinarians' in official correspondence (Quotations to be found in Pearson, loc. cit.).

23. In the 'Apologetical Narration' of the five (Independent) 'dissenting brethren' of the Westminster Synod the separation from the 'casuall and formall Christians' is placed in the foreground. This means, at first, only voluntaristic separatism, not renunciation of commercium. But Robinson, a strict Calvinist and advocate of the Dordrecht Synod (about him cf. Dexter, *Congregationalism*, p. 402) had originally held the opinion which he later softened, that the independent separatists must not have social intercourse with the others, even should they be *electi*, which was considered conceivable. However, most sects have avoided committing themselves overtly to this principle, and some have expressly rejected it, at least as a principle. Baxter, *Christian Directory*, vol. II, p. 100 (at the bottom of column 2), opines that, should not oneself but the housefather and parson, assume the responsibility, then one might acquiesce to praying together with an ungodly person. However, this is un-Puritan. The *mijdinge* [middle things] played a very important part in the radical Baptist sects in Holland during the seventeenth century.

24. This became strikingly obvious even in the discussions and struggles within the Amsterdam Refugee congregation at the beginning of the seventeenth century. Likewise in Lancashire the rejection of a *ministerial* church discipline, the demand for a lay rule in the church and for a church discipline enforced by laymen were decisive for the attitudes in the internal church struggles of Cromwell's times.

25. The appointment of the elders was the object of prolonged controversies in the Independent and Baptist communities, which will not concern us here.

26. The ordinance of the Long Parliament of 31 December 1646 was directed against this. It was intended as a stroke against the Independents. On the other hand, the principle of the liberty of prophesying

had also been vindicated in literary form by Robinson. From the Episcopalian standpoint Jeremy Taylor, *The Liberty of Prophesying* (1647), made concessions to it. Cromwell's 'tryers' requested that permission to prophesy depend on the certificate of six admitted members of the congregation, among whom were four laymen. During the early period of the English Reformation the 'exercises' and 'prophesyings' had not only been frequently tolerated by ardent Anglican bishops, but had been encouraged by them. In Scotland these were (in 1560) constituent elements of church activities; in 1571 they were introduced in Northampton. Other places were soon to follow. But Elizabeth persisted in suppressing them as a result of her proclamation of 1573 against Cartwright.

27. The charismatic revolutions of the sectarians (of the type of Fox and similar leaders) in the congregations always began with the fight against the office-holding prebendaries as 'hirelings' and with the fight for the apostolic principle of free preaching without remuneration for the speaker who is moved by the spirit. Heated disputes in Parliament took place between Goodwin, the congregationalist, and Prynne, who reproached him that, against his alleged principle, he had accepted a 'living,' whereas Goodwin declared acceptance only of what was given voluntarily. The principle that only *voluntary* contributions for the maintenance of ministers should be permissable is expressed in the petition of the Brownists to James I, in 1603 (point 71: hence the protest against 'Popish livings' and 'Jewish tithes').

28. In 1793 Methodism abolished differences between ordained and non-ordained preachers. Therewith, the non-ordained traveling preachers, and hence, the missionaries, who were the characteristic bearers of Methodism, were placed on an equal footing with the preachers still ordained by the Anglican church. But at the same time the monopoly of preaching in the whole circuit and of administering sacraments was reserved to the traveling preachers alone. (The autonomous administration of sacraments was then principally carried through, but still at hours different from those of the official church to which membership was still pretended now as before.) As, ever since 1768, preachers were forbidden to engage in ordinary civic occupations, a new 'clergy' emerged. Since 1836 formal ordination has taken place. Opposite the circuit preachers were the lay-recruited local preachers who took up preaching as a minor vocation. They had no right to administer sacraments and they had only local jurisdiction. None among these two categories of preachers donned an official garb.

29. Actually, in England at least, most of the 'circuits' have become little parishes and the travel of the preacher has become a fiction. Nevertheless, up to the very present, it has been upheld that the same minister must not serve the same circuit for more than three years. They were *professional* preachers. The 'local preachers,' from among whom the traveling preachers were recruited, were, however, people with a civic

occupation and with a license to preach, which (originally) was given for one year at a time. Their existence was necessary because of the abundance of services and of chapels. But above all, they were the backbone of the 'class'—organization and its curing of souls. Hence, they were actually the central organ of church discipline.

30. Among other things Cromwell's opposition to the 'Parliament of the Saints' became acute on the question of the universities (which with the radical elimination of all tithes and prebends would have collapsed). Cromwell could not decide to destroy these cultural institutions, which, however, then were meant especially to be institutions for the education of theologians.

31. An example is given by Gardiner, *Fall of the Monarchy*, vol. I, p. 380.

32. The Westminster Confession also (XXVI, I) establishes the principle of *inner and external* obligation to help one another. The respective rules are numerous among all sects.

33. Every case of failure to pay in early Methodism was investigated by a commission of brethren. To incur debts without the certain prospect of being able to pay them back was cause for exclusion—hence, the credit rating. Cf. the resolution of the Dutch synods quoted in note 9. The obligation to help one's brother in emergencies is determined, for example, in the Baptist Hanserd Knollys confession (c. 28) with the characteristic reservation that this should not prejudice the sanctity of property. Occasionally, and with great harshness (as in the Cambridge platform of 1647, edition of 1653, 7, no. VI) the elders are reminded of their duty to proceed against members who live *'without a calling'* or conduct themselves *'idly in their calling.'*

34. Among the Methodists these certificates of conduct originally had to be renewed every three months. The old Independents, as noted above, gave the Lord's Supper only to holders of tickets. Among the Baptists a newcomer to the community could be admitted to the congregation only upon a letter of recommendation from his former congregation: cf. the appendix to the edition of the Hanserd Knollys Confession of 1689 (West Chester, Pa., 1827). Even the three Amsterdam Baptist Communities at the beginning of the sixteenth century had the same system, which since then recurs everywhere. In Massachusetts since 1669, a certificate from the preacher and the select men concerning orthodoxy and *conduct* has been the attestation that the holder is qualified for acquiring political citizenship. This certificate replaced the admission to the Lord's Supper, which had originally been required.

35. Again we should like to stress emphatically this absolutely decisive point of the first of these two essays. (*The Protestant Ethics and the Spirit of Capitalism.*) It has been the fundamental mistake of my critics not to have taken notice of this very fact. In the discussion of the Ancient Hebrew Ethics in relation to the *doctrines* of Egyptian, Phoeni-

cian, Babylonian ethical systems we shall hit upon a very similar state of affairs.

36. Cf. among others the statement p. 166 in the *Protestant Ethic and the Spirit of Capitalism*. The formation of congregations among ancient Jewry, just as among early Christians, worked, each in its own way, in the same direction (among Jewry the decline of the social significance of the sib, as we shall see, is conditioned thereby, and Christianity during the early Middle Ages has had similar effects).

37. Cf. The *Livre des Métiers* of the Prévôt Étienne de Boileau of 1268 (éd. Lespinasse & Bonnardot in the *Histoire générale de Paris*) pp. 211, section 8; 215, section 4. These examples may stand for many others.

38. Here, in passing, we cannot analyze this rather involved causal relationship.

MAX WEBER'S INTRODUCTION
TO THE SOCIOLOGY OF RELIGION (1920)

A product of modern European civilization, studying
any problem of universal history, is bound to ask himself to what combination of circumstances the fact
should be attributed that in Western civilization, and in
Western civilization only, cultural phenomena have appeared which (as we like to think) lie in a line of development having *universal* significance and value.

Only in the West does science exist at a stage of
development which we recognize to-day as valid. Empirical knowledge, reflection on problems of the cosmos and of life, philosophical and theological wisdom
of the most profound sort, are not confined to it, though
in the case of the last the full development of a systematic theology must be credited to Christianity under the
influence of Hellenism, since there were only fragments
in Islam and in a few Indian sects. In short, knowledge
and observation of great refinement have existed elsewhere, above all in India, China, Babylonia, Egypt. But
in Babylonia and elsewhere astronomy lacked—which
makes its development all the more astounding—the
mathematical foundation which it first received from
the Greeks. The Indian geometry had no rational
proof; that was another product of the Greek intellect,
also the creator of mechanics and physics. The Indian
natural sciences, though well developed in observation,
lacked the method of experiment, which was, apart from
beginnings in antiquity, essentially a product of the
Renaissance, as was the modern laboratory. Hence
medicine, especially in India, though highly developed

In order to consistently reproduce the translator's original pagination, the
text of the translation begins on page 13.

in empirical technique, lacked a biological and particularly a biochemical foundation. A rational chemistry has been absent from all areas of culture except the West.

The highly developed historical scholarship of China did not have the method of Thucydides. Machiavelli, it is true, had predecessors in India; but all Indian political thought was lacking in a systematic method comparable to that of Aristotle, and, indeed, in the possession of rational concepts. Not all the anticipations in India (School of Mimamsa), nor the extensive codification especially in the Near East, nor all the Indian and other books of law, had the strictly systematic forms of thought, so essential to a rational jurisprudence, of the Roman law and of the Western law under its influence. A structure like the canon law is known only to the West.

A similar statement is true of art. The musical ear of other peoples has probably been even more sensitively developed than our own, certainly not less so. Polyphonic music of various kinds has been widely distributed over the earth. The co-operation of a number of instruments and also the singing of parts have existed elsewhere. All our rational tone intervals have been known and calculated. But rational harmonious music, both counterpoint and harmony, formation of the tone material on the basis of three triads with the harmonic third; our chromatics and enharmonics, not interpreted in terms of space, but, since the Renaissance, of harmony; our orchestra, with its string quartet as a nucleus, and the organization of ensembles of wind instruments; our bass accompaniment; our system of notation, which has made possible the composition and production of modern musical works, and thus their very survival; our sonatas, symphonies, operas; and finally, as means to all these, our fundamental instruments, the organ, piano, violin, etc.; all these things are known only in the Occident, although programme music, tone poetry, alteration of tones and chromatics, have existed in various musical traditions as means of expression.

In architecture, pointed arches have been used elsewhere as a means of decoration, in antiquity and in Asia; presumably the combination of pointed arch and cross-arched vault was not unknown in the Orient. But the rational use of the Gothic vault as a means of distributing pressure and of roofing spaces of all forms, and above all as the constructive principle of great monumental buildings and the foundation of a *style* extending to sculpture and painting, such as that created by our Middle Ages, does not occur elsewhere. The technical basis of our architecture came from the Orient. But the Orient lacked that solution of the problem of the dome and that type of classic rationalization of all art—in painting by the rational utilization of lines and spatial perspective—which the Renaissance created for us. There was printing in China. But a printed literature, designed *only* for print and only possible through it, and, above all, the Press and periodicals, have appeared only in the Occident. Institutions of higher education of all possible types, even some superficially similar to our universities, or at least academies, have existed (China, Islam). But a rational, systematic, and specialized pursuit of science, with trained and specialized personnel, has only existed in the West in a sense at all approaching its present dominant place in our culture. Above all is this true of the trained official, the pillar of both the modern State and of the economic life of the West. He forms a type of which there have heretofore only been suggestions, which have never remotely approached its present importance for the social order. Of course the official, even the specialized official, is a very old constituent of the most various societies. But no country and no age has ever experienced, in the same sense as the modern Occident, the absolute and complete dependence of its whole existence, of the political, technical, and economic conditions of its life, on a specially trained *organization* of officials. The most important functions of the everyday life of society have come to be in the hands of technically, commercially, and above all legally trained government officials.

Organization of political and social groups in feudal classes has been common. But even the feudal[1] state of *rex et regnum* in the Western sense has only been known to our culture. Even more are parliaments of periodically elected representatives, with government by demagogues and party leaders as ministers responsible to the parliaments, peculiar to us, although there have, of course, been parties, in the sense of organizations for exerting influence and gaining control of political power, all over the world. In fact, the State itself, in the sense of a political association with a rational, written constitution, rationally ordained law, and an administration bound to rational rules or laws, administered by trained officials, is known, in this combination of characteristics, only in the Occident, despite all other approaches to it.

And the same is true of the most fateful force in our modern life, capitalism. The impulse to acquisition, pursuit of gain, of money, of the greatest possible amount of money, has in itself nothing to do with capitalism. This impulse exists and has existed among waiters, physicians, coachmen, artists, prostitutes, dishonest officials, soldiers, nobles, crusaders, gamblers, and beggars. One may say that it has been common to all sorts and conditions of men at all times and in all countries of the earth, wherever the objective possibility of it is or has been given. It should be taught in the kindergarten of cultural history that this naïve idea of capitalism must be given up once and for all. Unlimited greed for gain is not in the least identical with capitalism, and is still less its spirit. Capitalism *may* even be identical with the restraint, or at least a rational tempering, of this irrational impulse. But capitalism is identical with the pursuit of profit, and forever *renewed* profit, by means of continuous, rational, capitalistic enterprise. For it must be so: in a wholly capitalistic order of society, an individual capitalistic enterprise which did not take advantage of its opportunities for profit-making would be doomed to extinction.

Let us now define our terms somewhat more carefully than is generally done. We will define a capitalistic economic action as one which rests on the expectation of profit by the utilization of opportunities for exchange, that is on (formally) peaceful chances of profit. Acquisition by force (formally and actually) follows its own particular laws, and it is not expedient, however little one can forbid this, to place it in the same category with action which is, in the last analysis, oriented to profits from exchange.[2] Where capitalistic acquisition is rationally pursued, the corresponding action is adjusted to calculations in terms of capital. This means that the action is adapted to a systematic utilization of goods or personal services as means of acquisition in such a way that, at the close of a business period, the balance of the enterprise in money assets (or, in the case of a continuous enterprise, the periodically estimated money value of assets) exceeds the capital, i.e. the estimated value of the material means of production used for acquisition in exchange. It makes no difference whether it involves a quantity of goods entrusted *in natura* to a travelling merchant, the proceeds of which may consist in other goods *in natura* acquired by trade, or whether it involves a manufacturing enterprise, the assets of which consist of buildings, machinery, cash, raw materials, partly and wholly manufactured goods, which are balanced against liabilities. The important fact is always that a calculation of capital in terms of money is made, whether by modern book-keeping methods or in any other way, however primitive and crude. Everything is done in terms of balances: at the beginning of the enterprise an initial balance, before every individual decision a calculation to ascertain its probable profitableness, and at the end a final balance to ascertain how much profit has been made. For instance, the initial balance of a *commenda*[3] transaction would determine an agreed money value of the assets put into it (so far as they were not in money form already), and a final balance would form the estimate on which to base the distribution of profit and loss at the end. So far as the transactions are rational, calculation underlies every single action of the partners. That a really accurate calculation or estimate may not exist, that the procedure is pure guess-work, or simply traditional and conventional, happens even to-day in every form of capitalistic enterprise where the circumstances do not demand strict accuracy. But these are points affecting only the *degree* of rationality of capitalistic acquisition.

For the purpose of this conception all that matters is that an actual adaptation of economic action to a comparison of money income with money expenses takes place, no matter how primitive the form. Now in this sense capitalism and capitalistic enterprises, even with a considerable rationalization of capitalistic calculation, have existed in all civilized countries of the earth, so far as economic documents permit us to judge. In China, India, Babylon, Egypt, Mediterranean antiquity, and the Middle Ages, as well as in modern times. These were not merely isolated ventures, but economic enterprises which were entirely dependent on the continual renewal of capitalistic undertakings, and even continuous operations. However, trade especially was for a long time not continuous like our own, but consisted essentially in a series of individual undertakings. Only gradually did the activities of even the large merchants acquire an inner cohesion (with branch organizations, etc.). In any case, the capitalistic enterprise and the capitalistic entrepreneur, not only as occasional but as regular entrepreneurs, are very old and were very widespread.

Now, however, the Occident has developed capitalism both to a quantitative extent, and (carrying this quantitative development) in types, forms, and directions which have never existed elsewhere. All over the world there have been merchants, wholesale and retail, local and engaged in foreign trade. Loans of all kinds have been made, and there have been banks with the most various functions, at least comparable to ours of, say, the sixteenth century. Sea loans,[4] *commenda,* and transactions and associations similar to the *Kommanditgesellschaft,*[5] have all been widespread, even as continuous businesses. Whenever money finances of public bodies have existed, money-lenders have appeared, as in Babylon, Hellas, India, China, Rome. They have financed wars and piracy, contracts and building operations of all sorts. In overseas policy they have functioned as colonial entrepreneurs, as planters with slaves, or directly or indirectly forced labour, and have farmed domains, offices, and, above all, taxes. They have financed party leaders in elections and *condottieri* in civil wars. And, finally, they have been speculators in chances for pecuniary gain of all kinds. This kind of entrepreneur, the capitalistic adventurer, has existed everywhere. With the exception of trade and credit and banking transactions, their activities were predominantly of an irrational and speculative character, or directed to acquisition by force, above all the acquisition of booty, whether directly in war or in the form of continuous fiscal booty by exploitation of subjects.

The capitalism of promoters, large-scale speculators, concession hunters, and much modern financial capitalism even in peace time, but, above all, the capitalism especially concerned with exploiting wars, bears this stamp even in modern Western countries, and some, but only some, parts of large-scale international trade are closely related to it, to-day as always.

But in modern times the Occident has developed, in addition to this, a very different form of capitalism which has appeared nowhere else: the rational capitalistic organization of (formally) free labour. Only suggestions of it are found elsewhere. Even the organization of free labour reached a considerable degree of rationality only on plantations and to a very limited extent in the *Ergasteria* of antiquity. In the manors, manorial workshops, and domestic industries on estates with serf labour it was probably somewhat less developed. Even real domestic industries with free labour have definitely been proved to have existed in only a few isolated cases outside the Occident. The frequent use of day labourers led in a very few cases—especially State monopolies, which are, however, very different from modern industrial organization—to manufacturing organizations, but never to a rational organization of apprenticeship in the handicrafts like that of our Middle Ages.

Rational industrial organization, attuned to a regular market, and neither to political nor irrationally speculative opportunities for profit, is not, however, the only peculiarity of Western capitalism. The modern rational organization of the capitalistic enterprise would not have been possible without two other important factors in its development: the separation of business from the household, which completely dominates modern economic life, and closely connected with it, rational book-keeping. A spatial separation of places of work from those of residence exists elsewhere, as in the Oriental bazaar and in the *ergasteria* of other cultures. The development of capitalistic associations with their own accounts is also found in the Far East, the Near East, and in antiquity. But compared to the modern independence of business enterprises, those are only small beginnings. The reason for this was particularly that the indispensable requisites for this independence, our rational business book-keeping and our legal separation of corporate from personal property, were entirely lacking, or had only begun to develop.[6] The tendency everywhere else was for acquisitive enterprises to arise as parts of a royal or manorial *household* (of the *oikos),* which is, as Rodbertus has perceived, with all its superficial similarity, a fundamentally different, even opposite, development.

However, all these peculiarities of Western capitalism have derived their significance in the last analysis only from their association with the capitalistic organization of labour. Even what is generally called commercialization, the development of negotiable securities and the rationalization of speculation, the exchanges, etc., is connected with it. For without the rational capitalistic organization of labour, all this, so far as it was possible at all, would have nothing like the same significance, above all for the social structure and all the specific problems of the modern Occident connected with it. Exact calculation—the basis of everything else—is only possible on a basis of free labour.[7]

Max Weber's Introduction to the Sociology of Religion (1920)

And just as, or rather because, the world has known no rational organization of labour outside the modern Occident, it has known no rational socialism. Of course, there has been civic economy, a civic food-supply policy, mercantilism and welfare policies of princes, rationing, regulation of economic life, protectionism, and *laissez-faire* theories (as in China). The world has also known socialistic and communistic experiments of various sorts: family, religious, or military communism, State socialism (in Egypt), monopolistic cartels, and consumers' organizations. But although there have everywhere been civic market privileges, companies, guilds, and all sorts of legal differences between town and country, the concept of the citizen has not existed outside the Occident, and that of the bourgeoisie outside the modern Occident. Similarly, the proletariat as a class could not exist, because there was no rational organization of free labour under regular discipline. Class struggles between creditor and debtor classes; landowners and the landless, serfs, or tenants; trading interests and consumers or landlords, have existed everywhere in various combinations. But even the Western mediæval struggles between putters-out and their workers exist elsewhere only in beginnings. The modern conflict of the large-scale industrial entrepreneur and free-wage labourers was entirely lacking. And thus there could be no such problems as those of socialism.

Hence in a universal history of culture the central problem for us is not, in the last analysis, even from a purely economic view-point, the development of capitalistic activity as such, differing in different cultures only in form: the adventurer type, or capitalism in trade, war, politics, or administration as sources of gain. It is rather the origin of this sober bourgeois capitalism with its rational organization of free labour. Or in terms of cultural history, the problem is that of the origin of the Western bourgeois class and of its peculiarities, a problem which is certainly closely connected with that of the origin of the capitalistic organization of labour, but is not quite the same thing. For the bourgeois as a class existed prior to the development of the peculiar modern form of capitalism, though, it is true, only in the Western hemisphere.

Now the peculiar modern Western form of capitalism has been, at first sight, strongly influenced by the development of technical possibilities. Its rationality is to-day essentially dependent on the calculability of the most important technical factors. But this means fundamentally that it is dependent on the peculiarities of modern science, especially the natural sciences based on mathematics and exact and rational experiment. On the other hand, the development of these sciences and of the technique resting upon them now receives important stimulation from these capitalistic interests in its practical economic application. It is true that the origin of Western science cannot be attributed to such interests. Calculation, even with decimals, and algebra have been carried on in India, where the decimal system was invented. But it was only made use of by developing capitalism in the West, while in India it led to no modern arithmetic or book-keeping. Neither was the origin of mathematics and mechanics determined by capitalistic interests. But the *technical* utiliza-

24

tion of scientific knowledge, so important for the living conditions of the mass of people, was certainly encouraged by economic considerations, which were extremely favourable to it in the Occident. But this encouragement was derived from the peculiarities of the social structure of the Occident. We must hence ask, from *what* parts of that structure was it derived, since not all of them have been of equal importance?

Among those of undoubted importance are the rational structures of law and of administration. For modern rational capitalism has need, not only of the technical means of production, but of a calculable legal system and of administration in terms of formal rules. Without it adventurous and speculative trading capitalism and all sorts of politically determined capitalisms are possible, but no rational enterprise under individual initiative, with fixed capital and certainty of calculations. Such a legal system and such administration have been available for economic activity in a comparative state of legal and formalistic perfection only in the Occident. We must hence inquire where that law came from. Among other circumstances, capitalistic interests have in turn undoubtedly also helped, but by no means alone nor even principally, to prepare the way for the predominance in law and administration of a class of jurists specially trained in rational law. But these interests did not themselves create that law. Quite different forces were at work in this development. And why did not the capitalistic interests do the same in China or India? Why did not the scientific, the artistic, the political, or the economic development there enter upon that path of rationalization which is peculiar to the Occident?

For in all the above cases it is a question of the specific and peculiar rationalism of Western culture. Now by this term very different things may be understood, as the following discussion will repeatedly show. There is, for example, rationalization of mystical contemplation, that is of an attitude which, viewed from other departments of life, is specifically irrational, just as much as there are rationalizations of economic life, of technique, of scientific research, of military training, of law and administration. Furthermore, each one of these fields may be rationalized in terms of very different ultimate values and ends, and what is rational from one point of view may well be irrational from another. Hence rationalizations of the most varied character have existed in various departments of life and in all areas of culture. To characterize their differences from the view-point of cultural history it is necessary to know what departments are rationalized, and in what direction. It is hence our first concern to work out and to explain genetically the special peculiarity of Occidental rationalism, and within this field that of the modern Occidental form. Every such attempt at explanation must, recognizing the fundamental importance of the economic factor, above all take account of the economic conditions. But at the same time the opposite correlation must not be left out of consideration. For though the development of economic rationalism is partly dependent on rational technique and law, it is at the same time determined by the ability and disposition of men to adopt certain types of practical rational conduct. When these types have been obstructed by spiritual obstacles, the development of rational economic conduct has also met serious inner resistance. The magical and religious forces, and the ethical ideas of duty based upon them, have in the past always been among the most important formative influences on conduct. In the studies collected here we shall be concerned with these forces.[8]

Two older essays have been placed at the beginning which attempt, at one important point, to approach the side of the problem which is generally most difficult to grasp: the influence of certain religious ideas on the development of an economic spirit, or the *ethos* of an economic system. In this case we are dealing with the connection of the spirit of modern economic life with the rational ethics of ascetic Protestantism. Thus we treat here only one side of the causal chain. The later studies on the Economic Ethics of the World Religions attempt, in the form of a survey of the relations of the most important religions to economic life and to the social stratification of their environment, to follow out both causal relationships, so far as it is necessary in order to find points of comparison with the Occidental development. For only in this way is it possible to attempt a causal evaluation of those elements of the economic ethics of the Western religions which differentiate them from others, with a hope of attaining even a tolerable degree of approximation. Hence these studies do not claim to be complete analyses of cultures, however brief. On the contrary, in every culture they quite deliberately emphasize the elements in which it differs from Western civilization. They are, hence, definitely oriented to the problems which seem important for the understanding of Western culture from *this* view-point. With our object in view, any other procedure did not seem possible. But to avoid misunderstanding we must here lay special emphasis on the limitation of our purpose.

In another respect the uninitiated at least must be warned against exaggerating the importance of these investigations. The Sinologist, the Indologist, the Semitist, or the Egyptologist, will of course find no facts unknown to him. We only hope that he will find nothing definitely wrong in points that are essential. How far it has been possible to come as near this ideal as a non-specialist is able to do, the author cannot know. It is quite evident that anyone who is forced to rely on translations, and furthermore on the use and evaluation of monumental, documentary, or literary sources, has to rely himself on a specialist literature which is often highly controversial, and the merits of which he is unable to judge accurately. Such a writer must make modest claims for the value of his work. All the more so since the number of available translations of real sources (that is, inscriptions and documents) is, especially for China, still very small in comparison with what exists and is important. From all this follows the definitely provisional character of these studies, and especially of the parts dealing with Asia.[9] Only the specialist is entitled to a final judgment. And, naturally, it is only because expert studies with this special purpose and from this particular view-point have not hitherto been made, that the present ones have been written at all. They are destined to be superseded in a much more important sense than this can be said, as it can be, of all scientific work. But however objectionable it may be, such trespassing on other special fields cannot be avoided in comparative work. But one must take the consequences by resigning oneself to considerable doubts regarding the degree of one's success.

Fashion and the zeal of the *literati* would have us think that the specialist can to-day be spared, or degraded to a position subordinate to that of the seer. Almost all sciences owe something to dilettantes, often very valuable view-points. But dilettantism as a leading principle would be the end of science. He who yearns for seeing should go to the cinema, though it will be offered to him copiously to-day in literary form in the present field of investigation also.[10] Nothing is farther from the intent of these thoroughly serious studies than such an attitude. And, I might add, whoever wants a sermon should go to a conventicle. The question of the relative value of the cultures which are compared here will not receive a single word. It is true that the path of human destiny cannot but appall him who surveys a section of it. But he will do well to keep his small personal commentaries to himself, as one does at the sight of the sea or of majestic mountains, unless he knows himself to be called and gifted to give them expression in artistic or prophetic form. In most other cases the voluminous talk about intuition does nothing but conceal a lack of perspective toward the object, which merits the same judgment as a similar lack of perspective toward men.

Some justification is needed for the fact that ethnographical material has not been utilized to anything like the extent which the value of its contributions naturally demands in any really thorough investigation, especially of Asiatic religions. This limitation has not only been imposed because human powers of work are restricted. This omission has also seemed to be permissible because we are here necessarily dealing with the religious ethics of the classes which were the culture-bearers of their respective countries. We are concerned with the influence which *their* conduct has had. Now it is quite true that this can only be completely known in all its details when the facts from ethnography and folk-lore have been compared with it. Hence we must expressly admit and emphasize that this is a gap to which the ethnographer will legitimately object. I hope to contribute something to the closing of this gap in a systematic study of the Sociology of Religion.[11] But such an undertaking would have transcended the limits of this investigation with its closely circumscribed purpose. It has been necessary to be content with bringing out the points of comparison with our Occidental religions as well as possible.

Finally, we may make a reference to the *anthropological* side of the problem. When we find again and again that, even in departments of life apparently mutually independent, certain types of rationalization have developed in the Occident, and only there, it would be natural to suspect that the most important reason lay in differences of heredity. The author admits that he is inclined to think the importance of biological heredity very great. But in spite of the notable achievements of anthropological research, I see up to the present no way of exactly or even approximately measuring either the extent or, above all, the form of its influence on the development investigated here.

It must be one of the tasks of sociological and historical investigation first to analyse all the influences and
causal relationships which can satisfactorily be explained in terms of reactions to environmental conditions. Only then, and when comparative racial neurol-
ogy and psychology shall have progressed beyond
their present and in many ways very promising beginnings, can we hope for even the probability of a satisfactory answer to that problem.[12] In the meantime that
condition seems to me not to exist, and an appeal to
heredity would therefore involve a premature renunciation of the possibility of knowledge attainable now,
and would shift the problem to factors (at present) still
unknown.

THE PROTESTANT ETHIC
AND THE
SPIRIT OF CAPITALISM

PART I

THE PROBLEM

CHAPTER I

RELIGIOUS AFFILIATION AND SOCIAL STRATIFICATION[1]

A glance at the occupational statistics of any country of mixed religious composition brings to light with remarkable frequency[2] a situation which has several times provoked discussion in the Catholic press and literature,[3] and in Catholic congresses in Germany, namely, the fact that business leaders and owners of capital, as well as the higher grades of skilled labour, and even more the higher technically and commercially trained personnel of modern enterprises, are over-whelmingly Protestant.[4] This is true not only in cases where the difference in religion coincides with one of nationality, and thus of cultural development, as in Eastern Germany between Germans and Poles. The same thing is shown in the figures of religious affiliation almost wherever capitalism, at the time of its great expansion, has had a free hand to alter the social distribution of the population in accordance with its needs, and to determine its occupational structure. The more freedom it has had, the more clearly is the effect shown. It is true that the greater relative participation of Protestants in the ownership of capital,[5] in management, and the upper ranks of labour in great modern industrial and commercial enterprises,[6] may in part be explained in terms of historical circumstances[7] which extend far back into the past, and in which religious affiliation is not a cause of the economic conditions, but to a certain extent appears to be a result of them. Participation in the above economic functions usually involves some previous ownership of capital, and generally an expensive education; often both. These are to-day largely dependent on the possession of inherited wealth, or at least on a certain degree of material well-being. A number of those sections of the old Empire which were most highly developed economically and most favoured by natural resources and situation, in particular a majority of the wealthy towns, went over to Protestantism in the sixteenth century. The results of that circumstance favour the Protestants even to-day in their struggle for economic existence. There arises thus the historical question: why were the districts of highest economic development at the same time particularly favourable to a revolution in the Church? The answer is by no means so simple as one might think.

The emancipation from economic traditionalism appears, no doubt, to be a factor which would greatly strengthen the tendency to doubt the sanctity of the religious tradition, as of all traditional authorities. But it is necessary to note, what has often been forgotten, that the Reformation meant not the elimination of the Church's control over everyday life, but rather the substitution of a new form of control for the previous one. It meant the repudiation of a control which was very lax, at that time scarcely perceptible in practice, and hardly more than formal, in favour of a regulation of the whole of conduct which, penetrating to all departments of private and public life, was infinitely burdensome and earnestly enforced. The rule of the Catholic Church, "punishing the heretic, but indulgent to the sinner", as it was in the past even more than to-day, is now tolerated by peoples of thoroughly modern economic character, and was borne by the richest and economically most advanced peoples on earth at about the turn of the fifteenth century. The rule of Calvinism, on the other hand, as it was enforced in the sixteenth century in Geneva and in Scotland, at the turn of the sixteenth and seventeenth centuries in large parts of the Netherlands, in the seventeenth in New England, and for a time in England itself, would be for us the most absolutely unbearable form of ecclesiastical control of the individual which could possibly exist. That was exactly what large numbers of the old commercial aristocracy of those times, in Geneva as well as in Holland and England, felt about it. And what the reformers complained of in those areas of high economic development was not too much supervision of life on the part of the Church, but too little. Now how does it happen that at that time those countries which were most advanced economically, and within them the rising bourgeois middle classes, not only failed to resist this unexampled tyranny of Puritanism, but even developed a heroism in its defence? For bourgeois classes as such have seldom before and never since displayed heroism. It was "the last of our heroisms", as Carlyle, not without reason, has said.

But further, and especially important: it may be, as has been claimed, that the greater participation of Protestants in the positions of ownership and management in modern economic life may to-day be understood, in part at least, simply as a result of the greater material wealth they have inherited. But there are certain other phenomena which cannot be explained in the same way. Thus, to mention only a few facts: there is a great difference discoverable in Baden, in Bavaria, in Hungary, in the type of higher education which Catholic parents, as opposed to Protestant, give their children. That the percentage of Catholics among the students and graduates of higher educational institutions in general lags behind their proportion of the total population,[8] may, to be sure, be largely explicable in terms of inherited differences of wealth. But among the Catholic graduates themselves the percentage of those graduating from the institutions preparing, in particular, for technical studies and industrial and commercial occupations, but in general from those preparing for middle-class business life, lags still farther behind the percentage of Protestants.[9] On the other hand, Catholics prefer the sort of training which the humanistic Gymnasium affords. That is a circumstance to which the above explanation does not apply, but which, on the contrary, is one reason why so few Catholics are engaged in capitalistic enterprise.

Even more striking is a fact which partly explains the smaller proportion of Catholics among the skilled labourers of modern industry. It is well known that the factory has taken its skilled labour to a large extent from young men in the handicrafts; but this is much more true of Protestant than of Catholic journeymen. Among journeymen, in other words, the Catholics show a stronger propensity to remain in their crafts, that is they more often become master craftsmen, whereas the Protestants are attracted to a larger extent into the factories in order to fill the upper ranks of skilled labour and administrative positions.[10] The explanation of these cases is undoubtedly that the mental and spiritual peculiarities acquired from the environment, here the type of education favoured by the religious atmosphere of the home community and the parental home, have determined the choice of occupation, and through it the professional career.

The smaller participation of Catholics in the modern business life of Germany is all the more striking because it runs counter to a tendency which has been observed at all times[11] including the present. National or religious minorities which are in a position of subordination to a group of rulers are likely, through their voluntary or involuntary exclusion from positions of political influence, to be driven with peculiar force into economic activity. Their ablest members seek to satisfy the desire for recognition of their abilities in this field since there is no opportunity in the service of the State. This has undoubtedly been true of the Poles in Russia and Eastern Prussia, who have without question been undergoing a more rapid economic advance than in Galicia, where they have been in the ascendant. It has in earlier times been true of the Huguenots in France under Louis XIV, the Nonconformists and Quakers in England, and, last but not least, the Jew for two thousand years. But the Catholics in Germany have shown no striking evidence of such a result of their position. In the past they have, unlike the Protestants, undergone no particularly prominent economic development in the times when they were persecuted or only tolerated, either in Holland or in England. On the other hand, it is a fact that the Protestants (especi-

ally certain branches of the movement to be fully discussed later) both as ruling classes and as ruled, both
as majority and as minority, have shown a special tendency to develop economic rationalism which cannot
be observed to the same extent among Catholics either
in the one situation or in the other.[12] Thus the principal explanation of this difference must be sought in
the permanent intrinsic character of their religious beliefs, and not only in their temporary external histo-
rico-political situations.[13]

It will be our task to investigate these religions with
a view to finding out what peculiarities they have or
have had which might have resulted in the behaviour
we have described. On superficial analysis, and on the
basis of certain current impressions, one might be
tempted to express the difference by saying that the
greater other-worldliness of Catholicism, the ascetic
character of its highest ideals, must have brought up
its adherents to a greater indifference toward the good
things of this world. Such an explanation fits the
popular tendency in the judgment of both religions. On
the Protestant side it is used as a basis of criticism of
those (real or imagined) ascetic ideals of the Catholic
way of life, while the Catholics answer with the
accusation that materialism results from the secularization of all ideals through Protestantism. One recent
writer has attempted to formulate the difference of
their attitudes toward economic life in the following
manner: "The Catholic is quieter, having less of the
acquisitive impulse; he prefers a life of the greatest
possible security, even with a smaller income, to a life
of risk and excitement, even though it may bring the

chance of gaining honour and riches. The proverb says jokingly, 'either eat well or sleep well'. In the present case the Protestant prefers to eat well, the Catholic to sleep undisturbed."[14]

In fact, this desire to eat well may be a correct though incomplete characterization of the motives of many nominal Protestants in Germany at the present time. But things were very different in the past: the English, Dutch, and American Puritans were characterized by the exact opposite of the joy of living, a fact which is indeed, as we shall see, most important for our present study. Moreover, the French Protestants, among others, long retained, and retain to a certain extent up to the present, the characteristics which were impressed upon the Calvinistic Churches everywhere, especially under the cross in the time of the religious struggles. Nevertheless (or was it, perhaps, as we shall ask later, precisely on that account?) it is well known that these characteristics were one of the most important factors in the industrial and capitalistic development of France, and on the small scale permitted them by their persecution remained so. If we may call this seriousness and the strong predominance of religious interests in the whole conduct of life otherworldliness, then the French Calvinists were and still are at least as otherworldly as, for instance, the North German Catholics, to whom their Catholicism is undoubtedly as vital a matter as religion is to any other people in the world. Both differ from the predominant religious trends in their respective countries in much the same way. The Catholics of France are, in their lower ranks, greatly interested in the enjoyment of life,

41

in the upper directly hostile to religion. Similarly, the Protestants of Germany are to-day absorbed in worldly economic life, and their upper ranks are most indifferent to religion.[15] Hardly anything shows so clearly as this parallel that, with such vague ideas as that of the alleged otherworldliness of Catholicism, and the alleged materialistic joy of living of Protestantism, and others like them, nothing can be accomplished for our purpose. In such general terms the distinction does not even adequately fit the facts of to-day, and certainly not of the past. If, however, one wishes to make use of it at all, several other observations present themselves at once which, combined with the above remarks, suggest that the supposed conflict between other-worldliness, asceticism, and ecclesiastical piety on the one side, and participation in capitalistic acquisition on the other, might actually turn out to be an intimate relationship.

As a matter of fact it is surely remarkable, to begin with quite a superficial observation, how large is the number of representatives of the most spiritual forms of Christian piety who have sprung from commercial circles. In particular, very many of the most zealous adherents of Pietism are of this origin. It might be explained as a sort of reaction against mammonism on the part of sensitive natures not adapted to commercial life, and, as in the case of Francis of Assisi, many Pietists have themselves interpreted the process of their conversion in these terms. Similarly, the remarkable circumstance that so many of the greatest capitalistic entrepreneurs—down to Cecil Rhodes—have come from clergymen's families might be explained as a reaction against their ascetic upbringing. But this

form of explanation fails where an extraordinary capitalistic business sense is combined in the same persons
and groups with the most intensive forms of a piety
which penetrates and dominates their whole lives.
Such cases are not isolated, but these traits are characteristic of many of the most important Churches and
sects in the history of Protestantism. Especially Calvinism, wherever it has appeared,[16] has shown this combination. However little, in the time of the expansion of
the Reformation, it (or any other Protestant belief) was
bound up with any particular social class, it is characteristic and in a certain sense typical that in French
Huguenot Churches monks and business men (merchants, craftsmen) were particularly numerous among
the proselytes, especially at the time of the persecution.[17] Even the Spaniards knew that heresy (i.e. the
Calvinism of the Dutch) promoted trade, and this coincides with the opinions which Sir William Petty expressed in his discussion of the reasons for the capitalistic development of the Netherlands. Gothein[18] rightly
calls the Calvinistic diaspora the seed-bed of capitalistic economy.[19] Even in this case one might consider
the decisive factor to be the superiority of the French
and Dutch economic cultures from which these communities sprang, or perhaps the immense influence of
exile in the breakdown of traditional relationships.[20]
But in France the situation was, as we know from
Colbert's struggles, the same even in the seventeenth
century. Even Austria, not to speak of other countries,
directly imported Protestant craftsmen.

But not all the Protestant denominations seem to
have had an equally strong influence in this direction.

That of Calvinism, even in Germany, was among the strongest, it seems, and the reformed faith[21] more than the others seems to have promoted the development of the spirit of capitalism, in the Wupperthal as well as elsewhere. Much more so than Lutheranism, as comparison both in general and in particular instances, especially in the Wupperthal, seems to prove.[22] For Scotland, Buckle, and among English poets, Keats, have emphasized these same relationships.[23] Even more striking, as it is only necessary to mention, is the connection of a religious way of life with the most intensive development of business acumen among those sects whose otherworldliness is as proverbial as their wealth, especially the Quakers and the Mennonites. The part which the former have played in England and North America fell to the latter in Germany and the Netherlands. That in East Prussia Frederick William I tolerated the Mennonites as indispensable to industry, in spite of their absolute refusal to perform military service, is only one of the numerous well-known cases which illustrates the fact, though, considering the character of that monarch, it is one of the most striking. Finally, that this combination of intense piety with just as strong a development of business acumen, was also characteristic of the Pietists, is common knowledge.[24]

It is only necessary to think of the Rhine country and of Calw. In this purely introductory discussion it is unnecessary to pile up more examples. For these few already all show one thing: that the spirit of hard work, of progress, or whatever else it may be called, the awakening of which one is inclined to ascribe to

Protestantism, must not be understood, as there is a tendency to do, as joy of living nor in any other sense as connected with the Enlightenment. The old Protestantism of Luther, Calvin, Knox, Voet, had precious little to do with what to-day is called progress. To whole aspects of modern life which the most extreme religionist would not wish to suppress to-day, it was directly hostile. If any inner relationship between certain expressions of the old Protestant spirit and modern capitalistic culture is to be found, we must attempt to find it, for better or worse, not in its alleged more or less materialistic or at least anti-ascetic joy of living, but in its purely religious characteristics. Montesquieu says *(Esprit des Lois,* Book XX, chap. 7) of the English that they "had progressed the farthest of all peoples of the world in three important things: in piety, in commerce, and in freedom". Is it not possible that their commercial superiority and their adaptation to free political institutions are connected in some way with that record of piety which Montesquieu ascribes to them?

A large number of possible relationships, vaguely perceived, occur to us when we put the question in this way. It will now be our task to formulate what occurs to us confusedly as clearly as is possible, considering the inexhaustible diversity to be found in all historical material. But in order to do this it is necessary to leave behind the vague and general concepts with which we have dealt up to this point, and attempt to penetrate into the peculiar characteristics of and the differences between those great worlds of religious thought which have existed historically in the various branches of Christianity.

45

Before we can proceed to that, however, a few remarks are necessary, first on the peculiarities of the
phenomenon of which we are seeking an historical explanation, then concerning the sense in which such an
explanation is possible at all within the limits of these
investigations.

CHAPTER II

THE SPIRIT OF CAPITALISM

In the title of this study is used the somewhat pretentious phrase, the *spirit* of capitalism. What is to be understood by it? The attempt to give anything like a definition of it brings out certain difficulties which are in the very nature of this type of investigation.

If any object can be found to which this term can be applied with any understandable meaning, it can only be an historical individual, i.e. a complex of elements associated in historical reality which we unite into a conceptual whole from the standpoint of their cultural significance.

Such an historical concept, however, since it refers in its content to a phenomenon significant for its unique individuality, cannot be defined according to the formula *genus proximum, differentia specifica,* but it must be gradually put together out of the individual parts which are taken from historical reality to make it up. Thus the final and definitive concept cannot stand at the beginning of the investigation, but must come at the end. We must, in other words, work out in the course of the discussion, as its most important result, the best conceptual formulation of what we here understand by the spirit of capitalism, that is the best from the point of view which interests us here. This point of view (the one of which we shall speak later) is, further, by no means the only possible one from which the historical phenomena we are investigating can be analysed. Other standpoints would, for this as for every

47

historical phenomenon, yield other characteristics as the essential ones. The result is that it is by no means necessary to understand by the spirit of capitalism only what it will come to mean to *us* for the purposes of our analysis. This is a necessary result of the nature of historical concepts which attempt for their methodological purposes not to grasp historical reality in abstract general formulæ, but in concrete genetic sets of relations which are inevitably of a specifically unique and individual character.[1]

Thus, if we try to determine the object, the analysis and historical explanation of which we are attempting, it cannot be in the form of a conceptual definition, but at least in the beginning only a provisional description of what is here meant by the spirit of capitalism. Such a description is, however, indispensable in order clearly to understand the object of the investigation. For this purpose we turn to a document of that spirit which contains what we are looking for in almost classical purity, and at the same time has the advantage of being free from all direct relationship to religion, being thus, for our purposes, free of preconceptions.

"Remember, that *time* is money. He that can earn ten shillings a day by his labour, and goes abroad, or sits idle, one half of that day, though he spends but sixpence during his diversion or idleness, ought not to reckon *that* the only expense; he has really spent, or rather thrown away, five shillings besides.

"Remember, that *credit* is money. If a man lets his money lie in my hands after it is due, he gives me the interest, or so much as I can make of it during that time. This amounts to a considerable sum where a man has good and large credit, and makes good use of it.

"Remember, that money is of the prolific, generating nature. Money can beget money, and its offspring can beget more, and so on. Five shillings turned is six, turned again it is seven and threepence, and so on, till it becomes a hundred pounds. The more there is of it, the more it produces every turning, so that the profits rise quicker and quicker. He that kills a breeding-sow, destroys all her offspring to the thousandth generation. He that murders a crown, destroys all that it might have produced, even scores of pounds."

"Remember this saying, *The good paymaster is lord of another man's purse.* He that is known to pay punctually and exactly to the time he promises, may at any time, and on any occasion, raise all the money his friends can spare. This is sometimes of great use. After industry and frugality, nothing contributes more to the raising of a young man in the world than punctuality and justice in all his dealings; therefore never keep borrowed money an hour beyond the time you promised, lest a disappointment shut up your friend's purse for ever.

"The most trifling actions that affect a man's credit are to be regarded. The sound of your hammer at five in the morning, or eight at night, heard by a creditor, makes him easy six months longer; but if he sees you at a billiard-table, or hears your voice at a tavern, when you should be at work, he sends for his money the next day; demands it, before he can receive it, in a lump.

"It shows, besides, that you are mindful of what you

owe; it makes you appear a careful as well as an honest man, and that still increases your credit.

"Beware of thinking all your own that you possess, and of living accordingly. It is a mistake that many people who have credit fall into. To prevent this, keep an exact account for some time both of your expenses and your income. If you take the pains at first to mention particulars, it will have this good effect: you will discover how wonderfully small, trifling expenses mount up to large sums, and will discern what might have been, and may for the future be saved, without occasioning any great inconvenience."

"For six pounds a year you may have the use of one hundred pounds, provided you are a man of known prudence and honesty.

"He that spends a groat a day idly, spends idly above six pounds a year, which is the price for the use of one hundred pounds.

"He that wastes idly a groat's worth of his time per day, one day with another, wastes the privilege of using one hundred pounds each day.

"He that idly loses five shillings' worth of time, loses five shillings, and might as prudently throw five shillings into the sea.

"He that loses five shillings, not only loses that sum, but all the advantage that might be made by turning it in dealing, which by the time that a young man becomes old, will amount to a considerable sum of money."[2]

It is Benjamin Franklin who preaches to us in these sentences, the same which Ferdinand Kürnberger satirizes in his clever and malicious *Picture of American Culture* [3] as the supposed confession of faith of the Yankee. That it is the spirit of capitalism which here speaks in characteristic fashion, no one will doubt, however little we may wish to claim that everything which could be understood as pertaining to that spirit is contained in it. Let us pause a moment to consider this passage, the philosophy of which Kürnberger sums up in the words, "They make tallow out of cattle and money out of men". The peculiarity of this philosophy of avarice appears to be the ideal of the honest man of recognized credit, and above all the idea of a duty of the individual toward the increase of his capital, which is assumed as an end in itself. Truly what is here preached is not simply a means of making one's way in the world, but a peculiar ethic. The infraction of its rules is treated not as foolishness but as forgetfulness of duty. That is the essence of the matter. It is not mere business astuteness, that sort of thing is common enough, it is an ethos. *This* is the quality which interests us.

When Jacob Fugger, in speaking to a business associate who had retired and who wanted to persuade him to do the same, since he had made enough money and should let others have a chance, rejected that as pusillanimity and answered that "he (Fugger) thought otherwise, he wanted to make money as long as he could", [4] the spirit of his statement is evidently quite different from that of Franklin. What in the former case was an expression of commercial daring and a personal inclination morally neutral, [5] in the latter takes on the character of an ethically coloured maxim for the conduct of life. The concept spirit of capitalism is here used in this specific sense,[6] it is the spirit of modern capitalism. For that we are here dealing only with Western European and American capitalism is obvious from the way in which the problem was stated. Capitalism existed in China, India, Babylon, in the classic world, and in the Middle Ages. But in all these cases, as we shall see, this particular ethos was lacking.

Now, all Franklin's moral attitudes are coloured with utilitarianism. Honesty is useful, because it assures credit; so are punctuality, industry, frugality, and that is the reason they are virtues. A logical deduction from this would be that where, for instance, the appearance of honesty serves the same purpose, that would suffice, and an unnecessary surplus of this virtue would evidently appear to Franklin's eyes as unproductive waste. And as a matter of fact, the story in his autobiography of his conversion to those virtues,[7] or the discussion of the value of a strict maintenance of the appearance of modesty, the assiduous belittlement of one's own deserts in order to gain general recognition later,[8] confirms this impression. According to Franklin, those virtues, like all others, are only in so far virtues as they are actually useful to the individual, and the surrogate of mere appearance is always sufficient when it accomplishes the end in view. It is a conclusion which is inevitable for strict utilitarianism. The impression of many Germans that the virtues professed by Americanism are pure hypocrisy seems to have been confirmed by this striking case. But in fact the matter is not by any means so simple. Benjamin Franklin's own character, as it appears in the really unusual candidness of his autobiography, belies that suspicion. The circumstance that he ascribes his recognition of the utility of virtue to a divine revelation which was intended to lead him in the path of righteousness, shows that something more than mere garnishing for purely egocentric motives is involved.

In fact, the *summum bonum* of this ethic, the earning of more and more money, combined with the strict avoidance of all spontaneous enjoyment of life, is above all completely devoid of any eudæmonistic, not to say hedonistic, admixture. It is thought of so purely as an end in itself, that from the point of view of the happiness of, or utility to, the single individual, it appears entirely transcendental and absolutely irrational.[9] Man is dominated by the making of money, by acquisition as the ultimate purpose of his life. Economic acquisition is no longer subordinated to man as the means for the satisfaction of his material needs. This reversal of what we should call the natural relationship, so irrational from a naïve point of view, is evidently as definitely a leading principle of capitalism as it is foreign to all peoples not under capitalistic influence. At the same time it expresses a type of feeling which is closely connected with certain religious ideas. If we thus ask, *why* should "money be made out of men", Benjamin Franklin himself, although he was a colourless deist, answers in his autobiography with a quotation from the Bible, which his strict Calvinistic father drummed into him again and again in his youth: "Seest thou a man diligent in his business? He shall stand before kings" (Prov. xxii. 29). The earning of money within the modern economic order is, so long as it is done legally, the result and the expression of virtue and proficiency in a calling; and this virtue and proficiency are, as it is now not difficult to see, the real Alpha and Omega of Franklin's ethic, as expressed in the passages we have quoted, as well as in all his works without exception.[10]

And in truth this peculiar idea, so familiar to us today, but in reality so little a matter of course, of one's duty in a calling, is what is most characteristic of the social ethic of capitalistic culture, and is in a sense the fundamental basis of it. It is an obligation which the individual is supposed to feel and does feel towards the content of his professional[11] activity, no matter in what it consists, in particular no matter whether it appears on the surface as a utilization of his personal powers, or only of his material possessions (as capital).

Of course, this conception has not appeared only under capitalistic conditions. On the contrary, we shall later trace its origins back to a time previous to the advent of capitalism. Still less, naturally, do we maintain that a conscious acceptance of these ethical maxims on the part of the individuals, entrepreneurs or labourers, in modern capitalistic enterprises, is a condition of the further existence of present-day capitalism. The capitalistic economy of the present day is an immense cosmos into which the individual is born, and which presents itself to him, at least as an individual, as an unalterable order of things in which he must live. It forces the individual, in so far as he is involved in the system of market relationships, to conform to capitalistic rules of action. The manufacturer who in the long run acts counter to these norms, will just as inevitably be eliminated from the economic scene as the worker who cannot or will not adapt himself to them will be thrown into the streets without a job.

Thus the capitalism of to-day, which has come to dominate economic life, educates and selects the economic subjects which it needs through a process of economic survival of the fittest. But here one can easily see the limits of the concept of selection as a means of historical explanation. In order that a manner of life so well adapted to the peculiarities of capitalism could be selected at all, i.e. should come to dominate others, it had to originate somewhere, and not in isolated individuals alone, but as a way of life common to whole groups of men. This origin is what really needs explanation. Concerning the doctrine of the more naïve historical materialism, that such ideas originate as a reflection or superstructure of economic situations, we shall speak more in detail below. At this point it will suffice for our purpose to call attention to the fact that without doubt, in the country of Benjamin Franklin's birth (Massachusetts), the spirit of capitalism (in the sense we have attached to it) was present before the capitalistic order. There were complaints of a peculiarly calculating sort of profit-seeking in New England, as distinguished from other parts of America, as early as 1632. It is further undoubted that capitalism remained far less developed in some of the neighbouring colonies, the later Southern States of the United States of America, in spite of the fact that these latter were founded by large capitalists for business motives, while the New England colonies were founded by preachers

marginalia: Something that made this possible → employers will hire the best people. Alternative to economic traditionalism.

and seminary graduates with the help of small bourgeois, craftsmen and yeomen, for religious reasons. In this case the causal relation is certainly the reverse of that suggested by the materialistic standpoint.

But the origin and history of such ideas is much more complex than the theorists of the superstructure suppose. The spirit of capitalism, in the sense in which we are using the term, had to fight its way to supremacy against a whole world of hostile forces. A state of mind such as that expressed in the passages we have quoted from Franklin, and which called forth the applause of a whole people, would both in ancient times and in the Middle Ages[12] have been proscribed as the lowest sort of avarice and as an attitude entirely lacking in self-respect. It is, in fact, still regularly thus looked upon by all those social groups which are least involved in or adapted to modern capitalistic conditions. This is not wholly because the instinct of acquisition was in those times unknown or undeveloped, as has often been said. Nor because the *auri sacra fames,* the greed for gold, was then, or now, less powerful outside of bourgeois capitalism than within its peculiar sphere, as the illusions of modern romanticists are wont to believe. The difference between the capitalistic and precapitalistic spirits is not to be found at this point. The greed of the Chinese Mandarin, the old Roman aristocrat, or the modern peasant, can stand up to any comparison. And the *auri sacra fames* of a Neapolitan cab-driver or *barcaiuolo,* and certainly of Asiatic representatives of similar trades, as well as of the craftsmen of southern European or Asiatic countries, is, as anyone can find out for himself, very much more intense, and especially more unscrupulous than that of, say, an Englishman in similar circumstances.[13]

The universal reign of absolute unscrupulousness in the pursuit of selfish interests by the making of money has been a specific characteristic of precisely those countries whose bourgeois-capitalistic development, measured according to Occidental standards, has remained backward. As every employer knows, the lack *of coscienziosità* of the labourers[14] of such countries, for instance Italy as compared with Germany, has been, and to a certain extent still is, one of the principal obstacles to their capitalistic development. Capitalism cannot make use of the labour of those who practise the doctrine of undisciplined *liberum arbitrium,* any more than it can make use of the business man who seems absolutely unscrupulous in his dealings with others, as we can learn from Franklin. Hence the difference does not lie in the degree of development of any impulse to make money. The *auri sacra fames* is as old as the history of man. But we shall see that those who submitted to it without reserve as an uncontrolled impulse, such as the Dutch sea-captain who "would go through hell for gain, even though he scorched his sails", were by no means the representatives of that attitude of mind from which the specifically modern capitalistic spirit as a mass phenomenon is derived, and that is what matters. At all periods of history, wherever it was possible, there has been ruthless acquisition, bound to no ethical norms whatever. Like war and piracy, trade has often been unrestrained in its relations with foreigners and those outside the group. The double ethic has permitted here what was forbidden in dealings among brothers.

Capitalistic acquisition as an adventure has been at home in all types of economic society which have known trade with the use of money and which have offered it opportunities, through *commenda,* farming of taxes, State loans, financing of wars, ducal courts and officeholders. Likewise the inner attitude of the adventurer, which laughs at all ethical limitations, has been universal. Absolute and conscious ruthlessness in acquisition has often stood in the closest connection with the strictest conformity to tradition. Moreover, with the breakdown of tradition and the more or less complete extension of free economic enterprise, even to within the social group, the new thing has not generally been ethically justified and encouraged, but only tolerated as a fact. And this fact has been treated either as ethically indifferent or as reprehensible, but unfortunately unavoidable. This has not only been the normal attitude of all ethical teachings, but, what is more important, also that expressed in the practical action of the average man of pre-capitalistic times, pre-capitalistic in the sense that the rational utilization of capital in a permanent enterprise and the rational capitalistic organization of labour had not yet become dominant forces in the determination of economic activity. Now just this attitude was one of the strongest inner obstacles which the adaptation of men to the conditions of an ordered bourgeois-capitalistic economy has encountered everywhere.

The most important opponent with which the spirit of capitalism, in the sense of a definite standard of life claiming ethical sanction, has had to struggle, was that type of attitude and reaction to new situations which *opposite of the Spirit of capitalism*

we may designate as traditionalism. In this case also every attempt at a final definition must be held in abeyance. On the other hand, we must try to make the provisional meaning clear by citing a few cases. We will begin from below, with the labourers. One of the technical means which the modern employer uses in order to secure the greatest possible amount of work from his men is the device of piece-rates. In agriculture, for instance, the gathering of the harvest is a case where the greatest possible intensity of labour is called for, since, the weather being uncertain, the difference between high profit and heavy loss may depend on the speed with which the harvesting can be done. Hence a system of piece-rates is almost universal in this case. And since the interest of the employer in a speeding up of harvesting increases with the increase of the results and the intensity of the work, the attempt has again and again been made, by increasing the piece-rates of the workmen, thereby giving them an opportunity to earn what is for them a very high wage, to interest them in increasing their own efficiency. But a peculiar difficulty has been met with surprising frequency: raising the piece-rates has often had the result that not more but less has been accomplished in the same time, because the worker reacted to the increase not by increasing but by decreasing the amount of his work. A man, for instance, who at the rate of 1 mark per acre mowed 2½ acres per day and earned 2½ marks, when the rate was raised to 1.25 marks per acre mowed, not 3 acres, as he might easily have done, thus earning 3.75 marks, but only 2 acres, so that he could still earn the 2½ marks to which he was accustomed. The opportunity of earning more was less attractive than that of working less. He did not ask: how much can I earn in a day if I do as much work as possible? but: how much must I work in order to earn the wage, 2½ marks, which I earned before and which takes care of my traditional needs? This is an example of what is here meant by tradition-alism. A man does not "by nature" wish to earn more and more money, but simply to live as he is accustomed to live and to earn as much as is necessary for that purpose. Wherever modern capitalism has begun its work of increasing the productivity of human labour by increasing its intensity, it has encountered the immensely stubborn resistance of this leading trait of pre-capitalistic labour. And to-day it encounters it the more, the more backward (from a capitalistic point of view) the labouring forces are with which it has to deal.

Another obvious possibility, to return to our example, since the appeal to the acquisitive instinct through higher wage-rates failed, would have been to try the opposite policy, to force the worker by reduction of his wage-rates to work harder to earn the same amount than he did before. Low wages and high profits seem even to-day to a superficial observer to stand in corre-lation; everything which is paid out in wages seems to involve a corresponding reduction of profits. That road capitalism has taken again and again since its begin-ning. For centuries it was an article of faith, that low wages were productive, i.e. that they increased the ma-terial results of labour so that, as Pieter de la Cour, on this point, as we shall see, quite in the spirit of the old

Calvinism, said long ago, the people only work because and so long as they are poor.

But the effectiveness of this apparently so efficient method has its limits.[15] Of course the presence of a surplus population which it can hire cheaply in the labour market is a necessity for the development of capitalism. But though too large a reserve army may in certain cases favour its quantitative expansion, it checks its qualitative development, especially the transition to types of enterprise which make more intensive use of labour. Low wages are by no means identical with cheap labour.[16] From a purely quantitative point of view the efficiency of labour decreases with a wage which is physiologically insufficient, which may in the long run even mean a survival of the unfit. The present-day average Silesian mows, when he exerts himself to the full, little more than two-thirds as much land as the better paid and nourished Pomeranian or Mecklenburger, and the Pole, the further East he comes from, accomplishes progressively less than the German. Low wages fail even from a purely business point of view wherever it is a question of producing goods which require any sort of skilled labour, or the use of expensive machinery which is easily damaged, or in general wherever any great amount of sharp attention or of initiative is required. Here low wages do not pay, and their effect is the opposite of what was intended. For not only is a developed sense of responsibility absolutely indispensable, but in general also an attitude which, at least during working hours, is freed from continual calculations of how the customary wage may be earned with a maximum of comfort and a

61

minimum of exertion. Labour must, on the contrary, be performed as if it were an absolute end in itself, a calling. But such an attitude is by no means a product of nature. It cannot be evoked by low wages or high ones alone, but can only be the product of a long and arduous process of education. To-day, capitalism, once in the saddle, can recruit its labouring force in all industrial countries with comparative ease. In the past this was in every case an extremely difficult problem.[17] And even to-day it could probably not get along without the support of a powerful ally along the way, which, as we shall see below, was at hand at the time of its development.

What is meant can again best be explained by means of an example. The type of backward traditional form of labour is to-day very often exemplified by women workers, especially unmarried ones. An almost universal complaint of employers of girls, for instance German girls, is that they are almost entirely unable and unwilling to give up methods of work inherited or once learned in favour of more efficient ones, to adapt themselves to new methods, to learn and to concentrate their intelligence, or even to use it at all. Explanations of the possibility of making work easier, above all more profitable to themselves, generally encounter a complete lack of understanding. Increases of piece-rates are without avail against the stone wall of habit. In general it is otherwise, and that is a point of no little importance from our view-point, only with girls having a specifically religious, especially a Pietistic, background. One often hears, and statistical investigation confirms it,[18] that by far the best chances of economic education are found

62

among this group. The ability of mental concentration, as well as the absolutely essential feeling of obligation to one's job, are here most often combined with a strict economy which calculates the possibility of high earnings, and a cool self-control and frugality which enormously increase performance. This provides the most favourable foundation for the conception of labour as an end in itself, as a calling which is necessary to capitalism: the chances of overcoming traditionalism are greatest on account of the religious upbringing. This observation of present-day capitalism[19] in itself suggests that it is worth while to ask how this connection of adaptability to capitalism with religious factors may have come about in the days of the early development of capitalism. For that they were even then present in much the same form can be inferred from numerous facts. For instance, the dislike and the persecution which Methodist workmen in the eighteenth century met at the hands of their comrades were not solely nor even principally the result of their religious eccentricities, England had seen many of those and more striking ones. It rested rather, as the destruction of their tools, repeatedly mentioned in the reports, suggests, upon their specific willingness to work as we should say to-day.

However, let us again return to the present, and this time to the entrepreneur, in order to clarify the meaning of traditionalism in his case.

Sombart, in his discussions of the genesis of capitalism[20] has distinguished between the satisfaction of needs and acquisition as the two great leading principles in economic history. In the former case the attainment of the goods necessary to meet personal needs, in the latter a struggle for profit free from the limits set by needs, have been the ends controlling the form and direction of economic activity. What he calls the economy of needs seems at first glance to be identical with what is here described as economic traditionalism. That may be the case if the concept of needs is limited to traditional needs. But if that is not done, a number of economic types which must be considered capitalistic according to the definition of capital which Sombart gives in another part of his work,[21] would be excluded from the category of acquisitive economy and put into that of needs economy. Enterprises, namely, which are carried on by private entrepreneurs by utilizing capital (money or goods with a money value) to make a profit, purchasing the means of production and selling the product, i.e. undoubted capitalistic enterprises, may at the same time have a traditionalistic character. This has, in the course even of modern economic history, not been merely an occasional case, but rather the rule, with continual interruptions from repeated and increasingly powerful conquests of the capitalistic spirit. To be sure the capitalistic form of an enterprise and the spirit in which it is run generally stand in some sort of adequate relationship to each other, but not in one of necessary interdependence. Nevertheless, we provisionally use the expression spirit of (modern) capitalism[22] to describe that attitude which seeks profit rationally and systematically in the manner which we have illustrated by the example of Benjamin Franklin. This, however, is justified by the historical fact that that attitude of

mind has on the one hand found its most suitable expression in capitalistic enterprise, while on the other
the enterprise has derived its most suitable motive
force from the spirit of capitalism.

But the two may very well occur separately. Benjamin Franklin was filled with the spirit of capitalism
at a time when his printing business did not differ in
form from any handicraft enterprise. And we shall see
that at the beginning of modern times it was by no
means the capitalistic entrepreneurs of the commercial
aristocracy, who were either the sole or the predominant bearers of the attitude we have here called the
spirit of capitalism.[23] It was much more the rising
strata of the lower industrial middle classes. Even in
the nineteenth century its classical representatives were
not the elegant gentlemen of Liverpool and Hamburg,
with their commercial fortunes handed down for generations, but the self-made parvenus of Manchester and
Westphalia, who often rose from very modest circumstances. As early as the sixteenth century the situation
was similar; the industries which arose at that time
were mostly created by parvenus.[24]

The management, for instance, of a bank, a wholesale export business, a large retail establishment, or of
a large putting-out enterprise dealing with goods produced in homes, is certainly only possible in the form
of a capitalistic enterprise. Nevertheless, they may all
be carried on in a traditionalistic spirit. In fact, the
business of a large bank of issue cannot be carried
on in any other way. The foreign trade of whole epochs
has rested on the basis of monopolies and legal privileges
of strictly traditional character. In retail trade—and we

65

are not here talking of the small men without capital who are continually crying out for Government aid—the revolution which is making an end of the old traditionalism is still in full swing. It is the same development which broke up the old putting-out system, to which modern domestic labour is related only in form. How this revolution takes place and what is its significance may, in spite of the fact these things are so familiar, be again brought out by a concrete example.

Until about the middle of the past century the life of a putter-out was, at least in many of the branches of the Continental textile industry,[25] what we should to-day consider very comfortable. We may imagine its routine somewhat as follows: The peasants came with their cloth, often (in the case of linen) principally or entirely made from raw material which the peasant himself had produced, to the town in which the putter-out lived, and after a careful, often official, appraisal of the quality, received the customary price for it. The putter-out's customers, for markets any appreciable distance away, were middlemen, who also came to him, generally not yet following samples, but seeking traditional qualities, and bought from his warehouse, or, long before delivery, placed orders which were probably in turn passed on to the peasants. Personal canvassing of customers took place, if at all, only at long intervals. Otherwise correspondence sufficed, though the sending of samples slowly gained ground. The number of business hours was very moderate, perhaps five to six a day, sometimes considerably less; in the rush season, where there was one, more. Earnings were moderate; enough to lead a respectable life and in good times to put away a little. On the whole, relations among competitors were relatively good, with a large degree of agreement on the fundamentals of business. A long daily visit to the tavern, with often plenty to drink, and a congenial circle of friends, made life comfortable and leisurely.

The form of organization was in every respect capitalistic; the entrepreneur's activity was of a purely business character; the use of capital, turned over in the business, was indispensable; and finally, the objective aspect of the economic process, the book-keeping, was rational. But it was traditionalistic business, if one considers the spirit which animated the entrepreneur: the traditional manner of life, the traditional rate of profit, the traditional amount of work, the traditional manner of regulating the relationships with labour, and the essentially traditional circle of customers and the manner of attracting new ones. All these dominated the conduct of the business, were at the basis, one may say, of the *ethos* of this group of business men.

Now at some time this leisureliness was suddenly destroyed, and often entirely without any essential change in the form of organization, such as the transition to a unified factory, to mechanical weaving, etc. What happened was, on the contrary, often no more than this: some young man from one of the putting-out families went out into the country, carefully chose weavers for his employ, greatly increased the rigour of his supervision of their work, and thus turned them from peasants into labourers. On the other hand, he would begin to change his marketing methods by so far as possible going directly to the final consumer, would take the details into his own hands, would personally solicit customers, visiting them every year, and above all would adapt the quality of the product directly to their needs and wishes. At the same time he began to introduce the principle of low prices and large turnover. There was repeated what everywhere and always is the result of such a process of rationalization: those who would not follow suit had to go out of business. The idyllic state collapsed under the pressure of a bitter competitive struggle, respectable fortunes were made, and not lent out at interest, but always reinvested in the business. The old leisurely and comfortable attitude toward life gave way to a hard frugality in which some participated and came to the top, because they did not wish to consume but to earn, while others who wished to keep on with the old ways were forced to curtail their consumption.[26]

And, what is most important in this connection, it was not generally in such cases a stream of new money invested in the industry which brought about this revolution—in several cases known to me the whole revolutionary process was set in motion with a few thousands of capital borrowed from relations—but the new spirit, the spirit of modern capitalism, had set to work. The question of the motive forces in the expansion of modern capitalism is not in the first instance a question of the origin of the capital sums which were available for capitalistic uses, but, above all, of the development of the spirit of capitalism. Where it appears and is able to work itself out, it produces its own capital and monetary supplies as the means to its ends, but the reverse is not true.[27] Its entry on the scene was not generally peaceful. A flood of mistrust, sometimes of hatred, above all of moral indignation, regularly opposed itself to the first innovator. Often—I know of several cases of the sort—regular legends of mysterious shady spots in his previous life have been produced. It is very easy not to recognize that only an unusually strong character could save an entrepreneur of this new type from the loss of his temperate self-control and from both moral and economic shipwreck. Furthermore, along with clarity of vision and ability to act, it is only by virtue of very definite and highly developed ethical qualities that it has been possible for him to command the absolutely indispensable confidence of his customers and workmen. Nothing else could have given him the strength to overcome the innumerable obstacles, above all the infinitely more intensive work which is demanded of the modern entrepreneur. But these are ethical qualities of quite a different sort from those adapted to the traditionalism of the past.

And, as a rule, it has been neither dare-devil and unscrupulous speculators, economic adventurers such as we meet at all periods of economic history, nor simply great financiers who have carried through this change, outwardly so inconspicuous, but nevertheless so decisive for the penetration of economic life with the new spirit. On the contrary, they were men who had grown up in the hard school of life, calculating and daring at the same time, above all temperate and reliable, shrewd and completely devoted to their business, with strictly bourgeois opinions and principles.

One is tempted to think that these personal moral qualities have not the slightest relation to any ethical maxims, to say nothing of religious ideas, but that the essential relation between them is negative. The ability to free oneself from the common tradition, a sort of liberal enlightenment, seems likely to be the most suitable basis for such a business man's success. And to-day that is generally precisely the case. Any relationship between religious beliefs and conduct is generally absent, and where any exists, at least in Germany, it tends to be of the negative sort. The people filled with the spirit of capitalism to-day tend to be indifferent, if not hostile, to the Church. The thought of the pious boredom of paradise has little attraction for their active natures; religion appears to them as a means of drawing people away from labour in this world. If you ask them what is the meaning of their restless activity, why they are never satisfied with what they have, thus appearing so senseless to any purely worldly view of life, they would perhaps give the answer, if they know any at all: "to provide for my children and grandchildren". But more often and, since that motive is not peculiar to them, but was just as effective for the traditionalist, more correctly, simply: that business with its continuous work has become a necessary part of their lives. That is in fact the only possible motivation, but it at the same time expresses what is, seen from the view-point of personal happiness, so irrational about this sort of life, where a man exists for the sake of his business, instead of the reverse.

Of course, the desire for the power and recognition which the mere fact of wealth brings plays its part.

When the imagination of a whole people has once been turned toward purely quantitative bigness, as in the United States, this romanticism of numbers exercises an irresistible appeal to the poets among business men. Otherwise it is in general not the real leaders, and especially not the permanently successful entrepreneurs, who are taken in by it. In particular, the resort to entailed estates and the nobility, with sons whose conduct at the university and in the officers' corps tries to cover up their social origin, as has been the typical history of German capitalistic parvenu families, is a product of later decadence. The ideal type[28] of the capitalistic entrepreneur, as it has been represented even in Germany by occasional outstanding examples, has no relation to such more or less refined climbers. He avoids ostentation and unnecessary expenditure, as well as conscious enjoyment of his power, and is embarrassed by the outward signs of the social recognition which he receives. His manner of life is, in other words, often, and we shall have to investigate the historical significance of just this important fact, distinguished by a certain ascetic tendency, as appears clearly enough in the sermon of Franklin which we have quoted. It is, namely, by no means exceptional, but rather the rule, for him to have a sort of modesty which is essentially more honest than the reserve which Franklin so shrewdly recommends. He gets nothing out of his wealth for himself, except the irrational sense of having done his job well.

But it is just that which seems to the pre-capitalistic man so incomprehensible and mysterious, so unworthy and contemptible. That anyone should be able to make it the sole purpose of his life-work, to sink into the grave weighed down with a great material load of money and goods, seems to him explicable only as the product of a perverse instinct, the *auri sacra fames*.

At present under our individualistic political, legal, and economic institutions, with the forms of organization and general structure which are peculiar to our economic order, this spirit of capitalism might be understandable, as has been said, purely as a result of adaptation. The capitalistic system so needs this devotion to the calling of making money, it is an attitude toward material goods which is so well suited to that system, so intimately bound up with the conditions of survival in the economic struggle for existence, that there can to-day no longer be any question of a necessary connection of that acquisitive manner of life with any single *Weltanschauung*. In fact, it no longer needs the support of any religious forces, and feels the attempts of religion to influence economic life, in so far as they can still be felt at all, to be as much an unjustified interference as its regulation by the State. In such circumstances men's commercial and social interests do tend to determine their opinions and attitudes. Whoever does not adapt his manner of life to the conditions of capitalistic success must go under, or at least cannot rise. But these are phenomena of a time in which modern capitalism has become dominant and has become emancipated from its old supports. But as it could at one time destroy the old forms of mediæval regulation of economic life only in alliance with the growing power of the modern State, the same, we may say provisionally, may have been the case in its relations with religious forces. Whether and in what sense that was the case, it is our task to investigate. For that the conception of money-making as an end in itself to which people were bound, as a calling, was contrary to the ethical feelings of whole epochs, it is hardly necessary to prove. The dogma *Deo placere vix potest* which was incorporated into the canon law and applied to the activities of the merchant, and which at that time (like the passage in the gospel about interest)[29] was considered genuine, as well as St. Thomas's characterization of the desire for gain as *turpitudo* (which term even included unavoidable and hence ethically justified profit-making), already contained a high degree of concession on the part of the Catholic doctrine to the financial powers with which the Church had such intimate political relations in the Italian cities,[30] as compared with the much more radically anti-chrematistic views of comparatively wide circles. But even where the doctrine was still better accommodated to the facts, as for instance with Anthony of Florence, the feeling was never quite overcome, that activity directed to acquisition for its own sake was at bottom a *pudendum* which was to be tolerated only because of the unalterable necessities of life in this world.

Some moralists of that time, especially of the nominalistic school, accepted developed capitalistic business forms as inevitable, and attempted to justify them, especially commerce, as necessary. The *industria* developed in it they were able to regard, though not without contradictions, as a legitimate source of profit, and hence ethically unobjectionable. But the dominant doctrine rejected the spirit of capitalistic acquisition as *turpitudo,* or at least could not give it a positive ethical sanction. An ethical attitude like that of Benjamin Franklin would have been simply unthinkable. This was, above all, the attitude of capitalistic circles themselves. Their life-work was, so long as they clung to the tradition of the Church, at best something morally indifferent. It was tolerated, but was still, even if only on account of the continual danger of collision with the Church's doctrine on usury, somewhat dangerous to salvation. Quite considerable sums, as the sources show, went at the death of rich people to religious institutions as conscience money, at times even back to former debtors as *usura* which had been unjustly taken from them. It was otherwise, along with heretical and other tendencies looked upon with disapproval, only in those parts of the commercial aristocracy which were already emancipated from the tradition. But even sceptics and people indifferent to the Church often reconciled themselves with it by gifts, because it was a sort of insurance against the uncertainties of what might come after death, or because (at least according to the very widely held latter view) an external obedience to the commands of the Church was sufficient to insure salvation.[31] Here the either non-moral or immoral character of their action in the opinion of the participants themselves comes clearly to light.

Now, how could activity, which was at best ethically tolerated, turn into a calling in the sense of Benjamin Franklin? The fact to be explained historically is that in the most highly capitalistic centre of that time, in

Florence of the fourteenth and fifteenth centuries, the
money and capital market of all the great political
Powers, this attitude was considered ethically unjustifiable, or at best to be tolerated. But in the backwoods
small bourgeois circumstances of Pennsylvania in the
eighteenth century, where business threatened for simple lack of money to fall back into barter, where there
was hardly a sign of large enterprise, where only the
earliest beginnings of banking were to be found, the
same thing was considered the essence of moral conduct, even commanded in the name of duty. To speak
here of a reflection of material conditions in the ideal
superstructure would be patent nonsense. What was the
background of ideas which could account for the sort
of activity apparently directed toward profit alone as a
calling toward which the individual feels himself to
have an ethical obligation? For it was this idea which
gave the way of life of the new entrepreneur its ethical
foundation and justification.

The attempt has been made, particularly by Sombart, in what are often judicious and effective observations, to depict economic rationalism as the salient
feature of modern economic life as a whole. Undoubtedly with justification, if by that is meant the extension
of the productivity of labour which has, through the
subordination of the process of production to scientific
points of view, relieved it from its dependence upon the
natural organic limitations of the human individual.
Now this process of rationalization in the field of
technique and economic organization undoubtedly determines an important part of the ideals of life of
modern bourgeois society. Labour in the service of a

rational organization for the provision of humanity with material goods has without doubt always appeared to representatives of the capitalistic spirit as one of the most important purposes of their life-work. It is only necessary, for instance, to read Franklin's account of his efforts in the service of civic improvements in Philadelphia clearly to apprehend this obvious truth. And the joy and pride of having given employment to numerous people, of having had a part in the economic progress of his home town in the sense referring to figures of population and volume of trade which capitalism associated with the word, all these things obviously are part of the specific and undoubtedly idealistic satisfactions in life to modern men of business. Similarly it is one of the fundamental characteristics of an individualistic capitalistic economy that it is rationalized on the basis of rigorous calculation, directed with foresight and caution toward the economic success which is sought in sharp contrast to the hand-to-mouth existence of the peasant, and to the privileged traditionalism of the guild craftsman and of the adventurers' capitalism, oriented to the exploitation of political opportunities and irrational speculation.

It might thus seem that the development of the spirit of capitalism is best understood as part of the development of rationalism as a whole, and could be deduced from the fundamental position of rationalism on the basic problems of life. In the process Protestantism would only have to be considered in so far as it had formed a stage prior to the development of a purely rationalistic philosophy. But any serious attempt to carry this thesis through makes it evident that such a simple way of putting the question will not work, simply because of the fact that the history of rationalism shows a development which by no means follows parallel lines in the various departments of life. The rationalization of private law, for instance, if it is thought of as a logical simplification and rearrangement of the content of the law, was achieved in the highest hitherto known degree in the Roman law of late antiquity. But it remained most backward in some of the countries with the highest degree of economic rationalization, notably in England, where the Renaissance of Roman Law was overcome by the power of the great legal corporations, while it has always retained its supremacy in the Catholic countries of Southern Europe. The worldly rational philosophy of the eighteenth century did not find favour alone or even principally in the countries of highest capitalistic development. The doctrines of Voltaire are even to-day the common property of broad upper, and what is practically more important, middle-class groups in the Romance Catholic countries. Finally, if under practical rationalism is understood the type of attitude which sees and judges the world consciously in terms of the worldly interests of the individual ego, then this view of life was and is the special peculiarity of the peoples of the *liberum arbitrium,* such as the Italians and the French are in very flesh and blood. But we have already convinced ourselves that this is by no means the soil in which that relationship of a man to his calling as a task, which is necessary to capitalism, has pre-eminently grown. In fact, one may—this simple proposition, which is often forgotten, should be placed at the beginning of every study which essays to deal with rationalism—rationalize life from fundamentally different basic points of view and in very different directions. Rationalism is an historical concept which covers a whole world of different things. It will be our task to find out whose intellectual child the particular concrete form of rational thought was, from which the idea of a calling and the devotion to labour in the calling has grown, which is, as we have seen, so irrational from the standpoint of purely eudæmonistic self-interest, but which has been and still is one of the most characteristic elements of our capitalistic culture. We are here particularly interested in the origin of precisely the irrational element which lies in this, as in every conception of a calling.

CHAPTER III

LUTHER'S CONCEPTION OF THE CALLING

TASK OF THE INVESTIGATION

Now it is unmistakable that even in the German word *Beruf,* and perhaps still more clearly in the English *calling,* a religious conception, that of a task set by God, is at least suggested. The more emphasis is put upon the word in a concrete case, the more evident is the connotation. And if we trace the history of the word through the civilized languages, it appears that neither the predominantly Catholic peoples nor those of classical antiquity[1] have possessed any expression of similar connotation for what we know as a calling (in the sense of a life-task, a definite field in which to work), while one has existed for all predominantly Protestant peoples. It may be further shown that this is not due to any ethnical peculiarity of the languages concerned. It is not, for instance, the product of a Germanic spirit, but in its modern meaning the word comes from the Bible translations, through the spirit of the translator, not that of the original.[2] In Luther's translation of the Bible it appears to have first been used at a point in Jesus Sirach (xi. 20 and 21) precisely in our modern sense.[3] After that it speedily took on its present meaning in the everyday speech of all Protestant peoples, while earlier not even a suggestion of such a meaning could be found in the secular literature of any of them, and even, in religious writings, so far as I can ascertain, it is only found in one of the German mystics whose influence on Luther is well known.

Like the meaning of the word, the idea is new, a product of the Reformation. This may be assumed as generally known. It is true that certain suggestions of the positive valuation of routine activity in the world, which is contained in this conception of the calling, had already existed in the Middle Ages, and even in late Hellenistic antiquity. We shall speak of that later. But at least one thing was unquestionably new: the valuation of the fulfilment of duty in worldly affairs as the highest form which the moral activity of the individual could assume. This it was which inevitably gave every-day worldly activity a religious significance, and which first created the conception of a calling in this sense. The conception of the calling thus brings out that central dogma of all Protestant denominations which the Catholic division of ethical precepts into *præcepta* and *consilia* discards. The only way of living acceptably to God was not to surpass worldly morality in monastic asceticism, but solely through the fulfilment of the obligations imposed upon the individual by his position in the world. That was his calling.

Luther[4] developed the conception in the course of the first decade of his activity as a reformer. At first, quite in harmony with the prevailing tradition of the Middle Ages, as represented, for example, by Thomas Aquinas,[5] he thought of activity in the world as a thing of the flesh, even though willed by God. It is the indispensable natural condition of a life of faith, but in itself, like eating and drinking, morally neutral.[6] But with the development of the conception of *sola fide* in all its consequences, and its logical result, the increasingly sharp emphasis against the Catholic *consilia evangelica* of the monks as dictates of the devil, the calling grew in importance. The monastic life is not only quite devoid of value as a means of justification before God, but he also looks upon its renunciation of the duties of this world as the product of selfishness, withdrawing from temporal obligations. In contrast, labour in a calling appears to him as the outward expression of brotherly love. This he proves by the observation that the division of labour forces every individual to work for others, but his view-point is highly naïve, forming an almost grotesque contrast to Adam Smith's well-known statements on the same subject.[7] However, this justification, which is evidently essentially scholastic, soon disappears again, and there remains, more and more strongly emphasized, the statement that the fulfilment of worldly duties is under all circumstances the only way to live acceptably to God. It and it alone is the will of God, and hence every legitimate calling has exactly the same worth in the sight of God.[8]

That this moral justification of worldly activity was one of the most important results of the Reformation, especially of Luther's part in it, is beyond doubt, and may even be considered a platitude.[9] This attitude is worlds removed from the deep hatred of Pascal, in his contemplative moods, for all worldly activity, which he was deeply convinced could only be understood in terms of vanity or low cunning.[10] And it differs even more from the liberal utilitarian compromise with the world at which the Jesuits arrived. But just what the practical significance of this achievement of Protestantism was in detail is dimly felt rather than clearly perceived.

In the first place it is hardly necessary to point out that Luther cannot be claimed for the spirit of capitalism in the sense in which we have used that term above, or for that matter in any sense whatever. The religious circles which to-day most enthusiastically celebrate that great achievement of the Reformation are by no means friendly to capitalism in any sense. And Luther himself would, without doubt, have sharply repudiated any connection with a point of view like that of Franklin. Of course, one cannot consider his complaints against the great merchants of his time, such as the Fuggers,[11] as evidence in this case. For the struggle against the privileged position, legal or actual, of single great trading companies in the sixteenth and seventeenth centuries may best be compared with the modern campaign against the trusts, and can no more justly be considered in itself an expression of a traditionalistic point of view. Against these people, against the Lombards, the monopolists, speculators, and bankers patronized by the Anglican Church and the kings and parliaments of England and France, both the Puritans and the Huguenots carried on a bitter struggle.[12] Cromwell, after the battle of Dunbar (September 1650), wrote to the Long Parliament: "Be pleased to reform the abuses of all professions: and if there be any one that makes many poor to make a few rich, that suits not a Commonwealth." But, nevertheless, we will find Cromwell following a quite specifically capitalistic line of thought.[13] On the other hand, Luther's numerous statements against usury or interest in any form reveal a conception of the nature of capitalistic acquisition which, compared with that of late Scholasticism, is, from a capitalistic view-point, definitely backward.[14] Especially, of course, the doctrine of the sterility of money which Anthony of Florence had already refuted.

But it is unnecessary to go into detail. For, above all, the consequences of the conception of the calling in the religious sense for worldly conduct were susceptible to quite different interpretations. The effect of the Reformation as such was only that, as compared with the Catholic attitude, the moral emphasis on and the religious sanction of, organized worldly labour in a calling was mightily increased. The way in which the concept of the calling, which expressed this change, should develop further depended upon the religious evolution which now took place in the different Protestant Churches. The authority of the Bible, from which Luther thought he had derived his idea of the calling, on the whole favoured a traditionalistic interpretation. The old Testament, in particular, though in the genuine prophets it showed no sign of a tendency to excel worldly morality, and elsewhere only in quite isolated rudiments and suggestions, contained a similar religious idea entirely in this traditionalistic sense. Everyone should abide by his living and let the godless run after gain. That is the sense of all the statements which bear directly on worldly activities. Not until the Talmud is a partially, but not even then fundamentally, different attitude to be found. The personal attitude of Jesus is characterized in classical purity by the typical antique-Oriental plea: "Give us this day our daily bread." The element of radical repudiation of the world, as expressed in the $\mu\alpha\mu\omega\nu\hat{\alpha}\varsigma$ $\tau\hat{\eta}\varsigma$ $\dot{\alpha}\delta\iota\kappa\dot{\iota}\alpha\varsigma$,

83

excluded the possibility that the modern idea of a calling should be based on his personal authority.[15] In the apostolic era as expressed in the New Testament, especially in St. Paul, the Christian looked upon worldly activity either with indifference, or at least essentially traditionalistically; for those first generations were filled with eschatological hopes. Since everyone was simply waiting for the coming of the Lord, there was nothing to do but remain in the station and in the worldly occupation in which the call of the Lord had found him, and labour as before. Thus he would not burden his brothers as an object of charity, and it would only be for a little while. Luther read the Bible through the spectacles of his whole attitude; at the time and in the course of his development from about 1518 to 1530 this not only remained traditionalistic but became ever more so.[16]

In the first years of his activity as a reformer he was, since he thought of the calling as primarily of the flesh, dominated by an attitude closely related, in so far as the form of world[17]activity was concerned, to the Pauline eschatological indifference as expressed in I Cor. vii.[17] One may attain salvation in any walk of life; on the short pilgrimage of life there is no use in laying weight on the form of occupation. The pursuit of material gain beyond personal needs must thus appear as a symptom of lack of grace, and since it can apparently only be attained at the expense of others, directly reprehensible.[18] As he became increasingly involved in the affairs of the world, he came to value work in the world more highly. But in the concrete calling an individual pursued he saw more and more a special command of God to fulfil these particular duties which the Divine Will had imposed upon him. And after the conflict with the Fanatics and the peasant disturbances, the objective historical order of things in which the individual has been placed by God becomes for Luther more and more a direct manifestation of divine will.[19] The stronger and stronger emphasis on the providential element, even in particular events of life, led more and more to a traditionalistic interpretation based on the idea of Providence. The individual should remain once and for all in the station and calling in which God had placed him, and should restrain his worldly activity within the limits imposed by his established station in life. While his economic traditionalism was originally the result of Pauline indifference, it later became that of a more and more intense belief in divine providence,[20] which identified absolute obedience to God's will,[21] with absolute acceptance of things as they were. Starting from this background, it was impossible for Luther to establish a new or in any way fundamental connection between worldly activity and religious principles.[22] His acceptance of purity of doctrine as the one infallible criterion of the Church, which became more and more irrevocable after the struggles of the 'twenties, was in itself sufficient to check the development of new points of view in ethical matters.

Thus for Luther the concept of the calling remained traditionalistic.[23] His calling is something which man has to accept as a divine ordinance, to which he must adapt himself. This aspect outweighed the other idea which was also present, that work in the calling was a, or rather *the,* task set by God.[24] And in its further development, orthodox Lutheranism emphasized this aspect still more. Thus, for the time being, the only ethical result was negative; worldly duties were no longer subordinated to ascetic ones; obedience to authority and the acceptance of things as they were, were preached.[25] In this Lutheran form the idea of a calling had, as will be shown in our discussion of mediæval religious ethics, to a considerable extent been anticipated by the German mystics. Especially in Tauler's equalization of the values of religious and worldly occupations, and the decline in valuation of the traditional forms of ascetic practices[26] on account of the decisive significance of the ecstatic-contemplative absorption of the divine spirit by the soul. To a certain extent Lutheranism means a step backward from the mystics, in so far as Luther, and still more his Church, had, as compared with the mystics, partly undermined the psychological foundations for a rational ethics. (The mystic attitude on this point is reminiscent partly of the Pietest and partly of the Quaker psychology of faith.[27]) That was precisely because he could not but suspect the tendency to ascetic self-discipline of leading to salvation by works, and hence he and his Church were forced to keep it more and more in the background.

Thus the mere idea of the calling in the Lutheran sense is at best of questionable importance for the problems in which we are interested. This was all that was meant to be determined here.[28] But this is not in the least to say that even the Lutheran form of the re-newal of the religious life may not have had some prac-tical significance for the objects of our investigation; quite the contrary. Only that significance evidently cannot be derived directly from the attitude of Luther and his Church to worldly activity, and is perhaps not altogether so easily grasped as the connection with other branches of Protestantism. It is thus well for us next to look into those forms in which a relation between practical life and a religious motivation can be more easily perceived than in Lutheranism. We have already called attention to the conspicuous part played by Calvinism and the Protestant sects in the history of capitalistic development. As Luther found a different spirit at work in Zwingli than in himself, so did his spiritual successors in Calvinism. And Catholicism has to the present day looked upon Calvinism as its real opponent.

Now that may be partly explained on purely political grounds. Although the Reformation is unthinkable without Luther's own personal religious development, and was spiritually long influenced by his personality, without Calvinism his work could not have had permanent concrete success. Nevertheless, the reason for this common repugnance of Catholics and Lutherans lies, at least partly, in the ethical peculiarities of Calvinism. A purely superficial glance shows that there is here quite a different relationship between the religious life and earthly activity than in either Catholicism or Lutheranism. Even in literature motivated purely by religious factors that is evident. Take for instance the end of the *Divine Comedy,* where the poet in Paradise stands speechless in his passive contemplation of the secrets of God, and compare it with the poem which has come to be called the *Divine Comedy of Puritanism.* Milton closes the last song of *Paradise*

Lost after describing the *expulsion* from paradise as follows:—

"They, looking back, all the eastern side beheld
Of paradise, so late their happy seat,
Waved over by that flaming brand; the gate
With dreadful faces thronged and fiery arms.
Some natural tears they dropped, but wiped them soon:
The world was all before them, there to choose
Their place of rest, and Providence their guide."

And only a little before Michael had said to Adam:

. . . "Only add
Deeds to thy knowledge answerable; add faith;
Add virtue, patience, temperance; add love,
By name to come called Charity, the soul
Of all the rest: then wilt thou not be loth
To leave this Paradise, but shall possess
A Paradise within thee, happier far."

One feels at once that this powerful expression of the Puritan's serious attention to this world, his acceptance of his life in the world as a task, could not possibly have come from the pen of a mediæval writer. But it is just as uncongenial to Lutheranism, as expressed for instance in Luther's and Paul Gerhard's chorales. It is now our task to replace this vague feeling by a somewhat more precise logical formulation, and to investigate the fundamental basis of these differences. The appeal to national character is generally a mere confession of ignorance, and in this case it is entirely untenable. To ascribe a unified national character to the Englishmen of the seventeenth century would be simply to falsify history. Cavaliers and Roundheads did not appeal to each other simply as two parties, but as radically distinct species of men, and whoever looks into the matter carefully must agree with them.[29] On the other hand, a difference of character between the English merchant adventurers and the old Hanseatic merchants is not to be found; nor can any other fundamental difference between the English and German characters at the end of the Middle Ages, which cannot easily be explained by the differences of their political history.[30] It was the power of religious influence, not alone, but more than anything else, which created the differences of which we are conscious today.[31]

We thus take as our starting-point in the investigation of the relationship between the old Protestant ethic and the spirit of capitalism the works of Calvin, of Calvinism, and the other Puritan sects. But it is not to be understood that we expect to find any of the founders or representatives of these religious movements considering the promotion of what we have called the spirit of capitalism as in any sense the end of his life-work. We cannot well maintain that the pursuit of worldly goods, conceived as an end in itself, was to any of them of positive ethical value. Once and for all it must be remembered that programmes of ethical reform never were at the centre of interest for any of the religious reformers (among whom, for our purposes, we must include men like Menno, George Fox, and Wesley). They were not the founders of societies for ethical culture nor the proponents of humanitarian projects for social reform or cultural ideals. The salvation of the soul and that alone was the centre of their life and work. Their ethical ideals and the practical results of their doctrines were all based on that alone, and were the consequences of purely religious motives. We shall thus have to admit that the cultural consequences of the Reformation were to a great extent, perhaps in the particular aspects with which we are dealing predominantly, unforeseen and even unwished-for results of the labours of the reformers. They were often far removed from or even in contradiction to all that they themselves thought to attain.

The following study may thus perhaps in a modest way form a contribution to the understanding of the manner in which ideas become effective forces in history. In order, however, to avoid any misunderstanding of the sense in which any such effectiveness of purely ideal motives is claimed at all, I may perhaps be permitted a few remarks in conclusion to this introductory discussion.

In such a study, it may at once be definitely stated, no attempt is made to evaluate the ideas of the Reformation in any sense, whether it concern their social or their religious worth. We have continually to deal with aspects of the Reformation which must appear to the truly religious consciousness as incidental and even superficial. For we are merely attempting to clarify the part which religious forces have played in forming the developing web of our specifically worldly modern culture, in the complex interaction of innumerable different historical factors. We are thus inquiring only to what extent certain characteristic features of this culture can be imputed to the influence of the Reformation. At the same time we must free ourselves from the idea that it is possible to deduce the Reformation, as a historically necessary result, from certain economic changes. Countless historical circumstances, which cannot be reduced to any economic law, and are not susceptible of economic explanation of any sort, especially purely political processes, had to concur in order that the newly created Churches should survive at all.

On the other hand, however, we have no intention whatever of maintaining such a foolish and doctrinaire thesis[32] as that the spirit of capitalism (in the provisional sense of the term explained above) could only have arisen as the result of certain effects of the Reformation, or even that capitalism as an economic system is a creation of the Reformation. In itself, the fact that certain important forms of capitalistic business organization are known to be considerably older than the Reformation is a sufficient refutation of such a claim. On the contrary, we only wish to ascertain whether and to what extent religious forces have taken part in the qualitative formation and the quantitative expansion of that spirit over the world. Furthermore, what concrete aspects of our capitalistic culture can be traced to them? In view of the tremendous confusion of interdependent influences between the material basis, the forms of social and political organization, and the ideas current in the time of the Reformation, we can only proceed by investigating whether and at what points certain correlations between forms of religious belief and practical ethics can be worked out. At the same time we shall as far as possible clarify the manner and the general *direction* in which, by virtue of those relationships, the religious movements have influenced the development of material culture. Only when this has been determined with reasonable accuracy can the attempt be made to estimate to what extent the historical development of modern culture can be attributed to those religious forces and to what extent to others.

PART II

THE PRACTICAL ETHICS OF THE
ASCETIC BRANCHES OF
PROTESTANTISM

CHAPTER IV

THE RELIGIOUS FOUNDATIONS OF
WORLDLY ASCETICISM

In history there have been four principal forms of ascetic Protestantism (in the sense of word here used): (1) Calvinism in the form which it assumed in the main area of its influence in Western Europe, especially in the seventeenth century; (2) Pietism; (3) Methodism; (4) the sects growing out of the Baptist movement.[1] None of these movements was completely separated from the others, and even the distinction from the non-ascetic Churches of the Reformation is never perfectly clear. Methodism, which first arose in the middle of the eighteenth century within the Established Church of England, was not, in the minds of its founders, intended to form a new Church, but only a new awakening of the ascetic spirit within the old. Only in the course of its development, especially in its extension to America, did it become separate from the Anglican Church.

Pietism first split off from the Calvinistic movement in England, and especially in Holland. It remained loosely connected with orthodoxy, shading off from it by imperceptible gradations, until at the end of the seventeenth century it was absorbed into Lutheranism under Spener's leadership. Though the dogmatic adjustment was not entirely satisfactory, it remained a movement within the Lutheran Church. Only the faction dominated by Zinzendorf, and affected by lingering Hussite and Calvinistic influences within the

Moravian brotherhood, was forced, like Methodism against its will, to form a peculiar sort of sect. Calvinism and Baptism were at the beginning of their development sharply opposed to each other. But in the Baptism of the latter part of the seventeenth century they were in close contact. And even in the Independent sects of England and Holland at the beginning of the seventeenth century the transition was not abrupt. As Pietism shows, the transition to Lutheranism is also gradual, and the same is true of Calvinism and the Anglican Church, though both in external character and in the spirit of its most logical adherents the latter is more closely related to Catholicism. It is true that both the mass of the adherents and especially the staunchest champions of that ascetic movement which, in the broadest sense of a highly ambiguous word, has been called Puritanism,[2] did attack the foundations of Anglicanism; but even here the differences were only gradually worked out in the course of the struggle. Even if for the present we quite ignore the questions of government and organization which do not interest us here, the facts are just the same. The dogmatic differences, even the most important, such as those over the doctrines of predestination and justification, were combined in the most complex ways, and even at the beginning of the seventeenth century regularly, though not without exception, prevented the maintenance of unity in the Church. Above all, the types of moral conduct in which we are interested may be found in a similar manner among the adherents of the most various denominations, derived from any one of the four sources mentioned above, or a combination of several of them. We shall see that similar ethical maxims may be correlated with very different dogmatic foundations. Also the important literary tools for the saving of souls, above all the casuistic compendia of the various denominations, influenced each other in the course of time; one finds great similarities in them, in spite of very great differences in actual conduct.

It would almost seem as though we had best completely ignore both the dogmatic foundations and the ethical theory and confine our attention to the moral practice so far as it can be determined. That, however, is not true. The various different dogmatic roots of ascetic morality did no doubt die out after terrible struggles. But the original connection with those dogmas has left behind important traces in the later undogmatic ethics; moreover, only the knowledge of the original body of ideas can help us to understand the connection of that morality with the idea of the afterlife which absolutely dominated the most spiritual men of that time. Without its power, overshadowing everything else, no moral awakening which seriously influenced practical life came into being in that period.

We are naturally not concerned with the question of what was theoretically and officially taught in the ethical compendia of the time, however much practical significance this may have had through the influence of Church discipline, pastoral work, and preaching.[3] We are interested rather in something entirely different: the influence of those psychological sanctions which, originating in religious belief and the practice of religion, gave a direction to practical conduct and held the individual to it. Now these sanctions were to a large extent derived from the peculiarities of the religious ideas behind them. The men of that day were occupied with abstract dogmas to an extent which itself can only be understood when we perceive the connection of these dogmas with practical religious interests. A few observations on dogma,[4] which will seem to the nontheological reader as dull as they will hasty and superficial to the theologian, are indispensable. We can of course only proceed by presenting these religious ideas in the artificial simplicity of ideal types, as they could at best but seldom be found in history. For just because of the impossibility of drawing sharp boundaries in historical reality we can only hope to understand their specific importance from an investigation of them in their most consistent and logical forms.

A. CALVINISM

Now Calvinism[5] was the faith[6] over which the great political and cultural struggles of the sixteenth and seventeenth centuries were fought in the most highly developed countries, the Netherlands, England, and France. To it we shall hence turn first. At that time, and in general even to-day, the doctrine of predestination was considered its most characteristic dogma. It is true that there has been controversy as to whether it is the most essential dogma of the Reformed Church or only an appendage. Judgments of the importance of a historical phenomenon may be judgments of value or faith, namely, when they refer to what is alone interesting, or alone in the long run valuable in it. Or, on the other hand, they may refer to its influence on other historical processes as a causal factor. Then we are concerned with judgments of historical imputation. If now we start, as we must do here, from the latter standpoint and inquire into the significance which is to be attributed to that dogma by virtue of its cultural and historical consequences, it must certainly be rated very highly.[7] The movement which Oldenbarneveld led was shattered by it. The schism in the English Church became irrevocable under James I after the Crown and the Puritans came to differ dogmatically over just this doctrine. Again and again it was looked upon as the real element of political danger in Calvinism and attacked as such by those in authority.[8] The great synods of the seventeenth century, above all those of Dordrecht and Westminster, besides numerous smaller ones, made its elevation to canonical authority the central purpose of their work. It served as a rallying-point to countless heroes of the Church militant, and in both the eighteenth and the nineteenth centuries it caused schisms in the Church and formed the battle-cry of great new awakenings. We cannot pass it by, and since to-day it can no longer be assumed as known to all educated men, we can best learn its content from the authoritative words of the Westminster Confession of 1647, which in this regard is simply repeated by both Independent and Baptist creeds.

"Chapter IX (of Free Will), No. 3. Man, by his fall into a state of sin, hath wholly lost all ability of will to any spiritual good accompanying salvation. So that a natural man, being altogether averse from that Good, and dead in sin, is not able, by his own strength, to convert himself, or to prepare himself thereunto.

"Chapter III (of God's Eternal Decree), No. 3. By the decree of God, for the manifestation of His glory, some men and angels are predestinated unto everlasting life, and others foreordained to everlasting death.

"No. 5. Those of mankind that are predestinated unto life, God before the foundation of the world was laid, according to His eternal and immutable purpose, and the secret counsel and good pleasure of His will, hath chosen in Christ unto everlasting glory, out of His mere free grace and love, without any foresight of faith or good works, or perseverance in either of them, or any other thing in the creature as conditions, or causes moving Him thereunto, and all to the praise of His glorious grace.

"No. 7. The rest of mankind God was pleased, according to the unsearchable counsel of His own will, whereby He extendeth, or with-holdeth mercy, as He pleaseth, for the glory of His sovereign power over His creatures, to pass by, and to ordain them to dishonour and wrath for their sin, to the praise of His glorious justice.

"Chapter X (of Effectual Calling), No. 1. All those whom God hath predestinated unto life, and those only, He is pleased in His appointed and accepted time effectually to call, by His word and spirit (out of that state of sin and death, in which they are by nature) . . . taking away their heart of stone, and giving unto them an heart of flesh; renewing their wills, and by His almighty power determining them to that which is good. . . .

"Chapter V (of Providence), No. 6. As for those wicked and ungodly men, whom God as a righteous judge, for former sins doth blind and harden, from them He not only with-holdeth His grace, whereby they might have been enlightened in their understandings and wrought upon in their hearts, but sometimes also withdraweth the gifts which they had and exposeth them to such objects as their corruption makes occasion of sin: and withal, gives them over to their own lusts, the temptations of the world, and the power of Satan: whereby it comes to pass that they harden themselves, even under those means, which God useth for the softening of others."[9]

"Though I may be sent to Hell for it, such a God will never command my respect", was Milton's well-known opinion of the doctrine.[10] But we are here concerned not with the evaluation, but the historical significance of the dogma. We can only briefly sketch the question of how the doctrine originated and how it fitted into the framework of Calvinistic theology.

Two paths leading to it were possible. The phenomenon of the religious sense of grace is combined, in the most active and passionate of those great worshippers which Christianity has produced again and again since Augustine, with the feeling of certainty that that grace is the sole product of an objective power, and not in the least to be attributed to personal worth. The powerful feeling of light-hearted assurance, in which the tremendous pressure of their sense of sin is released, apparently breaks over them with elemental force and destroys every possibility of the belief that this overpowering gift of grace could owe anything to their own co-operation or could be connected with achieve-ments or qualities of their own faith and will. At the time of Luther's greatest religious creativeness, when he was capable of writing his *Freiheit eines Christenmenschen,* God's secret decree was also to him most definitely the sole and ultimate source of his state of religious grace.[11] Even later he did not formally abandon it. But not only did the idea not assume a central position for him, but it receded more and more into the background, the more his position as responsible head of his Church forced him into practical politics. Melancthon quite deliber-ately avoided adopting the dark and dangerous teaching in the Augsburg Confession, and for the Church fathers of Lutheranism it was an article of faith that grace was revocable (*amissibilis*), and could be won again by penitent humility and faith-ful trust in the word of God and in the sacraments.

With Calvin the process was just the opposite; the sig-nificance of the doctrine for him increased,[12] perceptibly in the course of his polemical controversies with theo-logical opponents. It is not fully developed until the third edition of his *Institutes,* and only gained its position of central prominence after his death in the great strug-gles which the Synods of Dordrecht and Westminster sought to put an end to. With Calvin the *decretum horribile* is derived not, as with Luther, from religious experience, but from the logical necessity of his thought; therefore its importance increases with every increase in the logical consistency of that religious thought. The interest of it is solely in God, not in man; God does not exist for men, but men for the sake of

God.[13] All creation, including of course the fact, as it undoubtedly was for Calvin, that only a small proportion of men are chosen for eternal grace, can have any meaning only as means to the glory and majesty of God. To apply earthly standards of justice to His sovereign decrees is meaningless and an insult to His Majesty,[14] since He and He alone is free, i.e. is subject to no law. His decrees can only be understood by or even known to us in so far as it has been His pleasure to reveal them. We can only hold to these fragments of eternal truth. Everything else, including the meaning of our individual destiny, is hidden in dark mystery which it would be both impossible to pierce and presumptuous to question.

For the damned to complain of their lot would be much the same as for animals to bemoan the fact they were not born as men. For everything of the flesh is separated from God by an unbridgeable gulf and deserves of Him only eternal death, in so far as He has not decreed otherwise for the glorification of His Majesty. We know only that a part of humanity is saved, the rest damned. To assume that human merit or guilt play a part in determining this destiny would be to think of God's absolutely free decrees, which have been settled from eternity, as subject to change by human influence, an impossible contradiction. The Father in heaven of the New Testament, so human and understanding, who rejoices over the repentance of a sinner as a woman over the lost piece of silver she has found, is gone. His place has been taken by a transcendental being, beyond the reach of human understanding, who with His quite incomprehensible decrees has decided the fate of every individual and regulated the tiniest details of the cosmos from eternity.[15] God's grace is, since His decrees cannot change, as impossible for those to whom He has granted it to lose as it is unattainable for those to whom He has denied it.

In its extreme inhumanity this doctrine must above all have had one consequence for the life of a generation which surrendered to its magnificent consistency. That was a feeling of unprecedented inner loneliness of the single individual.[16] In what was for the man of the age of the Reformation the most important thing in life, his eternal salvation, he was forced to follow his path alone to meet a destiny which had been decreed for him from eternity. No one could help him. No priest, for the chosen one can understand the word of God only in his own heart. No sacraments, for though the sacraments had been ordained by God for the increase of His glory, and must hence be scrupulously observed, they are not a means to the attainment of grace, but only the subjective *externa subsidia* of faith. No Church, for though it was held that *extra ecclesiam nulla salus* in the sense that whoever kept away from the true Church could never belong to God's chosen band,[17] nevertheless the membership of the external Church included the doomed. They should belong to it and be subjected to its discipline, not in order thus to attain salvation, that is impossible, but because, for the glory of God, they too must be forced to obey His commandments. Finally, even no God. For even Christ had died only for the elect,[18] for whose benefit God had decreed His martyrdom from eternity. This, the complete elimination of salvation through the

Church and the sacraments (which was in Lutheranism by no means developed to its final conclusions), was what formed the absolutely decisive difference from Catholicism.

That great historic process in the development of religions, the elimination of magic from the world[19] which had begun with the old Hebrew prophets and, in conjunction with Hellenistic scientific thought, had repudiated all magical means to salvation as superstition and sin, came here to its logical conclusion. The genuine Puritan even rejected all signs of religious ceremony at the grave and buried his nearest and dearest without song or ritual in order that no superstition, no trust in the effects of magical and sacramental forces on salvation, should creep in.[20]

There was not only no magical means of attaining the grace of God for those to whom God had decided to deny it, but no means whatever. Combined with the harsh doctrines of the absolute transcendentality of God and the corruption of everything pertaining to the flesh, this inner isolation of the individual contains, on the one hand, the reason for the entirely negative attitude of Puritanism to all the sensuous and emotional elements in culture and in religion, because they are of no use toward salvation and promote sentimental illusions and idolatrous superstitions. Thus it provides a basis for a fundamental antagonism to sensuous culture of all kinds.[21] On the other hand, it forms one of the roots of that disillusioned and pessimistically inclined individualism[22] which can even to-day be identified in the national characters and the institutions of the peoples with a Puritan past, in such a striking

contrast to the quite different spectacles through which
the Enlightenment later looked upon men.[23] We can
clearly identify the traces of the influence of the doctrine of predestination in the elementary forms of conduct and attitude toward life in the era with which we
are concerned, even where its authority as a dogma
was on the decline. It was in fact only the most extreme form of that exclusive trust in God in which we
are here interested. It comes out for instance in the
strikingly frequent repetition, especially in the English
Puritan literature, of warnings against any trust in the
aid of friendship of men.[24] Even the amiable Baxter
counsels deep distrust of even one's closest friend, and
Bailey directly exhorts to trust no one and to say nothing compromising to anyone. Only God should be
your confidant.[25] In striking contrast to Lutheranism,
this attitude toward life was also connected with the
quiet disappearance of the private confession, of which
Calvin was suspicious only on account of its possible
sacramental misinterpretation, from all the regions of
fully developed Calvinism. That was an occurrence of
the greatest importance. In the first place it is a symptom of the type of influence this religion exercised.
Further, however, it was a psychological stimulus to
the development of their ethical attitude. The means to
a periodical discharge of the emotional sense of sin[26]
was done away with.

Of the consequences for the ethical conduct of
everyday life we speak later. But for the general
religious situation of a man the consequences are evident. In spite of the necessity of membership in the
true Church[27] for salvation, the Calvinist's intercourse

with his God was carried on in deep spiritual isolation. To see the specific results[28] of this peculiar atmosphere, it is only necessary to read Bunyan's *Pilgrim's Progress,*[29] by far the most widely read book of the whole Puritan literature. In the description of Christian's attitude after he had realized that he was living in the City of Destruction and he had received the call to take up his pilgrimage to the celestial city, wife and children cling to him, but stopping his ears with his fingers and crying, "life, eternal life", he staggers forth across the fields. No refinement could surpass the naïve feeling of the tinker who, writing in his prison cell, earned the applause of a believing world, in expressing the emotions of the faithful Puritan, thinking only of his own salvation. It is expressed in the unctuous conversations which he holds with fellow-seekers on the way, in a manner somewhat reminiscent of Gottfried Keller's *Gerechte Kammacher.* Only when he himself is safe does it occur to him that it would be nice to have his family with him. It is the same anxious fear of death and the beyond which we feel so vividly in Alfonso of Liguori, as Döllinger has described him to us. It is worlds removed from that spirit of proud worldliness which Machiavelli expresses in relating the fame of those Florentine citizens who, in their struggle against the Pope and his excommunication, had held "Love of their native city higher than the fear for the salvation of their souls". And it is of course even farther from the feelings which Richard Wagner puts into the mouth of Siegmund before his fatal combat, "Grüsse mir Wotan, grüsse mir Wallhall—Doch von Wallhall's spröden Wonnen sprich du wahrlich mir nicht". But the effects of this fear on Bunyan and Liguori are characteristically different. The same fear which drives the latter to every conceivable self-humiliation spurs the former on to a restless and systematic struggle with life. Whence comes this difference?

It seems at first a mystery how the undoubted superiority of Calvinism in social organization can be connected with this tendency to tear the individual away from the closed ties with which he is bound to this world.[30] But, however strange it may seem, it follows from the peculiar form which the Christian brotherly love was forced to take under the pressure of the inner isolation of the individual through the Calvinistic faith. In the first place it follows dogmatically.[31] The world exists to serve the glorification of God and for that purpose alone. The elected Christian is in the world only to increase this glory of God by fulfilling His commandments to the best of his ability. But God requires social achievement of the Christian because He wills that social life shall be organized according to His commandments, in accordance with that purpose. The social[32] activity of the Christian in the world is solely activity *in majorem gloriam Dei*. This character is hence shared by labour in a calling which serves the mundane life of the community. Even in Luther we found specialized labour in callings justified in terms of brotherly love. But what for him remained an uncertain, purely intellectual suggestion became for the Calvinists a characteristic element in their ethical system. Brotherly love, since it may only be practised for the glory of God[33] and not in the service of the flesh,[34] is expressed in the first place in the fulfilment of the daily tasks given by the *lex naturæ;* and in the process this fulfilment assumes a peculiarly objective and impersonal character, that of service in the interest of the rational organization of our social environment. For the wonderfully purposeful organization and arrangement of this cosmos is, according both to the revelation of the Bible and to natural intuition, evidently designed by God to serve the utility of the human race. This makes labour in the service of impersonal social usefulness appear to promote the glory of God and hence to be willed by Him. The complete elimination of the theodicy problem and of all those questions about the meaning of the world and of life, which have tortured others, was as self-evident to the Puritan as, for quite different reasons, to the Jew, and even in a certain sense to all the non-mystical types of Christian religion.

To this economy of forces Calvinism added another tendency which worked in the same direction. The conflict between the individual and the ethic (in Sören Kierkegaard's sense) did not exist for Calvinism, although it placed the individual entirely on his own responsibility in religious matters. This is not the place to analyse the reasons for this fact, or its significance for the political and economic rationalism of Calvinism. The source of the utilitarian character of Calvinistic ethics lies here, and important peculiarities of the Calvinistic idea of the calling were derived from the same source as well.[35] But for the moment we must return to the special consideration of the doctrine of predestination.

For us the decisive problem is: How was this doctrine borne[36] in an age to which the after-life was not only more important, but in many ways also more certain, than all the interests of life in this world?[37] The question, <u>Am I one of the elect</u>? <u>must sooner or later have arisen for every believer and have forced all other interests into the background</u>. And how can I be sure of this state of grace?[38] For Calvin himself this was not a problem. He felt himself to be a chosen agent of the Lord, and was certain of his own salvation. Accordingly, to the question of how the individual can be certain of his own election, he has at bottom only the answer that we should be content with the knowledge that God has chosen and depend further only on that implicit trust in Christ which is the result of true faith. He rejects in principle the assumption that one can learn from the conduct of others whether they are chosen or damned. It is an unjustifiable attempt to force God's secrets. The elect differ externally in this life in no way from the damned[39]; and even all the subjective experiences of the chosen are, as *ludibria spiritus sancti,* possible for the damned with the single exception of that *finaliter* expectant, trusting faith. The elect thus are and remain God's invisible Church.

Quite naturally this attitude was impossible for his followers as early as Beza, and, above all, for the broad mass of ordinary men. For them the *certitudo salutis* in the sense of the recognizability of the state of grace necessarily became of absolutely dominant importance.[40] So, wherever the doctrine of predestination was held, the question could not be suppressed whether there were any infallible criteria by which membership in the *electi* could be known. Not only has this question continually had a central importance in the development of the Pietism which first arose on the basis of the Reformed Church; it has in fact in a certain sense at times been fundamental to it. But when we consider the great political and social importance of the Reformed doctrine and practice of the Communion, we shall see how great a part was played during the whole seventeenth century outside of Pietism by the possibility of ascertaining the state of grace of the individual. On it depended, for instance, his admission to Communion, i.e. to the central religious ceremony which determined the social standing of the participants.

It was impossible, at least so far as the question of a man's own state of grace arose, to be satisfied[41] with Calvin's trust in the testimony of the expectant faith resulting from grace, even though the orthodox doctrine had never formally abandoned that criterion.[42] Above all, practical pastoral work, which had immediately to deal with all the suffering caused by the doctrine, could not be satisfied. It met these difficulties in various ways.[43] So far as predestination was not reinterpreted, toned down, or fundamentally abandoned,[44] two principal, mutually connected, types of pastoral advice appear. On the one hand it is held to be an absolute duty to consider oneself chosen, and to combat all doubts as temptations of the devil,[45] since lack of self-confidence is the result of insufficient faith, hence of imperfect grace. The exhortation of the apostle to make fast one's own call is here interpreted as a duty to attain certainty of one's own election and justification in the daily struggle of life. In the place of the humble sinners to whom Luther promises grace if they trust themselves to God in penitent faith are bred those self-confident saints[46] whom we can rediscover in the hard Puritan merchants of the heroic age of capitalism and in isolated instances down to the present. On the other hand, in order to attain that self-confidence intense worldly activity is recommended as the most suitable means.[47] It and it alone disperses religious doubts and gives the certainty of grace.

That worldly activity should be considered capable of this achievement, that it could, so to speak, be considered the most suitable means of counteracting feelings of religious anxiety, finds its explanation in the fundamental peculiarities of religious feeling in the Reformed Church, which come most clearly to light in its differences from Lutheranism in the doctrine of justification by faith. These differences are analysed so subtly and with such objectivity and avoidance of value-judgments in Schneckenburger's excellent lectures,[48] that the following brief observations can for the most part simply rest upon his discussion.

The highest religious experience which the Lutheran faith strives to attain, especially as it developed in the course of the seventeenth century, is the *unio mystica* with the deity.[49] As the name itself, which is unknown to the Reformed faith in this form, suggests, it is a feeling of actual absorption in the deity, that of a real entrance of the divine into the soul of the believer. It is qualitatively similar to the aim of the contemplation of the German mystics and is characterized by its passive search for the fulfilment of the yearning for rest in God.

Now the history of philosophy shows that religious belief which is primarily mystical may very well be compatible with a pronounced sense of reality in the field of empirical fact; it may even support it directly on account of the repudiation of dialectic doctrines. Furthermore, mysticism may indirectly even further the interests of rational conduct. Nevertheless, the positive valuation of external activity is lacking in its relation to the world. In addition to this, Lutheranism combines the *unio mystica* with that deep feeling of sin-stained unworthiness which is essential to preserve *the pœnitentia quotidiana* of the faithful Lutheran, thereby maintaining the humility and simplicity indispensable for the forgiveness of sins. The typical religion of the Reformed Church, on the other hand, has from the beginning repudiated both this purely inward emotional piety of Lutheranism and the Quietist escape from everything of Pascal. A real penetration of the human soul by the divine was made impossible by the absolute transcendentality of God compared to the flesh: *finitum non est capax infinite.* The community of the elect with their God could only take place and be perceptible to them in that God worked (*operatur*) through them and that they were conscious of it. That is, their action originated from the faith caused by God's grace, and this faith in turn justified itself by the quality of that action. Deep-lying differences of the most important conditions of salvation[50] which apply to the classification of all practical religious activity appear here. The religious believer can make himself sure of his state of grace either in that he feels himself to be the vessel of the Holy Spirit or the tool of the divine will. In the former case his religious life tends to mysticism and emotionalism, in the latter to ascetic action; Luther stood close to the former type, Calvinism belonged definitely to the latter. The Calvinist also wanted to be saved *sola fide.* But since Calvin viewed all pure feelings and emotions, no matter how exalted they might seem to be, with suspicion,[51] faith had to be proved by its objective results in order to provide a firm foundation for the *certitudo salutis.* It must be a *fides efficax,*[52] the call to salvation an effectual calling (expression used in Savoy Declaration).

If we now ask further, by what fruits the Calvinist thought himself able to identify true faith? the answer is: by a type of Christian conduct which served to increase the glory of God. Just what does so serve is to be seen in his own will as revealed either directly through the Bible or indirectly through the purposeful order of the world which he has created (*lex naturæ*).[53] Especially by comparing the condition of one's own soul with that of the elect, for instance the patriarchs, according to the Bible, could the state of one's own grace be known.[54] Only one of the elect really has the *fides efficax,*[55] only he is able by virtue of his rebirth (*regeneratio*) and the resulting sanctification (*sanctificatio*) of his whole life, to augment the glory of God by real, and not merely apparent, good works. It was through the consciousness that his conduct, at least in its fundamental character and constant ideal (*propositum obœdientiæ*), rested on a power[56] within himself working for the glory of God; that it is not only willed of God but rather done by God[57] that he attained the highest good towards which this religion strove, the certainty of salvation.[58] That it was attainable was proved by 2 Cor. xiii. 5.[59] Thus, however useless good works might be as a means of attaining salvation, for even the elect remain beings of the flesh, and everything they do falls infinitely short of divine standards, nevertheless, they are indispensable as a sign of election.[60] They are the technical means, not of purchasing salvation, but of getting rid of the fear of damnation. In this sense they are occasionally referred to as directly necessary for salvation[61] or the *possessio salutis* is made conditional on them.[62]

In practice this means that God helps those who help themselves.[63] Thus the Calvinist, as it is sometimes put, himself creates[64] his own salvation, or, as would be more correct, the conviction of it. But this creation cannot, as in Catholicism, consist in a gradual accumulation of individual good works to one's credit, but rather in a systematic self-control which at every moment stands before the inexorable alternative, chosen or damned. This brings us to a very important point in our investigation.

It is common knowledge that Lutherans have again and again accused this line of thought, which was worked out in the Reformed Churches and sects with increasing clarity,[65] of reversion to the doctrine of salvation by works.[66] And however justified the protest of the accused against identification of their dogmatic position with the Catholic doctrine, this accusation has surely been made with reason if by it is meant the practical consequences for the everyday life of the average Christian of the Reformed Church.[67] For a more intensive form of the religious valuation of moral action than that to which Calvinism led its adherents has perhaps never existed. But what is important for the practical significance of this sort of salvation by works must be sought in a knowledge of the particular qualities which characterized their type of ethical conduct and distinguished it from the everyday life of an average Christian of the Middle Ages. The difference may well be formulated as follows: the normal mediæval Catholic layman[68] lived ethically, so to speak, from hand to mouth. In the first place he conscientiously fulfilled his traditional duties. But beyond that minimum his good works did not necessarily form a connected, or at least not a rationalized, system of life, but rather remained a succession of individual acts. He could use them as occasion demanded, to atone for particular sins, to better his chances for salvation, or, toward the end of his life, as a sort of insurance premium. Of course the Catholic ethic was an ethic of intentions. But the concrete *intentio* of the single act determined its value. And the single good or bad action was credited to the doer determining his temporal and eternal fate. Quite realistically the Church recognized that man was not an absolutely clearly defined unity to be judged one way or the other, but that his moral life was normally subject to conflicting motives and his action contradictory. Of course, it required as an ideal a change of life in principle. But it weakened just this requirement (for the average) by one of its most important means of power and education, the sacrament of absolution, the function of which was connected with the deepest roots of the peculiarly Catholic religion.

116

The rationalization of the world, the elimination of magic as a means to salvation,[69] the Catholics had not carried nearly so far as the Puritans (and before them the Jews) had done. To the Catholic[70] the absolution of his Church was a compensation for his own imperfection. The priest was a magician who performed the miracle of transubstantiation, and who held the key to eternal life in his hand. One could turn to him in grief and penitence. He dispensed atonement, hope of grace, certainty of forgiveness, and thereby granted release from that tremendous tension to which the Calvinist was doomed by an inexorable fate, admitting of no mitigation. For him such friendly and human comforts did not exist. He could not hope to atone for hours of weakness or of thoughtlessness by increased good will at other times, as the Catholic or even the Lutheran could. The God of Calvinism demanded of his believers not single good works, but a life of good works combined into a unified system.[71] There was no place for the very human Catholic cycle of sin, repentance, atonement, release, followed by renewed sin. Nor was there any balance of merit for a life as a whole which could be adjusted by temporal punishments or the Churches' means of grace.

The moral conduct of the average man was thus deprived of its planless and unsystematic character and subjected to a consistent method for conduct as a whole. It is no accident that the name of Methodists stuck to the participants in the last great revival of Puritan ideas in the eighteenth century just as the term Precisians, which has the same meaning, was applied to their spiritual ancestors in the seventeenth century.[72]

For only by a fundamental change in the whole meaning of life at every moment and in every action[73] could the effects of grace transforming a man from the *status naturæ* to the *status gratiæ* be proved.

The life of the saint was directed solely toward a transcendental end, salvation. But precisely for that reason it was thoroughly rationalized in this world and dominated entirely by the aim to add to the glory of God on earth. Never has the precept *omnia in majorem dei gloriam* been taken with more bitter seriousness.[74] Only a life guided by constant thought could achieve conquest over the state of nature. Descartes's *cogito ergo sum* was taken over by the contemporary Puritans with this ethical reinterpretation.[75] It was this rationalization which gave the Reformed faith its peculiar ascetic tendency, and is the basis both of its relationship[76] to and its conflict with Catholicism. For naturally similar things were not unknown to Catholicism.

Without doubt Christian asceticism, both outwardly and in its inner meaning, contains many different things. But it has had a definitely rational character in its highest Occidental forms as early as the Middle Ages, and in several forms even in antiquity. The great historical significance of Western monasticism, as contrasted with that of the Orient, is based on this fact, not in all cases, but in its general type. In the rules of St. Benedict, still more with the monks of Cluny, again with the Cistercians, and most strongly the Jesuits, it has become emancipated from planless otherworldliness and irrational self-torture. It had developed a systematic method of rational conduct with the purpose of overcoming the *status naturæ,* to free man from the power of irrational impulses and his dependence on the world and on nature. It attempted to subject man to the supremacy of a purposeful Will,[77] to bring his actions under constant self-control with a careful consideration of their ethical consequences. Thus it trained the monk, objectively, as a worker in the service of the kingdom of God, and thereby further, subjectively, assured the salvation of his soul. This active self-control, which formed the end of the *exercitia* of St. Ignatius and of the rational monastic virtues everywhere,[78] was also the most important practical ideal of Puritanism.[79] In the deep contempt with which the cool reserve of its adherents is contrasted, in the reports of the trials of its martyrs, with the undisciplined blustering of the noble prelates and officials[80] can be seen that respect for quiet self-control which still distinguishes the best type of English or American gentleman to-day.[81] To put it in our terms[82]: The Puritan, like every rational type of asceticism, tried to enable a man to maintain and act upon his constant motives, especially those which it taught him itself, against the emotions. In this formal psychological sense of the term it tried to make him into a personality. Contrary to many popular ideas, the end of this asceticism was to be able to lead an alert, intelligent life: the most urgent task the destruction of spontaneous, impulsive enjoyment, the most important means was to bring order into the conduct of its adherents. All these important points are emphasized in the rules of Catholic monasticism as strongly[83] as in the principles of conduct of the Calvinist.[84] On this methodical control over the whole man rests the enormous expansive power of both, especially the ability of Calvinism as against Lutheranism to defend the cause of Protestantism as the Church militant.

On the other hand, the difference of the Calvinistic from the mediæval asceticism is evident. It consisted in the disappearance of the *consilia evangelica* and the accompanying transformation of asceticism to activity within the world. It is not as though Catholicism had restricted the methodical life to monastic cells. This was by no means the case either in theory or in practice. On the contrary, it has already been pointed out that, in spite of the greater ethical moderation of Catholicism, an ethically unsystematic life did not satisfy the highest ideals which it had set up even for the life of the layman.[85] The tertiary order of St. Francis was, for instance, a powerful attempt in the direction of an ascetic penetration of everyday life, and, as we know, by no means the only one. But, in fact, works like the *Nachfolge Christi* show, through the manner in which their strong influence was exerted, that the way of life preached in them was felt to be something higher than the everyday morality which sufficed as a minimum, and that this latter was not measured by such standards as Puritanism demanded. Moreover, the practical use made of certain institutions of the Church, above all of indulgences inevitably counteracted the tendencies toward systematic worldly asceticism. For that reason it was not felt at the time of the Reformation to be merely an unessential abuse, but one of the most fundamental evils of the Church.

But the most important thing was the fact that the man who, *par excellence*, lived a rational life in the religious sense was, and remained, alone the monk. Thus asceticism, the more strongly it gripped an individual, simply served to drive him farther away from everyday life, because the holiest task was definitely to surpass all worldly morality.[86] Luther, who was not in any sense fulfilling any law of development, but acting upon his quite personal experience, which was, though at first somewhat uncertain in its practical consequences, later pushed farther by the political situation, had repudiated that tendency, and Calvinism simply took this over from him.[87] Sebastian Franck struck the central characteristic of this type of religion when he saw the significance of the Reformation in the fact that now every Christian had to be a monk all his life. The drain of asceticism from everyday worldly life had been stopped by a dam, and those passionately spiritual natures which had formerly supplied the highest type of monk were now forced to pursue their ascetic ideals within mundane occupations.

But in the course of its development Calvinism added something positive to this, the idea of the necessity of proving one's faith in worldly activity.[88] Therein it gave the broader groups of religiously inclined people a positive incentive to asceticism. By founding its ethic in the doctrine of predestination, it substituted for the spiritual aristocracy of monks outside of and above the world the spiritual aristocracy of the predestined saints of God within the world.[89] It was an aristocracy which, with its *character indelebilis,* was divided from the eternally damned remainder of humanity by a more impassable and in its invisibility more terrifying gulf,[90] than separated the monk of the

Middle Ages from the rest of the world about him, a gulf which penetrated all social relations with its sharp brutality. This consciousness of divine grace of the elect and holy was accompanied by an attitude toward the sin of one's neighbour, not of sympathetic understanding based on consciousness of one's own weakness, but of hatred and contempt for him as an enemy of God bearing the signs of eternal damnation.[91] This sort of feeling was capable of such intensity that it sometimes resulted in the formation of sects. This was the case when, as in the Independent movement of the seventeenth century, the genuine Calvinist doctrine that the glory of God required the Church to bring the damned under the law, was outweighed by the conviction that it was an insult to God if an unregenerate soul should be admitted to His house and partake in the sacraments, or even, as a minister, administer them.[92] Thus, as a consequence of the doctrine of proof, the Donatist idea of the Church appeared, as in the case of the Calvinistic Baptists. The full logical consequence of the demand for a pure Church, a community of those proved to be in a state of grace, was not often drawn by forming sects. Modifications in the constitution of the Church resulted from the attempt to separate regenerate from unregenerate Christians, those who were from those who were not prepared for the sacrament, to keep the government of the Church or some other privilege in the hands of the former, and only to ordain ministers of whom there was no question.[93]

The norm by which it could always measure itself, of which it was evidently in need, this asceticism naturally found in the Bible. It is important to note that the well-known bibliocracy of the Calvinists held the moral precepts of the Old Testament, since it was fully as authentically revealed, on the same level of esteem as those of the New. It was only necessary that they should not obviously be applicable only to the historical circumstances of the Hebrews, or have been specifically denied by Christ. For the believer, the law was an ideal though never quite attainable norm[94] while Luther, on the other hand, originally had prized freedom from subjugation to the law as a divine privilege of the believer.[95] The influence of the God-fearing but perfectly unemotional wisdom of the Hebrews, which is expressed in the books most read by the Puritans, the Proverbs and the Psalms, can be felt in their whole attitude toward life. In particular, its rational suppression of the mystical, in fact the whole emotional side of religion, has rightly been attributed by Sanford[96] to the influence of the Old Testament. But this Old Testament rationalism was as such essentially of a small bourgeois, traditionalistic type, and was mixed not only with the powerful pathos of the prophets, but also with elements which encouraged the development of a peculiarly emotional type of religion even in the Middle Ages.[97] It was thus in the last analysis the peculiar, fundamentally ascetic, character of Calvinism itself which made it select and assimilate those elements of Old Testament religion which suited it best.

Now that systematization of ethical conduct which the asceticism of Calvinistic Protestantism had in common with the rational forms of life in the Catholic orders is expressed quite superficially in the way in which the conscientious Puritan continually super-vised[98] his own state of grace. To be sure, the relig-ious account-books in which sins, temptations, and progress made in grace were entered or tabulated were common to both the most enthusiastic Reformed cir-cles[99] and some parts of modern Catholicism (espe-cially in France), above all under the influence of the Jesuits. But in Catholicism it served the purpose of completeness of the confession, or gave the *directeur de l'âme* a basis for his authoritarian guidance of the Christian (mostly female). The Reformed Christian, however, felt his own pulse with its aid. It is men-tioned by all the moralists and theologians, while Ben-jamin Franklin's tabulated statistical book-keeping on his progress in the different virtues is a classic exam-ple.[100] On the other hand, the old mediæval (even an-cient) idea of God's book-keeping is carried by Bun-yan to the characteristically tasteless extreme of com-paring the relation of a sinner to his God with that of customer and shopkeeper. One who has once got into debt may well, by the product of all his virtuous acts, succeed in paying off the accumulated interest but never the principal.[101]

As he observed his own conduct, the later Puritan also observed that of God and saw His finger in all the details of life. And, contrary to the strict doctrine of Calvin, he always knew why God took this or that measure. The process of sanctifying life could thus al-most take on the character of a business enterprise.[102] A thoroughgoing Christianization of the whole of life was the consequence of this methodical quality of ethical conduct into which Calvinism as distinct from Lutheranism forced men. That this rationality was decisive in its influence on practical life must always be borne in mind in order rightly to understand the influence of Calvinism. On the one hand we can see that it took this element to exercise such an influence at all. But other faiths as well necessarily had a similar influence when their ethical motives were the same in this decisive point, the doctrine of proof.

So far we have considered only Calvinism, and have thus assumed the doctrine of predestination as the dogmatic background of the Puritan morality in the sense of methodically rationalized ethical conduct. This could be done because the influence of that dogma in fact extended far beyond the single religious group which held in all respects strictly to Calvinistic principles, the Presbyterians. Not only the Independent Savoy Declaration of 1658, but also the Baptist Confession of Hanserd Knolly of 1689 contained it, and it had a place within Methodism. Although John Wesley, the great organizing genius of the movement, was a believer in the universality of Grace, one of the great agitators of the first generation of Methodists and their most consistent thinker, Whitefield, was an adherent of the doctrine. The same was true of the circle around Lady Huntingdon, which for a time had considerable influence. It was this doctrine in its magnificent consistency which, in the fateful epoch of the seventeenth century, upheld the belief of the militant defenders of the holy life that they were weapons in the hand of God, and executors of His providential Will.[103] Moreover, it prevented a premature collapse into a purely utilitarian doctrine of good works in this world which would never have been capable of motivating such tremendous sacrifices for non-rational ideal ends.

The combination of faith in absolutely valid norms with absolute determinism and the complete transcendentality of God was in its way a product of great genius. At the same time it was, in principle, very much more modern than the milder doctrine, making greater concessions to the feelings which subjected God to the moral law. Above all, we shall see again and again how fundamental is the idea of proof for our problem. Since its practical significance as a psychological basis for rational morality could be studied in such purity in the doctrine of predestination, it was best to start there with the doctrine in its most consistent form. But it forms a recurring framework for the connection between faith and conduct in the denominations to be studied below. Within the Protestant movement the consequences which it inevitably had for the ascetic tendencies of the conduct of its first adherents form in principle the strongest antithesis to the relative moral helplessness of Lutheranism. The Lutheran *gratia amissibilis,* which could always be regained through penitent contrition evidently, in itself, contained no sanction for what is for us the most important result of ascetic Protestantism, a systematic rational ordering of the moral life as a whole.[104] The Lutheran faith thus left the spontaneous vitality of impulsive action and naïve emotion more nearly unchanged. The motive to constant self-control and thus to a deliberate regulation of one's own life, which the gloomy doctrine of Calvinism gave, was lacking. A religious genius like Luther could live in this atmosphere of openness and freedom without difficulty and, so long as his enthusiasm was powerful enough, without danger of falling back into the *status naturalis.* That simple, sensitive, and peculiarly emotional form of piety, which is the ornament of many of the highest types of Lutherans, like their free and spontaneous morality, finds few parallels in genuine Puritanism, but many more in the mild Anglicanism of such men as Hooker, Chillingsworth, etc. But for the everyday Lutheran, even the able one, nothing was more certain than that he was only temporarily, as long as the single confession or sermon affected him, raised above the *status naturalis.*

There was a great difference which was very striking to contemporaries between the moral standards of the courts of Reformed and of Lutheran princes, the latter often being degraded by drunkenness and vulgarity.[105] Moreover, the helplessness of the Lutheran clergy, with their emphasis on faith alone, against the ascetic Baptist movement, is well known. The typical German quality often called good nature (*Gemütlichkeit*) or naturalness contrasts strongly, even in the facial expressions of people, with the effects of that thorough destruction of the spontaneity of the *status naturalis* in the Anglo-American atmosphere, which Germans are accustomed to judge unfavourably as narrowness, unfreeness, and inner constraint. But the differences of conduct, which are very striking, have clearly originated in the lesser degree of ascetic penetration of life in Lutheranism as distinguished from Calvinism. The antipathy of every spontaneous child of nature to everything ascetic is expressed in those feelings. The fact is that Lutheranism, on account of its doctrine of grace, lacked a psychological sanction of systematic conduct to compel the methodical rationalization of life.

This sanction, which conditions the ascetic character of religion, could doubtless in itself have been furnished by various different religious motives, as we shall soon see. The Calvinistic doctrine of predestination was only one of several possibilities. But nevertheless we have become convinced that in its way it had not only a quite unique consistency, but that its psychological effect was extraordinarily powerful.[106] In comparison with it the non-Calvinistic ascetic movements, considered purely from the view-point of the religious motivation of asceticism, form an attenuation of the inner consistency and power of Calvinism.

But even in the actual historical development the situation was, for the most part, such that the Calvinistic form of asceticism was either imitated by the other ascetic movements or used as a source of inspiration or of comparison in the development of their divergent principles. Where, in spite of a different doctrinal basis, similar ascetic features have appeared, this has generally been the result of Church organization. Of this we shall come to speak in another connection.[107]

B. PIETISM

Historically the doctrine of predestination is also the starting-point of the ascetic movement usually known as Pietism. In so far as the movement remained within the Reformed Church, it is almost impossible to draw the line between Pietistic and non-Pietistic Calvinists.[108] Almost all the leading representatives of Puritanism are sometimes classed among the Pietists. It is even quite legitimate to look upon the whole connection between predestination and the doctrine of proof, with its fundamental interest in the attainment of the *certitudo salutis* as discussed above, as in itself a Pietistic development of Calvin's original doctrines. The occurrence of ascetic revivals within the Reformed Church was, especially in Holland, regularly accompanied by a regeneration of the doctrine of predestination which had been temporarily forgotten or not strictly held to. Hence for England it is not customary to use the term Pietism at all.[109]

But even the Continental (Dutch and Lower Rhenish) Pietism in the Reformed Church was, at least fundamentally, just as much a simple intensification of the Reformed asceticism as, for instance, the doctrines of Bailey. The emphasis was placed so strongly on the *praxis pietatis* that doctrinal orthodoxy was pushed into the background; at times, in fact, it seemed quite a matter of indifference. Those predestined for grace could occasionally be subject to dogmatic error as well as to other sins and experience showed that often those Christians who were quite uninstructed in the theology of the schools exhibited the fruits of faith most clearly, while on the other hand it became evident that mere knowledge of theology by no means guaranteed the proof of faith through conduct.[110]

Thus election could not be proved by theological learning at all.[111] Hence Pietism, with a deep distrust of the Church of the theologians,[112] to which—this is characteristic of it—it still belonged officially, began to gather the adherents of the *praxis pietatis* in conventicles removed from the world.[113] It wished to make the invisible Church of the elect visible on this earth. Without going so far as to form a separate sect, its members attempted to live, in this community, a life freed from all the temptations of the world and in all its details dictated by God's will, and thus to be made certain of their own rebirth by external signs manifested in their daily conduct. Thus the *ecclesiola* of the true converts—this was common to all genuinely Pietistic groups—wished, by means of intensified asceticism, to enjoy the blissfulness of community with God in this life.

Now this latter tendency had something closely related to the Lutheran *unio mystica,* and very often led to a greater emphasis on the emotional side of religion than was acceptable to orthodox Calvinism. In fact this may, from our view-point, be said to be the decisive characteristic of the Pietism which developed within the Reformed Church. For this element of emotion, which was originally quite foreign to Calvinism, but on the other hand related to certain mediæval forms of religion, led religion in practice to strive for the enjoyment of salvation in this world rather than to engage in the ascetic struggle for certainty about the future world. Moreover, the emotion was capable of such intensity, that religion took on a positively hysterical character, resulting in the alternation which is familiar from examples without number and neuropathologically understandable, of half-conscious states of religious ecstasy with periods of nervous exhaustion, which were felt as abandonment by God. The effect was the direct opposite of the strict and temperate discipline under which men were placed by the systematic life of holiness of the Puritan. It meant a weakening of the inhibitions which protected the rational personality of the Calvinist from his passions.[114] Similarly it was possible for the Calvinistic idea of the depravity of the flesh, taken emotionally, for instance in the form of the so-called worm-feeling, to lead to a deadening of enterprise in worldly activity.[115] Even the doctrine of predestination could lead to fatalism if, contrary to the predominant tendencies of rational Calvinism, it were made the object of emotional contemplation.[116] Finally, the desire to separate the elect from the world could, with a strong emotional intensity, lead to a sort of monastic community life of half-communistic character, as the history of Pietism, even within the Reformed Church, has shown again and again.[117]

But so long as this extreme effect, conditioned by this emphasis on emotion, did not appear, as long as Reformed Pietism strove to make sure of salvation within the everyday routine of life in a worldly calling, the practical effect of Pietistic principles was an even stricter ascetic control of conduct in the calling, which provided a still more solid religious basis for the ethic of the calling, than the mere worldly respectability of the normal Reformed Christian, which was felt by the superior Pietist to be a second-rate Christianity. The religious aristocracy of the elect, which developed in every form of Calvinistic asceticism, the more seriously it was taken, the more surely, was then organized, in Holland, on a voluntary basis in the form of conventicles within the Church. In English Puritanism, on the other hand, it led partly to a virtual differentiation between active and passive Christians within the Church organization, and partly, as has been shown above, to the formation of sects.

On the other hand, the development of German Pietism from a Lutheran basis, with which the names of Spener, Francke, and Zinzendorf are connected, led away from the doctrine of predestination. But at the same time it was by no means outside the body of ideas of which that dogma formed the logical climax, as is especially attested by Spener's own account of the influence which English and Dutch Pietism had upon him, and is shown by the fact that Bailey was read in his first conventicles.[118]

From our special point of view, at any rate, Pietism meant simply the penetration of methodically controlled and supervised, thus of ascetic, conduct into the non-Calvinistic denominations.[119] But Lutheranism necessarily felt this rational asceticism to be a foreign element, and the lack of consistency in German Pietistic doctrines was the result of the difficulties growing out of that fact. As a dogmatic basis of systematic religious conduct Spener combines Lutheran ideas with the specifically Calvinistic doctrine of good works as such which are undertaken with the "intention of doing honour to God".[120] He also has a faith, suggestive of Calvinism, in the possibility of the elect attaining a relative degree of Christian perfection.[121] But the theory lacked consistency. Spener, who was strongly influenced by the Mystics,[122] attempted, in a rather uncertain but essentially Lutheran manner, rather to describe the systematic type of Christian conduct which was essential to even his form of Pietism than to justify it. He did not derive the *certitudo salutis* from sanctification; instead of the idea of proof, he adopted Luther's somewhat loose connection between faith and works, which has been discussed above.[123]

But again and again, in so far as the rational and ascetic element of Pietism outweighed the emotional, the ideas essential to our thesis maintained their place. These were: (1) that the methodical development of one's own state of grace to a higher and higher degree of certainty and perfection in terms of the law was a sign of grace[124]; and (2) that "God's Providence works through those in such a state of perfection", i.e. in that He gives them His signs if they wait patiently and deliberate methodically.[125] Labour in a calling was also the ascetic activity *par excellence* for A. H. Francke[126]; that God Himself blessed His chosen ones through the success of their labours was as undeniable to him as we shall find it to have been to the Puritans.

And as a substitute for the double decree Pietism worked out ideas which, in a way essentially similar to Calvinism, though milder, established an aristocracy of the elect[127] resting on God's especial grace, with all the psychological results pointed out above. Among them belongs, for instance, the so-called doctrine of Terminism,[128] which was generally (though unjustly) attributed to Pietism by its opponents. It assumes that grace is offered to all men, but for everyone either once at a definite moment in his life or at some moment for the last time.[129] Anyone who let that moment pass was beyond the help of the universality of grace; he was in the same situation as those neglected by God in the Calvinistic doctrine. Quite close to this theory was the idea which Francke took from his personal experience, and which was very widespread in Pietism, one may even say predominant, that grace could only become effective under certain unique and peculiar circumstances, namely, after previous repentance.[130] Since, according to Pietist doctrine, not everyone was capable of such experiences, those who, in spite of the use of the ascetic methods recommended by the Pictists to bring it about, did not attain it, remained in the eyes of the regenerate a sort of passive Christian. On the other hand, by the creation of a method to induce repentance even the attainment of divine grace became in effect an object of rational human activity.

Moreover, the antagonism to the private confessional, which, though not shared by all—for instance, not by Francke—was characteristic of many Pietists, especially, as the repeated questions in Spener show, of Pietist pastors, resulted from this aristocracy of grace. This antagonism helped to weaken its ties with Lutheranism. The visible effects on conduct of grace gained through repentance formed a necessary criterion for admission to absolution; hence it was impossible to let *contritio* alone suffice.[131]

Zinzendorf's conception of his own religious position, even though it vacillated in the face of attacks from orthodoxy, tended generally toward the instrumental idea. Beyond that, however, the doctrinal standpoint of this remarkable religious dilettante, as Ritschl calls him, is scarcely capable of clear formula-

tion in the points of importance for us.[132] He repeatedly designated himself a representative of Pauline-Lu-
theran Christianity; hence he opposed the Pietistic type
associated with Jansen with its adherence to the law.
But the Brotherhood itself in practice upheld, as early
as its Protocol of August 12, 1729, a standpoint which
in many respects closely resembled that of the Calvinistic aristocracy of the elect.[133] And in spite of his repeated avowals of Lutheranism,[134] he permitted and
encouraged it. The famous stand of attributing the Old
Testament to Christ, taken on November 12, 1741,
was the outward expression of somewhat the same attitude. However, of the three branches of the Brotherhood, both the Calvinistic and the Moravian accepted
the Reformed ethics in essentials from the beginning.
And even Zinzendorf followed the Puritans in expressing to John Wesley the opinion that even though a
man himself could not, others could know his state of
grace by his conduct.[135]

But on the other hand, in the peculiar piety of
Herrnhut, the emotional element held a very prominent
place. In particular Zinzendorf himself continually attempted to counteract the tendency to ascetic sanctification in the Puritan sense[136] and to turn the interpretation of good works in a Lutheran direction.[137] Also
under the influence of the repudiation of conventicles
and the retention of the confession, there developed an
essentially Lutheran dependence on the sacraments.
Moreover, Zinzendorf's peculiar principle that the
childlikeness of religious feeling was a sign of its
genuineness, as well as the use of the lot as a means
of revealing God's will, strongly counteracted the

influence of rationality in conduct. On the whole, within the sphere of influence of the Count,[138] the anti-rational, emotional elements predominated much more in the religion of the Herrnhuters than elsewhere in Pietism.[139] The connection between morality and the forgiveness of sins in Spangenberg's *Idea fides fratrum* is as loose[140] as in Lutheranism generally. Zinzendorf's repudiation of the Methodist pursuit of perfection is part, here as everywhere, of his fundamentally eudæmonistic ideal of having men experience eternal bliss (he calls it happiness) emotionally in the present,[141] instead of encouraging them by rational labour to make sure of it in the next world.[142]

Nevertheless, the idea that the most important value of the Brotherhood as contrasted with other Churches lay in an active Christian life, in missionary, and, which was brought into connection with it, in professional work in a calling,[143] remained a vital force with them. In addition, the practical rationalization of life from the standpoint of utility was very essential to Zinzendorf's philosophy.[144] It was derived for him, as for other Pietists, on the one hand from his decided dislike of philosophical speculation as dangerous to faith, and his corresponding preference for empirical knowledge[145]; on the other hand, from the shrewd common sense of the professional missionary. The Brotherhood was, as a great mission centre, at the same time a business enterprise. Thus it led its members into the paths of worldly asceticism, which everywhere first seeks for tasks and then carries them out carefully and systematically. However, the glorification of the apostolic poverty, of the disciples[146] chosen by God through predestination, which was derived from the example of the apostles as missionaries, formed another obstacle. It meant in effect a partial revival of the *consilia evangelica*. The development of a rational economic ethic similar to the Calvinistic was certainly retarded by these factors, even though, as the development of the Baptist movement shows, it was not impossible, but on the contrary subjectively strongly encouraged by the idea of work solely for the sake of the calling.

All in all, when we consider German Pietism from the point of view important for us, we must admit a vacillation and uncertainty in the religious basis of its asceticism which makes it definitely weaker than the iron consistency of Calvinism, and which is partly the result of Lutheran influences and partly of its emotional character. To be sure, it is very one-sided to make this emotional element the distinguishing characteristic of Pietism as opposed to Lutheranism.[147] But compared to Calvinism, the rationalization of life was necessarily less intense because the pressure of occupation with a state of grace which had continually to be proved, and which was concerned for the future in eternity, was diverted to the present emotional state. The place of the self-confidence which the elect sought to attain, and continually to renew in restless and successful work at his calling, was taken by an attitude of humility and abnegation.[148] This in turn was partly the result of emotional stimulus directed solely toward spiritual experience; partly of the Lutheran institution of the confession, which, though it was often looked upon with serious doubts by Pietism, was still generally tolerated.[149] All this shows the influence of the peculiarly Lutheran conception of salvation by the forgiveness of sins and not by practical sanctification. In place of the systematic rational struggle to attain and retain certain knowledge of future (otherworldly) salvation comes here the need to feel reconciliation and community with God now. Thus the tendency of the pursuit of present enjoyment to hinder the rational organization of economic life, depending as it does on provision for the future, has in a certain sense a parallel in the field of religious life.

Evidently, then, the orientation of religious needs to present emotional satisfaction could not develop so powerful a motive to rationalize worldly activity, as the need of the Calvinistic elect for proof with their exclusive preoccupation with the beyond. On the other hand, it was considerably more favourable to the methodical penetration of conduct with religion than the traditionalistic faith of the orthodox Lutheran, bound as it was to the Word and the sacraments. On the whole Pietism from Francke and Spener to Zinzendorf tended toward increasing emphasis on the emotional side. But this was not in any sense the expression of an immanent law of development. The differences resulted from differences of the religious (and social) environments from which the leaders came. We cannot enter into that here, nor can we discuss how the peculiarities of German Pietism have affected its social and geographical extension.[150] We must again remind ourselves that this emotional Pietism of course shades off into the way of life of the Puritan elect by quite gradual stages. If we can, at least provisionally, point out any practical consequence of the difference, we may say that the virtues favoured by Pietism were more those on the one hand of the faithful official, clerk, labourer, or domestic worker,[151] and on the other of the predominantly patriarchal employer with a pious condescension (in Zinzendorf's manner). Calvinism, in comparison, appears to be more closely related to the hard legalism and the active enterprise of bourgeois-capitalistic entrepreneurs.[152] Finally, the purely emotional form of Pietism is, as Ritschl[153] has pointed out, a religious dilettantism for the leisure classes. However far this characterization falls short of being exhaustive, it helps to explain certain differences in the character (including the economic character) of peoples which have been under the influence of one or the other of these two ascetic movements.

C. METHODISM

The combination of an emotional but still ascetic type of religion with increasing indifference to or repudiation of the dogmatic basis of Calvinistic asceticism is characteristic also of the Anglo-American movement corresponding to Continental Pietism, namely Methodism.[154] The name in itself shows what impressed contemporaries as characteristic of its adherents: the methodical, systematic nature of conduct for the purpose of attaining the *certitudo salutis*. This was from the beginning the centre of religious aspiration for this movement also, and remained so. In spite of all the differences, the undoubted relationship to certain branches of German Pietism[155] is shown above all by the fact that the method was used primarily to bring about the emotional act of conversion. And the emphasis on feeling, in John Wesley awakened by Moravian and Lutheran influences, led Methodism, which from the beginning saw its mission among the masses, to take on a strongly emotional character, especially in America. The attainment of repentance under certain circumstances involved an emotional struggle of such intensity as to lead to the most terrible ecstasies, which in America often took place in a public meeting. This formed the basis of a belief in the undeserved possession of divine grace and at the same time of an immediate consciousness of justification and forgiveness.

Now this emotional religion entered into a peculiar alliance, containing no small inherent difficulties, with the ascetic ethics which had for good and all been stamped with rationality by Puritanism. For one thing, unlike Calvinism, which held everything emotional to be illusory, the only sure basis for the *certitudo salutis* was in principle held to be a pure feeling of absolute certainty of forgiveness, derived immediately from the testimony of the spirit, the coming of which could be definitely placed to the hour. Added to this is Wesley's doctrine of sanctification which, though a decided departure from the orthodox doctrine, is a logical development of it. According to it, one reborn in this manner can, by virtue of the divine grace already working in him, even in this life attain sanctification, the consciousness of perfection in the sense of freedom from sin, by a second, generally separate and often sudden spiritual transformation. However difficult of attainment this end is, generally not till toward the end of one's life, it must inevitably be sought, because it finally guarantees the *certitudo salutis* and substitutes a serene confidence for the sullen worry of the Calvinist.[156] And it distinguishes the true convert in his own eyes and those of others by the fact that sin at least no longer has power over him.

In spite of the great significance of self-evident feeling, righteous conduct according to the law was thus naturally also adhered to. Whenever Wesley attacked the emphasis on works of his time, it was only to revive the old Puritan doctrine that works are not the cause, but only the means of knowing one's state of grace, and even this only when they are performed solely for the glory of God. Righteous conduct alone did not suffice, as he had found out for himself. The feeling of grace was necessary in addition. He himself sometimes described works as a condition of grace, and in the Declaration of August 9, 1771,[157] he emphasized that he who performed no good works was not a true believer. In fact, the Methodists have always maintained that they did not differ from the Established Church in doctrine, but only in religious practice. This emphasis on the fruits of belief was mostly justified by I John iii, 9; conduct is taken as a clear sign of rebirth.

But in spite of all that there were difficulties.[158] For those Methodists who were adherents of the doctrine of predestination, to think of the *certitido salutis* as appearing in the immediate feeling[159] of grace and perfection instead of the consciousness of grace which grew out of ascetic conduct in continual proof of faith—

since then the certainty of the *perservantia* depended only on the single act of repentance—meant one of two things. For weak natures there was a fatalistic interpretation of Christian freedom, and with it the breakdown of methodical conduct; or, where this path was rejected, the self-confidence of the righteous man[160] reached untold heights, an emotional intensification of the Puritan type. In the face of the attacks of opponents, the attempt was made to meet these consequences. On the one hand by increased emphasis on the normative authority of the Bible and the indispensability of proof[161]; on the other by, in effect, strengthening Wesley's anti-Calvinistic faction within the movement with its doctrine that grace could be lost. The strong Lutheran influences to which Wesley was exposed[162] through the Moravians strengthened this tendency and increased the uncertainty of the religious basis of the Methodist ethics.[163] In the end only the concept of regeneration, an emotional certainty of salvation as the immediate result of faith, was definitely maintained as the indispensable foundation of grace; and with it sanctification, resulting in (at least virtual) freedom from the power of sin, as the consequent proof of grace. The significance of external means of grace, especially the sacraments, was correspondingly diminished. In any case, the general awakening which followed Methodism everywhere, for example in New England, meant a victory for the doctrine of grace and election.[164]

Thus from our view-point the Methodist ethic appears to rest on a foundation of uncertainty similar to Pietism. But the aspiration to the higher life, the second blessedness, served it as a sort of makeshift for the doctrine of predestination. Moreover, being English in origin, its ethical practice was closely related to that of English Puritanism, the revival of which it aspired to be.

The emotional act of conversion was methodically induced. And after it was attained there did not follow a pious enjoyment of community with God, after the manner of the emotional Pietism of Zinzendorf, but the emotion, once awakened, was directed into a rational struggle for perfection. Hence the emotional character of its faith did not lead to a spiritualized religion of feeling like German Pietism. It has already been shown by Schneckenburger that this fact was connected with the less intensive development of the sense of sin (partly directly on account of the emotional experience of conversion), and this has remained an accepted point in the discussion of Methodism. The fundamentally Calvinistic character of its religious feeling here remained decisive. The emotional excitement took the form of enthusiasm which was only occasionally, but then powerfully stirred, but which by no means destroyed the otherwise rational character of conduct.[165] The regeneration of Methodism thus created only a supplement to the pure doctrine of works, a religious basis for ascetic conduct after the doctrine of predestination had been given up. The signs given by conduct which formed an indispensable means of ascertaining true conversion, even its condition as Wesley occasionally says, were in fact just the same as those of Calvinism. As a late product[166] we can, in the following discussion, generally neglect Methodism, as it added nothing new to the development[167] of the idea of calling.

D. THE BAPTIST SECTS

The Pietism of the Continent of Europe and the Methodism of the Anglo-Saxon peoples are, considered both in their content of ideas and their historical significance, secondary movements.[168] On the other hand, we find a second independent source of Protestant asceticism besides Calvinism in the Baptist movement and the sects[169] which, in the course of the sixteenth and seventeenth centuries, came directly from it or adopted its forms of religious thought, the Baptists, Mennonites, and, above all, the Quakers.[170] With them we approach religious groups whose ethics rest upon a basis differing in principle from the Calvinistic doctrine. The following sketch, which only emphasizes what is important for us, can give no true impression of the diversity of this movement. Again we lay the principal emphasis on the development in the older capitalistic countries.

The feature of all these communities, which is both historically and in principle most important, but whose influence on the development of culture can only be made quite clear in a somewhat different connection, is something with which we are already familiar, the believer's Church.[171] This means that the religious community, the visible Church in the language of the Reformation Churches,[172] was no longer looked upon as a sort of trust foundation for supernatural ends, an institution, necessarily including both the just and the unjust, whether for increasing the glory of God (Calvinistic) or as a medium for bringing the means of salvation to men (Catholic and Lutheran), but

solely as a community of personal believers of the re-
born, and only these. In other words, not as a Church
but as a sect.[173] This is all that the principle, in itself
purely external, that only adults who have personally
gained their own faith should be baptized, is meant to
symbolize.[174] The justification through this faith was
for the Baptists, as they have insistently repeated in all
religious discussions, radically different from the idea
of work in the world in the service of Christ, such as
dominated the orthodox dogma of the older Protestantism.[175] It consisted rather in taking spiritual possession
of His gift of salvation. But this occurred through individual revelation, by the working of the Divine Spirit
in the individual, and only in that way. It was offered
to everyone, and it sufficed to wait for the Spirit, and
not to resist its coming by a sinful attachment to the
world. The significance of faith in the sense of knowledge of the doctrines of the Church, but also in that of
a repentant search for divine grace, was consequently
quite minimized, and there took place, naturally with
great modifications, a renaissance of Early Christian
pneumatic doctrines. For instance, the sect to which
Menno Simons in his *Fondamentboek* (1539) gave
the first reasonably consistent doctrine, wished, like
the other Baptist sects, to be the true blameless
Church of Christ; like the apostolic community, con-
sisting entirely of those personally awakened and
called by God. Those who have been born again,
and they alone, are brethren of Christ, because
they, like Him, have been created in spirit directly
by God.[176] A strict avoidance of the world, in the
sense of all not strictly necessary intercourse with

worldly people, together with the strictest bibliocracy in the sense of taking the life of the first generations of Christians as a model, were the results for the first Baptist communities, and this principle of avoidance of the world never quite disappeared so long as the old spirit remained alive.[177]

As a permanent possession, the Baptist sects retained from these dominating motives of their early period a principle with which, on a somewhat different foundation, we have already become acquainted in Calvinism, and the fundamental importance of which will again and again come out. They absolutely repudiated all idolatry of the flesh, as a detraction from the reverence due to God alone.[178] The Biblical way of life was conceived by the first Swiss and South German Baptists with a radicalism similar to that of the young St. Francis, as a sharp break with all the enjoyment of life, a life modelled directly on that of the Apostles. And, in truth, the life of many of the earlier Baptists is reminiscent of that of St. Giles. But this strict observation of Biblical precepts[179] was not on very secure foundations in its connection with the pneumatic character of the faith. What God had revealed to the prophets and apostles was not all that He could and would reveal. On the contrary, the continued life of the Word, not as a written document, but as the force of the Holy Spirit working in daily life, which speaks directly to any individual who is willing to hear, was the sole characteristic of the true Church. That, as Schwenkfeld taught as against Luther and later Fox against the Presbyterians, was the testimony of the early Christian communities. From this idea of the continuance of revelation developed the well-known doctrine, later consistently worked out by the Quakers, of the (in the last analysis decisive) significance of the inner testimony of the Spirit in reason and conscience. This did away, not with the authority, but with the sole authority, of the Bible, and started a development which in the end radically eliminated all that remained of the doctrine of salvation through the Church; for the Quakers even with Baptism and the Communion.[180]

The Baptist denominations along with the predestinationists, especially the strict Calvinists, carried out the most radical devaluation of all sacraments as means to salvation, and thus accomplished the religious rationalization of the world in its most extreme form. Only the inner light of continual revelation could enable one truly to understand even the Biblical revelations of God.[181] On the other hand, at least according to the Quaker doctrine which here drew the logical conclusion, its effects could be extended to people who had never known revelation in its Biblical form. The proposition *extra ecclesiam nulla salus* held only for this *in*visible Church of those illuminated by the Spirit. Without the inner light, the natural man, even the man guided by natural reason,[182] remained purely a creature of the flesh, whose godlessness was condemned by the Baptists, including the Quakers, almost even more harshly than by the Calvinists. On the other hand, the new birth caused by the Spirit, if we wait for it and open our hearts to it, may, since it is divinely caused, lead to a state of such complete conquest of the power of sin,[183] that relapses, to say nothing of the loss of the state of grace, become

147

practically impossible. However, as in Methodism at a later time, the attainment of that state was not thought of as the rule, but rather the degree of perfection of the individual was subject to development.

But all Baptist communities desired to be pure Churches in the sense of the blameless conduct of their members. A sincere repudiation of the world and its interests, and unconditional submission to God as speaking through the conscience, were the only un-challengeable signs of true rebirth, and a corresponding type of conduct was thus indispensable to salvation. And hence the gift of God's grace could not be earned, but only one who followed the dictates of his conscience could be justified in considering himself re-born. Good works in this sense were a *causa sine qua non*. As we see, this last reasoning of Barclay, to whose exposition we have adhered, was again the equivalent in practice of the Calvinistic doctrine, and was certainly developed under the influence of the Calvinistic asceticism, which surrounded the Baptist sects in England and the Netherlands. George Fox de-voted the whole of his early missionary activity to the preaching of its earnest and sincere adoption.

But, since predestination was rejected, the peculiarly rational character of Baptist morality rested psycho-logically above all on the idea of expectant waiting for the Spirit to descend, which even to-day is charac-teristic of the Quaker meeting, and is well analysed by Barclay. The purpose of this silent waiting is to overcome everything impulsive and irrational, the pas-sions and subjective interests of the natural man. He must be stilled in order to create that deep repose of the soul in which alone the word of God can be heard. Of course, this waiting might result in hysterical conditions, prophecy, and, as long as eschatological hopes survived, under certain circumstances even in an outbreak of chiliastic enthusiasm, as is possible in all similar types of religion. That actually happened in the movement which went to pieces in Münster.

But in so far as Baptism affected the normal workaday world, the idea that God only speaks when the flesh is silent evidently meant an incentive to the deliberate weighing of courses of action and their careful justification in terms of the individual conscience.[184] The later Baptist communities, most particularly the Quakers, adopted this quiet, moderate, eminently conscientious character of conduct. The radical elimination of magic from the world allowed no other psychological course than the practice of worldly asceticism. Since these communities would have nothing to do with the political powers and their doings, the external result also was the penetration of life in the calling with these ascetic virtues. The leaders of the earliest Baptist movement were ruthlessly radical in their rejection of worldliness. But naturally, even in the first generation, the strictly apostolic way of life was not maintained as absolutely essential to the proof of rebirth for everyone. Well-to-do bourgeois there were, even in this generation and even before Menno, who definitely defended the practical worldly virtues and the system of private property; the strict morality of the Baptists had turned in practice into the path prepared by the Calvinistic ethic.[185] This was simply because the road to the otherworldly monastic form of asceticism had been closed as unbiblical and savouring of salvation by works since Luther, whom the Baptists also followed in this respect.

Nevertheless, apart from the half-communistic communities of the early period, one Baptist sect, the so-called Dunckards *(Tunker, dompelaers),* has to this day maintained its condemnation of education and of every form of possession beyond that indispensable to life. And even Barclay looks upon the obligation to one's calling not in Calvinistic or even Lutheran terms, but rather Thomistically, as *naturali ratione,* the necessary consequence of the believers having to live in the world.[186]

This attitude meant a weakening of the Calvinistic conception of the calling similar to those of Spener and the German Pietists. But, on the other hand, the intensity of interest in economic occupations was considerably increased by various factors at work in the Baptist sects. In the first place, by the refusal to accept office in the service of the State, which originated as a religious duty following from the repudiation of everything worldly. After its abandonment in principle it still remained, at least for the Mennonites and Quakers, effective in practice, because the strict refusal to bear arms or to take oaths formed a sufficient disqualification for office. Hand in hand with it in all Baptists' denominations went an invincible antagonism to any sort of aristocratic way of life. Partly, as with the Calvinists, it was a consequence of the prohibition of all idolatry of the flesh, partly a result of the aforementioned unpolitical or even anti-political principles. The whole shrewd and conscientious rationality of

Baptist conduct was thus forced into non-political call-ings.

At the same time, the immense importance which was attributed by the Baptist doctrine of salvation to the rôle of the conscience as the revelation of God to the individual gave their conduct in worldly callings a character which was of the greatest significance for the development of the spirit of capitalism. We shall have to postpone its consideration until later, and it can then be studied only in so far as this is possible without entering into the whole political and social ethics of Protestant asceticism. But, to anticipate this much, we have already called attention to that most important principle of the capitalistic ethic which is generally formulated "honesty is the best policy".[187] Its classical document is the tract of Franklin quoted above. And even in the judgment of the seventeenth century the specific form of the worldly asceticism of the Baptists, especially the Quakers, lay in the practical adoption of this maxim.[188] On the other hand, we shall expect to find that the influence of Calvinism was exerted more in the direction of the liberation of energy for private acquisition. For in spite of all the formal legalism of the elect, Goethe's remark in fact applied often enough to the Calvinist: "The man of action is always ruth-less; no one has a conscience but an observer."[189]

A further important element which promoted the intensity of the worldly asceticism of the Baptist denominations can in its full significance also be considered only in another connection. Nevertheless, we may anticipate a few remarks on it to justify the order of presentation we have chosen. We have quite deliberately not taken as a starting-point the objective social institutions of the older Protestant Churches, and their ethical influences, especially not the very important Church discipline. We have preferred rather to take the results which subjective adoption of an ascetic faith might have had in the conduct of the individual. This was not only because this side of the thing has previously received far less attention than the other, but also because the effect of Church discipline was by no means always a similar one. On the contrary, the ecclesiastical supervision of the life of the individual, which, as it was practised in the Calvinistic State Churches, almost amounted to an inquisition, might even retard that liberation of individual powers which was conditioned by the rational ascetic pursuit of salvation, and in some cases actually did so.

The mercantilistic regulations of the State might develop industries, but not, or certainly not alone, the spirit of capitalism; where they assumed a despotic, authoritarian character, they to a large extent directly hindered it. Thus a similar effect might well have resulted from ecclesiastical regimentation when it became excessively despotic. It enforced a particular type of external conformity, but in some cases weakened the subjective motives of rational conduct. Any discussion of this point[190] must take account of the great difference between the results of the authoritarian moral discipline of the Established Churches and the corresponding discipline in the sects which rested on voluntary submission. That the Baptist movement everywhere and in principle founded sects and not Churches was certainly as favourable to the intensity of their asceticism as was the case, to differing degrees, with those Calvinistic, Methodist, and Pietist communities which were driven by their situations into the formation of voluntary groups.[191]

It is our next task to follow out the results of the Puritan idea of the calling in the business world, now that the above sketch has attempted to show its religious foundations. With all the differences of detail and emphasis which these different ascetic movements show in the aspects with which we have been concerned, much the same characteristics are present and important in all of them.[192] But for our purposes the decisive point was, to recapitulate, the conception of the state of religious grace, common to all the denominations, as a status which marks off its possessor from the degradation of the flesh, from the world.[193]

On the other hand, though the means by which it was attained differed for different doctrines, it could not be guaranteed by any magical sacraments, by relief in the confession, nor by individual good works. That was only possible by proof in a specific type of conduct unmistakably different from the way of life of the natural man. From that followed for the individual an incentive methodically to supervise his own state of grace in his own conduct, and thus to penetrate it with asceticism. But, as we have seen, this ascetic conduct meant a rational planning of the whole of one's life in accordance with God's will. And this asceticism was no longer an *opus supererogationis,* but something which could be required of everyone who would be certain of salvation. The religious life of the saints, as distinguished from the natural life, was—the most important point—no longer lived outside the world in monastic communities, but within the world and its institutions. This rationalization of conduct within this world, but for the sake of the world beyond, was the consequence of the concept of calling of ascetic Protestantism.

Christian asceticism, at first fleeing from the world into solitude, had already ruled the world which it had renounced from the monastery and through the Church. But it had, on the whole, left the naturally spontaneous character of daily life in the world untouched. Now it strode into the market-place of life, slammed the door of the monastery behind it, and undertook to penetrate just that daily routine of life with its methodicalness, to fashion it into a life in the world, but neither of nor for this world. With what result, we shall try to make clear in the following discussion.

*Capitalism is running out of Control - not Clear if going to stop devistation creating in the world. => making a link

CHAPTER V

worldly

ASCETICISM AND THE SPIRIT OF CAPITALISM

In order to understand the connection between the fundamental religious ideas of ascetic Protestantism and its maxims for everyday economic conduct, it is necessary to examine with especial care such writing as have evidently been derived from ministerial practice. For in a time in which the beyond meant everything, when the social position of the Christian depended upon his admission to the communion, the clergyman, through his ministry, Church discipline, and preaching, exercised an influence (as a glance at collections of *consilia, casus conscientiæ,* etc., shows) which we modern men are entirely unable to picture. In such a time the religious forces which express themselves through such channels are the decisive influences in the formation of national character.

For the purposes of this chapter, though by no means for all purposes, we can treat ascetic Protestantism as a single whole. But since that side of English Puritanism which was derived from Calvinism gives the most consistent religious basis for the idea of the calling, we shall, following our previous method, place one of its representatives at the centre of the discussion. Richard Baxter stands out above many other writers on Puritan ethics, both because of his eminently practical and realistic attitude, and, at the same time, because of the universal recognition accorded to his works, which have gone through many new editions and translations. He was a Presbyterian and an apologist of the Westminster Synod, but at the same time, like so many of the best spirits of his time, gradually grew away from the dogmas of pure Calvinism. At heart he opposed Cromwell's usurpation as he would any revolution. He was unfavourable to the sects and the fanatical enthusiasm of the saints, but was very broad-minded about external peculiarities and objective towards his opponents. He sought his field of labour most especially in the practical promotion of the moral life through the Church. In the pursuit of this end, as one of the most successful ministers known to history, he placed his services at the disposal of the Parliamentary Government, of Cromwell, and of the Restoration[1] until he retired from office under the last, before St. Bartholomew's day. His *Christian Directory* is the most complete compendium of Puritan ethics, and is continually adjusted to the practical experiences of his own ministerial activity. In comparison we shall make use of Spener's *Theologische Bedenken,* as representative of German Pietism, Barclay's *Apology* for the Quakers, and some other representatives of ascetic ethics,[2] which, however, in the interest of space, will be limited as far as possible.[3]

Now, in glancing at Baxter's *Saints' Everlasting Rest,* or his *Christian Directory,* or similar works of others,[4] one is struck at first glance by the emphasis placed, in the discussion of wealth[5] and its acquisition, on the ebionitic elements of the New Testament.[6] Wealth as such is a great danger; its temptations never end, and its pursuit[7] is not only senseless as compared with

156

the dominating importance of the Kingdom of God, but it is morally suspect. Here asceticism seems to have turned much more sharply against the acquisition of earthly goods than it did in Calvin, who saw no hindrance to the effectiveness of the clergy in their wealth, but rather a thoroughly desirable enhancement of their prestige. Hence he permitted them to employ their means profitably. Examples of the condemnation of the pursuit of money and goods may be gathered without end from Puritan writings, and may be contrasted with the late mediæval ethical literature, which was much more open-minded on this point.

Moreover, these doubts were meant with perfect seriousness; only it is necessary to examine them somewhat more closely in order to understand their true ethical significance and implications. The real moral objection is to relaxation in the security of possession,[8] the enjoyment of wealth with the consequence of idleness and the temptations of the flesh, above all of distraction from the pursuit of a righteous life. In fact, it is only because possession involves this danger of relaxation that it is objectionable at all. For the saints' everlasting rest is in the next world; on earth man must, to be certain of his state of grace, "do the works of him who sent him, as long as it is yet day". Not leisure and enjoyment, but only activity serves to increase the glory of God, according to the definite manifestations of His will.[9]

Waste of time is thus the first and in principle the deadliest of sins. The span of human life is infinitely short and precious to make sure of one's own election. Loss of time through sociability, idle talk,[10] luxury,[11] even more sleep than is necessary for health,[12] six to at most eight hours, is worthy of absolute moral condemnation.[13] It does not yet hold, with Franklin, that time is money, but the proposition is true in a certain spiritual sense. It is infinitely valuable because every hour lost is lost to labour for the glory of God.[14] Thus inactive contemplation is also valueless, or even directly reprehensible if it is at the expense of one's daily work.[15] For it is less pleasing to God than the active performance of His will in a calling.[16] Besides, Sunday is provided for that, and according to Baxter, it is always those who are not diligent in their callings who have no time for God when the occasion demands it.[17]

Accordingly, Baxter's principal work is dominated by the continually repeated, often almost passionate preaching of hard, continuous bodily or mental labour.[18] It is due to a combination of two different motives.[19] Labour is, on the one hand, an approved ascetic technique, as it always has been[20] in the Western Church, in sharp contrast not only to the Orient but to almost all monastic rules the world over.[21] It is in particular the specific defence against all those temptations which Puritanism united under the name of the unclean life, whose rôle for it was by no means small. The sexual asceticism of Puritanism differs only in degree, not in fundamental principle, from that of monasticism; and on account of the Puritan conception of marriage, its practical influence is more far-reaching than that of the latter. For sexual intercourse is permitted, even within marriage, only as the means willed by God for the increase of His glory according to the commandment, "Be fruitful and multiply."[22] Along with a moderate vegetable diet and cold baths, the same prescription is given for all sexual temptations as is used against religious doubts and a sense of moral unworthiness: "Work hard in your calling."[23] But the most important thing was that even beyond that labour came to be considered in itself[24] the end of life, ordained as such by God. St. Paul's "He who will not work shall not eat" holds unconditionally for everyone.[25] Unwillingness to work is symptomatic of the lack of grace."[26]

Here the difference from the mediæval view-point becomes quite evident. Thomas Aquinas also gave an interpretation of that statement of St. Paul. But for him[27] labour is only necessary *naturali ratione* for the maintenance of individual and community. Where this end is achieved, the precept ceases to have any meaning. Moreover, it holds only for the race, not for every individual. It does not apply to anyone who can live without labour on his possessions, and of course contemplation, as a spiritual form of action in the Kingdom of God, takes precedence over the commandment in its literal sense. Moreover, for the popular theology of the time, the highest form of monastic productivity lay in the increase of the *Thesaurus eccesiæ* through prayer and chant.

Now only do these exceptions to the duty to labour naturally no longer hold for Baxter, but he holds most emphatically that wealth does not exempt anyone from the unconditional command.[28] Even the wealthy shall not eat without working, for even though they do not need to labour to support their own need, there is God's commandment which they, like the poor, must obey.[29] For everyone without exception God's Providence has prepared a calling, which he should profess and in which he should labour. And this calling is not, as it was for the Lutheran,[30] a fate to which he must submit and which he must make the best of, but God's commandment to the individual to work for the divine glory. This seemingly subtle difference had far-reaching psychological consequences, and became connected with a further development of the providential interpretation of the economic order which had begun in scholasticism.

The phenomenon of the division of labour and occupations in society had, among others, been interpreted by Thomas Aquinas, to whom we may most conveniently refer, as a direct consequence of the divine scheme of things. But the places assigned to each man in this cosmos follow *ex causis naturalibus* and are fortuitous (contingent in the Scholastic terminology). The differentiation of men into the classes and occupations established through historical development became for Luther, as we have seen, a direct result of the divine will. The perseverance of the individual in the place and within the limits which God had assigned to him was a religious duty.[31] This was the more certainly the consequence since the relations of Lutheranism to the world were in general uncertain from the beginning and remained so. Ethical principles for the reform of the world could not be found in Luther's realm of ideas; in fact it never quite freed itself from Pauline indifference. Hence the world had to be accepted as it was, and this alone could be made a religious duty.

But in the Puritan view, the providential character of the play of private economic interests takes on a somewhat different emphasis. True to the Puritan tendency to pragmatic interpretations, the providential purpose of the division of labour is to be known by its fruits. On this point Baxter expresses himself in terms which more than once directly recall Adam Smith's well-known apotheosis of the division of labour.[32] The specialization of occupations leads, since it makes the development of skill possible, to a quantitative and qualitative improvement in production, and thus serves the common good, which is identical with the good of the greatest possible number. So far, the motivation is purely utilitarian, and is closely related to the customary view-point of much of the secular literature of the time.[33]

But the characteristic Puritan element appears when Baxter sets at the head of his discussion the statement that "outside of a well-marked calling the accomplishments of a man are only casual and irregular, and he spends more time in idleness than at work", and when he concludes it as follows: "and he [the specialized worker] will carry out his work in order while another remains in constant confusion, and his business knows neither time nor place[34] . . . therefore is a certain calling the best for everyone". Irregular work, which the ordinary labourer is often forced to accept, is often unavoidable, but always an unwelcome state of transition. A man without a calling thus lacks the systematic, methodical character which is, as we have seen, demanded by worldly asceticism.

The Quaker ethic also holds that a man's life in his calling is an exercise in ascetic virtue, a proof of his state of grace through his conscientiousness, which is expressed in the care[35] and method with which he pursues his calling. What God demands is not labour in itself, but rational labour in a calling. In the Puritan concept of the calling the emphasis is always placed on this methodical character of worldly asceticism, not, as with Luther, on the acceptance of the lot which God has irretrievably assigned to man.[36]

Hence the question whether anyone may combine several callings is answered in the affirmative, if it is useful for the common good or one's own,[37] and not injurious to anyone, and if it does not lead to unfaithfulness in one of the callings. Even a change of calling is by no means regarded as objectionable, if it is not thoughtless and is made for the purpose of pursuing a calling more pleasing to God,[38] which means, on general principles, one more useful.

It is true that the usefulness of a calling, and thus its favour in the sight of God, is measured primarily in moral terms, and thus in terms of the importance of the goods produced in it for the community. But a further, and, above all, in practice the most important, criterion is found in private profitableness.[39] For if that God, whose hand the Puritan sees in all the occurrences of life, shows one of His elect a chance of profit, he must do it with a purpose. Hence the faithful Christian must follow the call by taking advantage of the opportunity.[40] "If God show you a way in which you may lawfully get more than in another way (without wrong to your soul or to any other), if you refuse this, and choose the less gainful way, you cross one of the ends of your calling, and you refuse to be God's steward, and to accept His gifts and use them for Him when He requireth it: you may labour to be rich for God, though not for the flesh and sin."[41]

Wealth is thus bad ethically only in so far as it is a temptation to idleness and sinful enjoyment of life, and its acquisition is bad only when it is with the purpose of later living merrily and without care. But as a performance of duty in a calling it is not only morally permissible, but actually enjoined.[42] The parable of the servant who was rejected because he did not increase the talent which was entrusted to him seemed to say so directly.[43] To wish to be poor was, it was often argued, the same as wishing to be unhealthy[44]; it is objectionable as a glorification of works and derogatory to the glory of God. Especially begging, on the part of one able to work, is not only the sin of slothfulness, but a violation of the duty of brotherly love according to the Apostle's own word.[45]

The emphasis on the ascetic importance of a fixed calling provided an ethical justification of the modern specialized division of labour. In a similar way the providential interpretation of profit-making justified the activities of the business man.[46] The superior indulgence of the *seigneur* and the parvenu ostentation of the *nouveau riche* are equally detestable to asceticism. But, on the other hand, it has the highest ethical appreciation of the sober, middle-class, self-made man.[47] "God blesseth His trade" is a stock remark about those good men[48] who had successfully followed the divine hints. The whole power of the God of the Old Testament, who rewards His people for their obedience in this life,[49] necessarily exercised a similar influence on the Puritan who, following Baxter's advice, compared his own state of grace with that of the heroes of the Bible,[50] and in the process interpreted the statements of the Scriptures as the articles of a book of statutes.

Of course, the words of the Old Testament were not entirely without ambiguity. We have seen that Luther first used the concept of the calling in the secular sense in translating a passage from Jesus Sirach. But the book of Jesus Sirach belongs, with the whole atmosphere expressed in it, to those parts of the broadened Old Testament with a distinctly traditionalistic tendency, in spite of Hellenistic influences. It is characteristic that down to the present day this book seems to enjoy a special favour among Lutheran German peasants,[51] just as the Lutheran influence in large sections of German Pietism has been expressed by a preference for Jesus Sirach.[52]

The Puritans repudiated the Apocrypha as not inspired, consistently with their sharp distinction between things divine and things of the flesh.[53] But among the canonical books that of Job had all the more influence. On the one hand it contained a grand conception of the absolute sovereign majesty of God, beyond all human comprehension, which was closely related to that of Calvinism. With that, on the other hand, it combined the certainty which, though incidental for Calvin, came to be of great importance for Puritanism, that God would bless His own in this life—in the book of Job only—and also in the material sense.[54] The Oriental quietism, which appears in several of the finest verses of the Psalms and in the Proverbs, was interpreted away, just as Baxter did with the traditionalistic tinge of the passage in the ɪst Epistle to the Corinthians, so important for the idea of the calling.

But all the more emphasis was placed on those parts of the Old Testament which praise formal legality as a sign of conduct pleasing to God. They held the theory that the Mosaic Law had only lost its validity through Christ in so far as it contained ceremonial or purely historical precepts applying only to the Jewish people, but that otherwise it had always been valid as an expression of the natural law, and must hence be retained.[55] This made it possible, on the one hand, to eliminate elements which could not be reconciled with modern life. But still, through its numerous related features, Old Testament morality was able to give a powerful impetus to that spirit of self-righteous and sober legality which was so characteristic of the worldly asceticism of this form of Protestantism.[56]

Thus when authors, as was the case with several contemporaries as well as later writers, characterize the basic ethical tendency of Puritanism, especially in England, as English Hebraism[57] they are, correctly understood, not wrong. It is necessary, however, not to think of Palestinian Judaism at the time of the writing of the Scriptures, but of Judaism as it became under the influence of many centuries of formalistic, legalistic, and Talmudic education. Even then one must be very careful in drawing parallels. The general tendency of the older Judaism toward a naïve acceptance of life as such was far removed from the special characteristics of Puritanism. It was, however, just as far—and this ought not to be overlooked—from the economic ethics of mediæval and modern Judaism, in the traits which determined the positions of both in the development of the capitalistic ethos. The Jews stood on the side of the politically and speculatively oriented adventurous capitalism; their ethos was, in a word, that of pariah-capitalism. But Puritanism carried the ethos of the rational organization of capital and labour. It took over from the Jewish ethic only what was adapted to this purpose.

To analyse the effects on the character of peoples of the penetration of life with Old Testament norms—a tempting task which, however, has not yet satisfactorily been done even for Judaism[58]—would be impossible within the limits of this sketch. In addition to the relationships already pointed out, it is important for the general inner attitude of the Puritans, above all, that the belief that they were God's chosen people saw in them a great renaissance.[59] Even the kindly Baxter thanked God that he was born in England, and thus in the true Church, and nowhere else. This thankfulness for one's own perfection by the grace of God penetrated the attitude toward life[60] of the Puritan middle class, and played its part in developing that formalistic, hard, correct character which was peculiar to the men of that heroic age of capitalism.

Let us now try to clarify the points in which the Puritan idea of the calling and the premium it placed upon ascetic conduct was bound directly to influence the development of a capitalistic way of life. As we have seen, this asceticism turned with all its force against one thing: the spontaneous enjoyment of life and all it had to offer. This is perhaps most characteristically brought out in the struggle over the *Book of Sports*[61] which James I and Charles I made into law expressly as a means of counteracting Puritanism, and which the latter ordered to be read from all the pulpits. The fanatical opposition of the Puritans to the ordinances of the King, permitting certain popular amusements on Sunday outside of Church hours by law, was not only explained by the disturbance of the Sabbath rest, but also by resentment against the intentional diversion from the ordered life of the saint, which it caused. And, on his side, the King's threats of severe punishment for every attack on the legality of those sports were motivated by his purpose of breaking the anti-authoritarian ascetic tendency of Puritanism, which was so dangerous to the State. The feudal and monarchical forces protected the pleasure seekers against the rising middle-class morality and the anti-authoritarian ascetic conventicles, just as to-day capitalistic society tends to protect those willing to work against the class morality of the proletariat and the anti-authoritarian trade union.

As against this the Puritans upheld their decisive characteristic, the principle of ascetic conduct. For otherwise the Puritan aversion to sport, even for the Quakers, was by no means simply one of principle. Sport was accepted if it served a rational purpose, that of recreation necessary for physical efficiency. But as a means for the spontaneous expression of undisciplined impulses, it was under suspicion; and in so far as it became purely a means of enjoyment, or awakened pride, raw instincts or the irrational gambling instinct, it was of course strictly condemned. Impulsive enjoyment of life, which leads away both from work in a calling and from religion, was as such the enemy of rational asceticism, whether in the form of seigneurial

sports, or the enjoyment of the dance-hall or the pub-
lichouse of the common man.[62]

Its attitude was thus suspicious and often hostile to
the aspects of culture without any immediate religious
value. It is not, however, true that the ideals of Puritanism implied a solemn, narrow-minded contempt of
culture. Quite the contrary is the case at least for science, with the exception of the hatred of Scholasticism. Moreover, the great men of the Puritan movement were thoroughly steeped in the culture of the
Renaissance. The sermons of the Presbyterian divines
abound with classical allusions,[63] and even the Radicals, although they objected to it, were not ashamed to
display that kind of learning in theological polemics.
Perhaps no country was ever so full of graduates as
New England in the first generation of its existence. The
satire of their opponents, such as, for instance, Butler's
Hudibras, also attacks primarily the pedantry and highly
trained dialectics of the Puritans. This is partially due to
the religious valuation of knowledge which followed
from their attitude to the Catholic *fides implicita.*

But the situation is quite different when one looks
at non-scientific literature,[64] and especially the fine
arts. Here asceticism descended like a frost on the life
of "Merrie old England." And not only worldly merri-
ment felt its effect. The Puritan's ferocious hatred of
everything which smacked of superstition, of all survivals of magical or sacramental salvation, applied to
the Christmas festivities and the May Pole[65] and all
spontaneous religious art. That there was room in
Holland for a great, often uncouthly realistic art[66]
proves only how far from completely the authoritarian

moral discipline of that country was able to counteract the influence of the court and the regents (a class of *rentiers),* and also the joy in life of the parvenu bourgeoisie, after the short supremacy of the Calvinistic theocracy had been transformed into a moderate national Church, and with it Calvinism had perceptibly lost in its power of ascetic influence.[67]

The theatre was obnoxious to the Puritans,[68] and with the strict exclusion of the erotic and of nudity from the realm of toleration, a radical view of either literature or art could not exist. The conceptions of idle talk, of superfluities,[69] and of vain ostentation, all designations of an irrational attitude without objective purpose, thus not ascetic, and especially not serving the glory of God, but of man, were always at hand to serve in deciding in favour of sober utility as against any artistic tendencies. This was especially true in the case of decoration of the person, for instance clothing.[70] That powerful tendency toward uniformity of life, which to-day so immensely aids the capitalistic interest in the standardization of production,[71] had its ideal foundations in the repudiation of all idolatry of the flesh.[72]

Of course we must not forget that Puritanism included a world of contradictions, and that the instinctive sense of eternal greatness in art was certainly stronger among its leaders than in the atmosphere of the Cavaliers.[73] Moreover, a unique genius like Rembrandt, however little his conduct may have been acceptable to God in the eyes of the Puritans, was very strongly influenced in the character of his work by his religious environment.[74] But that does not alter the picture as a whole. In so far as the development of the Puritan tradition could, and in part did, lead to a powerful spiritualization of personality, it was a decided benefit to literature. But for the most part that benefit only accrued to later generations.

Although we cannot here enter upon a discussion of the influence of Puritanism in all these directions, we should call attention to the fact that the toleration of pleasure in cultural goods, which contributed to purely aesthetic or athletic enjoyment, certainly always ran up against one characteristic limitation: they must not cost anything. Man is only a trustee of the goods which have come to him through God's grace. He must, like the servant in the parable, give an account of every penny entrusted to him,[75] and it is at least hazardous to spend any of it for a purpose which does not serve the glory of God but only one's own enjoyment.[76] What person, who keeps his eyes open, has not met representatives of this view-point even in the present?[77] The idea of a man's duty to his possessions, to which he subordinates himself as an obedient steward, or even as an acquisitive machine, bears with chilling weight on his life. The greater the possessions the heavier, if the ascetic attitude toward life stands the test, the feeling of responsibility for them, for holding them undiminished for the glory of God and increasing them by restless effort. The origin of this type of life also extends in certain roots, like so many aspects of the spirit of capitalism, back into the Middle Ages.[78] But it was in the ethic of ascetic Protestantism that it first found a consistent ethical foundation. Its significance for the development of capitalism is obvious.[79]

This worldly Protestant asceticism, as we may

recapitulate up to this point, acted powerfully against the spontaneous enjoyment of possessions; it restricted consumption, especially of luxuries. On the other hand, it had the psychological effect of freeing the acquisition of goods from the inhibitions of traditionalistic ethics. It broke the bonds of the impulse of acquisition in that it not only legalized it, but (in the sense discussed) looked upon it as directly willed by God. The campaign against the temptations of the flesh, and the dependence on external things, was, as besides the Puritans the great Quaker apologist Barclay expressly says, not a struggle against the rational acquisition, but against the irrational use of wealth.

But this irrational use was exemplified in the outward forms of luxury which their code condmned as idolatry of the flesh,[80] however natural they had appeared to the feudal mind. On the other hand, they approved the rational and utilitarian uses of wealth which were willed by God for the needs of the individual and the community. They did not wish to impose mortification[81] on the man of wealth, but the use of his means for necessary and practical things. The idea of comfort characteristically limits the extent of ethically permissible expenditures. It is naturally no accident that the development of a manner of living consistent with that idea may be observed earliest and most clearly among the most consistent representatives of this whole attitude toward life. Over against the glitter and ostentation of feudal magnificence which, resting on an unsound economic basis, prefers a sordid elegance to a sober simplicity, they set the clean and solid comfort of the middle-class home as an ideal.[82]

On the side of the production of private wealth, asceticism condemned both dishonesty and impulsive avarice. What was condemned as covetousness, Mammonism, etc., was the pursuit of riches for their own sake. For wealth in itself was a temptation. But here asceticism was the power "which ever seeks the good but ever creates evil"[83]; what was evil in its sense was possession and its temptations. For, in conformity with the Old Testament and in analogy to the ethical valuation of good works, asceticism looked upon the pursuit of wealth as an end in itself as highly reprehensible; but the attainment of it as a fruit of labour in a calling was a sign of God's blessing. And even more important: the religious valuation of restless, continuous, systematic work in a worldly calling, as the highest means to asceticism, and at the same time the surest and most evident proof of rebirth and genuine faith, must have been the most powerful conceivable lever for the expansion of that attitude toward life which we have here called the spirit of capitalism.[84]

When the limitation of consumption is combined with this release of acquisitive activity, the inevitable practical result is obvious: accumulation of capital through ascetic compulsion to save.[85] The restraints which were imposed upon the consumption of wealth naturally served to increase it by making possible the productive investment of capital. How strong this influence was is not, unfortunately, susceptible of exact statistical demonstration. In New England the connection is so evident that it did not escape the eye of so discerning a historian as Doyle.[86] But also in Holland, which was really only dominated by strict

Calvinism for seven years, the greater simplicity of life in the more seriously religious circles, in combination with great wealth, led to an excessive propensity to accumulations.[87]

That, furthermore, the tendency which has existed everywhere and at all times, being quite strong in Germany to-day, for middle-class fortunes to be absorbed into the nobility, was necessarily checked by the Puritan antipathy to the feudal way of life, is evident. English Mercantilist writers of the seventeenth century attributed the superiority of Dutch capital to English to the circumstance that newly acquired wealth there did not regularly seek investment in land. Also, since it is not simply a question of the purchase of land, it did not there seek to transfer itself to feudal habits of life, and thereby to remove itself from the possibility of capitalistic investments.[88] The high esteem for agriculture as a peculiarly important branch of activity, also especially consistent with piety, which the Puritans shared, applied (for instance in Baxter) not to the landlord, but to the yeoman and fanner, in the eighteenth century not to the squire, but the rational cultivators.[89] Through the whole of English society in the time since the seventeenth century goes the conflict between the squirearchy, the representatives of "merrie old England", and the Puritan circles of widely varying social influence.[90] Both elements, that of an unspoiled naïve joy of life, and of a strictly regulated, reserved self-control, and conventional ethical conduct are even to-day combined to form the English national character.[91] Similarly, the early history of the North American Colonies is dominated by the sharp contrast of the adventurers, who wanted to set up plantations with the labour of indentured servants, and live as feudal lords, and the specifically middle-class outlook of the Puritans.[92]

As far as the influence of the Puritan outlook extended, under all circumstances—and this is, of course, much more important than the mere encouragement of capital accumulation—it favoured the development of a rational bourgeois economic life; it was the most important, and above all the only consistent influence in the development of that life. It stood at the cradle of the modern economic man.

To be sure, these Puritanical ideals tended to give way under excessive pressure from the temptations of wealth, as the Puritans themselves knew very well. With great regularity we find the most genuine adherents of Puritanism among the classes which were rising from a lowly status,[93] the small bourgeois and farmers, while the *beati possidentes,* even among Quakers, are often found tending to repudiate the old ideals.[94] It was the same fate which again and again befell the predecessor of this worldly asceticism, the monastic asceticism of the Middle Ages. In the latter case, when rational economic activity had worked out its full effects by strict regulation of conduct and limitation of consumption, the wealth accumulated either succumbed directly to the nobility, as in the time before the Reformation, or monastic discipline threatened to break down, and one of the numerous reformations became necessary.

In fact the whole history of monasticism is in a certain sense the history of a continual struggle with the problem of the secularizing influence of wealth. The same is true on a grand scale of the worldly

174

asceticism of Puritanism. The great revival of Methodism, which preceded the expansion of English industry toward the end of the eighteenth century, may well be compared with such a monastic reform. We may hence quote here a passage[95] from John Wesley himself which might well serve as a motto for everything which has been said above. For it shows that the leaders of these ascetic movements understood the seemingly paradoxical relationships which we have here analysed perfectly well, and in the same sense that we have given them.[96] He wrote:

"I fear, wherever riches have increased, the essence of religion has decreased in the same proportion. Therefore I do not see how it is possible, in the nature of things, for any revival of true religion to continue long. For religion must necessarily produce both industry and frugality, and these cannot but produce riches. But as riches increase, so will pride, anger, and love of the world in all its branches. How then is it possible that Methodism, that is, a religion of the heart, though it flourishes now as a green bay tree, should continue in this state? For the Methodists in every place grow diligent and frugal; consequently they increase in goods. Hence they proportionately increase in pride, in anger, in the desire of the flesh, the desire of the eyes, and the pride of life. So, although the form of religion remains, the spirit is swiftly vanishing away. Is there no way to prevent this—this continual decay of pure religion? We ought not to prevent people from being diligent and frugal; *we must exhort all Christians to gain all they can, and to save all they can; that is, in effect, to grow rich."* [97]

There follows the advice that those who gain all they can and save all they can should also give all they can, so that they will grow in grace and lay up a treasure in heaven. It is clear that Wesley here expresses, even in detail, just what we have been trying to point out.[98]

As Wesley here says, the full economic effect of those great religious movements, whose significance for economic development lay above all in their ascetic educative influence, generally came only after the peak of the purely religious enthusiasm was past. Then the intensity of the search for the Kingdom of God commenced gradually to pass over into sober economic virtue; the religious roots died out slowly, giving way to utilitarian worldliness. Then, as Dowden puts it, as in *Robinson Crusoe,* the isolated economic man who carries on missionary activities on the side[99] takes the place of the lonely spiritual search for the Kingdom of Heaven of Bunyan's pilgrim, hurrying through the market-place of Vanity.

When later the principle "to make the most of both worlds" became dominant in the end, as Dowden has remarked, a good conscience simply became one of the means of enjoying a comfortable bourgeois life, as is well expressed in the German proverb about the soft pillow. What the great religious epoch of the seventeenth century bequeathed to its utilitarian successor was, however, above all an amazingly good, we may even say a pharisaically good, conscience in the acquisition of money, so long as it took place legally. Every trace of the *deplacere vix potest* has disappeared.[100]

A specifically bourgeois economic ethic had grown up. With the consciousness of standing in the fullness of God's grace and being visibly blessed by Him, the bourgeois business man, as long as he remained within the bounds of formal correctness, as long as his moral conduct was spotless and the use to which he put his wealth was not objectionable, could follow his pecuniary interests as he would and feel that he was fulfilling a duty in doing so. The power of religious asceticism provided him in addition with sober, conscientious, and unusually industrious workmen, who clung to their work as to a life purpose willed by God.[101]

Finally, it gave him the comforting assurance that the unequal distribution of the goods of this world was a special dispensation of Divine Providence, which in these differences, as in particular grace, pursued secret ends unknown to men.[102] Calvin himself had made the much-quoted statement that only when the people, i.e. the mass of labourers and craftsmen, were poor did they remain obedient to God.[103] In the Netherlands (Pieter de la Court and others), that had been secularized to the effect that the mass of men only labour when necessity forces them to do so. This formulation of a leading idea of capitalistic economy later entered into the current theories of the productivity of low wages. Here also, with the dying out of the religious root, the utilitarian interpretation crept in unnoticed, in the line of development which we have again and again observed.

Mediæval ethics not only tolerated begging but actually glorified it in the mendicant orders. Even secular beggars, since they gave the person of means opportunity for good works through giving alms, were sometimes considered an estate and treated as such. Even the Anglican social ethic of the Stuarts was very close to this attitude. It remained for Puritan Asceticism to take part in the severe English Poor Relief Legislation which fundamentally changed the situation. And it could do that, because the Protestant sects and the strict Puritan communities actually did not know any begging in their own midst.[104]

On the other hand, seen from the side of the workers, the Zinzendorf branch of Pietism, for instance, glorified the loyal worker who did not seek acquisition, but lived according to the apostolic model, and was thus endowed with the *charisma*[105] of the disciples.[106] Similar ideas had originally been prevalent among the Baptists in an even more radical form.

Now naturally the whole ascetic literature of almost all denominations is saturated with the idea that faithful labour, even at low wages, on the part of those whom life offers no other opportunities, is highly pleasing to God. In this respect Protestant Asceticism added in itself nothing new. But it not only deepened this idea most powerfully, it also created the force which was alone decisive for its effectiveness: the psychological sanction of it through the conception of this labour as a calling, as the best, often in the last analysis the only means of attaining certainty of grace.[107] And on the other hand it legalized the exploitation of this specific willingness to work, in that it also interpreted the employer's business activity as a calling.[108] It is obvious how powerfully the exclusive search for the Kingdom of God only through the fulfilment of duty in the calling, and the strict asceticism which Church discipline naturally imposed, especially on the propertyless classes, was bound to affect the productivity of labour

178

in the capitalistic sense of the word. The treatment of labour as a calling became as characteristic of the modern worker as the corresponding attitude toward acquisition of the business man. It was a perception of this situation, new at his time, which caused so able an observer as Sir William Petty to attribute the economic power of Holland in the seventeenth century to the fact that the very numerous dissenters in that country (Calvinists and Baptists) "are for the most part thinking, sober men, and such as believe that Labour and Industry is their duty towards God".[109]

Calvinism opposed organic social organization in the fiscal-monopolistic form which it assumed in Anglicanism under the Stuarts, especially in the conceptions of Laud, this alliance of Church and State with the monopolists on the basis of a Christian-social ethical foundation. Its leaders were universally among the most passionate opponents of this type of politically privileged commercial, putting-out, and colonial capitalism. Over against it they placed the individualistic motives of rational legal acquisition by virtue of one's own ability and initiative. And, while the politically privileged monopoly industries in England all disappeared in short order, this attitude played a large and decisive part in the development of the industries which grew up in spite of and against the authority of the State.[110] The Puritans (Prynne, Parker) repudiated all connection with the large-scale capitalistic courtiers and projectors as an ethically suspicious class. On the other hand, they took pride in their own superior middle-class business morality, which formed the true reason for the persecutions to which they were

subjected on the part of those circles. Defoe proposed to win the battle against dissent by boycotting
bank credit and withdrawing deposits. The difference of the two types of capitalistic attitude went to
a very large extent hand in hand with religious differences. The opponents of the Nonconformists,
even in the eighteenth century, again and again ridi-
culed them for personifying the spirit of shopkeep-
ers, and for having ruined the ideals of old England.
Here also lay the difference of the Puritan economic
ethic from the Jewish; and contemporaries (Prynne)
knew well that the former and not the latter was the
bourgeois capitalistic ethic.[111]

One of the fundamental elements of the spirit of
modern capitalism, and not only of that but of all
modern culture: rational conduct on the basis of the
idea of the calling, was born–that is what this discussion has sought to demonstrate–from the spirit of
Christian asceticism. One has only to re-read the passage from Franklin, quoted at the beginning of this essay, in order to see that the essential elements of the
attitude which was there called the spirit of capitalism
are the same as what we have just shown to be the
content of the Puritan worldly asceticism,[112] only without the religious basis, which by Franklin's time had
died away. The idea that modern labour has an ascetic character is of course not new. Limitation to
specialized work, with a renunciation of the Faustian
universality of man which it involves, is a condition
of any valuable work in the modern world; hence
deeds and renunciation inevitably condition each other
today. This fundamentally ascetic trait of middle-class

life, if it attempts to be a way of life at all, and not simply the absence of any, was what Goethe wanted to teach, at the height of his wisdom, in the *Wander-jahren*, and in the end which he gave to the life of his *Faust*.[113] For him the realization meant a renunciation, a departure from an age of full and beautiful human-ity, which can no more be repeated in the course of our cultural development than can the flower of the Athenian culture of antiquity.

The Puritan wanted to work in a calling; we are forced to do so. For when asceticism was carried out of monastic cells into everyday life, and began to dominate worldly morality, it did its part in building the tremendous cosmos of the modern economic order. This order is now bound to the technical and eco-nomic conditions of machine production which to-day determine the lives of all the individuals who are born into this mechanism, not only those directly concerned with economic acquisition, with irresistible force. Per-haps it will so determine them until the last ton of fos-silized coal is burnt. In Baxter's view the care for ex-ternal goods should only lie on the shoulders of the "saint like a light cloak, which can be thrown aside at any moment."[114] But fate decreed that the cloak should become an iron cage.

Since asceticism undertook to remodel the world and to work out its ideals in the world, material goods have gained an increasing and finally an inexorable power over the lives of men as at no previous period in history. To-day the spirit of religious asceticism–whether finally, who knows?–has escaped from the cage. But victorious capitalism, since it rests on mechanical

18

[Handwritten annotations:]

system on buildings on pleasure.
your very burden of wishes
Asceticism did its part in building the Capitalist economy → building cosmos of economic order.

Looking for way of demon-strating that pre-destined go to heaven. Looking for a

Protestant minister

Care for external goods shouldn't be relied on.

We are the victims of capitalism and → Capitalism will never come to an end. Until all natural resources are exhausted.
work ethic → more important

Doom — what does he mean?

Capitalism

religion no longer needed

Economic order shapes who we are ⇒ Sets terms of how we are going to lead our life.

→ sport of being successful.

The Protestant Ethic and the Spirit of Capitalism

means of production

embarrassed

foundations, needs its support no longer. The rosy
blush of its laughing heir, the Enlightenment, seems
also to be irretrievably fading, and the idea of duty in
one's calling prowls about in our lives like the ghost
of dead religious beliefs. Where the fulfilment of the
calling cannot directly be related to the highest spiritual and cultural values, or when, on the other hand, it
need not be felt simply as economic compulsion, the
individual generally abandons the attempt to justify it
at all. In the field of its highest development, in the
United States, the pursuit of wealth, stripped of its religious and ethical meaning, tends to become associated with purely mundane passions, which often actually give it the character of sport.[115]

No one knows who will live in this cage in the future, or whether at the end of this tremendous development entirely new prophets will arise, or there will be
a great rebirth of old ideas and ideals, or, if neither,
mechanized petrification, embellished with a sort of
convulsive self-importance. For of the last stage of this
cultural development, it might well be truly said: "Specialists without spirit, sensualists without heart; this
nullity imagines that it has attained a level of civilization never before achieved."

But this brings us to the world of judgments of
value and of faith, with which this purely historical
discussion need not be burdened. The next task would
be rather to show the significance of ascetic rationalism, which has only been touched in the foregoing
sketch, for the content of practical social ethics, thus
for the types of organization and the functions of social groups from the conventicle to the State. Then its

182

Spiritual guidance → religious movement → Protestant ethic is fading

Become completely detached from any meaning → acquiring money as sport.

Dark rendering of modern life

no longer have a calling indulging in wealth

*religion no longer needed → has done its service

relations to humanistic rationalism,[116] its ideals of life and cultural influence; further to the development of philosophical and scientific empiricism, to technical development and to spiritual ideals would have to be analysed. Then its historical development from the mediæval beginnings of worldly asceticism to its dissolution into pure utilitarianism would have to be traced out through all the areas of ascetic religion. Only then could the quantitative cultural significance of ascetic Protestantism in its relation to the other plastic elements of modern culture be estimated.

Here we have only attempted to trace the fact and the direction of its influence to their motives in one, though a very important point. But it would also further be necessary to investigate how Protestant Asceticism was in turn influenced in its development and its character by the totality of social conditions, especially economic.[117] The modern man is in general, even with the best will, unable to give religious ideas a significance for culture and national character which they deserve. But it is, of course, not my aim to substitute for a one-sided materialistic an equally one-sided spiritualistic causal interpretation of culture and of history. Each is equally possible,[118] but each, if it does not serve as the preparation, but as the conclusion of an investigation, accomplishes equally little in the interest of historical truth.[119]

Started as a
religions motivation and
→ now a greed !!

NOTES

MAX WEBER'S INTRODUCTION TO THE SOCIOLOGY OF RELIGION

1. *Ständestaat.* The term refers to the late form taken by feudalism in Europe in its transition to absolute monarchy.—TRANSLATOR'S NOTE.

2. Here, as on some other points, I differ from our honoured master, Lujo Brentano (in his work to be cited later). Chiefly in regard to terminology, but also on questions of fact. It does not seem to me expedient to bring such different things as acquisition of booty and acquisition by management of a factory together under the same category; still less to designate every tendency to the acquisition of money as the spirit of capitalism as against other types of acquisition. The second sacrifices all precision of concepts, and the first the possibility of clarifying the specific difference between Occidental capitalism and other forms. Also in Simmel's *Philosophie des Geldes* money economy and capitalism are too closely identified, to the detriment of his concrete analysis. In the writings of Werner Sombart, above all in the second edition of his most important work, *Der moderne Kapitalismus,* the *differentia specifica* of Occidental capitalism–at least from the view-point of my problem–the rational organization of labour, is strongly overshadowed by genetic factors which have been operative everywhere in the world.

3. *Commenda* was a form of mediæval trading association, entered into *ad hoc* for carrying out one sea voyage. A producer or exporter of goods turned them over to another who took them abroad (on a ship provided sometimes by one party, sometimes by the other) and sold them, receiving a share in the profits. The expenses of the voyage were divided between the two in agreed proportion, while the original shipper bore the risk. See Weber, "Handelsgesellschaften im Mittelalter" *Gesammelte Aufsätze zur Sozial- und Wirtschaftsgeschichte,* pp. 323–8.—TRANSLATOR'S NOTE.

4. The sea loan, used in maritime commerce in the Middle Ages, was "a method of insuring against the risks of the sea without violating the prohibitions against usury. . . . When certain risky maritime ventures were to be undertaken, a certain sum . . . was obtained for the cargo belonging to such and such a person or capitalist. If the ship was lost, no repayment was exacted by the lender; if it reached port safely, the borrower paid a considerable premium, sometimes 50 per cent." Henri Sée, *Modern Capitalism,* p. 189.—TRANSLATOR'S NOTE.

5. A form of company between the partnership and the limited liability corporation. At least one of the participants is made liable without limit, while the others enjoy limitation of liability to the amount of their investment.—TRANSLATOR'S NOTE.

6. Naturally the difference cannot be conceived in absolute terms. The politically oriented capitalism (above all tax-farming) of Mediterranean and Oriental antiquity, and even of China and India, gave rise to rational, continuous enterprises whose book-keeping—though known to us only in pitiful fragments—probably had a rational character. Furthermore, the politically oriented adventurers' capitalism has been closely associated with rational bourgeois capitalism in the development of modern banks, which, including the Bank of England, have for the most part originated in transactions of a political nature, often connected with war. The difference between the characters of Paterson, for instance—a typical promoter—and of the members of the directorate of the Bank who gave the keynote to its permanent policy, and very soon came to be known as the "Puritan usurers of Grocers' Hall" is characteristic of it. Similarly, we have the aberration of the policy of this most solid bank at the time of the South Sea Bubble. Thus the two naturally shade off into each other. But the difference is there. The great promoters and financiers have no more created the rational organization of labour than—again in general and with individual exceptions—those other typical representatives of financial and political capitalism, the Jews. That was done, typically, by quite a different set of people.

7. For Weber's discussion of the ineffectiveness of slave labour, especially so far as calculation is concerned, see his essay, "Agrarverhältnisse im Altertum" in the volume *Gesammelte Aufsätze zur Sozial- und Wirtschaftsgeschichte.*—TRANSLATOR'S NOTE.

8. That is, in the whole series of *Aufsätze zur Religionssoziologie,* not only in the essay here translated. See translator's preface.—TRANSLATOR'S NOTE.

9. The remains of my knowledge of Hebrew are also quite inadequate.

10. I need hardly point out that this does not apply to attempts like that of Karl Jasper's (in his book *Psychologie der Weltanschauungen,* 1919), nor to Klages's *Charakterologie,* and similar studies which differ from our own in their point of departure. There is no space here for a criticism of them.

11. The only thing of this kind which Weber ever wrote is the section on "Religionssoziologie" in his large work *Wirtschaft und Gesellschaft.* It was left unfinished by him and does not really close the gap satisfactorily.—TRANSLATOR'S NOTE.

12. Some years ago an eminent psychiatrist expressed the same opinion to me.

CHAPTER I

1. From the voluminous literature which has grown up around this essay I cite only the most comprehensive criticisms. (1) F. Rachfahl, "Kalvinismus und Kapitalismus", *Internationale Wochenschrift für Wissenschaft, Kunst und Technik* (1909), Nos. 39–43. In

reply, my article: "Antikritisches zum Geist des Kapitalismus," *Archiv für Sozialwissenschaft und Sozialpolitik* (Tübingen), XX, 1910. Then Rachfahl's reply to that: "Nochmals Kalvinismus und Kapitalismus" 1910, Nos. 22–25, of the *Internationale Wochenschrift*. Finally my "Antikritisches Schlusswort", *Archiv*, XXXI. (Brentano, in the criticism presently to be referred to, evidently did not know of this last phase of the discussion, as he does not refer to it.) I have not incorporated anything in this edition from the somewhat unfruitful polemics against Rachfahl. He is an author whom I otherwise admire, but who has in this instance ventured into a field which he has not thoroughly mastered. I have only added a few supplementary references from my anti-critique, and have attempted, in new passages and footnotes, to make impossible any future misunderstanding. (2) W. Sombart, in his book *Der Bourgeois* (Munich and Leipzig, 1913, also translated into English under the title *The Quintessence of Capitalism,* London, 1915), to which I shall return in footnotes below. Finally (3) Lujo Brentano in Part II of the Appendix to his Munich address (in the Academy of Sciences, 1913) on *Die Anfänge des modernen Kapitalismus,* which was published in 1916. (Since Weber's death Brentano has somewhat expanded these essays and incorporated them into his recent book *Der wirtschaftende Mensch in der Geschichte.* —TRANSLATOR'S NOTE.) I shall also refer to this criticism in special footnotes in the proper places. I invite anyone who may be interested to convince himself by comparison that I have not in revision left out, changed the meaning of, weakened, or added materially different statements to, a single sentence of my essay which contained any essential point. There was no occasion to do so, and the development of my exposition will convince anyone who still doubts. The two latter writers engaged in a more bitter quarrel with each other than with me. Brentano's criticism of Sombart's book, *Die Juden und das Wirtschaftsleben,* I consider in many points well founded, but often very unjust, even apart from the fact that Brentano does not himself seem to understand the real essence of the problem of the Jews (which is entirely omitted from this essay, but will be dealt with later [in a later section of the *Religionssoziologie.*—TRANSLATOR'S NOTE]).

From theologians I have received numerous valuable suggestions in connection with this study. Its reception on their part has been in general friendly and impersonal, in spite of wide differences of opinion on particular points. This is the more welcome to me since I should not have wondered at a certain antipathy to the manner in which these matters must necessarily be treated here. What to a theologian is valuable in his religion cannot play a very large part in this study. We are concerned with what, from a religious point of view, are often quite superficial and unrefined aspects of religious life, but which, and precisely because they were superficial and unrefined, have often influenced outward behaviour most profoundly.

Another book which, besides containing many other things, is a very welcome confirmation of and supplement to this essay in so far as it deals with our problem, is the important work of E. Troeltsch, *Die Soziallehren der christlichen Kirchen und Gruppen* (Tübingen, 1912). It deals with the history of the ethics of Western Christianity from a very comprehensive point of view of its own. I here refer the reader to it for general comparison instead of making repeated references to special points. The author is principally concerned with the doctrines of religion, while I am interested rather in their practical results.

2. The exceptions are explained, not always, but frequently, by the fact that the religious leanings of the labouring force of an industry are naturally, in the first instance, determined by those of the locality in which the industry is situated, or from which its labour is drawn. This circumstance often alters the impression given at first glance by some statistics of religious adherence, for instance in the Rhine provinces. Furthermore, figures can naturally only be conclusive if individual specialized occupations are carefully distinguished in them. Otherwise very large employers may sometimes be grouped together with master craftsmen who work alone, under the category of "proprietors of enterprises". Above all, the fully developed capitalism of the present day, especially so far as the great unskilled lower strata of labour are concerned, has become independent of any influence which religion may have had in the past. I shall return to this point.

3. Compare, for instance, Schell, *Der Katholizismus als Prinzip des Fortschrittes* (Würzburg, 1897), p. 31, and V. Hertling, *Das Prinzip des Katholizismus und die Wissenschaft* (Freiburg, 1899), p. 58.

4. One of my pupils has gone through what is at this time the most complete statistical material we possess on this subject: the religious statistics of Baden. See Martin Offenbacher, "Konfession und soziale Schichtung", *Eine Studie über die wirtschaftliche Lage der Katholiken und Protestanten in Baden* (Tübingen und Leipzig, 1901), Vol. IV, part v, of the *Volkswirtschaftliche Abhandlungen der badischen Hochschulen.* The facts and figures which are used for illustration below are all drawn from this study.

5. For instance, in 1895 in Baden there was taxable capital available for the tax on returns from capital:

Per 1,000 Protestants . .   . .   . .   954,000 marks
Per 1,000 Catholics   . .   . .   . .   589,000 marks

It is true that the Jews, with over four millions per 1,000, were far ahead of the rest. (For details see Offenbacher, *op. cit.*, p. 21.)

6. On this point compare the whole discussion in Offenbacher's study.

7. On this point also Offenbacher brings forward more detailed evidence for Baden in his first two chapters.

8. The population of Baden was composed in 1895 as follows:

Notes

Protestants, 37.0 per cent.; Catholics, 61.3 per cent.; Jewish, 1.5 per cent. The students of schools beyond the compulsory public school stage were, however, divided as follows (Offenbacher, p. 16):

	Protestant.	Catholic.	Jews.
	Per Cent.	Per Cent.	Per Cent.
Gymnasien	43	46	9.5
Realgymnasien	69	31	9
Oberrealschulen	52	41	7
Realschulen	49	40	11
Höhere Bürgerschulen ..	51	37	12
Average	48	42	10

(In the *Gymnasium* the main emphasis is on the classics. In the *Realgymnasium* Greek is dropped and Latin reduced in favour of modern languages, mathematics and science. The *Realschule* and *Oberrealtschule* are similar to the latter except that Latin is dropped entirely in favour of modern languages. See G. E. Bolton, *The Secondary School System in Germany,* New York, 1900.—TRANSLATOR'S NOTE.)

The same thing may be observed in Prussia, Bavaria, Würtemberg, Alsace-Lorraine, and Hungary (see figures in Offenbacher, pp. 16 ff.).

9. See the figures in the preceding note, which show that the Catholic attendance at secondary schools, which is regularly less than the Catholic share of the total population by a third, only exceeds this by a few per cent. in the case of the grammar schools (mainly in preparation for theological studies). With reference to the subsequent discussion it may further be noted as characteristic that in Hungary those affiliated with the Reformed Church exceed even the average Protestant record of attendance at secondary schools. (See Offenbacher, p. 19, note.)

10. For the proofs see Offenbacher, p. 54, and the tables at the end of his study.

11. Especially well illustrated by passages in the works of Sir William Petty, to be referred to later.

12. Petty's reference to the case of Ireland is very simply explained by the fact that the Protestants were only involved in the capacity of absentee landlords. If he had meant to maintain more he would have been wrong, as the situation of the Scotch-Irish shows. The typical relationship between Protestantism and capitalism existed in Ireland as well as elsewhere. (On the Scotch-Irish see C. A. Hanna, *The Scotch-Irish,* two vols., Putnam, New York.)

13. This is not, of course, to deny that the latter facts have had exceedingly important consequences. As I shall show later, the fact

that many Protestant sects were small and hence homogeneous minorities, as were all the strict Calvinists outside of Geneva and New England, even where they were in possession of political power, was of fundamental significance for the development of their whole character, including their manner of participation in economic life. The migration of exiles of all the religions of the earth, Indian, Arabian, Chinese, Syrian, Phoenician, Greek, Lombard, to other countries as bearers of the commercial lore of highly developed areas, has been of universal occurrence and has nothing to do with our problem. Brentano, in the essay to which I shall often refer, *Die Anfänge des modernen Kapitalismus,* calls to witness his own family. But bankers of foreign extraction have existed at all times and in all countries as the representatives of commercial experience and connections. They are not peculiar to modern capitalism, and were looked upon with ethical mistrust by the Protestants (see below). The case of the Protestant families, such as the Muralts, Pestalozzi, etc., who migrated to Zurich from Locarno, was different. They very soon became identified with a specifically modern (industrial) type of capitalistic development.

14. Offenbacher, *op. cit.,* p. 58.

15. Unusually good observations on the characteristic peculiarities of the different religions in Germany and France, and the relation of these differences to other cultural elements in the conflict of nationalities in Alsace are to be found in the fine study of W. Wittich, "Deutsche und französische Kultur im Elsass". *Illustrierte Elsässische Rundschau* (1900, also published separately).

16. This, of course, was true only when some possibility of capitalistic development in the area in question was present.

17. On this point see, for instance, Dupin de St. André, "L'ancienne église réformée de Tours. Les membres de l'église", *Bull de la soc. de l'hist. du Protest.,* 4, p. 10. Here again one might, especially from the Catholic point of view, look upon the desire for emancipation from monastic or ecclesiastical control as the dominant motive. But against that view stands not only the judgment of contemporaries (including Rabelais), but also, for instance, the qualms of conscience of the first national synods of the Huguenots (for instance 1st Synod, C. partic. qu. 10 in Aymon, *Synod. Nat.,* p. 10), as to whether a banker might become an elder of the Church; and in spite of Calvin's own definite stand, the repeated discussions in the same bodies of the permissibility of taking interest occasioned by the questions of ultra-scrupulous members. It is partly explained by the number of persons having a direct interest in the question, but at the same time the wish to practise *usuraria pravitas* without the necessity of confession could not have been alone decisive. The same, see below, is true of Holland. Let it be said explicitly that the prohibition of interest in the canon law will play no part in this investigation.

Notes

18. Gothein, *Wirtschaftsgeschichte des Schwarzwaldes*, 1, p. 67.

19. In connection with this see Sombart's brief comments (*Der moderne Kapitalismus,* first edition, p. 380). Later, under the influence of a study of F. Keller (*Unternehmung und Mehrwert,* Publications of the Goerres-Gesellschaft, XII), which, in spite of many good observations (which in this connection, however, are not new), falls below the standard of other recent works of Catholic apologetics, Sombart, in what is in these parts in my opinion by far the weakest of his larger works (*Der Bourgeois*), has unfortunately maintained a completely untenable thesis, to which I shall refer in the proper place.

20. That the simple fact of a change of residence is among the most effective means of intensifying labour is thoroughly established (compare note 13 above). The same Polish girl who at home was not to be shaken loose from her traditional laziness by any chance of earning money, however tempting, seems to change her entire nature and become capable of unlimited accomplishment when she is a migratory worker in a foreign country. The same is true of migratory Italian labourers. That this is by no means entirely explicable in terms of the educative influence of the entrance into a higher cultural environment, although this naturally plays a part, is shown by the fact that the same thing happens where the type of occupation, as in agricultural labour, is exactly the same as at home. Furthermore, accommodation in labour barracks, etc., may involve a degradation to a standard of living which would never be tolerated at home. The simple fact of working in quite different surroundings from those to which one is accustomed breaks through the tradition and is the educative force. It is hardly necessary to remark how much of American economic development is the result of such factors. In ancient times the similar significance of the Babylonian exile for the Jews is very striking, and the same is true of the Parsees. But for the Protestants, as is indicated by the undeniable difference in the economic characteristics of the Puritan New England colonies from Catholic Maryland, the Episcopal South, and mixed Rhode Island, the influence of their religious belief quite evidently plays a part as an independent factor. Similarly in India, for instance, with the Jains.

21. It is well known in most of its forms to be a more or less moderated Calvinism or Zwinglianism.

22. In Hamburg, which is almost entirely Lutheran, the only fortune going back to the seventeenth century is that of a well-known Reformed family (kindly called to my attention by Professor A. Wahl).

23. It is thus not new that the existence of this relationship is maintained here. Lavelye, Matthew Arnold, and others already perceived it. What is new, on the contrary, is the quite unfounded denial of it. Our task here is to explain the relation.

24. Naturally this does not mean that official Pietism, like other religious tendencies, did not at a later date, from a patriarchal point

of view, oppose certain progressive features of capitalistic development, for instance, the transition from domestic industry to the factory system. What a religion has sought after as an ideal, and what the actual result of its influence on the lives of its adherents has been, must be sharply distinguished, as we shall often see in the course of our discussion. On the specific adaptation of Pietists to industrial labour, I have given examples from a Westphalian factory in my article, "Zür Psychophysik der gewerblichen Arbeit", *Archiv für Sozialwissenschaft und Sozialpolitik,* XXVIII, and at various other times.

CHAPTER II

1. These passages represent a very brief summary of some aspects of Weber's methodological views. At about the same time that he wrote this essay he was engaged in a thorough criticism and revaluation of the methods of the Social Sciences, the result of which was a point of view in many ways different from the prevailing one, especially outside of Germany. In order thoroughly to understand the significance of this essay in its wider bearings on Weber's sociological work as a whole it is necessary to know what his methodological aims were. Most of his writings on this subject have been assembled since his death (in 1920) in the volume *Gesammelte Aufsätze zur Wissenschaftslehre.* A shorter exposition of the main position is contained in the opening chapters of *Wirtschaft und Gesellschaft, Grundriss der Sozialökonomik,* III.—TRANSLATOR'S NOTE.

2. The final passage is from *Necessary Hints to Those That Would Be Rich* (written 1736, Works, Sparks edition, II, p. 80), the rest from *Advice to a Young Tradesman* (written 1748, Sparks edition, II, pp. 87 ff.). The italics in the text are Franklin's.

3. *Der Amerikamüde* (Frankfurt, 1855), well known to be an imaginative paraphrase of Lenau's impressions of America. As a work of art the book would to-day be somewhat difficult to enjoy, but it is incomparable as a document of the (now long since blurred over) differences between the German and the American outlook, one may even say of the type of spiritual life which, in spite of everything, has remained common to all Germans, Catholic and Protestant alike, since the German mysticism of the Middle Ages, as against the Puritan capitalistic valuation of action.

4. Sombart has used this quotation as a motto for his section dealing with the genesis of capitalism (*Der moderne Kapitalismus,* first edition, I, p. 193. See also p. 390).

5. Which quite obviously does not mean either that Jacob Fugger was a morally indifferent or an irreligious man, or that Benjamin Franklin's ethic is completely covered by the above quotations. It scarcely required Brentano's quotations (*Die Anfänge des modernen Kapitalismus,* pp. 150 ff.) to protect this well-known philanthropist

from the misunderstanding which Brentano seems to attribute to me. The problem is just the reverse: how could such a philanthropist come to write these particular sentences (the especially characteristic form of which Brentano has neglected to reproduce) in the manner of a moralist?

6. This is the basis of our difference from Sombart in stating the problem. Its very considerable practical significance will become clear later. In anticipation, however, let it be remarked that Sombart has by no means neglected this ethical aspect of the capitalistic entrepreneur. But in his view of the problem it appears as a result of capitalism, whereas for our purposes we must assume the opposite as an hypothesis. A final position can only be taken up at the end of the investigation. For Sombart's view see *op. cit.,* pp. 357, 380, etc. His reasoning here connects with the brilliant analysis given in Simmel's *Philosophie des Geldes* (final chapter). Of the polemics which he has brought forward against me in his *Bourgeois* I shall come to speak later. At this point any thorough discussion must be postponed.

7. "I grew convinced that truth, sincerity, and integrity in dealings between man and man were of the utmost importance to the felicity of life; and I formed written resolutions, which still remain in my journal book to practise them ever while I lived. Revelation had indeed no weight with me as such; but I entertained an opinion that, though certain actions might not be bad because they were forbidden by it, or good because it commanded them, yet probably these actions might be forbidden because they were bad for us, or commanded because they were beneficial to us in their own nature, all the circumstances of things considered." *Autobiography* (ed. F. W. Pine, Henry Holt, New York, 1916), p. 112.

8. "I therefore put myself as much as I could out of sight and started it"—that is the project of a library which he had initiated—"as a scheme of a *number of friends,* who had requested me to go about and propose it to such as they thought lovers of reading. In this way my affair went on smoothly, and I ever after practised it on such occasions; and from my frequent successes, can heartily recommend it. The present little sacrifice of your vanity will afterwards be amply repaid. If it remains awhile uncertain to whom the merit belongs, someone more vain than yourself will be encouraged to claim it, and then even envy will be disposed to do you justice by plucking those assumed feathers and restoring them to their right owner." *Autobiography,* p. 140.

9. Brentano *(op. cit.,* pp. 125, 127, note 1) takes this remark as an occasion to criticize the later discussion of "that rationalization and discipline" to which worldly asceticism[1] has subjected men. That,

---

1. This seemingly paradoxical term has been the best translation I could find for Weber's *innerweltliche* Askese, which means asceticism practised

he says, is a rationalization toward an irrational mode of life. He is, in fact, quite correct. A thing is never irrational in itself, but only from a particular rational point of view. For the unbeliever every religious way of life is irrational, for the hedonist every ascetic standard, no matter whether, measured with respect to its particular basic values, that opposing asceticism is a rationalization. If this essay makes any contribution at all, may it be to bring out the complexity of the only superficially simple concept of the rational.

10. In reply to Brentano's (*Die Anfänge des modernen Kapitalismus,* pp. 150 ff.) long and somewhat inaccurate apologia for Franklin, whose ethical qualities I am supposed to have misunderstood, I refer only to this statement, which should, in my opinion, have been sufficient to make that apologia superfluous.

11. The two terms profession and calling I have used in translation of the German *Beruf,* whichever seemed best to fit the particular context. Vocation does not carry the ethical connotation in which Weber is interested. It is especially to be remembered that profession in this sense is not contrasted with business, but it refers to a particular attitude toward one's occupation, no matter what that occupation may be. This should become abundantly clear from the whole of Weber's argument.—TRANSLATOR'S NOTE.

12. I make use of this opportunity to insert a few anti-critical remarks in advance of the main argument. Sombart (*Bourgeois*) makes the untenable statement that this ethic of Franklin is a word-for-word repetition of some writings of that great and versatile genius of the Renaissance, Leon Battista Alberti, who besides theoretical treatises on Mathematics, Sculpture, Painting, Architecture, and Love (he was personally a woman-hater), wrote a work in four books on household management (*Della Famiglia*). (Unfortunately, I have not at the time of writing been able to procure the edition of Mancini, but only the older one of Bonucci.) The passage from Franklin is printed above word for word. Where then are corresponding passages to be found in Alberti's work, especially the maxim "time is money", which stands at the head, and the exhortations which follow it? The only passage which, so far as I know, bears the slightest resemblance to it is found towards the end of the first book of *Della Famiglia* (ed. Bonucci, II, p. 353), where Alberti speaks in very general terms of money as the *nervus rerum* of the household, which must hence

---

within the world as contrasted with *ausserweltliche Askese,* which withdraws from the world (for instance into a monastery). Their precise meaning will appear in the course of Weber's discussion. It is one of the prime points of his essay that asceticism does not need to flee from the world to be ascetic. I shall consistently employ the terms worldly and otherworldly to denote the contrast between the two kinds of asceticism.—TRANSLATOR'S NOTE.

Notes

be handled with special care, just as Cato spoke in *De Re Rustica.* To treat Alberti, who was very proud of his descent from one of the most distinguished cavalier families of Florence (*Nobilissimi Cavalieri, op. cit.,* pp. 213, 228, 247, etc.), as a man of mongrel blood who was filled with envy for the noble families because his illegitimate birth, which was not in the least socially disqualifying, excluded him as a bourgeois from association with the nobility, is quite incorrect. It is true that the recommendation of large enterprises as alone worthy of a *nobile è onesta famiglia* and a *libero è nobile animo,* and as costing less labour is characteristic of Alberti (p. 209; compare *Del governo della Famiglia,* IV, p. 55, as well as p. 116 in the edition for the Pandolfini). Hence the best thing is a putting-out business for wool and silk. Also an ordered and painstaking regulation of his household, i.e. the limiting of expenditure to income. This is the *santa masserizia,* which is thus primarily a principle of maintenance, a given standard of life, and not of acquisition (as no one should have understood better than Sombart). Similarly, in the discussion of the nature of money, his concern is with the management of consumption funds (money or *possessioni),* not with that of capital; all that is clear from the expression of it which is put into the mouth of Gianozzo. He recommends, as protection against the uncertainty of *fortuna,* early habituation to continuous activity, which is also (pp. 73–4) alone healthy in the long run, *in cose magnifiche è ample,* and avoidance of laziness, which always endangers the maintenance of one's position in the world. Hence a careful study of a suitable trade in case of a change of fortune, but every *opera mercenaria* is unsuitable *(op. cit.,* I, p. 209). His idea of *tranquillita dell' animo* and his strong tendency toward the Epicurean λάθε βιώσας *(vivere a sè stesso,* p. 262); especially his dislike of any office (p. 258) as a source of unrest, of making enemies, and of becoming involved in dishonourable dealings; the ideal of life in a country villa; his nourishment of vanity through the thought of his ancestors; and his treatment of the honour of the family (which on that account should keep its fortune together in the Florentine manner and not divide it up) as a decisive standard and ideal—all these things would in the eyes of every Puritan have been sinful idolatry of the flesh, and in those of Benjamin Franklin the expression of incomprehensible aristocratic nonsense. Note, further, the very high opinion of literary things (for the *industria* is applied principally to literary and scientific work), which is really most worthy of a man's efforts. And the expression of the *masserizia,* in the sense of "rational conduct of the household" as the means of living independently of others and avoiding destitution, is in general put only in the mouth of the illiterate Gianozzo as of equal value. Thus the origin of this concept, which comes (see below) from monastic ethics, is traced back to an old priest (p. 249).

Now compare all this with the ethic and manner of life of Benjamin

Franklin, and especially of his Puritan ancestors; the works of the Renaissance *littérateur* addressing himself to the humanistic aristocracy, with Franklin's works addressed to the masses of the lower middle class (he especially mentions clerks) and with the tracts and sermons of the Puritans, in order to comprehend the depth of the difference. The economic rationalism of Alberti, everywhere supported by references to ancient authors, is most clearly related to the treatment of economic problems in the works of Xenophon (whom he did not know), of Cato, Varro, and Columella (all of whom he quotes), except that especially in Cato and Varro, *acquisition* as such stands in the foreground in a different way from that to be found in Alberti. Furthermore, the very occasional comments of Alberti on the use of the *fattori,* their division of labour and discipline, on the unreliability of the peasants, etc., really sound as if Cato's homely wisdom were taken from the field of the ancient slave-using household and applied to that of free labour in domestic industry and the metayer system. When Sombart (whose reference to the Stoic ethic is quite misleading) sees economic rationalism as "developed to its farthest conclusions" as early as Cato, he is, with a correct interpretation, not entirely wrong. It is possible to unite the *diligens pater familias* of the Romans with the ideal of the *massajo* of Alberti under the same category. It is above all characteristic for Cato that a landed estate is valued and judged as an object for the investment of consumption funds. The concept of *industria,* on the other hand, is differently coloured on account of Christian influence. And there is just the difference. In the conception of *industria,* which comes from monastic asceticism and which was developed by monastic writers, lies the seed of an *ethos* which was fully developed later in the Protestant worldly asceticism. Hence, as we shall often point out, the relationship of the two, which, however, is less close to the official Church doctrine of St. Thomas than to the Florentine and Siennese mendicant-moralists. In Cato and also in Alberti's own writings this *ethos* is lacking; for both it is a matter of worldly wisdom, not of ethic. In Franklin there is also a utilitarian strain. But the ethical quality of the sermon to young business men is impossible to mistake, and that is the characteristic thing. A lack of care in the handling of money means to him that one so to speak murders capital embryos, and hence it is an ethical defect.

An inner relationship of the two (Alberti and Franklin) exists in fact only in so far as Alberti, whom Sombart calls pious, but who actually, although he took the sacraments and held a Roman benefice, like so many humanists, did not himself (except for two quite colourless passages) in any way make use of religious motives as a justification of the manner of life he recommended, had not yet, Franklin on the other hand no longer, related his recommendation of economy to religious conceptions. Utilitarianism, in Alberti's preference for

Notes

wool and silk manufacture, also the mercantilist social utilitarianism "that many people should be given employment" (see Alberti, *op. cit.,* p. 292,), is in this field at least formally the sole justification for the one as for the other. Alberti's discussions of this subject form an excellent example of the sort of economic rationalism which really existed as a reflection of economic conditions, in the work of authors interested purely in "the thing for its own sake" everywhere and at all times; in the Chinese classicism and in Greece and Rome no less than in the Renaissance and the age of the Enlightenment. There is no doubt that just as in ancient times with Cato, Varro, and Columella, also here with Alberti and others of the same type, especially in the doctrine of *industria,* a sort of economic rationality is highly developed. But how can anyone believe that such a literary *theory* could develop into a revolutionary force at all comparable to the way in which a religious belief was able to set the sanctions of salvation and damnation on the fulfillment of a particular (in this case methodically rationalized) manner of life? What, as compared with it, a really religiously oriented rationalization of conduct looks like, may be seen, outside of the Puritans of all denominations, in the cases of the Jains, the Jews, certain ascetic sects of the Middle Ages, the Bohemian Brothers (an offshoot of the Hussite movement), the Skoptsi and Stundists in Russia, and numerous monastic orders, however much all these may differ from each other.

The essential point of the difference is (to anticipate) that an ethic based on religion places certain psychological sanctions (not of an economic character) on the maintenance of the attitude prescribed by it, sanctions which, so long as the religious belief remains alive, are highly effective, and which mere worldly wisdom like that of Alberti does not have at its disposal. Only in so far as these sanctions work, and, above all, in the direction in which they work, which is often very different from the doctrine of the theologians, does such an ethic gain an independent influence on the conduct of life and thus on the economic order. This is, to speak frankly, the point of this whole essay, which I had not expected to find so completely overlooked.

Later on I shall come to speak of the theological moralists of the late Middle Ages, who were relatively friendly to capital (especially Anthony of Florence and Bernhard of Siena), and whom Sombart has also seriously misinterpreted. In any case Alberti did not belong to that group. Only the concept of *industria* did he take from monastic lines of thought, no matter through what intermediate links. Alberti, Pandolfini, and their kind are representatives of that attitude which, in spite of all its outward obedience, was inwardly already emancipated from the tradition of the Church. With all its resemblance to the current Christian ethic, it was to a large extent of the antique pagan character, which Brentano thinks I have ignored in its significance for the development of modern economic thought (and also modern economic policy). That I do not deal with its influence here is quite true. It would be out of place in a study of the Protestant ethic and the spirit of capitalism. But, as will appear in a different connection, far from denying its significance, I have been and am for good reasons of the opinion that its sphere and direction of influence were entirely different from those of the Protestant ethic (of which the spiritual ancestry, of no small practical importance, lies in the sects and in the ethics of Wyclif and Hus). It was not the mode of life of the rising bourgeoisie which was influenced by this other attitude, but the policy of statesmen and princes; and these two partly, but by no means always, convergent lines of development should for purposes of analysis be kept perfectly distinct. So far as Franklin is concerned, his tracts of advice to business men, at present used for school reading in America, belong in fact to a category of works which have influenced practical life, far more than Alberti's large book, which hardly became known outside of learned circles. But I have expressly denoted him as a man who stood beyond the direct influence of the Puritan view of life, which had paled considerably in the meantime, just as the whole English enlightenment, the relations of which to Puritanism have often been set forth.

13. Unfortunately Brentano (*op. cit.*) has thrown every kind of struggle for gain, whether peaceful or warlike, into one pot, and has then set up as the specific criterion of capitalistic (as contrasted, for instance, with feudal) profit-seeking, its acquisitiveness of *money* (instead of land). Any further differentiation, which alone could lead to a clear conception, he has not only refused to make, but has made against the concept of the spirit of (modern) capitalism which we have formed for our purposes, the (to me) incomprehensible objection that it already includes in its assumptions what is supposed to be proved.

14. Compare the, in every respect, excellent observations of Sombart, *Die deutsche Volkswirtschaft im 19ten Jahrhundert,* p. 123. In general I do not need specially to point out, although the following studies go back in their most important points of view to much older work, how much they owe in their development to the mere existence of Sombart's important works, with their pointed formulations and this even, perhaps especially, where they take a different road. Even those who feel themselves continually and decisively disagreeing with Sombart's views, and who reject many of his theses, have the duty to do so only after a thorough study of his work.

15. Of course we cannot here enter into the question of where these limits lie, nor can we evaluate the familiar theory of the relation between high wages and the high productivity of labour which was first suggested by Brassey, formulated and maintained theoretically by Brentano, and both historically and theoretically by Schulze Gaevernitz. The discussion was again opened by Hasbach's penetrating studies *(Schmollers Jahrbuch,* 1903, pp. 385–91 and 417 ff.),

and is not yet finally settled. For us it is here sufficient to assent to the fact which is not, and cannot be, doubted by anyone, that low wages and high profits, low wages and favourable opportunities for industrial development, are at least not simply identical, that generally speaking training for capitalistic culture, and with it the possibility of capitalism as an economic system,are not brought about simply through mechanical financial operations. All examples are purely illustrative.

16. It must be remembered that this was written twenty-five years ago, when the above statement was by no means the commonplace that it is now, even among economists, to say nothing of business men.—TRANS-LATOR'S NOTE.

17. The establishment even of capitalistic industries has hence often not been possible without large migratory movements from areas of older culture. However correct Sombart's remarks on the difference between the personal skill and trade secrets of the handicraftsman and the scientific, objective modern technique may be, at the time of the rise of capitalism the difference hardly existed. In fact the, so to speak, ethical qualities of the capitalistic workman (and to a certain extent also of the entrepreneur) often had a higher scarcity value than the skill of the craftsman, crystallized in traditions hundreds of years old. And even present-day industry is not yet by any means entirely independent in its choice of location of such qualities of the population, acquired by long-standing tradition and education in intensive labour. It is congenial to the scientific prejudices of to-day, when such a dependence is observed to ascribe it to congenital racial qualities rather than to tradition and education, in my opinion with very doubtful validity.

18. See my "Zur Psychophysik der gewerblichen Arbeit", *Archiv für Sozialwissenschaft und Sozialpolitik,* XXVIII.

19. The foregoing observations might be misunderstood. The tendency of a well-known type of business man to use the belief that "religion must be maintained for the people" for his own purpose, and the earlier not uncommon willingness of large numbers, especially of the Lutheran clergy, from a general sympathy with authority, to offer themselves as black police when they wished to brand the strike as sin and trade unions as furtherers of cupidity, all these are things with which our present problem has nothing to do. The factors discussed in the text do not concern occasional but very common facts, which, as we shall see, continually recur in a typical manner.

20. *Der moderne Kapitalismus,* first edition, I, p. 62.

21. *Ibid.,* p. 195.

22. Naturally that of the modern rational enterprise peculiar to the Occident, not of the sort of capitalism spread over the world for three thousand years, from China, India, Babylon, Greece, Rome, Florence, to the present, carried on by usurers, military contractors,

traders in offices, tax-farmers, large merchants, and financial magnates. See the Introduction.

23. The assumption is thus by no means justified *a priori,* that is all I wish to bring out here, that on the one hand the technique of the capitalistic enterprise, and on the other the spirit of professional work which gives to capitalism its expansive energy, must have had their original roots in the same social classes. Similarly with the social relationships of religious beliefs. Calvinism was historically one of the agents of education in the spirit of capitalism. But in the Netherlands, the large moneyed interests were, for reasons which will be discussed later, not predominately adherents of strict Calvinism, but Arminians. The rising middle and small bourgeoisie, from which entrepreneurs were principally recruited, were for the most part here and elsewhere typical representatives both of capitalistic ethics and of Calvinistic religion. But that fits in very well with our present thesis: there were at all times large bankers and merchants. But a rational capitalistic organization of industrial labour was never known until the transition from the Middle Ages to modern times took place.

24. On this point see the good Zurich dissertation of J. Maliniak (1913).

25. The following picture has been put together as an ideal type from conditions found in different industrial branches and at different places. For the purposes of illustration which it here serves, it is of course of no consequence that the process has not in any one of the examples we have in mind taken place in precisely the manner we have described.

26. For this reason, among others, it is not by chance that this first period of incipient (economic) rationalism in German industry was accompanied by certain other phenomena, for instance the catastrophic degradation of taste in the style of articles of everyday use.

27. This is not to be understood as a claim that changes in the supply of the precious metals are of no economic importance.

28. This is only meant to refer to the type of entrepreneur (business man) whom we are making the object of our study, not any empirical average type. On the concept of the ideal type see my discussion in the *Archiv für Sozialwissenschaft und Sozialpolitik,* XIX, No. I. (Republished since Weber's death in the *Gesammelte Aufsätze zur Wissenschaftslehre.* The concept was first thoroughly developed by Weber himself in these essays, and is likely to be unfamiliar to non-German readers. It is one of the most important aspects of Weber's methodological work, referred to in a note above.—TRANSLATOR'S NOTE.)

29. This is perhaps the most appropriate place to make a few remarks concerning the essay of F. Keller, already referred to (volume 12 of the publications of the Görres-Gesellschaft), and Sombart's observations (*Der Bourgeois*) in following it up, so far as they are relevant in the present context. That an author should criti-

cize a study in which the canonical prohibition of interest (except in one incidental remark which has no connection with the general argument) is not even mentioned, on the assumption that this prohibition of interest, which has a parallel in almost every religious ethic in the world, is taken to be the decisive criterion of the difference between the Catholic and Protestant ethics, is almost inconceivable. One should really only criticize things which one has read, or the argument of which, if read, one has not already forgotten. The campaign against *usuraria pravitas* runs through both the Huguenot and the Dutch Church history of the sixteenth century; Lombards, i.e. bankers, were by virtue of that fact alone often excluded from communion (see Chap. I, note 17). The more liberal attitude of Calvin (which did not, however, prevent the inclusion of regulations against usury in the first plan of the ordinances) did not gain a definite victory until Salmasius. Hence the difference did not lie at this point; quite the contrary. But still worse are the author's own arguments on this point. Compared to the works of Funck and other Catholic scholars (which he has not, in my opinion, taken as fully into consideration as they deserve), and the investigations of Endemann, which, however obsolete in certain points to-day, are still fundamental, they make a painful impression of superficiality. To be sure, Keller has abstained from such excesses as the remarks of Sombart (*Der Bourgeois,* p. 321) that one noticed how the "pious gentlemen" (Bernard of Siena and Anthony of Florence) "wished to excite the spirit of enterprise by every possible means", that is, since they, just like nearly everyone else concerned with the prohibition of interest, interpreted it in such a way as to exempt what we should call the productive investment of capital. That Sombart, on the one hand, places the Romans among the heroic peoples, and on the other, what is for his work as a whole an impossible contradiction, considers economic rationalism to have been developed to its final consequences in Cato (p. 267), may be mentioned by the way as a symptom that this is a book with a thesis in the worst sense.

He has also completely misrepresented the significance of the prohibition of interest. This cannot be set forth here in detail. At one time it was often exaggerated, then strongly underestimated, and now, in an era which produces Catholic millionaires as well as Protestant, has been turned upside down for apologetic purposes. As is well known, it was not, in spite of Biblical authority, abolished until the last century by order of the *Congregatio S. Officii,* and then only *temporum ratione habita* and indirectly, namely, by forbidding confessors to worry their charges by questions about *usuraria pravitas,* even though no claim to obedience was given up in case it should be restored. Anyone who has made a thorough study of the extremely complicated history of the doctrine cannot claim, considering the endless controversies over, for instance, the justification of the purchase of bonds, the discounting of notes and various other contracts (and above all considering the order of the *Congregatio S. Officii,* mentioned above, concerning a municipal loan), that the prohibition of interest was only intended to apply to emergency loans, nor that it had the intention of preserving capital, or that it was even an aid to capitalistic enterprise (p. 25). The truth is that the Church came to reconsider the prohibition of interest comparatively late. At the time when this happened the forms of purely business investment were not loans at fixed interest rate, but the *fœnus nauticum, commenda, societas maris,* and the *dare ad proficuum de mari* (a loan in which the shares of gain and loss were adjusted according to degrees of risk), and were, considering the character of the return on loans to productive enterprise, necessarily of that sort. These were not (or only according to a few rigorous canonists) held to fall under the ban, but when investment at a definite rate of interest and discounting became possible and customary, the first sort of loans also encountered very troublesome difficulties from the prohibition, which led to various drastic measures of the merchant guilds (black lists). But the treatment of usury on the part of the canonists was generally purely legal and formal, and was certainly free from any such tendency to protect capital as Keller ascribes to it. Finally, in so far as any attitude towards capitalism as such can be ascertained, the decisive factors were: on the one hand, a traditional, mostly inarticulate hostility towards the growing power of capital which was impersonal, and hence not readily amenable to ethical control (as it is still reflected in Luther's pronouncements about the Fuggers and about the banking business); on the other hand, the necessity of accommodation to practical needs. But we cannot discuss this, for, as has been said, the prohibition of usury and its fate can have at most a symptomatic significance for us, and that only to a limited degree.

The economic ethic of the Scotists, and especially of certain mendicant theologians of the fourteenth century, above all Bernhard of Siena and Anthony of Florence, that is monks with a specifically rational type of asceticism, undoubtedly deserves a separate treatment, and cannot be disposed of incidentally in our discussion. Otherwise I should be forced here, in reply to criticism, to anticipate what I have to say in my discussion of the economic ethics of Catholicism in its positive relations to capitalism. These authors attempt, and in that anticipate some of the Jesuits, to present the profit of the merchant as a reward for his *industria* and thus ethically to justify it. (Of course, even Keller cannot claim more.)

The concept and the approval of *industria* come, of course, in the last analysis from monastic asceticism, probably also from the idea of *masserizia,* which Alberti, as he himself says through the mouth of Gianozzo, takes over from clerical sources. We shall later speak more fully of the sense in which the monastic ethics is a forerunner of the worldly ascetic denominations of Protestantism. In Greece, among the Cynics, as shown by late-Hellenic tombstone inscriptions, and, with an entirely different background, in Egypt, there were suggestions of similar ideas. But what is for us the most important thing is entirely lacking both here and in the case of Alberti. As we shall see later, the characteristic Protestant conception of the proof of one's own salvation, the *certitudo salutis* in a calling, provided the psychological sanctions which this religious belief put behind the *industria*. But that Catholicism could not supply, because its means to salvation were different. In effect these authors are concerned with an ethical doctrine, not with motives to practical action, dependent on the desire for salvation. Furthermore, they are, as is very easy to see, concerned with concessions to practical necessity, not, as was worldly asceticism, with deductions from fundamental religious postulates. (Incidentally, Anthony and Bernhard have long ago been better dealt with than by Keller.) And even these concessions have remained an object of controversy down to the present. Nevertheless the significance of these monastic ethical conceptions as symptoms is by no means small.

But the real roots of the religious ethics which led the way to the modern conception of a calling lay in the sects and the heterodox movements, above all in Wyclif; although Brodnitz (*Englische Wirtschaftsgeschichte*), who thinks his influence was so great that Puritanism found nothing left for it to do, greatly overestimates his significance. All that cannot be gone into here. For here we can only discuss incidentally whether and to what extent the Christian ethic of the Middle Ages had in fact already prepared the way for the spirit of capitalism.

30. The words μηδὲν ἀπελπίζοντες (Luke vi.35) and the translation of the Vulgate, *nihil inde sperantes,* are thought (according to A. Merx) to be a corruption of μηδένα ἀπελπίζοντες (or *meminem desperantes*), and thus to command the granting of loans to all brothers, including the poor, without saying anything at all about interest. The passage *Deo placere vix potest* is now thought to be of Arian origin (which, if true, makes no difference to our contentions).

31. How a compromise with the prohibition of usury was achieved is shown, for example, in Book I, chapter 65, of the statutes of the *Arte di Calimala* (at present I have only the Italian edition in Emiliani Guidici, *Stor. dei Com. Ital.,* III, p. 246). "Procurino i consoli con quelli frate, che parrà loro, che perdono si faccia e come fare si possa il meglio per l'amore di ciascuno, del dono, merito o guiderdono, ovvero interesse per l'anno presente e secondo che altra volta fatto fue." It is thus a way for the guild to secure exemption for its members on account of their official positions, without defiance of authority. The suggestions immediately following, as well as the immediately preceding idea to book all interest and profits as gifts, are very characteristic of the amoral attitude towards profits on

capital. To the present stock exchange black list against brokers who hold back the difference between top price and actual selling price, often corresponded the outcry against those who pleaded before the ecclesiastical court with the *exceptio usurariæ, pravitatis.*

CHAPTER III

1. Of the ancient languages, only Hebrew has any similar concept. Most of all in the word מְלָאכָה. It is used for sacerdotal functions (Exod. xxxv. 21; Neh. xi. 22; I Chron. ix. 13; xxiii. 4; xxvi. 30), for business in the service of the king (especially I Sam. viii. 16; I Chron. iv. 23; xxix. 6), for the service of a royal official (Esther iii. 9; ix. 3), of a superintendent of labour (2 Kings xii. 12), of a slave (Gen. xxxix. II), of labour in the fields (I Chron. xxvii. 26), of craftsmen (Exod. xxxi. 5; xxxv. 21; Kings vii. 14), for traders (Psa. cvii. 23), and for worldly activity of any kind in the passage, Sirach xi. 20, to be discussed later. The word is derived from the root לְאַךְ, to send, thus meaning originally a task. That it originated in the ideas current in Solomon's bureaucratic kingdom of serfs *(Fronstaat),* built up as it was according to the Egyptian model, seems evident from the above references. In meaning, however, as I learn from A. Merx, this root concept had become lost even in antiquity. The word came to be used for any sort of labour, and in fact became fully as colourless as the German *Beruf,* with which it shared the fate of being used primarily for mental and not manual functions. The expression (חק), assignment, task, lesson, which also occurs in Sirach xi. 20, and is translated in the Septuagint with διθήκη, is also derived from the terminology of the servile bureaucratic regime of the time, as is רֹבֵד־יֹם (Exod. v. 13, cf. Exod. v. 14), where the Septuagint also uses διαθήκη for task. In Sirach xliii.10 it is rendered in the Septuagint with κρίμα. In Sirach xi. 20 it is evidently used to signify the fulfillment of God's commandments, being thus related to our calling. On this passage in Jesus Sirach reference may here be made to Smend's well-known book on Jesus Sirach, and for the words διαθήκη, ἔργον, πόνος, to his *Index zur Weisheit des Jesus Sirach* (Berlin, 1907). As is well known, the Hebrew text of the Book of Sirach was lost, but has been rediscovered by Schechter, and in part supplemented by quotations from the Talmud. Luther did not possess it, and these two Hebrew concepts could not have had any influence on his use of language. (See below on Prov. xxii. 29.)

In Greek there is no term corresponding in ethical connotation to the German or English words at all. Where Luther, quite in the spirit of the modern usage (see below), translates Jesus Sirach xi. 20 and 21, *bleibe in deinem Beruf,* the Septuagint has at one point ἔργον, at the other, which however seems to be an entirely corrupt passage,

Notes

πόνος (the Hebrew original speaks of the shining of divine help!). Otherwise in antiquity τὰ προσήκοντο is used in the general sense of duties. In the works of the Stoics κάματος occasionally carries similar connotations, though its linguistic source is indifferent (called to my attention by A. Dieterich). All other expressions (such as τάξις, etc.) have no ethical implications.

In Latin what we translate as calling, a man's sustained activity under the division of labour, which is thus (normally) his source of income and in the long run the economic basis of his existence, is, aside from the colourless *opus*, expressed with an ethical content, at least similar to that of the German word, either by *officium* (from *opificium,* which was originally ethically colourless, but later, as especially in Seneca *de benef,* IV, p. 18, came to mean *Beruf*); or by *munus*, derived from the compulsory obligations of the old civic community; or finally by *professio.* This last word was also characteristically used in this sense for public obligations, probably being derived from the old tax declarations of the citizens. But later it came to be applied in the special modern sense of the liberal professions (as in *professio bene dicendit*), and in this narrower meaning had a significance in every way similar to the German *Beruf,* even in the more spiritual sense of the word, as when Cicero says of someone "non intelligit quid profiteatur", in the sense of "he does not know his real profession". The only difference is that it is, of course, definitely secular without any religious connotation. That is even more true of *ars,* which in Imperial times was used for handicraft. The Vulgate translates the above passages from Jesus Sirach, at one point with *opus*, the other (verse 21) with *locus,* which in this case means something like social station. The addition of *mandaturam tuorum* comes from the ascetic Jerome, as Brentano quite rightly remarks, without, however, here or elsewhere, calling attention to the fact that this was characteristic of precisely the ascetic use of the term, before the Reformation in an otherworldly, afterwards in a worldly, sense. It is furthermore uncertain from what text Jerome's translation was made. An influence of the old liturgical meaning of מְלָאכָה does not seem to be impossible.

In the Romance languages only the Spanish *vocacion* in the sense of an inner call to something, from the analogy of a clerical office, has a connotation partly corresponding to that of the German word, but it is never used to mean calling in the external sense. In the Romance Bible translations the Spanish *vocacion,* the Italian *vocazione* and *chiamamento,* which otherwise have a meaning partly corresponding to the Lutheran and Calvinistic usage to be discussed presently, are used only to translate the κλῆσις of the New Testament, the call of the Gospel to eternal salvation, which in the Vulgate is *vocatio.* Strange to say, Brentano, *op. cit.,* maintains that this fact, which I have myself adduced to defend my view, is evidenced for the existence of the concept of the calling in the sense which it had later, before the Reformation. But it is nothing of the kind. κλῆσις had to be translated by *vocatio*. But where and when in the Middle Ages was it used in our sense? The fact of this translation, and in spite of it, the lack of any application of the word to worldly callings is what is decisive. *Chiamamento* is used in this manner along with *vocazione* in the Italian Bible translation of the fifteenth century, which is printed in the *Collezione di opere inedite e rare* (Bologna, 1887), while the modern Italian translations use the latter alone. On the other hand, the words used in the Romance languages for calling in the external worldly sense of regular acquisitive activity carry, as appears from all the dictionaries and from a report of my friend Professor Baist (of Freiburg), no religious connotation whatever. This is so no matter whether they are derived from *ministerium* or *officium,* which originally had a certain religious colouring, or from *ars, professio* and *implicare* (*impeigo*), from which it has been entirely absent from the beginning. The passages in Jesus Sirach mentioned above, where Luther used *Beruf*, are translated: in French, v. 20, *office;* v. 21, *labeur* (Calvinistic translation); Spanish, v. 20, *obra;* V. 21, *lugar* (following the Vulgate); recent translations, *posto* (Protestant). The Protestants of the Latin countries, since they were minorities, did not exercise, possibly without even making the attempt, such a creative influence over their respective languages as Luther did over the still less highly rationalized (in an academic sense) German official language.

2. On the other hand, the *Augsburg Confession* only contains the idea implicitly and but partially developed. Article XVI (ed. by Kolde, p. 43) teaches: "Meanwhile it (the Gospel) does not dissolve the ties of civil or domestic economy, but strongly enjoins us to maintain them as ordinances of God and in such ordinances (*ein jeder nach seinem Beruf*) to exercise charity." (Translated by Rev. W. H. Teale, Leeds, 1842.)

(In Latin it is only "et in talibus ordinationibus exercere caritatem". The English is evidently translated directly from the Latin, and does not contain the idea which came into the German version.—TRANSLATOR'S NOTE.)

The conclusion drawn, that one must obey authority, shows that here *Beruf* is thought of, at least primarily, as an objective order in the sense of the passage in 1 Cor. vii. 20.

And Article XXVII (Kolde, p. 83) speaks of *Beruf* (Latin *in vocatione sua*) only in connection with estates ordained by God: clergy, magistrates, princes, lords, etc. But even this is true only of the German version of the *Konkordienbuch,* while in the German *Ed. princeps* the sentence is left out.

Only in Article XXVI (Kolde, p. 81) is the word used in a sense which at least includes our present meaning: "that he did chastise his body, not to deserve by that discipline remission of sin, but to

Notes

have his body in bondage and apt to spiritual things, and to do his calling". Translated by Richard Taverner, Philadelphia Publications Society, 1888. (Latin *juxta vocationem suam.*)

3. According to the lexicons, kindly confirmed by my colleagues Professors Braune and Hoops, the word *Beruf* (Dutch *beroep*, English *calling*, Danish *kald,* Swedish *kallelse*) does not occur in any of the languages which now contain it in its present worldly (secular) sense before Luther's translation of the Bible. The Middle High German, Middle Low German, and Middle Dutch words, which sound like it, all mean the same as *Ruf* in modern German, especially inclusive, in late mediæval times, of the calling (vocation) of a candidate to a clerical benefice by those with the power of appointment. It is a special case which is also often mentioned in the dictionaries of the Scandinavian languages. The word is also occasionally used by Luther in the same sense. However, even though this special use of the word may have promoted its change of meaning, the modern conception of *Beruf* undoubtedly goes linguistically back to the Bible translations by Protestants, and any anticipation of it is only to be found, as we shall see later, in Tauler (died 1361). All the languages which were fundamentally influenced by the Protestant Bible translations have the word, all of which this was not true (like the Romance languages) do not, or at least not in its modern meaning.

Luther renders two quite different concepts with *Beruf.* First the Pauline κλῆσις in the sense of the call to eternal salvation through God. Thus: I Cor. i. 26; Eph. i. 18; iv. 1,4; 2 Thess. i. 11; Heb. iii. 1; 2 Peter i.10. All these cases concern the purely religious idea of the call through the Gospel taught by the apostle; the word κλῆσις has nothing to do with worldly callings in the modern sense. The German Bibles before Luther use in this case *ruffunge* (so in all those in the Heidelberg Library), and sometimes instead of "von Gott geruffet" say "von Gott gefordert". Secondly, however, he, as we have already seen, translates the words in Jesus Sirach discussed in the previous note (in the Septuagint ἔν τῷ ἔργῳ σου παλαιώθητι and καὶ ἔμμενε τῷ πόνῳ σου), with "beharre in deinem Beruf" and "bliebe in de inem Beruf" instead of "bliebe bei deiner Arbeit". The later (authorized) Catholic translations (for instance that of Fleischütz, Fulda, 1781) have (as in the New Testament passages) simply followed him. Luther's translation of the passage in the Book of Sirach is, so far as I know, the first case in which the German word *Beruf* appears in its present purely secular sense.The preceding exhortation, verse 20, στῆθι εν διαθήκῃ σου, he translates "bliebe in Gottes Wort" although Sirach xiv. 1 and xliii. 10 show that, corresponding to the Hebrew חק , which (according to quotations in the Talmud) Sirach used, διαθήκη really did mean something similar to our calling, namely one's fate or assigned task. In its later and present sense the word *Beruf* did not exist in the German language, nor, so far as I can learn, in the works of the older Bible translators or preachers. The German Bibles before Luther rendered the passage from Sirach with *Werk*. Berthold of Regensburg, at the points in his sermons where the modern would say *Beruf*, uses the word *Arbeit*. The usage was thus the same as in antiquity. The first passage I know, in which not *Beruf* but *Ruf* (as a translation of κλῆσις) is applied to purely worldly labour, is in the fine sermon of Tauler on Ephesians iv (Works, Basle edition, f. 117.v), of peasants who *misten* go: they often fare better "so sie folgen einfeltiglich irem Ruff denn die geistlichen Menschen, die auf ihren *Ruf* nicht Acht haben". The word in this sense did not find its way into everyday speech. Although Luther's usage at first vacillates between *Ruf* and *Beruf* (see *Werke*, Erlangen edition, p. 51), that he was directly influenced by Tauler is by no means certain, although the *Freiheit eines Christenmenschen* is in many respects similar to this sermon of Tauler. But in the purely worldly sense of Tauler, Luther did not use the word *Ruf*. (This against Denifle, *Luther*, p. 163.)

Now evidently Sirach's advice in the version of the Septuagint contains, apart from the general exhortation to trust in God, no suggestion of a specifically religious valuation of secular labour in a calling. The term πόνος, toil, in the corrupt second passage would be rather the opposite, if it were not corrupted. What Jesus Sirach says simply corresponds to the exhortation of the psalmist (Psa. xxxvii. 3), "Dwell in the land, and feed on his faithfulness" as also comes out clearly in the connection with the warning not to let oneself be blinded with the works of the godless, since it is easy for God to make a poor man rich. Only the opening exhortation to remain in the רח (verse 20) has a certain resemblance to the κλῆσις of the Gospel, but here Luther did not use the word *Beruf* for the Greek διαθήκη. The connection between Luther's two seemingly quite unrelated uses of the word *Beruf* is found in the first letter to the Corinthians and its translation.

In the usual modern editions, the whole context in which the passage stands is as follows, I Cor. vii. 17 (English, King James version [American revision, 1901]): "(17) Only as the Lord hath distributed to each man, as God hath called each, so let him walk. And so ordain I in all churches. (18) Was any man called being circumcised? let him not become uncircumcised. Hath any man been called in uncircumcision? let him not be circumcised. (19) Circumcision is nothing and uncircumcision is nothing; but the keeping of the commandments of God. (20) Let each man abide in that calling wherein he was called (ἐν τῇ κλήσει ᾗ ἐκλήθη; an undoubted Hebraism, as Professor Merx tells me). (21) Wast thou called being a bond-servant? care not for it; nay even if thou canst become free use it rather. (22) For he that was called in the Lord being a bondservant is the Lord's freedman; likewise he that was called being free is

Notes

Christ's bondservant. (23) Ye were bought with a price; become not bondservants of men. (24) Brethren, let each man, wherein he was called, therein abide with God."

In verse 29 follows the remark that time is shortened, followed by the well-known commandments motivated by eschatological expectations: (31) to possess women as though one did not have them, to buy as though one did not have what one had bought, etc. In verse 20 Luther, following the older German translations, even in 1523 in his exigesis of this chapter, renders κλῆσις with *Beruf,* and interprets it with *Stand.* (Erlangen ed., LI, p. 51.)

In fact it is evident that the word κλῆσις at this point, and only at this, corresponds approximately to the Latin *status* and the German *Stand* (status of marriage, status of a servant, etc.). But of course not as Brentano, *op. cit.,* p. 137, assumes, in the modern sense of *Beruf.* Brentano can hardly have read this passage, or what I have said about it, very carefully. In a sense at least suggesting it this word, which is etymologically related to ἐκκλησία, an assembly which has been called, occurs in Greek literature, so far as the lexicons tell, only once in a passage from Dionysius of Halicarnassus, where it corresponds to the Latin *classis,* a word borrowed from the Greek, meaning that part of the citizenry which has been called to the colours. Theophylaktos (eleventh-twelfth century) interprets I Cor. vii. 20: ἐν οἴῳ βίῳ καὶ ἐν οἴῳ τάγματι καὶ πολιτεύματι ὢν ἐπίστευσεν. (My colleague Professor Deissmann called my attention to this passage.) Now, even in our passage, κλῆσις does not correspond to the modern *Beruf.* But having translated κλῆσις with *Beruf* in the eschatologically motivated exhortation, that everyone should remain in his present status, Luther, when he later came to translate the Apocrypha, would naturally, on account of the similar content of the exhortations alone, also use *Beruf* for πόνος in the traditionalistic and anti-chrematistic commandment of Jesus Sirach, that everyone should remain in the same business. This is what is important and characteristic. The passage in I Cor. vii. 17 does not, as has been pointed out, use κλῆσις at all in the sense of *Beruf,* a definite field of activity.

In the meantime (or about the same time), in the *Augsburg Confession,* the Protestant dogma of the uselessness of the Catholic attempt to excel worldly morality was established, and in it the expression "einem jeglichen nach seinem Beruf" was used (see previous note). In Luther's translation, both this and the positive valuation of the order in which the individual was placed, as holy, which was gaining ground just about the beginning of the 1530's, stand out. It was a result of his more and more sharply defined belief in special Divine Providence, even in the details of life, and at the same time of his increasing inclination to accept the existing order of things in the world as immutably willed by God. *Vocatio,* in the traditional Latin, meant the divine call to a life of holiness, especially in a monastery or as a priest. But now, under the influence of this dogma, life in a worldly calling came for Luther to have the same connotation. For he now translated πόνος and ἔργον in Jesus Sirach with *Beruf,* for which, up to that time, there had been only the (Latin) analogy, coming from the monastic translation. But a few years earlier, in Prov. xxii. 29, he had still translated the Hebrew מְלָאכָה, which was the original of ἔργον in the Greek text of Jesus Sirach, and which, like the German *Beruf* and the Scandinavian *kald, kallelse,* originally related to a *spiritual* call (*Beruf*), as in other passages (Gen. xxxix. 11), with *Geschäft* (Septuagint ἔργον, Vulgate *opus,* English Bibles *business,* and correspondingly in the Scandinavian and all the other translations before me).

The word *Beruf,* in the modern sense which he had finally created, remained for the time being entirely Lutheran. To the Calvinists the Apocrypha are entirely uncanonical. It was only as a result of the development which brought the interest in proof of salvation to the fore that Luther's concept was taken over, and then strongly emphasized by them. But in their first (Romance) translations they had no such word available, and no power to create one in the usage of a language already so stereotyped.

As early as the sixteenth century the concept of *Beruf* in its present sense became established in secular literature. The Bible translators before Luther had used the word *Berufung* for κλῆσις (as for instance in the Heidelberg versions of 1462–66 and 1485), and the Eck translation of 1537 says "in dem Ruf, worin er beruft ist". Most of the later Catholic translators directly follow Luther. In England, the first of all, Wyclif's translation (1382), used *cleping* (the Old English word which was later replaced by the borrowed *calling).* It is quite characteristic of the Lollard ethics to use a word which already corresponded to the later usage of the Reformation. Tyndale's translation of 1534, on the other hand, interprets the idea in terms of *status:* "in the same state wherein he was called" as also does the Geneva Bible of 1557. Cranmer's official translation of 1539 substituted *calling* f o r *state,* while the (Catholic) Bible of Rheims (1582), as well as the Anglican Court Bibles of the Elizabethan era, characteristically return to vocation, following the Vulgate.

That for England, Cranmer's Bible translation is the source of the Puritan conception of calling in the sense of *Beruf,* trade, has already, quite correctly, been pointed out by Murray. As early as the middle of the sixteenth century calling is used in that sense. In 1588 unlawful callings are referred to, and in 1603 greater callings in the sense of higher occupations, etc. (see Murray). Quite remarkable is Brentano's idea *(op. cit.,* p. 139), that in the Middle Ages *vocatio* was not translated with *Beruf,* and that this concept was not known, because only a free man could engage in a *Beruf,* and freemen, in the middle-class professions, did not exist at that time. Since the

Notes

whole social structure of the mediæval crafts, as opposed to those of antiquity, rested upon free labour, and, above all, almost all the merchants were freemen, I do not clearly understand this thesis.

4. Compare with the following the instructive discussion in K. Eger, *Die Anschauung Luthers vom Beruf* (Giessen, 1900). Perhaps its only serious fault, which is shared by almost all other theological writers, is his insufficiently clear analysis of the concept of *lex naturæ*. On this see E. Troeltsch in his review of Seeberg's *Dogmengeschichte,* and now above all in the relevant parts of his *Soziallehren der christlichen Kirchen.*

5. For when Thomas Aquinas represents the division of men into estates and occupational groups as the work of divine providence, by that he means the objective cosmos of society. But that the individual should take up a particular calling (as we should say; Thomas, however, says *ministerium* or *officium*) is due to *causæ naturales. Quæst. quodlibetal,* VII, Art. 17c: "Hæc autem diversificatio hominum in diversis officiis contingit primo ex divina providentia, quæ ita hominum status distribuit . . . secundo etiam ex causis naturalibus, ex quibus contingit, quod in diversis hominibus sunt diversæ inclinationes ad diversa officia. . . ."

Quite similar is Pascal's view when he says that it is chance which determines the choice of a calling. See on Pascal, A. Koester, *Die Ethik Pascals* (1907). Of the organic systems of religious ethics, only the most complete of them, the Indian, is different in this respect. The difference between the Thomistic and the Protestant ideas of the call ing is so evident that we may dismiss it for the present with the above quotation. This is true even as between the Thomistic and the later Lutheran ethics, which are very similar in many other respects, especially in their emphasis on Providence. We shall return later to a discussion of the Catholic view-point. On Thomas Aquinas, see Maurenbrecher, *Thomas von Aquino's Stellung zum Wirtschaftsleben seiner Zeit,* 1888. Otherwise, where Luther agrees with Thomas in details, he has probably been influenced rather by the general doctrines of Scholasticism than by Thomas in particular. For, according to Denifle's investigations, he seems really not to have known Thomas very well. See Denifle, *Luther und Luthertum* (1903), p. 501, and on it, Koehler, *Ein Wort zu Denifles Luther* (1904), p. 25.

6. In *Von der Freiheit eines Christenmenschen,* (1) the double nature of man is used for the justification of worldly duties in the sense of the *lex naturæ* (here the natural order of the world). From that it follows (Erlangen edition, 27, p. 188) that man is inevitably bound to his body and to the social community. (2) In this situation he will (p. 96: this is a second justification), if he is a believing Christian, decide to repay God's act of grace, which was done for pure love, by love of his neighbour. With this very loose connection between faith and love is combined (3) (p. 190) the old ascetic justification

of labour as a means of securing to the inner man mastery over the body. (4) Labour is hence, as the reasoning is continued with another appearance of the idea of *lex naturæ* in another sense (here, natural morality), an original instinct given by God to Adam (before the fall), which he has obeyed "solely to please God". Finally (5) (pp. 161 and 199), there appears, in connection with Matt. vii. i8 f., the idea that good work in one's ordinary calling is and must be the result of the renewal of life, caused by faith, without, however, developing the most important Calvinistic idea of proof. The powerful emotion which dominates the work explains the presence of such contradictory ideas.

7. "It is not from the benevolence of the butcher, the brewer, or the baker, that we expect our dinner, but from their regard to their own interest. We address ourselves, not to their humanity, but to their self-love; and never talk to them of our own necessities, but of their advantages" (*Wealth of Nations,* Book I, chap. ii).

8. "Omnia enim per te operabitur (Deus), mulgebit per te vaccam et servilissima quæque *opera faciet, ac maxima pariter et minima ipsi grata erunt" (Exigesis of Genesis, Opera lat. exeget.,* ed. Elsperger, VII, p. 213). The idea is found before Luther in Tauler, who holds the spiritual and the worldly *Ruf* to be in principle of equal value. The difference from the Thomistic view is common to the German mystics and Luther. It may be said that Thomas, principally to retain the moral value of contemplation, but also from the view-point of the mendicant friar, is forced to interpret Paul's doctrine that "if a man will not work he shall not eat" in the sense that labour, which is of course necessary *lege naturæ,* is imposed upon the human race as a whole, but not on all individuals. The gradation in the value of forms of labour, from the *opera servilia* of the peasants upwards, is connected with the specific character of the mendicant friars, who were for material reasons bound to the town as a place of domicile. It was equally foreign to the German mystics and to Luther, the peasant's son; both of them, while valuing all occupations equally, looked upon their order of rank as willed by God. For the relevant passages in Thomas see Maurenbrecher, *op. cit.,* pp. 65 ff.

9. It is astonishing that some investigators can maintain that such a change could have been without effect upon the actions of men. I confess my inability to understand such a view.

10. "Vanity is so firmly imbedded in the human heart that a camp-follower, a kitchen-helper, or a porter, boast and seek admirers. . . . (Faugeres edition, I, p. 208. Compare Koester, *op. cit.,* pp. 17, 136 ff.). On the attitude of Port Royal and the Jansenists to the calling, to which we shall return, see now the excellent study of Dr. Paul Honigsheim, *Die Staats- und Soziallehren der franözischen Jansenisten im 17ten Jahrhundert* (Heidelberg Historical Dissertation, 1914. It is a separately printed part of a more comprehensive work on the *Vorgeschichte der französischen Aufklärung.* Compare especially pp. 138 ff.).

Notes

11. Apropos of the Fuggers, he thinks that it "cannot be right and godly for such a great and regal fortune to be piled up in the lifetime of one man". That is evidently the peasant's mistrust of capital. Similarly (*Grosser Sermon vom Wucher,* Erlangen edition, XX, p. 109) investment in securities he considers ethically undesirable, because it is "ein neues behendes erfunden Ding"—i.e. because it is to him economically incomprehensible; somewhat like margin trading to the modern clergyman.

12. The difference is well worked out by H. Levy (in his study, *Die Grundlagen des ökonomischen Liberalismus in der Geschichte der englischen Volkswirtschaft,* Jena, 1912). Compare also, for instance, the petition of the Levellers in Cromwell's army of 1653 against monopolies and companies, given in Gardiner, *Commonwealth,* II, p. 179. Laud's regime, on the other hand, worked for a Christian, social, economic organization under the joint leadership of Crown and Church, from which the King hoped for political and fiscal-monopolistic advantages. It was against just this that the Puritans were struggling.

13. What I understand by this may be shown by the example of the proclamation addressed by Cromwell to the Irish in 1650, with which he opened his war against them and which formed his reply to the manifestos of the Irish (Catholic) clergy of Clonmacnoise of December 4 and 13, 1649. The most important sentences follow: "Englishmen had good inheritances (namely in Ireland) which many of them purchased with their money . . . they had good leases from Irishmen for long time to come, great stocks thereupon, houses and plantations erected at their cost and charge. . . . You broke the union . . . at a time when Ireland was in perfect peace and when, through the example of English industry, through commerce and traffic, that which was in the nation's hands was better to them than if all Ireland had been in their possession. . . . Is God, will God be with you? I am confident He will not."

This proclamation, which is suggestive of articles in the English Press at the time of the Boer War, is not characteristic, because the capitalistic interests of Englishmen are held to be the justification of the war. That argument could, of course, have just as well been made use of, for instance, in a quarrel between Venice and Genoa over their respective spheres of influence in the Orient (which, in spite of my pointing it out here, Brentano, *op. cit.,* p. 142, strangely enough holds against me). On the contrary, what is interesting in the document is that Cromwell, with the deepest personal conviction, as everyone who knows his character will agree, bases the moral justification of the subjection of the Irish, in calling God to witness, on the fact that English capital has taught the Irish to work. (The proclamation is in Carlyle, and is also reprinted and analysed in Gardiner, *History of the Commonwealth,* I, pp. 163 f.)

14. This is not the place to follow the subject farther. Compare the authors cited in Note 16 below.

15. Compare the remarks in Jülicher's fine book, *Die Gleichnisreden Jesu,* II, pp. 108, 636 f.

16. With what follows, compare above all the discussion in Eger, *op. cit.* Also Schneckenburger's fine work, which is even to-day not yet out of date *(Vergleichende Darstellung der lutherischen und reformierten Lehrbegriffe,* Grüder, Stuttgart, 1855). Luthardt's *Ethik Luthers,* p. 84 of the first edition, the only one to which I have had access, gives no real picture of the development. Further compare Seeberg, *Dogmengeschichte,* II, pp. 262 ff. The article on *Beruf* in the *Realenzyklopädie für protestantische Theologie und Kirche* is valueless. Instead of a scientific analysis of the conception and its origin, it contains all sorts of rather sentimental observations on all possible subjects, such as the position of women, etc. Of the economic literature on Luther, I refer here only to Schmoller's studies ("Geschichte der Nationalökonomischen Ansichten in Deutschland während der Reformationszeit", *Zeitschrift f. Staatswiss,* XVI, 1860); Wiskemann's prize essay (1861); and the study of Frank G. Ward ("Darstellung und Würdigung von Luthers Ansichten vom Staat und seinen wirtschaftlichen Aufgaben", *Conrads Abhandlungenz,* XXI, Jena, 1898). The literature on Luther in commemoration of the anniversary of the Reformation, part of which is excellent, has, so far as I can see, made no definite contribution to this particular problem. On the social ethics of Luther (and the Lutherans) compare, of course, the relevant parts of Troeltsch's *Soziallehren.*

17. *Analysis of the Seventh Chapter of the First Epistle to the Corinthians,* 1523, Erlangen edition, LI, p. 1. Here Luther still interprets the idea of the freedom of every calling before God in the sense of this passage, so as to emphasize (1) that certain human institutions should be repudiated (monastic vows, the prohibition of mixed marriages, etc.), (2) that the fulfillment of traditional worldly duties to one's neighbour (in itself indifferent before God) is turned into a commandment of brotherly love. In fact this characteristic reasoning (for instance pp. 55, 56) fundamentally concerns the question of the dualism of the *lex naturæ* in its relations with divine justice.

18. Compare the passage from *Von Kaufhandlung und Wucher,* which Sombart rightly uses as a motto for his treatment of the handicraft spirit (= traditionalism): "Darum musst du dir fürsetzen, nichts denn deine ziemliche Nahrung zu suchen in solchem Handel, danach Kost, Mühe, Arbeit und Gefahr rechnen und überschlagen und also dann die Ware selbst setzen, steigern oder niedern, dass du solcher Arbeit und Mühe Lohn davon hasst." The principle is formulated in a thoroughly Thomistic spirit.

19. As early as the letter to H. von Sternberg of 1530, in which he dedicates the Exigesis of the 117th Psalm to him, the estate of the

Notes

lower nobility appears to him, in spite of its moral degradation, as ordained of God (Erlangen edition, XL, pp. 282 ff.). The decisive influence of the Münzer disturbances in developing this view-point can clearly be seen in the letter (p. 282). Compare also Eger, *op. cit.,* p. 150.

20. Also in the analysis of the 111th Psalm, verses 5 and 6 (Erlangen edition, XL, pp. 215–16), written in 1530, the starting-point is the polemics against withdrawal from the world into monasteries. But in this case the *lex naturæ* (as distinct from positive law made by the Emperor and the Jurists) is directly identical with divine justice. It is God's ordinance, and includes especially the division of the people into classes (p. 215). The equal value of the classes is emphasized, but only in the sight of God.

21. As taught especially in the works *Von Konzilien und Kirchen* (1539) and *Kurzer Bekenntnis vom heiligen Sakrament (1545).*

22. How far in the background of Luther's thought was the most important idea of proof of the Christian in his calling and his worldly conduct, which dominated Calvinism, is shown by this passage from *Von Konzilien und Kirchen* (1539, Erlangen edition, XXV, p. 376): "Besides these seven principal signs there are more superficial ones by which the holy Christian Church can be known. If we are not unchaste nor drunkards, proud, insolent, nor extravagant, but chaste, modest, and temperate." According to Luther these signs are not so infallible as the others (purity of doctrine, prayer, etc.). "Because certain of the heathen have borne themselves so and sometimes even appeared holier than Christians." Calvin's personal position was, as we shall see, not very different, but that was not true of Puritanism. In any case, for Luther the Christian serves God only *in vocatione,* not *per vocationem* (Eger, pp. 117 ff.). Of the idea of proof, on the other hand (more, however, in its Pietistic than its Calvinistic form), there are at least isolated suggestions in the German mystics (see for instance in Seeberg, *Dogmengeschichte, p.* 195, the passage from Suso, as well as those from Tauler quoted above), even though it was understood only in a psychological sense.

23. His final position is well expressed in some parts of the exegesis of Genesis (in the *op. lat. exeget.* edited by Elsperger).

Vol. IV, p. 109: "Neque hæc fuit levis tentatio, intentum esse suæ vocationi et de aliis non esse curiosum. . . . Paucissimi sunt, qui sua sorte vivant contenti . . . (p. III). Nostrum autem est, ut vocanti Deo pareamus . . . (p. 112). Regula igitur hæc servanda est, ut unusquisque maneat in sua vocatione et suo dono contentus vivat, de aliis autem non sit curiosus." In effect that is thoroughly in accordance with Thomas Aquinas's formulation of traditionalism *(Secundæ secundæ,* Quest. 118, Art. i): " Unde necesse est, quod bonum hominis circa ea consistat in quadam mensura, dum scilicet homo . . . quærit habere exteriores divitas, prout sunt necessari' ad vitam ejus secundum suam conditionem. Et ideo in excessu hujus mensuræ

215

consistit peccatum, dum scilicet aliquis supra debitum modum vult eas vel acquirere vel retinere, quod pertinet ad avaritiam." The sinfulness of the pursuit of acquisition beyond the point set by the needs of one's station in life is based by Thomas on the *lex naturæ* as revealed by the purpose (ratio) of external goods; by Luther, on the other hand, on God's will. On the relation of faith and the calling in Luther see also Vol. VII, p. 225: " . . . quando es fidelis, tum placent Deo etiam physica, carnalia, animalia, officia, sive edas, sive bibas, sive vigiles, sive dormias, quæ mere corporalia et animalia sunt. Tanta res est fides. . . . Verum est quidem, placere Deo etiam in impiis sedulitatem et industriam in officio [This activity in practical life is a virtue *lege naturæ*] sed obstat incredulitas et vana gloria, ne possint opera sua referre ad gloriam Dei [reminiscent of Calvinistic ways of speaking]. . . . Merentur igitur etiam impiorum bona opera in hac quidem vita præmia sua [as distinct from Augustine's 'vitia specie virtutum palliata'] sed non numerantur, non colliguntur in altero."

24. In the *Kirchenpostille* it runs (Erlangen edition, X, pp. 233, 235–6):"Everyone is called to some calling." He should wait for this call (on p. 236 it even becomes command) and serve God in it. God takes pleasure not in man's achievements but in his obedience in this respect.

25. This explains why, in contrast to what has been said above about the effects of Pietism on women workers, modern business men sometimes maintain that strict Lutheran domestic workers to-day often, for instance in Westphalia, think very largely in traditional terms. Even without going over to the factory system, and in spite of the temptation of higher earnings, they resist changes in methods of work, and in explanation maintain that in the next world such trifles won't matter anyway. It is evident that the mere fact of Church membership and belief is not in itself of essential significance for conduct as a whole. It has been much more concrete religious values and ideals which have influenced the development of capitalism in its early stages and, to a lesser extent, still do.

26. Compare Tauler, Basle edition, *Bl.*, pp. 161 ff.

27. Compare the peculiarly emotional sermon of Tauler referred to above, and the following one, 17, 18, verse 20.

28. Since this is the sole purpose of these present remarks on Luther, I have limited them to a brief preliminary sketch, which would, of course, be wholly inadequate as an appraisal of Luther's influence as a whole.

29. One who shared the philosophy of history of the Levellers would be in the fortunate position of being able to attribute this in turn to racial differences. They believed themselves to be the defenders of the Anglo-Saxon birthright, against the descendants of William the Conqueror and the Normans. It is astonishing enough that it

Notes

has not yet occurred to anyone to maintain that the plebeian Roundheads were round-headed in the anthropometric sense!

30. Especially the English national pride, a result of Magna Charta and the great wars. The saying, so typical to-day, "She looks like an English girl" on seeing any pretty foreign girl, is reported as early as the fifteenth century.

31. These differences have, of course, persisted in England as well. Especially the Squirearchy has remained the centre of "merrie old England" down to the present day, and the whole period since the Reformation may be looked upon as a struggle of the two elements in English society. In this point I agree with M. J. Bonn's remarks (in the *Frankfurter Zeitung*) on the excellent study of v. Schulze-Gaevernitz on British Imperialism. Compare H. Levy in the *Archiv für Sozialwissenschaft und Sozialpolitik,* 46, 3.

32. In spite of this and the following remarks, which in my opinion are clear enough, and have never been changed, I have again and again been accused of this.

CHAPTER IV

1. Zwinglianism we do not discuss separately, since after a short lease of power it rapidly lost in importance. Arminianism, the dogmatic peculiarity of which consisted in the repudiation of the doctrine of predestination in its strict form, and which also repudiated worldly asceticism, was organized as a sect only in Holland (and the United States). In this chapter it is without interest to us, or has only the negative interest of having been the religion of the merchant patricians in Holland (see below). In dogma it resembled the Anglican Church and most of the Methodist denominations. Its Erastian position (i.e. upholding the sovereignty of the State even in Church matters) was, however, common to all the authorities with purely political interests: the Long Parliament in England, Elizabeth, the Dutch States-General, and, above all, Oldenbarnereldt.

2. On the development of the concept of Puritanism see, above all, Sanford, *Studies and Reflections of the Great Rebellion,* p. 65 f. When we use the expression it is always in the sense which it took on in the popular speech of the seventeenth century, to mean the ascetically inclined religious movements in Holland and England without distinction of Church organization or dogma, thus including Independents, Congregationalists, Baptists, Mennonites, and Quakers.

3. This has been badly misunderstood in the discussion of these questions. Especially Sombart, but also Brentano, continually cite the ethical writers (mostly those of whom they have heard through me) as codifications of rules of conduct without ever asking which of them were supported by psychologically effective religious sanctions.

4. I hardly need to emphasize that this sketch, so far as it is concerned solely with the field of dogma, falls back everywhere on the formulations of the literature of the history of the Church and of doctrine. It makes no claim whatever to originality. Naturally I have attempted, so far as possible, to acquaint myself with the sources for the history of the Reformation. But to ignore in the process the intensive and acute theological research of many decades, instead of, as is quite indispensable, allowing oneself to be led from it to the sources, would have been presumption indeed. I must hope that the necessary brevity of the sketch has not led to incorrect formulations, and that I have at least avoided important misunderstandings of fact. The discussion contributes something new for those familiar with theological literature only in the sense that the whole is, of course, considered from the point of view of our problem. For that reason many of the most important points, for instance the rational character of this asceticism and its significance for modern life, have naturally not been emphasized by theological writers.

This aspect, and in general the sociological side, has, since the appearance of this study, been systematically studied in the work of E. Troeltsch, mentioned above, whose *Gerhard und Melanchthon,* as well as numerous reviews in the *Gött. Gel. Anz.,* contained several preliminary studies to his great work. For reasons of space the references have not included everything which has been used, but for the most part only those works which that part of the text follows, or which are directly relevant to it. These are often older authors, where our problems have seemed closer to them. The insufficient pecuniary resources of German libraries have meant that in the provinces the most important source materials or studies could only be had from Berlin or other large libraries on loan for very short periods. This is the case with Voët, Baxter, Tymermans, Wesley, all the Methodist, Baptist, and Quaker authors, and many others of the earlier writers not contained in the *Corpus Reformatorum.* For any thorough study the use of English and American libraries is almost indispensable. But for the following sketch it was necessary (and possible) to be content with material available in Germany. In America recently the characteristic tendency to deny their own sectarian origins has led many university libraries to provide little or nothing new of that sort of literature. It is an aspect of the general tendency to the secularization of American life which will in a short time have dissolved the traditional national character and changed the significance of many of the fundamental institutions of the country completely and finally. It is now necessary to fall back on the small orthodox sectarian colleges.

5. On Calvin and Calvinism, besides the fundamental work of Kampschulte, the best source of information is the discussion of Erick Marcks (in his *Coligny*). Campbell, *The Puritans in Holland,*

Notes

England, and America (2 vols.), is not always critical and unprejudiced. A strongly partisan anti-Calvinistic study is Pierson, *Studien over Johan Calvijn*. For the development in Holland compare, besides Motley, the Dutch classics, especially Groen van Prinsterer, *Geschiedenis v.h. Vaderland; La Hollande et l'influence de Calvin* (1864); *Le parti anti-révolutionnaire et confessionnel dans l'eglise des P.B.* (1860) (for modern Holland); further, above all, Fruin's *Tien jaren mit den tachtigjarigen oorlog,* and especially Naber, *Calvinist of Libertijntsch.* Also W. J. F. Nuyens, *Gesch. der kerkel. an pol. geschillen in de Rep. d. Ver. Prov.* (Amsterdam, 1886); A. Köhler, *Die Niederl. ref. Kirche* (Erlangen, 1856), for the nineteenth century. For France, besides Polenz, now Baird, *Rise of the Huguenots.* For England, besides Carlyle, Macaulay, Masson, and, last but not least, Ranke, above all, now the various works of Gardiner and Firth. Further, Taylor, *A Retrospect of the Religious Life in England* (1854), and the excellent book of Weingarten, *Die englischen Revolutionskirchen.* Then the article on the English Moralists by E. Troeltsch in the *Realenzyklöpadie für protestantische Theologie und Kirche,* third edition, and of course his *Soziallehren.* Also E. Bernstein's excellent essay in the *Geschichte des Sozialismus* (Stuttgart, 1895, I, p. 50 ff.). The best bibliography (over seven thousand titles) is in Dexter, *Congregationalism of the Last Three Hundred Years* (principally, though not exclusively, questions of Church organization). The book is very much better than Price *(History of Nonconformism).* Skeats, and others. For Scotland see, among others, Sack, *Die Kirche von Schottland* (1844), and the literature on John Knox. For the American colonies the outstanding work is Doyle, *The English in America.* Further, Daniel Wait Howe, *The Puritan Republic;* J. Brown, *The Pilgrim Fathers of New England and their Puritan Successors* (third edition, Revell). Further references will be given later.

For the differences of doctrine the following presentation is especially indebted to Schneckenburger's lectures cited above. Ritschl's fundamental work, *Die christliche Lehre von der Rechtfertigung und Versöhnung* (references to Vol. III of third edition), in its mixture of historical method with judgments of value, shows the marked peculiarities of the author, who with all his fine acuteness of logic does not always give the reader the certainty of objectivity. Where, for instance, he differs from Schneckenburger's interpretation I am often doubtful of his correctness, however little I presume to have an opinion of my own. Further, what he selects out of the great variety of religious ideas and feelings as the Lutheran doctrine often seems to be determined by his own preconceptions. It is what Ritschl himself conceives to be of permanent value in Lutheranism. It is Lutheranism as Ritschl would have had it, not always as it was. That the works of Karl Müller, Seeberg, and others have everywhere been made use of it is unnecessary to mention particularly. If in the following I have condemned the reader as well as myself to the penitence of a malignant growth of footnotes, it has been done in order to give especially the non-theological reader an opportunity to check up the validity of this sketch by the suggestion of related lines of thought.

6. In the following discussion we are not primarily interested in the origin, antecedents, or history of these ascetic movements, but take their doctrines as given in a state of full development.

7. For the following discussion I may here say definitely that we are not studying the personal views of Calvin, but Calvinism, and that in the form to which it had evolved by the end of the sixteenth and in the seventeenth centuries in the great areas where it had a decisive influence and which were at the same time the home of capitalistic culture. For the present, Germany is neglected entirely, since pure Calvinism never dominated large areas here. Reformed is, of course, by no means identical with Calvinistic.

8. Even the Declaration agreed upon between the University of Cambridge and the Archbishop of Canterbury on the 7th Article of the Anglican Confession, the so-called Lambeth Article of 1595, which (contrary to the official version) expressly held that there was also predestination to eternal death, was not ratified by the Queen. The Radicals (as in *Hanserd Knolly's Confession*) laid special emphasis on the express predestination to death (not only the admission of damnation, as the milder doctrine would have it).

9. *Westminster Confession*, fifth official edition, London, 1717. Compare the Savoy and the (American) *Hanserd Knolly's Declarations*. On predestination and the Huguenots see, among others, Polenz, I, pp. 545 ff.

10. On Milton's theology see the essay of Eibach in the *Theol. Studien und Kritiken*, 1879. Macaulay's essay on it, on the occasion of Sumner's translation of the *Doctrina Christiana*, rediscovered in 1823 (Tauchnitz edition, 185, pp. 1 ff.), is superficial. For more detail see the somewhat too schematic six-volume English work of Masson, and the German biography of Milton by Stern which rests upon it. Milton early began to grow away from the doctrine of predestination in the form of the double decree, and reached a wholly free Christianity in his old age. In his freedom from the tendencies of his own time he may in a certain sense be compared to Sebastian Franck. Only Milton was a practical and positive person, Franck predominantly critical. Milton is a Puritan only in the broader sense of the rational organization of his life in the world in accordance with the divine will, which formed the permanent inheritance of later times from Calvinism. Franck could be called a Puritan in much the same sense. Both, as isolated figures, must remain outside our investigation.

11. "Hic est fides summus gradus; credere Deum esse clementum,

qui tam paucos salvat, justum, qui sua voluntate nos damnabiles facit" is the text of the famous passage in *De servo arbitrio*.

12. The truth is that both Luther and Calvin believed fundamentally in a double God (see Ritschl's remarks in *Geschichte des Pietismus* and Köstlin, *Gott* in *Realenzyklopädie für protestantische Theologie und Kirche*, third edition), the gracious and kindly Father of the New Testament, who dominates the first books of the *Institutio Christiana*, and behind him the *Deus absconditus* as an arbitrary despot. For Luther, the God of the New Testament kept the upper hand, because he avoided reflection on metaphysical questions as useless and dangerous, while for Calvin the idea of a transcendental God won out. In the popular development of Calvinism, it is true, this idea could not be maintained, but what took his place was not the Heavenly Father of the New Testament but the Jehovah of the Old.

13. Compare on the following: Scheibe, *Calvins Prädestinationslehre* (Halle, 1897). On Calvinistic theology in general, Heppe, *Dogmatik der evangelisch-reformierten Kirche* (Elberfeld, 1861).

14. *Corpus Reformatorum*, LXXVII, pp. 186 ff.

15. The preceding exposition of the Calvinistic doctrine can be found in much the same form as here given, for instance in Hoornbeek's *Theologia practica* (Utrecht, 1663), L. II, c. 1; *de predestinatione*, the section stands characteristically directly under the heading *De Deo*. The Biblical foundation for it is principally the first chapter of the Epistle to the Ephesians. It is unnecessary for us here to analyse the various inconsistent attempts to combine with the predestination and providence of God the responsibility and free will of the individual. They began as early as in Augustine's first attempt to develop the doctrine.

16. "The deepest community (with God) is found not in institutions or corporations or churches, but in the secrets of a solitary heart", as Dowden puts the essential point in his fine book *Puritan and Anglican* (p. 234). This deep spiritual loneliness of the individual applied as well to the Jansenists of Port Royal, who were also predestinationists.

17. "Contra qui huiusmodi cœtum [namely a Church which maintains a pure doctrine, sacraments, and Church discipline] contemnunt . . . salutis suæ certi esse non possunt; et qui in illo contemtu perseverat electus non est." Olevian, *De subst. fœd.*, p. 222.

18. "It is said that God sent His Son to save the human race, but that was not His purpose, He only wished to help a few out of their degradation—I say unto you that God died only for the elect" (sermon held in 1609 at Broek, near Rogge, Wtenbogaert, II, p. 9. Compare Nuyens, *op. cit.*, II, p. 232). The explanation of the rôle of Christ is also confused in *Hanserd Knolly's Confession.* It is everywhere assumed that God did not need His instrumentality.

19. *Entzauberung der Welt.* On this process see the other essays in my *Wirtschaftsethik der Weltreligionen*. The peculiar position of the

old Hebrew ethic, as compared with the closely related ethics of Egypt and Babylon, and its development after the time of the prophets, rested, as is shown there, entirely on this fundamental fact, the rejection of sacramental magic as a road to salvation. (This process is for Weber one of the most important aspects of the broader process of rationalization, in which he sums up his philosophy of history. See various parts of *Wirtschaft und Gesellschaft* and H. Grab, *Der Begriff des Rationalen bei Max Weber.*—TRANSLATOR'S NOTE.)

20. Similarly the most consistent doctrine held that baptism was required by positive ordinance, but was not necessary to salvation. For that reason the strictly Puritan Scotch and English Independents were able to maintain the principle that children of obvious reprobates should not be baptized (for instance, children of drunkards). An adult who desired to be baptized, but was not yet ripe for the communion, the Synod of Edam of 1586 (Art. 32, 1) recommended should be baptized only if his conduct were blameless, and he should have placed his desires *sonder superstitie.*

21. This negative attitude toward all sensuous culture is, as Dowden, *op. cit.,* shows, a very fundamental element of Puritanism.

22. The expression individualism includes the most heterogeneous things imaginable. What is here understood by it will, I hope, be clear from the following discussion. In another sense of the word, Lutheranism has been called individualistic, because it does not attempt any ascetic regulation of life. In yet another quite different sense the word is used, for example, by Dietrich Schafer when in his study, "Zur Beurteilung des Wormser Konkordats", *Abh. d. Berl. Akad.* (1905), he calls the Middle Ages the era of pronounced individuality because, for the events relevant for the historian, irrational factors then had a significance which they do not possess to-day. He is right, but so perhaps are also those whom he attacks in his remarks, for they mean something quite different, when they speak of individuality and individualism. Jacob Burchhardt's brilliant ideas are to-day at least partly out of date, and a thorough analysis of these concepts in historical terms would at the present time be highly valuable to science. Quite the opposite is, of course, true when the play impulse causes certain historians to define the concept in such a way as to enable them to use it as a label for any epoch of history they please.

23. And in a similar, though naturally less sharp, contrast to the later Catholic doctrine. The deep pessimism of Pascal, which also rests on the doctrine of predestination, is, on the other hand, of Jansenist origin, and the resulting individualism of renunciation by no means agrees with the official Catholic position. See the study by Honigsheim on the French Jansenists, referred to in Chap. III, note 10.

24. The same holds for the Jansenists.

25. Bailey, *Praxis pietatis* (German edition, Leipzig, 1724), p. 187. Also P. J. Spener in his *Theologische Bedenken* (according to third

edition, Halle, 1712) adopts a similar standpoint. A friend seldom gives advice for the glory of God, but generally for mundane (though not necessarily egotistical) reasons. "He [the knowing man] is blind in no man's cause, but best sighted in his own. He confines himself to the circle of his own affairs and thrusts not his fingers into needless fires. He sees the falseness of it [the world] and therefore learns to trust himself ever, others so far as not to be damaged by their disappointment" is the philosophy of Thomas Adarns (*Works of the Puritan Divines,* p. 11). Bailey (*Praxis pietatis,* p. 176) further recommends every morning before going out among people to imagine oneself going into a wild forest full of dangers, and to pray God for the "cloak of foresight and righteousness". This feeling is characteristic of all the ascetic denominations without exception, and in the case of many Pietists led directly to a sort of hermit's life within the world. Even Spangenberg in the (Moravian) *Idea fides fratum,* p. 382, calls attention with emphasis to Jer. xvii. 5: "Cursed is the man who trusteth in man." To grasp the peculiar misanthropy of this attitude, note also Hoornbeek's remarks (*Theologia practica,* I, p. 882) on the duty to love one's enemy: "Denique hoc magis nos ulcisimur, quo proximum, inultum nobis, tradimus ultori Deo—Quo quis plus se ulscitur, eo minus id pro ipso agit Deus." It is the same transfer of vengeance that is found in the parts of the Old Testament written after the exile; a subtle intensification and refinement of the spirit of revenge compared to the older "eye for an eye". On brotherly love, see below, note 34.

26. Of course the confessional did not have only that effect. The explanations, for instance, of Muthmann, *Z. f. Rel. Psych.,* I, Heft 2, p. 65, are too simple for such a highly complex psychological problem as the confessional.

27. This is a fact which is of especial importance for the interpretation of the psychological basis of Calvinistic social organizations. They all rest on spiritually individualistic, rational motives. The individual never enters emotionally into them. The glory of God and one's own salvation always remain above the threshold of consciousness. This accounts for certain characteristic features of the social organization of peoples with a Puritan past even to-day.

28. The fundamentally anti-authoritarian tendency of the doctrine, which at bottom undermined every responsibility for ethical conduct or spiritual salvation on the part of Church or State as useless, led again and again to its proscription, as, for instance, by the States-General of the Netherlands. The result was always the formation of conventicles (as after 1614).

29. On Bunyan compare the biography of Froude in the *English Men of Letters* series, also Macaulay's superficial sketch *(Miscel. Works,* II, p. 227). Bunyan was indifferent to the denominational distinctions within Calvinism, but was himself a strict Calvinistic Baptist.

The Protestant Ethic and the Spirit of Capitalism

30. It is tempting to refer to the undoubted importance for the social character of Reformed Christianity of the necessity for salvation, following from the Calvinistic idea of "incorporation into the body of Christ" (Calvin, *Instit. Christ,* III, II, 10), of reception into a community conforming to the divine prescriptions. From our point of view, however, the centre of the problem is somewhat different. That doctrinal tenet could have been developed in a Church of purely institutional character *(anstaltmässig),* and, as is well known, this did happen. But in itself it did not possess the psychological force to awaken the initiative to form such communities nor to imbue them with the power which Calvinism possessed. Its tendency to form a community worked itself out very largely in the world outside the Church organizations ordained by God. Here the belief that the Christian proved (see below) his state of grace by action *in majorem Dei gloriam* was decisive, and the sharp condemnation of idolatry of the flesh and of all dependence on personal relations to other men was bound unperceived to direct this energy into the field of objective (impersonal) activity. The Christian who took the proof of his state of grace seriously acted in the service of God's ends, and these could only be impersonal. Every purely emotional, that is not rationally motivated, personal relation of man to man easily fell in the Puritan, as in every ascetic ethic, under the suspicion of idolatry of the flesh. In addition to what has already been said, this is clearly enough shown for the case of friendship by the following warning: "It is an irrational act and not fit for a rational creature to love any one farther than reason will allow us. . . . It very often taketh up men's minds so as to hinder their love of God" (Baxter, *Christian Directory,* IV, p. 253). We shall meet such arguments again and again.

The Calvinist was fascinated by the idea that God in creating the world, including the order of society, must have willed things to be objectively purposeful as a means of adding to His glory; not the flesh for its own sake, but the organization of the things of the flesh under His will. The active energies of the elect, liberated by the doctrine of predestination, thus flowed into the struggle to rationalize the world. Especially the idea that the public welfare, or as Baxter *(Christian Directory,* IV, p. 262) puts it, quite in the sense of later liberal rationalism, "The good of the many" (with a somewhat forced reference to Rom. ix. 3), was to be preferred to any personal or private good of the individual, followed, although not in itself new, for Puritanism from the repudiation of idolatry of the flesh. The traditional American objection to performing personal service is probably connected, besides the other important causes resulting from democratic feelings, at least indirectly with that tradition. Similarly, the relative immunity of formerly Puritan peoples to C'sarism, and, in general, the subjectively free attitude of the English to their great statesmen as compared with many things which we

224

have experienced since 1878 in Germany positively and negatively. On the one hand, there is a greater willingness to give the great man his due, but, on the other, a repudiation of an hysterical idolization of him and of the naïve idea that political obedience could be due anyone from thankfulness. On the sinfulness of the belief in authority, which is only permissible in the form of an impersonal authority, the Scriptures, as well as of an excessive devotion to even the most holy and virtuous of men, since that might interfere with obedience to God, see Baxter, *Christian Directory* (second edition, 1678), I, p. 56. The political consequences of the renunciation of idolatry of the flesh and the principle which was first applied only to the Church but later to life in general, that God alone should rule, do not belong in this investigation.

31. Of the relation between dogmatic and practical psychological consequence we shall often have to speak. That the two are not identical it is hardly necessary to remark.

32. Social, used of course without any of the implications attached to the modern sense of the word, meaning simply activity within the Church, politics, or any other social organization.

33. "Good works performed for any other purpose than the glory of God are sinful" *(Hanserd Knolly's Confession,* chap. xvi).

34. What such an impersonality of brotherly love, resulting from the orientation of life solely to God's will, means in the field of religious group life itself may be well illustrated by the attitude of the China Inland Mission and the International Missionaries Alliance (see Warneck, *Gesch. d. prot. Missionären, pp.* 99, 111). At tremendous expense an army of missionaries was fitted out, for instance one thousand for China alone, in order by itinerant preaching to offer the Gospel to all the heathen in a strictly literal sense, since Christ had commanded it and made His second coming dependent on it. Whether these heathen should be converted to Christianity and thus attain salvation, even whether they could understand the language in which the missionary preached, was a matter of small importance and could be left to God, Who alone could control such things. According to Hudson Taylor (see Warneck, *op. cit.),* China has about fifty million families; one thousand missionaries could each reach fifty families per day (!) or the Gospel could be presented to all the Chinese in less than three years. It is precisely the same manner in which, for instance, Calvinism carried out its Church discipline. The end was not the salvation of those subject to it, which was the affair of God alone (in practice their own) and could not be in any way influenced by the means at the disposal of the Church, but simply the increase of God's glory. Calvinism as such is not responsible for those feats of missionary zeal, since they rest on an interdenominational basis. Calvin himself denied the duty of sending missions to the heathen since a further expansion of the

Church is *unius Dei opus*. Nevertheless, they obviously originate in the ideas, running through the whole Puritan ethic, according to which the duty to love one's neighbour is satisfied by fulfilling God's commandments to increase His glory. The neighbour thereby receives all that is due him, and anything further is God's affair. Humanity in relation to one's neighbour has, so to speak, died out. That is indicated by the most various circumstances.

Thus, to mention a remnant of that atmosphere, in the field of charity of the Reformed Church, which in certain respects is justly famous, the Amsterdam orphans, with (in the twentieth century!) their coats and trousers divided vertically into a black and a red, or a red and a green half, a sort of fool's costume, and brought in parade formation to church, formed, for the feelings of the past, a highly uplifting spectacle. It served the glory of God precisely to the extent that all personal and human feelings were necessarily insulted by it. And so, as we shall see later, even in all the details of private life. Naturally all that signified only a tendency and we shall later ourselves have to make certain qualifications. But as one very important tendency of this ascetic faith, it was necessary to point it out here.

35. In all these respects the ethic of Port Royal, although predestinationist, takes quite a different standpoint on account of its mystical and otherworldly orientation, which is in so far Catholic (see Honigsheim, *op. cit.*).

36. Hundeshagen (*Beitr. z. Kirchenverfassungsgesch. u. Kirchenpolitik,* 1864, I, p. 37) takes the view, since often repeated, that predestination was a dogma of the theologians, not a popular doctrine. But that is only true if the people is identified with the mass of the uneducated lower classes. Even then it has only limited validity. Köhler (*op. cit.*) found that in the forties of the nineteenth century just those masses (meaning the *petite bourgeoisie* of Holland) were thoroughly imbued with predestination. Anyone who denied the double decree was to them a heretic and a condemned soul. He himself was asked about the time of his rebirth (in the sense of predestination). Da Costa and the separation of de Kock were greatly influenced by it. Not only Cromwell, in whose case Zeller (*Das Theologische System Zwinglis,* p. 17) has already shown the effects of the dogma most effectively, but also his army knew very well what it was about. Moreover, the canons of the synods of Dordrecht and Westminster were national questions of the first importance. Cromwell's tryers and ejectors admitted only believers in predestination, and Baxter (*Life,* I, p. 72), although he was otherwise its opponent, considers its effect on the quality of the clergy to be important. That the Reformed Pietists, the members of the English and Dutch conventicles, should not have understood the doctrine is quite impossible. It was precisely what drove them together to seek the *certitudo salutis*.

Notes

What significance the doctrine of predestination does or does not have when it remains a dogma of the theologians is shown by perfectly orthodox Catholicism, to which it was by no means strange as an esoteric doctrine under various forms. What is important is that the idea of the individual's obligation to consider himself of the elect and prove it to himself was always denied. Compare for the Catholic doctrine, for instance, A. Van Wyck, *Tract. de præstinatione* (Cologne, 1708). To what extent Pascal's doctrine of predestination was correct, we cannot inquire here.

Hundeshagen, who dislikes the doctrine, evidently gets his impressions primarily from German sources. His antipathy is based on the purely deductive opinion that it necessarily leads to moral fatalism and antinomianism. This opinion has already been refuted by Zeller, *op. cit.* That such a result was possible cannot, of course, be denied. Both Melanchthon and Wesley speak of it. But it is characteristic that in both cases it is combined with an emotional religion of faith. For them, lacking the rational idea of proof, this consequence was in fact not unnatural.

The same consequences appeared in Islam. But why? Because the Mohammedan idea was that of predetermination, not predestination, and was applied to fate in this world, not in the next. In consequence the most important thing, the proof of the believer in predestination, played no part in Islam. Thus only the fearlessness of the warrior (as in the case of *moira*) could result, but there were no consequences for rationalization of life; there was no religious sanction for them. See the (Heidelberg) theological dissertation of F. Ullrich, *Die Vorherbestimmungslehre im Islam u. Christenheit,* 1900. The modifications of the doctrine which came in practice, for instance Baxter, did not disturb it in essence so long as the idea that the election of God, and its proof, fell upon the concrete individual, was not shaken. Finally, and above all, all the great men of Puritanism (in the broadest sense) took their departure from this doctrine, whose terrible seriousness deeply influenced their youthful development. Milton like, in declining order it is true, Baxter, and, still later, the free-thinker Franklin. Their later emancipation from its strict interpretation is directly parallel to the development which the religious movement as a whole underwent in the same direction. And all the great religious revivals, at least in Holland, and most of those in England, took it up again.

37. As is true in such a striking way of the basic atmosphere of Bunyan's *Pilgrim's Progress.*

38. This question meant less to the later Lutheran, even apart from the doctrine of predestination, than to the Calvinist. Not because he was less interested in the salvation of his soul, but because, in the form which the Lutheran Church had taken, its character as an institution for salvation (*Heilsanstalt*) came to the fore. The individual

thus felt himself to be an object of its care and dependent on it. The problem was first raised within Lutheranism characteristically enough through the Pietist movement. The question of *certitudo salutis itself* has, however, for every non-sacramental religion of salvation, whether Buddhism, Jainism, or anything else, been absolutely fundamental; that must not be forgotten. It has been the origin of all psychological drives of a purely religious character.

39. Thus expressly in the letter to Bucer, *Corp. Ref.* 29, p. 883 f. Compare with that again Scheibe, *op. cit.,* p. 30.

40. The *Westminster Confession* (XVIII, p. 2) also assures the elect of indubitable certainty of grace, although with all our activity we remain useless servants and the struggle against evil lasts one's whole life long. But even the chosen one often has to struggle long and hard to attain the *certitudo* which the consciousness of having done his duty gives him and of which a true believer will never entirely be deprived.

41. The orthodox Calvinistic doctrine referred to faith and the consciousness of community with God in the sacraments, and mentioned the "other fruits of the Spirit" only incidentally. See the passages in Heppe, *op. cit.,* p. 425. Calvin himself most emphatically denied that works were indications of favour before God, although he, like the Lutherans, considered them the fruits of belief (*Instit. Christ,* III, 2, 37, 38). The actual evolution to the proof of faith through works, which is characteristic of asceticism, is parallel to a gradual modification of the doctrines of Calvin. As with Luther, the true Church was first marked off primarily by purity of doctrine and sacraments, but later the *disciplinia* came to be placed on an equal footing with the other two. This evolution may be followed in the passages given by Heppe, *op. cit.,* pp. 194–5, as well as in the manner in which Church members were acquired in the Netherlands by the end of the sixteenth century (express subjection by agreement to Church discipline as the principal prerequisite).

42. For example, Olevian, *De substantia fœderis gratuiti inter Deum et electos (1585),* p. 257; Heidegger, *Corpus Theologiœ,* XXIV, p. 87; and other passages in Heppe, *Dogmatik der ev. ref. Kirche* (1861), p. 425.

43. On this point see the remarks of Schneckenburger, *op. cit.,* p. 48.

44. Thus, for example, in Baxter the distinction between mortal and venial sin reappears in a truly Catholic sense. The former is a sign of the lack of grace which can only be attained by the conversion of one's whole life. The latter is not incompatible with grace.

45. As held in many different shades by Baxter, Bailey, Sedgwick, Hoornbeek. Further see examples given by Schneckenburger, *op. cit.,* p. 262.

46. The conception of the state of grace as a sort of social estate (somewhat like that of the ascetics of the early Church) is very common.

Notes

See for instance Schortinghuis, *Het innige Christendom* (1740 proscribed by the States-General)!

47. Thus, as we shall see later, in countless passages, especially the conclusion, of Baxter's *Christian Directory*. This recommendation of worldly activity as a means of overcoming one's own feeling of moral inferiority is reminiscent of Pascal's psychological interpretation of the impulse of acquisition and ascetic activity as means to deceive oneself about one's own moral worthlessness. For him the belief in predestination and the conviction of the original sinfulness of everything pertaining to the flesh resulted only in renunciation of the world and the recommendation of contemplation as the sole means of lightening the burden of sin and attaining certainty of salvation. Of the orthodox Catholic and the Jansenist versions of the idea of calling an acute analysis has been made by Dr. Paul Honigsheim in the dissertation cited above (part of a larger study, which it is hoped will be continued). The Jansenists lacked every trace of a connection between certainty of salvation and worldly activity. Their concept of calling has, even more strongly than the Lutheran or even the orthodox Catholic, the sense of acceptance of the situation in life in which one finds oneself, sanctioned not only, as in Catholicism by the social order, but also by the voice of one's own conscience (Honigsheim, *op. cit.*, pp. 139 ff.).

48. The very lucidly written sketch of Lobstein in the *Festgabe für H. Holtzmann*, which starts from his view-point, may also be compared with the following. It has been criticized for too sharp an emphasis on the *certitudo salutis*. But just at this point Calvin's theology must be distinguished from Calvinism, the theological system from the needs of religious practice. All the religious movements which have affected large masses have started from the question, "How can I become certain of my salvation?" As we have said, it not only plays a central part in this case but in the history of all religions, even in India. And could it well be otherwise?

49. Of course it cannot be denied that the full development of this conception did not take place until late Lutheran times (Prætorius, Nicolai, Meisner). It is present, however, even in Johannes Gerhard, quite in the sense meant here. Hence Ritschl in Book IV of his *Geschichte des Pietismus* (II, pp. 3 ff.) interprets the introduction of this concept into Lutheranism as a Renaissance or an adoption of Catholic elements. He does not deny (p. 10) that the problem of individual salvation was the same for Luther as for the Catholic Mystics, but he believes that the solution was precisely opposite in the two cases. I can, of course, have no competent opinion of my own. That the atmosphere of *Die Freiheit eines Christenmenschen* is different, on the one hand, from the sweet flirtation with the *liebem Jesulein* of the later writers, and on the other from Tauler's religious feeling, is naturally obvious to anyone. Similarly the retention of

the mystic-magical element in Luther's doctrines of the Communion certainly has different religious motives from the Bernhardine piety, the "Song of Songs feeling" to which Ritschl again and again returns as the source of the bridal relations with Christ. But might not, among other things, that doctrine of the Communion have favoured the revival of mystical religious emotions? Further, it is by no means accurate to say that (p. 11, *op. cit.*) the freedom of the mystic consisted entirely in isolation from the world. Especially Tauler has, in passages which from the point of view of the psychology of religion are very interesting, maintained that the order which is thereby brought into thoughts concerning worldly activities is one practical result of the nocturnal contemplation which he recommends, for instance, in case of insomnia. "Only thereby [the mystical union with God at night before going to sleep] is reason clarified and the brain strengthened, and man is the whole day the more peacefully and divinely guided by virtue of the inner discipline of having truly united himself with God: then all his works shall be set in order. And thus when a man has forewarned (= prepared) himself of his work, and has placed his trust in virtue; then if he comes into the world, his works shall be virtuous and divine" (*Predigten,* fol. 318). Thus we see, and we shall return to the point, that mystic contemplation and a rational attitude toward the calling are not in themselves mutually contradictory. The opposite is only true when the religion takes on a directly hysterical character, which has not been the case with all mystics nor even all Pietists.

50. On this see the introduction to the following essays on the *Wirtschaftsethik der Weltreligionen* (not included in this translation: German in *Gesammelte Aufsätze zur Religionssoziologie.*—TRANSLATOR'S NOTE).

51. In this assumption Calvinism has a point of contact with official Catholicism. But for the Catholics there resulted the necessity of the sacrament of repentance; for the Reformed Church that of practical proof through activity in the world.

52. See, for instance, Beza *(De prædestinat doct. ex præeclect.* in Rom 9a, Raph. Eglino exc. 1584), p. 133: "Sicut ex operibus vere bonis ad sanctificationis donum, a sanctificatione ad fidem—ascendimus: ita ex certis illis effectis non quamvis vocationem, sed efficacem illam et ex hac vocatione electionem et ex electione donum prædestinationis in Christo tam firmam quam immotus est Dei thronus certissima connexione effectorum et causarum colligimus. . . ." Only with regard to the signs of damnation is it necessary to be careful, since it is a matter of final judgment. On this point the Puritans first differed. See further the thorough discussion of Schneckenburger, *op. cit.,* who to be sure only cites a limited category of literature. In the whole Puritan literature this aspect comes out. "It will not be said, did you believe?—but: were you Doers or Talkers only?" says Bunyan. According to Baxter *(The Saints' Everlasting Rest,* chap. xii),

Notes

who teaches the mildest form of predestination, faith means subjection to Christ in heart and in deed. "Do what you are able first, and then complain of God for denying you grace if you have cause" was his answer to the objection that the will was not free and God alone was able to insure salvation (*Works of the Puritan Divines*, IV, p.155). The investigation of Fuller (the Church historian) was limited to the one question of practical proof and the indications of his state of grace in his conduct. The same with Howe in the passage referred to elsewhere. Any examination of the *Works of the Puritan Divines* gives ample proofs.

Not seldom the conversion to Puritanism was due to Catholic ascetic writings, thus, with Baxter, a Jesuit tract. These conceptions were not wholly new compared with Calvin's own doctrine (*Instit. Christ,* chap. 1, original edition of 1536, pp. 97, 113). Only for Calvin himself the certainty of salvation could not be attained in this manner (p. 147). Generally one referred to 1 John iii. 5 and similar passages. The demand for *fides efficax* is not—to anticipate—limited to the Calvinists. Baptist confessions of faith deal, in the article on predestination, similarly with the fruits of faith ("and that its—of regeneration—proper evidence appears in the holy fruits of repentance and faith and newness of life"—Article 7 of the Confession printed in *the Baptist Church Manual* by J. N. Brown, D.D., Philadelphia,. *Am. Bapt. Pub. Soc.).* In the same way the tract (under Mennonite influence), *Oliif-Tacxken,* which the Harlem Synod adopted in 1649, begins on page 1 with the question of how the children of God are to be known, and answers (p. 10): "Nu al is't dat dasdanigh vruchtbare ghelove alleene zii het seker fondamentale kennteeken—om de conscientien der gelovigen in het nieuwe verbondt der genade Gods te versekeren."

53. Of the significance of this for the material content of social ethics some hint has been given above. Here we are interested not in the content, but in the motives of moral action.

54. How this idea must have promoted the penetration of Puritanism with the Old Testament Hebrew spirit is evident.

55. Thus the Savoy Declaration says of the members of the *ecclesia pura* that they are "saints by effectual calling, visibly manifested by their profession and walking".

56. "A Principle of Goodness" Charnock in the *Works of the Puritan Divines,* p. 175.

57. Conversion is, as Sedgwick puts it, an "exact copy of the decree of predestination". And whoever is chosen is also called to obedience and made capable of it, teaches Bailey. Only those whom God calls to His faith (which is expressed in their conduct) are true believers, not merely temporary believers, according to the (Baptist) Confession of Hanserd Knolly.

58. Compare, for instance, the conclusion to Baxter's *Christian Directory.*

The Protestant Ethic and the Spirit of Capitalism

59. Thus, for instance, Charnock, *Self-Examination,* p. 183, in refutation of the Catholic doctrine of *dubitatio.*

60. This argument recurs again and again in Hoornbeek, *Theologia practica.* For instance, I, p. 160; II, pp. 70, 72, 182.

61. For instance, the *Conf. Helvet,* 16, says "et improprie his [the works] *salus adtribuitur".*

62. With all the above compare Schneckenburger, pp. 80 ff.

63. Augustine is supposed to have said "si non es prædestinatus, fac ut præstineris".

64. One is reminded of a saying of Goethe with essentially the same meaning: "How can a man know himself? Never by observation, but through action. Try to do your duty and you will know what is in you. And what is your duty? Your daily task."

65. For though Calvin himself held that saintliness must appear on the surface *(Instit. Christ,* IV, pp. 1, 2, 7, 9), the dividing-line between saints and sinners must ever remain hidden from human knowledge. We must believe that where God's pure word is alive in a Church, organized and administered according to His law, some of the elect, even though we do not know them, are present.

66. The Calvinistic faith is one of the many examples in the history of religions of the relation between the logical and the psychological consequences for the practical religious attitude to be derived from certain religious ideas. Fatalism is, of course, the only logical consequence of predestination. But on account of the idea of proof the psychological result was precisely the opposite. For essentially similar reasons the followers of Nietzsche claim a positive ethical significance for the idea of eternal recurrence. This case, however, is concerned with responsibility for a future life which is connected with the active individual by no conscious thread of continuity, while for the Puritan it was *tua res agitur.* Even Hoornbeek *(Theologia pratica,* I, p. 159) analyses the relation between predestination and action well in the language of the times. The *electi* are, on account of their election, proof against fatalism because in their rejection of it they prove themselves "quos ipsa electio sollicitos reddit et diligentes officiorum". The practical interests cut off the fatalistic consequences of logic (which, however, in spite of everything occasionally did break through).

But, on the other hand, the content of ideas of a religion is, as Calvinism shows, far more important than William James *(Varieties of Religious Experience,* 1902, p. 444 f) is inclined to admit. The significance of the rational element in religious metaphysics is shown in classical form by the tremendous influence which especially the logical structure of the Calvinistic concept of God exercised on life. If the God of the Puritans has influenced history as hardly another before or since, it is principally due to the attributes which the power of thought had given him. James's pragmatic valuation of the significance of religious ideas according to their influence on life is inci-

232

dentally a true child of the world of ideas of the Puritan home of that eminent scholar. The religious experience as such is of course irrational, like every experience. In its highest, mystical form it is even the experience κατ' ἐξοχὴν, and, as James has well shown, is distinguished by its absolute incommunicability. It has a specific character and appears as knowledge, but cannot be adequately reproduced by means of our lingual and conceptual apparatus. It is further true that every religious experience loses some of its content in the attempt of rational formulation, the further the conceptual formulation goes, the more so. That is the reason for many of the tragic conflicts of all rational theology, as the Baptist sects of the seventeenth century already knew. But that irrational element, which is by no means peculiar to religious experience, but applies (in different senses and to different degrees) to every experience, does not prevent its being of the greatest practical importance, of what particular type the system of ideas is, that captures and moulds the immediate experience of religion in its own way. For from this source develop, in times of great influence of the Church on life and of strong interest in dogmatic considerations within it, most of those differences between the various religions in their ethical consequences which are of such great practical importance. How unbelievably intense, measured by present standards, the dogmatic interests even of the layman were, everyone knows who is familiar with the historical sources. We can find a parallel to-day only in the at bottom equally superstitious belief of the modern proletariat in what can be accomplished and proved by science.

67. Baxter, *The Saints' Everlasting Rest*, I, p. 6, answers to the question: "Whether to make salvation our end be not mercenary or legal? It is properly mercenary when we expect it as wages for work done. . . . Otherwise it is only such a mercenarism as Christ commandeth . . . and if seeking Christ be mercenary, I desire to be so mercenary." Nevertheless, many Calvinists who are considered orthodox do not escape falling into a very crass sort of mercenariness. According to Bailey, *Praxis pietatis*, p. 262, alms are a means of escaping temporal punishment. Other theologians urged the damned to perform good works, since their damnation might thereby become somewhat more bearable, but the elect because God will then not only love them without cause but *ob causam,* which shall certainly sometime have its reward. The apologists have also made certain small concessions concerning the significance of good works for the degree of salvation (Schneckenburger, *op. cit.,* p. 101).

68. Here also it is absolutely necessary, in order to bring out the characteristic differences, to speak in terms of ideal types, thus in a certain sense doing violence to historical reality. But without this a clear formulation would be quite impossible considering the complexity of the material. In how far the differences which we here draw as sharply as possible were merely relative, would have to be discussed separately. It is, of course, true that the official Catholic

doctrine, even in the Middle Ages, itself set up the ideal of a systematic sanctification of life as a whole. But it is just as certain (1) that the normal practice of the Church, directly on account of its most effective means of discipline, the confession, promoted the unsystematic way of life discussed in the text, and further (2) that the fundamentally rigorous and cold atmosphere in which he lived and the absolute isolation of the Calvinist were utterly foreign to mediæval lay Catholicism.

69. The absolutely fundamental importance of this factor will, as has already once been pointed out, gradually become clear in the essays on the *Wirtschaftsethik der Weltreligionen.*

70. And to a certain extent also to the Lutheran. Luther did not wish to eliminate this last vestige of sacramental magic.

71. Compare, for instance, Sedgwick, *Buss- und Gnadenlehre* (German by Roscher, 1689). The repentant man has a fast rule to which he holds himself exactly, ordering thereby his whole life and conduct (p. 596). He lives according to the law, shrewdly, wakefully, and carefully (p. 596). Only a permanent change in the whole man can, since it is a result of predestination, cause this (p. 852). True repentance is always expressed in conduct (p. 361). The difference between only morally good work and *opera spiritualia* lies, as Hoornbeek (*op. cit.,* I, IX, chap. ii) explains, in the fact that the latter are the results of a regenerate life (*op. cit.,* I, p. 160). A continuous progress in them is discernible which can only be achieved by the supernatural influence of God's grace (p. 150). Salvation results from the transformation of the whole man through the grace of God (p. 190 f.). These ideas are common to all Protestantism, and are of course found in the highest ideals of Catholicism as well. But their consequences could only appear in the Puritan movements of worldly asceticism, and above all only in those cases did they have adequate psychological sanctions.

72. The latter name is, especially in Holland, derived from those who modelled their lives precisely on the example of the Bible (thus with Voet). Moreover, the name Methodists occurs occasionally among the Puritans in the seventeenth century.

73. For, as the Puritan preachers emphasize (for instance Bunyan in the *Pharisee and the Publican, Works of the Puritan Divines,* p. 126), every single sin would destroy everything which might have been accumulated in the way of merit by good works in a lifetime, if, which is unthinkable, man were alone able to accomplish anything which God should necessarily recognize as meritorious, or even could live in perfection for any length of time. Thus Puritanism did not think as did Catholicism in terms of a sort of account with calculation of the balance, a simile which was common even in antiquity, but of the definite alternative of grace or damnation held for a life as a whole. For suggestions of the bank account idea see note 102 below.

Notes

74. Therein lies the distinction from the mere Legality and Civility which Bunyan has living as associates of Mr. Worldly-Wiseman in the City called Morality.

75. Charnock, *Self-Examination* (*Works of the Puritan Divines,* p. 172): "Reflection and knowledge of self is a prerogative of a rational nature." Also the footnote: "Cogito, ergo sum, is the first principle of the new philosophy."

76. This is not yet the place to discuss the relationship of the theology of Duns Scotus to certain ideas of ascetic Protestantism. It never gained official recognition, but was at best tolerated and at times proscribed. The later specific repugnance of the Pietists to Aristotelean philosophy was shared by Luther, in a somewhat different sense, and also by Calvin in conscious antagonism to Catholicism (cf. *Instit. Christ,* II, chap. xii, p. 4; IV, chap. xvii, p. 24). The "primacy of the will" as Kahl has put it, is common to all these movements.

77. Thus, for instance, the article on "Asceticism" in the Catholic *Church Lexicon* defines its meaning entirely in harmony with its highest historical manifestations. Similarly Seeberg in the *Realenzyklopädie für protestantische Theologie und Kirche.* For the purpose of this study we must be allowed to use the concept as we have done. That it can be defined in other ways, more broadly as well as more narrowly, and is generally so defined, I am well aware.

78. In Hudibras (*1st Song,* 18, 19) the Puritans are compared with the bare-foot Franciscans. A report of the Genoese Ambassador, Fieschi, calls Cromwell's army an assembly of monks.

79. In view of the close relationship between otherworldly monastic asceticism and active worldly asceticism, which I here expressly maintain, I am surprised to find Brentano (*op. cit.,* p. 134 and elsewhere) citing the ascetic labour of the monks and its recommendation against me. His whole "Exkurs" against me culminates in that. But that continuity is, as anyone can see, a fundamental postulate of my whole thesis: the Reformation took rational Christian asceticism and its methodical habits out of the monasteries and placed them in the service of active life in the world. Compare the following discussion, which has not been altered.

80. So in the many reports of the trials of Puritan heretics cited in Neal's *History of the Puritans* and Crosby's *English Baptists.*

81. Sanford, *op. cit.* (and both before and after him many others), has found the origin of the ideal of reserve in Puritanism. Compare on that ideal also the remarks of James Bryce on the American college in Vol. II of his *American Commonwealth.* The ascetic principle of self-control also made Puritanism one of the fathers of modern military discipline. (On Maurice of Orange as a founder of modern army organization, see Roloff, *Preuss. Jahrb.,* 1903, III, p. 255.) Cromwell's Ironsides, with cocked pistols in their hands, and approaching the enemy at a brisk trot without shooting, were not the superiors of

the Cavaliers by virtue of their fierce passion, but, on the contrary, through their cool self-control, which enabled their leaders always to keep them well in hand. The knightly storm-attack of the Cavaliers, on the other hand, always resulted in dissolving their troops into atoms. See Firth, *Cromwell's Army.*

82. See especially Windelband, *Ueber Willensfreiheit,* pp. 77 ff.

83. Only not so unmixed. Contemplation, sometimes combined with emotionalism, is often combined with these rational elements. But again contemplation itself is methodically regulated.

84. According to Richard Baxter everything is sinful which is contrary to the reason given by God as a norm of action. Not only passions which have a sinful content, but all feelings which are senseless and intemperate as such. They destroy the countenance and, as things of the flesh, prevent us from rationally directing all action and feeling to God, and thus insult Him. Compare what is said of the sinfulness of anger (*Christian Directory,* second edition, 1698, p. 285. Tauler is cited on p. 287). On the sinfulness of anxiety, *Ebenda,* I, p. 287. That it is idolatry if our appetite is made the "rule or measure of eating" is maintained very emphatically (*op. cit.,* I, pp. 310, 316, and elsewhere). In such discussions reference is made everywhere to the Proverbs and also to Plutarch's *De tranquilitate Animi,* and not seldom to ascetic writings of the Middle Ages: St. Bernard, Bonaventura, and others. The contrast to "who does not love wine, women, and song . . ." could hardly be more sharply drawn than by the extension of the idea of idolatry to all sensuous pleasures, so far as they are not justified by hygienic considerations, in which case they (like sport within these limits, but also other recreations) are permissible. See below (Chapter V) for further discussion. Please note that the sources referred to here and elsewhere are neither dogmatic nor edifying works, but grew out of practical ministry, and thus give a good picture of the direction which its influence took.

85. I should regret it if any evaluation of one or the other form of religion should be read into this discussion. We are not concerned with that here. It is only a question of the influence of certain things which, from a purely religious point of view, are perhaps incidental, but important for practical conduct.

86. On this, see especially the article "Moralisten, englische" by E. Troeltsch, in the *Realenzyklopädie für protestantische Theologie und Kirche,* third edition.

87. How much influence quite definite religious ideas and situations, which seem to be historical accidents, have had is shown unusually clearly by the fact that in the circles of Pietism of a Reformed origin the lack of monasteries was occasionally directly regretted, and that the communistic experiments of Labadie and others were simply a substitute for monastic life.

88. As early even as several confessions of the time of the Reformation. Even Ritschl (*Pietismus,* I, p. 258 f.) does not deny, although he looks upon the later development as a deterioration of the ideas of the Reformation, that, for instance, in *Conf. Gall.* 25, 26, *Conf. Belg.* 29, *Conf. Helv.* post, 17, the true Reformed Church was defined by definitely empirical attributes, and that to this true Church believers were not accounted without the attribute of moral activity. (See above, note 42.)

89. "Bless God that we are not of the many" (Thomas Adams, *Works of the Puritan Divines,* p. 138).

90. The idea of the birthright, so important in history, thus received an important confirmation in England. "The firstborn which are written in heaven. . . . As the firstborn is not to be defeated in his inheritance, and the enrolled names are never to be obliterated, so certainly they shall inherit eternal life" (Thomas Adams, *Works of the Puritan Divines,* p. xiv).

91. The Lutheran emphasis on penitent grief is foreign to the spirit of ascetic Calvinism, not in theory, but definitely in practice. For it is of no ethical value to the Calvinist; it does not help the damned, while for those certain of their election, their own sin, so far as they admit it to themselves, is a symptom of backwardness in development. Instead of repenting of it they hate it and attempt to overcome it by activity for the glory of God. Compare the explanation of Howe (Cromwell's chaplain 1656–58) in *Of Men's Enmity against God and of Reconciliation between God and Man* (*Works of English Puritan Divines,* p. 237): "The carnal mind is enmity against God. It is the mind, therefore, not as speculative merely, but as practical and active that must be renewed" and, p. 246: "Reconciliation . . . must begin in (1) a deep conviction . . . of your former enmity. . . . I have been alienated from God. . . . (2) (p. 251) a clear and lively apprehension of the monstrous iniquity and wickedness thereof." The hatred here is that of sin, not of the sinner. But as early as the famous letter of the Duchess Renata d'Este (Leonore's mother) to Calvin, in which she speaks of the hatred which she would feel toward her father and husband if she became convinced they belonged to the damned, is shown the transfer to the person. At the same time it is an example of what was said above [pp. 104–6] of how the individual became loosed from the ties resting on his natural feelings, for which the doctrine of predestination was responsible.

92. "None but those who give evidence of being regenerate or holy persons ought to be received or counted fit members of visible Churches. Where this is wanting, the very essence of a Church is lost" as the principle is put by Owen, the Independent-Calvinistic Vice-Chancellor of Oxford under Cromwell (*Inv. into the Origin of Ev. Ch.*). Further, see the following essay (not translated here.—TRANSLATOR).

93. See following essay.

94. *Cat. Genev.,* p. 149. Bailey, *Praxis pietatis,* p. 125: "In life we should act as though no one but Moses had authority over us."

95. "The law appears to the Calvinist as an ideal norm of action. It oppresses the Lutheran because it is for him unattainable." In the Lutheran catechism it stands at the beginning in order to arouse the necessary humility, in the Reformed catechism it generally stands after the Gospel. The Calvinists accused the Lutherans of having a "virtual reluctance to becoming holy" (Möhler), while the Lutherans accused the Calvinists of an "unfree servitude to the law" and of arrogance.

96. *Studies and Reflections of the Great Rebellion,* pp. 79 f.

97. Among them the Song of Songs is especially noteworthy. It was for the most part simply ignored by the Puritans. Its Oriental eroticism has influenced the development of certain types of religion, such as that of St. Bernard.

98. On the necessity of this self-observation, see the sermon of Charnock, already referred to, on 2 Cor. xiii. 5, *Works of the Puritan Divines,* pp. 161 ff.

99. Most of the theological moralists recommended it. Thus Baxter, *Christian Directory,* II, pp. 77 ff., who, however, does not gloss over its dangers.

100. Moral book-keeping has, of course, been widespread elsewhere. But the emphasis which was placed upon it as the sole means of knowledge of the eternal decree of salvation or damnation was lacking, and with it the most important psychological sanction for care and exactitude in this calculation.

101. This was the significant difference from other attitudes which were superficially similar.

102. Baxter (*Saints' Everlasting Rest,* chap. xii) explains God's invisibility with the remark that just as one can carry on profitable trade with an invisible foreigner through correspondence, so is it possible by means of holy commerce with an invisible God to get possession of the one priceless pearl. These commercial similes rather than the forensic ones customary with the older moralists and the Lutherans are thoroughly characteristic of Puritanism, which in effect makes man buy his own salvation. Compare further the following passage from a sermon: "We reckon the value of a thing by that which a wise man will give for it, who is not ignorant of it nor under necessity. Christ, the Wisdom of God, gave Himself, His own precious blood, to redeem souls, and He knew what they were and had no need of them" (Matthew Henry, *The Worth of the Soul, Works of the, Puritan Divines,* p. 313).

103. In contrast to that, Luther himself said: "Weeping goes before action and suffering excells all accomplishment" (*Weinen geht vor Wirken und Leiden übertrifft alles tun*).

104. This is also shown most clearly in the development of the ethical theory of Lutheranism. On this see Hoennicke, *Studien zur*

Notes

altprotestantischen Ethik (Berlin, 1902), and the instructive review of it by E. Troeltsch, *Gött. Gel. Anz.,* 1902, No. 8. The approach of the Lutheran doctrine, especially to the older orthodox Calvinistic, was in form often very close. But the difference of religious background was always apparent. In order to establish a connection between morality and faith, Melanchthon had placed the idea of repentance in the foreground. Repentance through the law must precede faith, but good works must follow it, otherwise it cannot be the truly justifying faith—almost a Puritan formula. Melanchthon admitted a certain degree of perfection to be attainable on earth. He had, in fact, originally taught that justification was given in order to make men capable of good works, and in increasing perfection lay at least the relative degree of blessedness which faith could give in this world. Also later Lutheran theologians held that good works are the necessary fruits of faith, that faith results in a new external life, just as the Reformed preachers did. The question in what good works consist Melanchthon, and especially the later Lutherans, answered more and more by reference to the law. There remained of Luther's original doctrines only the lesser degree of seriousness with which the Bible, especially the particular norms of the Old Testament, was taken. The decalogue re mained, as a codification of the most important ideas of the natural moral law, the essential norm of human action. But there was no firm link connecting its legal validity with the more and more strongly emphasized importance of faith for justification, because this faith (see above) had a fundamentally different psychological character from the Calvinistic.

The true Lutheran standpoint of the early period had to be abandoned by a Church which looked upon itself as an institution for salvation. But another had not been found. Especially was it impossible, for fear of losing their dogmatic foundation (*sola fide!*), to accept the ascetic rationalization of conduct as the moral task of the individual. For there was no motive to give the idea of proof such a significance as it attained in Calvinism through the doctrine of predestination. Moreover, the magical interpretation of the sacraments, combined with the lack of this doctrine, especially the association of the *regeneratio* or at least its beginning with baptism, necessarily, assuming as it did the universality of grace, hindered the development of methodical morality. For it weakened the contrast between the state of nature and the state of grace, especially when combined with the strong Lutheran emphasis on original sin. No less important was the entirely forensic interpretation of the act of justification which assumed that God's decrees might be changed through the influence of particular acts of repentance of the converted sinner. And that was just the element to which Melanchthon gave increasing emphasis. The whole development of his doctrine, which gave increasing weight to repentance, was intimately connected with his

239

profession of the freedom of the will. That was what primarily determined the *un*methodical character of Lutheran conduct.

Particular acts of grace for particular sins, not the development of an aristocracy of saints creating the certainty of their own salvation, was the necessary form salvation took for the average Lutheran, as the retention of the confession proves. Thus it could develop neither a morality free from the law nor a rational asceticism in terms of the law. Rather the law remained in an unorganic proximity to faith as an ideal, and, moreover, since the strict dependence on the Bible was avoided as suggesting salvation by works, it remained uncertain, vague, and, above all, unsystematic in its content. Their conduct remained, as Troeltsch has said of their ethical theory, a "sum of mere beginnings which never quite materialized"; which, "taught in particular, uncertain, and unrelated maxims" did not succeed in "working out an articulate system of conduct" but formed essentially, following the development through which Luther himself (see above) had gone, a resignation to things as they were in matters both small and great. The resignation of the Germans to foreign cultures, their rapid change of nationality, of which there is so much complaint, is clearly to be attributed, along with certain political circumstances in the history of the nation, in part to the results of this influence, which still affects all aspects of our life. The subjective assimilation of culture remained weak because it took place primarily by means of a passive absorption of what was authoritatively presented.

105. On these points, see the gossipy book of Tholuck, *Vorgeschichte des Rationalismus.*

106. On the quite different results of the Mohammedan doctrine of predestination (or rather predetermination) and the reasons for it, see the theological dissertation (Heidelberg) of F. Ulirich, *Die Vorherbestimmungslehre im Islam u. Ch.,* 1912. On that of the Jansenists, see P. Honigsheim, *op. cit.*

107. See the following essay in this collection (not translated here).

108. Ritschl, *Geschichte des Pietismus,* I, p. 152, attempts to distinguish them for the time before Labadie (only on the basis of examples from the Netherlands) (1) in that the Pietists formed conventicles; (2) they held the doctrine of the "worthlessness of existence in the flesh" in a "manner contrary to the Protestant interests in salvation"; (3) "the assurance of grace in the tender relationship with the Lord Jesus" was sought in an un-Calvinistic manner. The last criterion applies for this early period only to one of the cases with which he deals. The idea of worthlessness of the flesh was in itself a true child of the Calvinistic spirit, and only where it led to practical renunciation of the world was it antagonistic to normal Protestantism. The conventicles, finally, had been established to a certain extent (especially for catechistic purposes) by the Synod of Dordrecht itself. Of the criteria of Pietism analysed

in Ritschl's previous discussion, those worth considering are (1) the greater precision with which the letter of the Bible was followed in all external affairs of life, as Gisbert Voet for a time urged; (2) the treatment of justification and reconciliation with God, not as ends in themselves, but simply as means toward a holy ascetic life as can be seen perhaps in Lodensteyn, but as is also suggested by Melanchthon [see above, note 104]; (3) the high value placed on repentance as a sign of true regeneration, as was first taught by W. Teellinck; (4) abstention from communion when unregenerate persons partake of it (of which we shall speak in another connection). Connected with that was the formation of conventicles with a revival of prophecy, i.e. interpretation of the Scriptures by laymen, even women. That went beyond the limits set by the canons of Dordrecht.

Those are all things forming departures, sometimes considerable, from both the doctrine and practice of the Reformers. But compared with the movements which Ritschl does not include in his treatment, especially the English Puritans, they form, except for No. 3, only a continuation of tendencies which lay in the whole line of development of this religion. The objectivity of Ritschl's treatment suffers from the fact that the great scholar allows his personal attitude towards the Church or, perhaps better, religious policy, to enter in, and, in his antipathy to all peculiarly ascetic forms of religion, interprets any development in that direction as a step back into Catholicism. But, like Catholicism, the older Protestantism included all sorts and conditions of men. But that did not prevent the Catholic Church from repudiating rigorous worldly asceticism in the form of Jansenism; just as Pietism repudiated the peculiar Catholic Quietism of the seventeenth century. From our special view-point Pietism differs not in degree, but in kind from Calvinism only when the increasing fear of the world leads to flight from ordinary economic life and the formation of monastic-communistic conventicles (Labadie). Or, which has been attributed to certain extreme Pietists by their contemporaries, they were led deliberately to neglect worldly duties in favour of contemplation. This naturally happened with particular frequency when contemplation began to assume the character which Ritschl calls Bernardism, because it suggests St. Bernard's interpretation of the Song of Songs: a mystical, emotional form of religion seeking the *unio mystica* with an esoteric sexual tinge. Even from the view-point of religious psychology alone this is undoubtedly something quite different from Calvinism, including its ascetic form exemplified by men like Voet. Ritschl, however, everywhere attempts to connect this quietism with the Pietist asceticism and thus to bring the latter under the same indictment; in doing so he puts his finger on every quotation from Catholic mysticism or asceticism which he can find in Pietist literature. But English and Dutch moralists and theologians who are quite beyond suspicion cite Bernard, Bonaventura, and Thomas à Kempis. The relationship of all the Reformation Churches to the Catholic past was very complex and, according to the point of view which is emphasized, one or another appears most closely related to Catholicism or certain sides of it.

109. The illuminating article on "Pietism" by Mirbt in the third edition of the *Realenzyklopädie für protestantische Theologie und Kirche,* treats the origin of Pietism, leaving its Protestant antecedents entirely on one side, as a purely personal religious experience of Spener, which is somewhat improbable. As an introduction to Pietism, Gustav Freytag's description in *Bilder der deutschen Vergangenheit* is still worth reading. For the beginnings of English Pietism in the contemporary literature, compare W. Whitaker, *Prima Institutio disciplinaque pietatis* (1570).

110. It is well known that this attitude made it possible for Pietism to be one of the main forces behind the idea of toleration. At this point we may insert a few remarks on that subject. In the West its historical origin, if we omit the humanistic indifference of the Enlightenment, which in itself has never had great practical influence, is to be found in the following principal sources: (1) Purely political expediency (type: William of Orange). (2) Mercantilism (especially clear for the City of Amsterdam, but also typical of numerous cities, landlords, and rulers who received the members of sects as valuable for economic progress). (3) The radical wing of Calvinism. Predestination made it fundamentally impossible for the State really to promote religion by intolerance. It could not thereby save a single soul. Only the idea of the glory of God gave the Church occasion to claim its help in the suppression of heresy. Now the greater the emphasis on the membership of the preacher, and all those that partook of the communion, in the elect, the more intolerable became the interference of the State in the appointment of the clergy. For clerical positions were often granted as benefices to men from the universities only because of their theological training, though they might be personally unregenerate. In general, any interference in the affairs of the religious community by those in political power, whose conduct might often be unsatisfactory, was resented. Reformed Pietism strengthened this tendency by weakening the emphasis on doctrinal orthodoxy and by gradually undermining the principle of *extra ecclesiam nulla salus.*

Calvin had regarded the subjection of the damned to the divine supervision of the Church as alone consistent with the glory of God; in New England the attempt was made to constitute the Church as an aristocracy of proved saints. Even the radical Independents, however, repudiated every interference of temporal or any sort of hierarchical powers with the proof of salvation which was only possible within the individual community. The idea that the glory of God requires the subjection of the damned to the discipline of

Notes

the Church was gradually superseded by the other idea, which was present from the beginning and became gradually more prominent, that it was an insult to His glory to partake of the Communion with one rejected by God. That necessarily led to voluntarism, for it led to the believers' Church the religious community which included only the twice-born. Calvinistic Baptism, to which, for instance, the leader of the Parliament of Saints Praisegod Barebones belonged, drew the consequences of this line of thought with great emphasis. Cromwell's army upheld the liberty of conscience and the parliament of saints even advocated the separation of Church and State, because its members were good Pietists, thus on positive religious grounds. (4) The Baptist sects, which we shall discuss later, have from the beginning of their history most strongly and consistently maintained the principle that only those personally regenerated could be admitted to the Church. Hence they repudiated every conception of the Church as an institution (*Anstalt*) and every interference of the temporal power. Here also it was for positive religious reasons that unconditional toleration was advocated.

The first man who stood out for absolute toleration and the separation of Church and State, almost a generation before the Baptists and two before Roger Williams, was probably John Browne. The first declaration of a Church group in this sense appears to be the resolution of the English Baptists in Amsterdam of 1612 or 1613: "The magistrate is not to middle with religion or matters of conscience . . . because Christ is the King and Law-giver of the Church and conscience." The first official document of a Church which claimed the positive protection of liberty of conscience by the State as a right was probably Article 44 of the Confession of the Particular Baptists of 1644.

Let it be emphatically stated again that the idea sometimes brought forward, that toleration as such was favourable to capitalism, is naturally quite wrong. Religious toleration is neither peculiar to modern times nor to the West. It has ruled in China, in India, in the great empires of the Near East in Hellenistic times, in the Roman Empire and the Mohammedan Empires for long periods to a degree only limited by reasons of political expediency (which form its limits to-day also !) which was attained nowhere in the world in the sixteenth and seventeenth centuries. Moreover, it was least strong in those areas which were dominated by Puritanism, as, for instance, Holland and Zeeland in their period of political and economic expansion or in Puritan old or New England. Both before and after the Reformation, religious intolerance was peculiarly characteristic of the Occident as of the Sassanian Empire. Similarly, it has prevailed in China, Japan, and India at certain particular times, though mostly for political reasons. Thus toleration as such certainly has nothing whatever to do with capitalism. The real question is, Who benefited by it? Of the consequences of the believers' Church we shall speak further in the following article.

111. This idea is illustrated in its practical application by Cromwell's tryers, the examiners of candidates for the position of preacher. They attempted to ascertain not only the knowledge of theology, but also the subjective state of grace of the candidate. See also the following article.

112. The characteristic Pietistic distrust of Aristotle and classical philosophy in general is suggested in Calvin himself (compare *Instit. Christ,* II, chap. ii, p. 4; III, chap. xxiii, p. 5; IV, chap. xvii, p. 24). Luther in his early days distrusted it no less, but that was later changed by the humanistic influence (especially of Melanchthon) and the urgent need of ammunition for apologetic purposes. That everything necessary for salvation was contained in the Scriptures plainly enough for even the untutored was, of course, taught by the Westminster Confession (chap. i, No. 7.), in conformity with the whole Protestant tradition.

113. The official Churches protested against this, as, for example, in the shorter catechism of the Scotch Presbyterian Church of 1648, sec. vii. Participation of those not members of the same family in family devotions was forbidden as interference with the prerogatives of the office. Pietism, like every ascetic community-forming movement, tended to loosen the ties of the individual with domestic patriarchalism, with its interest in the prestige of office.

114. We are here for good reasons intentionally neglecting discussion of the psychological, in the technical sense of the word, aspect of these religious phenomena, and even its terminology has been as far as possible avoided. The firmly established results of psychology, including psychiatry, do not as present go far enough to make them of use for the purposes of the historical investigation of our problems without prejudicing historical judgments. The use of its terminology would only form a temptation to hide phenomena which were immediately understandable, or even sometimes trivial, behind a veil of foreign words, and thus give a false impression of scientific exactitude, such as is unfortunately typical of Lamprecht. For a more serious attempt to make use of psychological concepts in the interpretation of certain historical mass phenomena, see W. Hellpach, *Grundlinien zu einer Psychologie der Hysterie,* chap. xii, as well as his *Nervosität und Kultur.* I cannot here attempt to explain that in my opinion even this many-sided writer has been harmfully influenced by certain of Lamprecht's theories. How completely worthless, as compared with the older literature, Lamprecht's schematic treatment of Pietism is (in Vol. VII of the *Deutsche Geschichte*) everyone knows who has the slightest acquaintance with the literature.

115. Thus with the adherents of Schortinghuis's *Innige Christendom.* In the history of religion it goes back to the verse about the servant of God in Isaiah and the 22nd Psalm.

Notes

116. This appeared occasionally in Dutch Pietism and then under the influence of Spinoza.

117. Labadie, Teersteegen, etc.

118. Perhaps this appears most clearly when he (Spener!) disputes the authority of the Government to control the conventicles except in cases of disorder and abuses, because it concerns a fundamental right of Christians guaranteed by apostolic authority (*Theologische Bedenken,* II, pp. 81 f.). That is, in principle, exactly the Puritan standpoint regarding the relations of the individual to authority and the extent to which individual rights, which follow *ex jure divino* and are therefore inalienable, are valid. Neither this heresy, nor the one mentioned farther on in the text, has escaped Ritschl (*Pietismus,* II, pp. 115, 157). However unhistorical the positivistic (not to say philistine) criticism to which he has subjected the idea of natural rights to which we are nevertheless indebted for not much less than everything which even the most extreme reactionary prizes as his sphere of individual freedom, we naturally agree entirely with him that in both cases an organic relationship to Spener's Lutheran standpoint is lacking.

The conventicles (*collegia pietitatis*) themselves, to which Spener's famous *pia desideria* gave the theoretical basis, and which he founded in practice, corresponded closely in essentials to the English prophesyings which were first practised in John of Lasco's London Bible Classes (1547), and after that were a regular feature of all forms of Puritanism which revolted against the authority of the Church. Finally, he bases his well-known repudiation of the Church discipline of Geneva on the fact that its natural executors, the third estate (*status 'conomicus:* the Christian laity), were not even a part of the organization of the Lutheran Church. On the other hand, in the discussion of excommunication the lay members' recognition of the Consistorium appointed by the prince as representatives of the third estate is weakly Lutheran.

119. The name Pietism in itself, which first occurs in Lutheran territory, indicates that in the opinion of contemporaries it was characteristic of it that a methodical business was made out of *pietas.*

120. It is, of course, granted that though this type of motivation was primarily Calvinistic it is not exclusively such. It is also found with special frequency in some of the oldest Lutheran Church constitutions.

121. In the sense of Heb. v. 13, 14. Compare Spener, *Theologische Bedenken,* I, p. 306.

122. Besides Bailey and Baxter (see *Consilia theologica* III, 6, I; II, 47; 3, 6), Spener was especially fond of Thomas à Kempis, and even more of Tauler—whom he did not entirely understand (*op. cit.,* III, 61, 1, No. 1). For detailed discussion of the latter, see *op. cit.,* I, 1, 1 No. 7. For him Luther is derived directly from Tauler.

123. See in Ritschl, *op. cit.*, II, p. 113. He did not accept the repentance of the later Pietists (and of Luther) as the sole trustworthy indication of true conversion (*Theologische Bedenkent*, III, p. 476). On sanctification as the fruit of thankfulness in the belief of forgiveness, a typically Lutheran idea, see passages cited by Ritschl, *op. cit.*, p. 115, note 2. On the *certitudo salutis* see, on the one hand, *Theologische Bedenken*, I, p. 324: "true belief is not so much felt emotionally as known by its fruits" (love and obedience to God); on the other, *Theologische Bedenken*, I, p. 335 f.: "As far as anxiety that they should be assured of salvation and grace is concerned, it is better to trust to our books, the Lutheran, than to the English writings." But on the nature of sanctification he was at one with the English view-point.

124. Of this the religious account books which A. H. Francke recommended were external symptoms. The methodical practice and habit of virtue was supposed to cause its growth and the separation of good from evil. This is the principal theme of Francke's book, *Von des Christen Vollkommenheit.*

125. The difference between this rational Pietist belief in Providence and its orthodox interpretation is shown characteristically in the famous controversy between the Pietists of Halle and the orthodox Lutheran Löscher. Löscher in his *Timotheus Verinus* goes so far as to contrast everything that is attained by human action with the decrees of Providence. On the other hand, Francke's consistent view was that the sudden flash of clarity over what is to happen, which comes as a result of quiet waiting for decision, is to be considered as "God's hint" quite analogous to the Quaker psychology, and corresponding to the general ascetic idea that rational methods are the way to approach nearer to God. It is true that Zinzendorf, who in one most vital decision entrusted the fate of his community to lot, was far from Francke's form of the belief in Providence. Spener, *Theologische Bedenken*, I, p. 314, referred to Tauler for a description of the Christian resignation in which one should bow to the divine will, and not cross it by hasty action on one's own responsibility, essentially the position of Francke. Its effectiveness as compared to Puritanism is essentially weakened by the tendency of Pietism to seek peace in this world, as can everywhere be clearly seen. "First righteousness, then peace", as was said in opposition to it in 1904 by a leading Baptist (G. White in an address to be referred to later) in formulating the ethical programme of his denomination (*Baptist Handbook*, 1904, p. 107).

126. *Lect. paraenet.*, IV, p. 271.

127. Ritschl's criticism is directed especially against this continually recurrent idea. See the work of Francke containing the doctrine which has already been referred to. (See note 124 above.)

128. It occurs also among English Pietists who were not adherents of predestination, for instance Goodwin. On him and others compare

Notes

Heppe, *Geschichte des Pietismus in der reformierten Kirche* (Leiden, 1879), a book which even with Ritschl's standard work cannot yet be dispensed with for England, and here and there also for the Netherlands. Even in the nineteenth century in the Netherlands Köhler, *Die Niederl. ref. Kirche,* was asked about the exact time of his rebirth.

129. They attempted thus to counteract the lax results of the Lutheran doctrine of the recoverability of grace (especially the very frequent conversion *in extremis*).

130. Against the corresponding necessity of knowing the day and hour of conversion as an indispensable sign of its genuineness. See Spener, *Theologische Bedenken,* II, 6, 1, p. 197. Repentance was as little known to him as Luther's *terrores conscientiæ* to Melanchthon.

131. At the same time, of course, the anti-authoritarian interpretation of the universal priesthood, typical of all asceticism, played a part. Occasionally the minister was advised to delay absolution until proof was given of genuine repentance which, as Ritschl rightly says, was in principle Calvinistic.

132. The essential points for our purposes are most easily found in Plitt, *Zinzendorf's Theologie* (3 vols., Gotha, 1869), I, pp. 325, 345, 381, 412, 429, 433 f, 444, 448, II, pp. 372, 381, 385, 409 f., III, pp. 131, 167, 176. Compare also Bernh. Becker, *Zinzendorf und sein Christentum* (Leipzig, 1900), Book III, chap. iii.

133. "In no religion do we recognize as brothers those who have not been washed in the blood of Christ and continue thoroughly changed in the sanctity of the Spirit. We recognize no evident (= visible) Church of Christ except where the Word of God is taught in purity and where the members live in holiness as children of God following its precepts." The last sentence, it is true, is taken from Luther's smaller catechism but, as Ritschl points out, there it serves to answer the question how the Name of God shall be made holy, while here it serves to delimit the Church of the saints.

134. It is true that he only considered the Augsburg Confession to be a suitable document of the Lutheran Christian faith if, as he expressed it in his disgusting terminology, a *Wundbrühe* had been poured upon it. To read him is an act of penitence because his language, in its insipid melting quality, is even worse than the frightful Christo-turpentine of F. T. Vischer (in his polemics with the Munich *christoterpe*).

135. See Plitt, *op. cit.,* I, p. 346. Even more decisive is the answer, quoted in Plitt, *op. cit.,* I, p. 381, to the question whether good works are necessary to salvation. "Unnecessary and harmful to the attainment of salvation, but after salvation is attained so necessary that he who does not perform them is not really saved." Thus here also they are not the cause of salvation, but the sole means of recognizing it.

136. For instance, through those caricatures of Christian freedom which Ritschl, *op. cit.,* III, p. 381, so severely criticizes.

137. Above all in the greater emphasis on the idea of retributive punishment in the doctrine of salvation, which, after the repudiation of his missionary attempts by the American sects, he made the basis of his method of sanctification. After that he places the retention of childlikeness and the virtues of humble resignation in the foreground as the end of Herrnhut asceticism, in sharp contrast to the inclination of his own community to an asceticism closely analogous to the Puritan.

138. Which, however, had its limits. For this reason alone it is wrong to attempt to place Zinzendorf's religion in a scheme of social psychological evolutionary stages, as Lamprecht does. Furthermore, however, his whole religious attitude is influenced by nothing more strongly than the fact that he was a Count with an outlook fundamentally feudal. Further, the emotional side of it would, from the point of view of social psychology, fit just as well into the period of the sentimental decadence of chivalry as in that of sensitiveness. If social psychology gives any clue to its difference from West European rationalism, it is most likely to be found in the patriarchal traditionalism of Eastern Germany.

139. This is evident from Zinzendorf's controversy with Dippel just as, after his death, the doctrines of the Synod of 1764 bring out the character of the Herrnhut community as an institution for salvation. See Ritschl's criticism, *op. cit.,* III, p. 443 f.

140. Compare, for instance, §§151, 153, 160. That sanctification may not take place in spite of true penitence and the forgiveness of sins is evident, especially from the remarks on p. 311, and agrees with the Lutheran doctrine of salvation just as it is in disagreement with that of Calvinism (and Methodism).

141. Compare Zinzendorf's opinion, cited in Plitt, *op. cit.,* II, p. 345. Similarly Spangenberg, *Idea Fidei,* p. 325.

142. Compare, for instance, Zinzendorf's remark on Matt. XX. 28, cited by Plitt, *op. cit.,* III, p. 131: "When I see a man to whom God has given a great gift, I rejoice and gladly avail myself of the gift. But when I note that he is not content with his own, but wishes to increase it further, I consider it the beginning of that person's ruin." In other words, Zinzendorf denied, especially in his conversation with John Wesley in 1743, that there could be progress in holiness, because he identified it with justification and found it only in the emotional relationship to Christ, (Plitt, I, p. 413). In place of the sense of being the instrument of God comes the possession of the divine; mysticism, not asceticism (in the sense to be discussed in the introduction to the following essays) (not here translated.—TRANSLATOR'S NOTE). As is pointed out there, a present, worldly state of mind is naturally what the Puritan really seeks for also. But for him the state which he interprets as the *certitudo salutis* is the feeling of being an active instrument.

Notes

143. But which, precisely on account of this mystical tendency, did not receive a consistent ethical justification. Zinzendorf rejects Luther's idea of divine worship in the calling as the decisive reason for performing one's duty in it. It is rather a return for the "Saviour's loyal services" (Plitt, II, p. 411).

144. His saying that "a reasonable man should not be without faith and a believer should not be unreasonable" is well known. See his *Sokrates, d. i. Aufrichtige Anzeige verschiedener nicht sowohl unbekannter als vielmehr in Abfall geratener Hauptwahrheiten* (1725). Further, his fondness for such authors as Bayle.

145. The decided propensity of Protestant asceticism for empiricism, rationalized on a mathematical basis, is well known, but cannot be further analysed here. On the development of the sciences in the direction of mathematically rationalized exact investigation, the philosophical motives of it and their contrast to Bacon's viewpoint, see Windelband, *Geschichte der Philosophie,* pp. 305–7, especially the remark on p. 305, which rightly denies that modern natural science can be understood as the product of material and technical interests. Highly important relationships exist, of course, but they are much more complex. See further Windelband, *Neuere Phil.,* I, pp. 40 ff. For the attitude of Protestant asceticism the decisive point was, as may perhaps be most clearly seen in Spener's *Theologische Bedemken,* I, p. 232; III, p. 260, that just as the Christian is known by the fruits of his belief, the knowledge of God and His designs can only be attained through a knowledge of His works. The favourite science of all Puritan, Baptist, or Pietist Christianity was thus physics, and next to it all those other natural sciences which used a similar method, especially mathematics. It was hoped from the empirical knowledge of the divine laws of nature to ascend to a grasp of the essence of the world, which on account of the fragmentary nature of the divine revelation, a Calvinistic idea, could never be attained by the method of metaphysical speculation. The empiricism of the seventeenth century was the means for asceticism to seek God in nature. It seemed to lead to God, philosophical speculation away from Him. In particular Spener considers the Aristotelean philosophy to have been the most harmful element in Christian tradition. Every other is better, especially the Platonic: *Cons. Theol.,* III, 6, 1, Dist. 2, No. 13. Compare further the following characteristic passage: "Unde pro Cartesio quid dicam non habeo [he had not read him], semper tamen optavi et opto, ut Deus viros excitet, qui veram philosophiam vel tandem oculis sisterent in qua nullius hominis attenderetur auctoritas, sed sana tantum magistri nescia ratio", Spener, *Cons. Theol.,* II, 5, No. 2. The significance of this attitude of ascetic Protestantism for the development of education, especially technical education, is well known. Combined with the attitude to *fides implicita* they furnished a pedagogical programme.

The Protestant Ethic and the Spirit of Capitalism

146. "That is a type of men who seek their happiness in four main-ways: (1) to be insignificant, despised, and abased; (2) to neglect all things they do not need for the service of their Lord; (3) either to possess nothing or to give away again what they receive; (4) to work as wage la-bourers, not for the sake of the wage, but of the calling in the service of the Lord and their neighbour" (*Rel. Reden,* II, p. 180; Plitt, *op. cit.,* 1, p. 449). Not everyone can or may become a disciple, but only those who re-ceive the call of the Lord. But according to Zinzendorf's own confession (Plitt, *op. cit.,* I, p. 449) there still remain difficulties, for the Sermon on the Mount applies formally to all. The resemblance of this free universal-ity of love to the old Baptist ideals is evident.

147. An emotional intensification of religion was by no means entirely unknown to Lutheranism even in its later period. Rather the ascetic ele-ment, the way of life which the Lutheran suspected of being salvation by works, was the fundamental difference in this case.

148. A healthy fear is a better sign of grace than certainty, says Spener, *Theologische Bedenken,* I, p. 324. In the Puritan writers we, of course, also find emphatic warnings against false certainty; but at least the doctrine of predestination, so far as its influence determined religious practice, always worked in the opposite direction.

149. The psychological effect of the confessional was everywhere to relieve the individual of responsibility for his own conduct, that is why it was sought, and that weakened the rigorous consistency of the demands of asceticism.

150. How important at the same time, even for the form of the Pietist faith, was the part played by purely political factors, has been indicated by Ritschl in his study of Würtemberg Pietism.

151. See Zinzendorf's statement [quoted above, note 146].

152. Of course Calvinism, in so far as it is genuine, is also patriar-chal. The connection, for instance, of the success of Baxter's activities with the domestic character of industry in Kidderminster is evident from his autobiography. See the passage quoted in the *Works of the Puritan Divines,* p. 38: "The town liveth upon the weaving of Kidder-minster stuffs, and as they stand in their loom, they can set a book be-fore them, or edify each other. . . ." Nevertheless, there is a difference between patriarchalism based on Pietism and on the Calvinistic and es-pecially the Baptist ethics. This problem can only be discussed in an-other connection.

153. *Lehre von der Rechtfertigung und Versöhnung,* third edition, I, p. 598. That Frederick William I called Pietism a religion for the leisure class is more indicative of his own Pietism than that of Spener and Francke. Even this king knew very well why he had opened his realm to the Pietists by his declaration of toleration.

154. As an introductiont to Methodism the excellent article *Methodis-mus* by Loofs in the *Realenzyklopädie für protestantische Theolo-*

250

Notes

gie und Kirche is particularly good. Also the works of Jacoby (especially the *Handbuch des Methodismus*), Kolde, Jüngst, and Southey are useful. On Wesley: Tyerman, *Life and Times of John Wesley* is popular. One of the best libraries on the history of Methodism is that of Northwestern University, Evanston, Ill. A sort of link between classical Puritanism and Methodism was formed by the religious poet Isaac Watts, a friend of the chaplain of Oliver Cromwell (Howe) and then of Richard Cromwell. Whitefield is said to have sought his advice (cf. Skeats, *op. cit.,* pp. 254 f.).

155. Apart from the personal influence of the Wesleys the similarity is historically determined, on the one hand, by the decline of the dogma of predestination, on the other by the powerful revival of the *sola fide* in the founders of Methodism, especially motivated by its specific missionary character. This brought forth a modified rejuvenation of certain mediæval methods of revival preaching and combined them with Pietistic forms. It certainly does not belong in a general line of development toward subjectivism, since in this respect it stood behind not only Pietism, but also the Bernardine religion of the Middle Ages.

156. In this manner Wesley himself occasionally characterized the effect of the Methodist faith. The relationship to Zinzendorf's *Glückseligkeit* is evident.

157. Given in Watson's *Life of Wesley,* p. 331 (German edition).

158. J. Schneckenburger, *Vorlesungen über die Lehrbegriffe der kleinen protestantischen Kirchenparteien,* edited by Hundeshagen (Frankfurt, 1863), p. 147.

159. Whitefield, the leader of the predestinationist group which after his death dissolved for lack of organization, rejected Wesley's doctrine of perfection in its essentials. In fact, it is only a makeshift for the real Calvinistic idea of proof.

160. Schneckenburger, *op. cit.,* p. 145. Somewhat different in Loofs, *op. cit.* Both results are typical of all similar religious phenomena.

161. Thus in the conference of 1770. The first conference of 1744 had already recognized that the Biblical words came "within a hair" of Calvinism on the one hand and Antinomianism on the other. But since they were so obscure it was not well to be separated by doctrinal differences so long as the validity of the Bible as a practical norm was upheld.

162. The Methodists were separated from the Herrnhuters by their doctrine of the possibility of sinless perfection, which Zinzendorf, in particular, rejected. On the other hand, Wesley felt the emotional element in the Herrnhut religion to be mysticism and branded Luther's interpretation of the law as blasphemous. This shows the barrier which existed between Lutheranism and every kind of rational religious conduct.

163. John Wesley emphasizes the fact that everywhere, among Quakers, Presbyterians, and High Churchmen, one must believe in

dogmas, except in Methodism. With the above, compare the rather summary discussion in Skeats, *History of the Free Churches of England,
1688–1851.*

164. Compare Dexter, *Congregationalism,* pp. 455 ff.

165. Though naturally it might interfere with it, as is to-day the case
among the American negroes. Furthermore, the often definitely pathologi-
cal character of Methodist emotionalism as compared to the relatively
mild type of Pietism may possibly, along with purely historical reasons
and the publicity of the process, be connected with the greater ascetic
penetration of life in the areas where Methodism is widespread. Only a
neurologist could decide that.

166. Loofs, *op. cit.,* p. 750, strongly emphasizes the fact that
Methodism is distinguished from other ascetic movements in that it
came after the English Enlightenment, and compares it with the
(surely much less pronounced) German Renaissance of Pietism in the
first third of the nineteenth century. Nevertheless, it is permissible,
following Ritschl, *Lehre von der Rechtfertigung und Versöhnung,* pp.
568 f., to retain the parallel with the Zinzendorf form of Pietism,
which, unlike that of Spener and Francke, was already itself a reaction
against the Enlightenment. However, this reaction takes a very different course in Methodism from that of the Herrnhuters, at least so far
as they were influenced by Zinzendorf.

167. But which, as is shown by the passage from John Wesley (below,
p. 175), it developed in the same way and with the same effect as the
other ascetic denominations.

168. And, as we have seen, milder forms of the consistent ascetic ethics of Puritanism; while if, in the popular manner, one wished to interpret
these religious conceptions as only exponents or reflections of capitalistic
institutions, just the opposite would have to be the case.

169. Of the Baptists only the so-called General Baptists go back to the
older movement. The Particular Baptists were, as we have pointed out already, Calvinists, who in principle limited Church membership to the regenerate, or at least personal believers, and hence remained in principle
voluntarists and opponents of any State Church. Under Cromwell, no
doubt, they were not always consistent in practice. Neither they nor the
General Baptists, however important they are as the bearers of the Baptist
tradition, give us any occasion for an especial dogmatic analysis here.
That the Quakers, though formally a new foundation of George Fox
and his associates, were fundamentally a continuation of the Baptist
tradition, is beyond question. The best introduction to their history, including their relations to Baptists and Mennonites, is Robert Barclay,
The Inner Life of the Religious Societies of the Commonwealth, 1876.
On the history of the Baptists, compare, among others, H. M. Dexter,
The True Story of John Smyth, the Se-Baptist, as told by himself and his
contemporaries, Boston, 1881 (also J. C. Lang in *The Baptist Quarterly*

Notes

Review, 1883, p. 1); J. Murch, *A History of the Presb. and Gen. Bapt. Church in the West of England,* London, 1835; A. H. Newman, *History of the Baptist Church in the U.S.,* New York, 1894 (*Am. Church Hist. Series,* vol. 2); Vedder, *A Short History of the Baptists,* London, 1897; E. B. Bax, *Rise and Fall of the Anabaptists,* New York, 1902; G. Lorimer, *The Baptists in History,* 1902; J. A. Seiss, *The Baptist System Examined,* Lutheran Publication Society, 1902; further material in the *Baptist Handbook,* London, 1896 ff.; *Baptist Manuals,* Paris, 1891–93; *The Baptist Quarterly Review;* and the *Bibliotheca Sacra,* Oberlin, 1900.

The best Baptist library seems to be that of Colgate College in the State of New York. For the history of the Quakers the collection in Devonshire House in London is considered the best (not available to me). The official modern organ of orthodoxy is the *American Friend,* edited by Professor Jones; the best Quaker history that of Rowntree. In addition: Rufus B. Jones, *George Fox, an Autobiography,* Phila., 1903; Alton C. Thomas, *A History of the Society of Friends in America,* Phila., 1895; Edward Grubbe, *Social Aspects of the Quaker Faith,* London, 1899. Also the copious and excellent biographical literature.

170. It is one of the many merits of Karl Müller's *Kirchengeschichte* to have given the Baptist movement, great in its way, even though outwardly unassuming, the place it deserved in his work. It had suffered more than any other from the pitiless persecution of all the Churches, because it wished to be a sect in the specific sense of that word. Even after five generations it was discredited before the eyes of all the world by the debacle of the related eschatological experiment in Münster. And, continually oppressed and driven underground, it was long after its origin before it attained a consistent formulation of its religious doctrines. Thus it produced even less theology than would have been consistent with its principles, which were themselves hostile to a specialized development of its faith in God as a science. That was not very pleasing to the older professional theologians, even in its own time, and it made little impression on them. But many more recent ones have taken the same attitude. In Ritschl, *Pietismus,* I, pp. 22 f., the rebaptizers are not very adequately, in fact, rather contemptuously, treated. One is tempted to speak of a theological bourgeois standpoint. That, in spite of the fact that Cornelius's fine work *(Geschichte des Münsterschen Aufruhrs)* had been available for decades.

Here also Ritschl everywhere sees a retrogression from his standpoint toward Catholicism, and suspects direct influences of the radical wing of the Franciscan tradition. Even if such could be proved in a few cases, these threads would be very thin. Above all, the historical fact was probably that the official Catholic Church, wherever the worldly asceticism of the laity went as far as the formation of conventicles, regarded it with the utmost suspicion and attempted to encourage the formation of orders, thus outside the world, or to attach it as asceticism of the second grade to the existing orders and bring it under control. Where this did not succeed, it felt the danger that the practice of subjectivist ascetic morality might lead to the denial of authority and to heresy, just as, and with the same justification, the Elizabethan Church felt toward the half-Pietistic prophesying Bible conventicles, even when their conformism was undoubted; a feeling which was expressed by the Stuarts in their *Book of Sports,* of which later. The history of numerous heretical movements, including, for instance, the Humiliati and the Beguins, as well as the fate of St. Francis, are the proofs of it. The preaching of the mendicant friars, especially the Franciscans, probably did much to prepare the way for the ascetic lay morality of Calvinist-Baptist Protestantism. But the numerous close relationships between the asceticism of Western monasticism and the ascetic conduct of Protestantism, the importance of which must continually be stressed for our particular problems, are based in the last analysis on the fact that important factors are necessarily common to every asceticism on the basis of Biblical Christianity. Furthermore, every asceticism, no matter what its faith, has need of certain tried methods of subduing the flesh.

Of the following sketch it may further be remarked that its brevity is due to the fact that the Baptist ethic is of only very limited importance for the problem considered primarily in this study, the development of the religious background of the bourgeois idea of the calling. It contributed nothing new whatever to it. The much more important social aspect of the movement must for the present remain untouched. Of the history of the older Baptist movement, we can, from the view-point of our problem, present here only what was later important for the development of the sects in which we are interested: Baptists, Quakers, and, more incidentally, Mennonites.

171. See above [note 92].

172. On their origin and changes, see A. Ritschl in his *Gesammelte Aufsätze,* pp. 69 f.

173. Naturally the Baptists have always repudiated the designation of a sect. They form *the* Church in the sense of the Epistle to the Ephesians v. 27. But in our terminology they form a sect not only because they lack all relation to the State. The relation between Church and State of early Christianity was even for the Quakers (Barclay) their ideal; for to them, as to many Pietists, only a Church under the Cross was beyond suspicion of its purity. But the Calvinists as well, *faute de mieux,* similarly even the Catholic Church in the same circumstances, were forced to favour the separation of Church and State under an unbelieving State or under the Cross. Neither were they a sect, because induction to membership in the Church took

Notes

place *de facto* through a contract between the congregation and the candidates. For that was formally the case in the Dutch Reformed communities (as a result of the original political situation) in accordance with the old Church constitution (see v. Hoffmann, *Kirchenverfassungsrecht der niederl. Reformierten,* Leipzig, 1902).

On the contrary, it was because such a religious community could only be voluntarily organized as a sect, not compulsorily as a Church, if it did not wish to include the unregenerate and thus depart from the Early Christian ideal. For the Baptist communities it was an essential of the very idea of their Church, while for the Calvinists it was an historical accident. To be sure, that the latter were also urged by very definite religious motives in the direction of the believers' Church has already been indicated. On the distinction between Church and sect, see the following essay. The concept of sect which I have adopted here has been used at about the same time and, I assume, independently from me, by Kattenbusch in the *Realenzyklopädie für protestantische Theologie und Kirche* (Article *Sekte*). Troeltsch in his *Die Soziallehren der christlichen Kirchen und Gruppen* accepts it and discusses it more in detail. See also below, the introduction to the essays on the *Wirtschaftsethik der Weltreligionen.*

174. How important this symbol was, historically, for the conservation of the Church community, since it was an unambiguous and unmistakable sign, has been very clearly shown by Cornelius, *op. cit.*

175. Certain approaches to it in the Mennonites' doctrine of justification need not concern us here.

176. This idea is perhaps the basis of the religious interest in the discussion of questions like the incarnation of Christ and his relationship to the Virgin Mary, which, often as the sole purely dogmatic part, stands out so strangely in the oldest documents of Baptism (for instance the confessions printed in Cornelius, *op. cit.,* Appendix to Vol. II. On this question, see K. Müller, *Kirchengeschichte,* II, 1, p. 330). The difference between the christology of the Reformed Church and the Lutheran (in the doctrine of the so-called *communicatio idiomatum*) seems to have been based on similar religious interests.

177. It was expressed especially in the original strict avoidance even of everyday intercourse with the excommunicated, a point at which even the Calvinists, who in principle held the opinion that worldly affairs were not affected by spiritual censure, made large concessions. See the following essay.

178. How this principle was applied by the Quakers to seemingly trivial externals (refusal to remove the hat, to kneel, bow, or use formal address) is well known. The basic idea is to a certain extent characteristic of all asceticism. Hence the fact that true asceticism is always hostile to authority. In Calvinism it appeared in the principle that only Christ should rule in the Church. In the case of Pietism one may think of Spener's attempts to find a Biblical justification of

titles. Catholic asceticism, so far as ecclesiastical authority was concerned, broke through this tendency in its oath of obedience, by interpreting obedience itself in ascetic terms. The overturning of this principle in Protestant asceticism is the historical basis of the peculiarities of even the contemporary democracy of the peoples influenced by Puritanism as distinct from that of the Latin spirit. It is also part of the historical background of that lack of respect of the American which is, as the case may be, so irritating or so refreshing.

179. No doubt this was true from the beginning for the Baptists essentially only of the New Testament, not to the same extent of the Old. Especially the Sermon on the Mount enjoyed a peculiar prestige as a programme of social ethic in all denominations.

180. Even Schwenkfeld had considered the outward performance of the sacraments an *adiaphoron,* while the General Baptists and the Mennonites held strictly to Baptism and the Communion, the Mennonites to the washing of feet in addition. On the other hand, for the predestinationists the depreciation, in fact for all except the communion—one may even say the suspicion—in which the sacraments were held, went very far. See the following essay. .

181. On this point the Baptist denominations, especially the Quakers (Barclay, *Apology for the True Christian Divinity,* fourth edition, London, 1701, kindly placed at my disposal by Eduard Bernstein), referred to Calvin's statements in the *Instit. Christ,* III, p. 2, where in fact quite unmistakable suggestions of Baptist doctrine are to be found. Also the older distinction between the Word of God as that which God had revealed to the patriarchs, the prophets, and the apostles, and the Holy Scriptures as that part of it which they had written down, was, even though there was no historical connection, intimately related to the Baptist conception of revelation. The mechanical idea of inspiration, and with it the strict bibliocracy of the Calvinists, was just as much the product of their development in one direction in the course of the sixteenth century as the doctrine of the inner light of the Quakers, derived from Baptist sources, was the result of a directly opposite development. The sharp differentiation was also in this case partly a result of continual disputes.

182. That was emphasized strongly against certain tendencies of the Socinians. The natural reason knows nothing whatever of God (Barclay, *op. cit.,* p. 102). That meant that the part played by the *lex naturæ* elsewhere in Protestantism was altered. In principle there could be no general rules, no moral code, for the calling which everyone had, and which is different for every individual, is revealed to him by God through his conscience. We should do, not the good in the general sense of natural reason, but God's will as it is written in our hearts and known through the conscience (Barclay, pp. 73, 76). This irrationality of morality, derived from the exaggerated

Notes

contrast between the divine and the flesh, is expressed in these fundamental tenets of Quaker ethics: "What a man does contrary to his faith, though his faith may be wrong, is in no way acceptable to God—though the thing might have been lawful to another" (Barclay, p. 487). Of course that could not be upheld in practice. The "moral and perpetual statutes acknowledged by all Christians" are, for instance, for Barclay the limit of toleration. In practice the contemporaries felt their ethic, with certain peculiarities of its own, to be similar to that of the Reformed Pietists. "Everything good in the Church is suspected of being Quakerism" as Spener repeatedly points out. It thus seems that Spener envied the Quakers this reputation. *Cons. Theol.,* III, 6, 1, Dist. 2, No. 64. The repudiation of oaths on the basis of a passage in the Bible shows that the real emancipation from the Scriptures had not gone far. The significance for social ethics of the principle, "Do unto others as you would that they should do unto you" which many Quakers regarded as the essence of the whole Christian ethics, need not concern us here.

183. The necessity of assuming this possibility Barclay justifies because without it "there should never be a place known by the Saints wherein they might be free of doubting and despair, which—is most absurd". It is evident that the *certitudo salutis* depends upon it. Thus Barclay, *op. cit.,* p. 20.

184. There thus remains a difference in type between the Calvinistic and the Quaker rationalization of life. But when Baxter formulates it by saying that the spirit is supposed by the Quakers to act upon the soul as on a corpse, while the characteristically formulated Calvinistic principle is "reason and spirit are conjunct principles" (*Christian Directory,* II, p. 76), the distinction was no longer valid for his time in this form.

185. Thus in the very careful articles "Menno" and "Mennoniten" by Cramer in the *Realenzyklopädie für Protestantische Theologie und Kirche,* especially p. 604. However excellent these articles are, the article "Baptisten" in the same encyclopedia is not very penetrating and in part simply incorrect. Its author does not know, for instance, the *Publications of the Hanserd Knolly's Society,* which are indispensable for the history of Baptism.

186. Thus Barclay, *op. cit.,* p. 404, explains that eating, drinking, and acquisition are natural, not spiritual acts, which may be performed without the special sanction of God. The explanation is in reply to the characteristic objection that if, as the Quakers teach, one cannot pray without a special motion of the Spirit, the same should apply to ploughing. It is, of course, significant that even in the modern resolutions of Quaker Synods the advice is sometimes given to retire from business after acquiring a sufficient fortune, in order, withdrawn from the bustle of the world, to be able to live in devotion to the Kingdom of God alone. But the same idea certainly occurs

occasionally in other denominations, including Calvinism. That betrays the fact that the acceptance of the bourgeois practical ethics by these movements was the worldly application of an asceticism which had originally fled from the world.

187. Veblen in his suggestive book *The Theory of Business Enterprise* is of the opinion that this motto belongs only to early capitalism. But economic supermen, who, like the present captains of industry, have stood beyond good and evil, have always existed, and the statement is still true of the broad underlying strata of business men.

188. We may here again expressly call attention to the excellent remarks of Eduard Bernstein, *op. cit.* To Kautsky's highly schematic treatment of the Baptist movement and his theory of heretical communism in general (in the first volume of the same work) we shall return on another occasion.

189. "In civil actions it is good to be as the many, in religious to be as the best" says, for example, Thomas Adams (*Works of the Puritan Divines*, p. 138). That sounds somewhat more drastic than it is meant to be. It means that the Puritan honesty is formalistic legality, just as the uprightness which the sometime Puritan people like to claim as a national virtue is something specifically different from the German *Ehrlichkeit*. Some good remarks on the subject from the educational standpoint may be found in the *Preuss. Jahrb.*, CXII (1903), p. 226. The formalism of the Puritan ethic is in turn the natural consequence of its relation to the law.

190. Something is said on this in the following essay.

191. This is the reason for the economic importance of the ascetic Protestant, but not Catholic, minorities.

192. That the difference of dogmatic basis was not inconsistent with the adoption of the most important interest in proof is to be explained in the last analysis by the historical peculiarities of Christianity in general which cannot be discussed here.

193. "Since God hath gathered us to be a people" says Barclay, *op. cit.*, p. 357. I myself heard a Quaker sermon at Haverford College which laid great emphasis on the interpretation of saints as meaning separate.

CHAPTER V

1. See the excellent sketch of his character in Dowden, *op. cit.* A passable introduction to Baxter's theology, after he had abandoned a strict belief in the double decree, is given in the introduction to the various extracts from his works printed in the *Works of the Puritan Divines* (by Jenkyn). His attempt to combine universal redemption and personal election satisfied no one. For us it is important only that he even then held to personal election, i.e. to

Notes

the most important point for ethics in the doctrine of predestination. On the other hand, his weakening of the forensic view of redemption is important as being suggestive of baptism.

2. Tracts and sermons by Thomas Adams, John Howe, Matthew Henry, J. Janeway, Stuart Charnock, Baxter, Bunyan, have been collected in the ten volumes of the *Works of the Puritan Divines* (London, 1845–8), though the choice is often somewhat arbitrary. Editions of the works of Bailey, Sedgwick, and Hoornbeek have already been referred to.

3. We could just as well have included Voet and other continental representatives of worldly asceticism. Brentano's view that the whole development was purely Anglo-Saxon is quite wrong. My choice is motivated mainly (though not exclusively) by the wish to present the ascetic movement as much as possible in the second half of the seventeenth century, immediately before the change to utilitarianism. It has unfortunately been impossible, within the limits of this sketch, to enter upon the fascinating task of presenting the characteristics of ascetic Protestantism through the medium of the biographical literature; the Quakers would in this connection be particularly important, since they are relatively little known in Germany.

4. For one might just as well take the writings of Gisbert Voet, the proceedings of the Huguenot Synods, or the Dutch Baptist literature. Sombart and Brentano have unfortunately taken just the ebionitic parts of Baxter, which I myself have strongly emphasized, to confront me with the undoubted capitalistic backwardness of his doctrines. But (1) one must know this whole literature thoroughly in order to use it correctly, and (2) not overlook the fact that I have attempted to show how, in spite of its anti-mammonistic doctrines, the spirit of this ascetic religion nevertheless, just as in the monastic communities, gave birth to economic rationalism because it placed a premium on what was most important for it: the fundamentally ascetic rational motives. That fact alone is under discussion and is the point of this whole essay.

5. Similarly in Calvin, who was certainly no champion of bourgeois wealth (see the sharp attacks on Venice and Antwerp in *Jes. Opp.,* III, 140a, 308a).

6. *Saints' Everlasting Rest,* chaps. x, xii. Compare Bailey (*Praxis Pietatis,* p. 182) or Matthew Henry (*The Worth of the Soul, Works of the Puritan Divines,* p. 319). "Those that are eager in pursuit of worldly wealth despise their Soul, not only because the Soul is neglected and the body preferred before it, but because it is employed in these pursuits" (Psa. cxxvii. 2). On the same page, however, is the remark to be cited below about the sinfulness of all waste of time, especially in recreations. Similarly in almost the whole religious literature of English-Dutch Puritanism. See, for instance, Hoornbeek's (*op. cit.,* L, X, ch. 18, 18) Phillipics against *avaritia.* This writer is also

affected by sentimental pietistic influences. See the praise of *tranquillitas animi* which is much more pleasing to God than the *sollicitudo* of this world. Also Bailey, referring to the well-known passage in Scripture, is of the opinion that "A rich man is not easily saved" (*op. cit.,* p. 182). The Methodist catechisms also warn against "gathering treasure on this earth". For Pietism this is quite obvious, as also for the Quakers. Compare Barclay (*op. cit.,* p. 517), " . . . and therefore beware of such temptations as to use their callings as an engine to be richer".

7. For not wealth alone, but also the impulsive pursuit of it (or what passed as such) was condemned with similar severity. In the Netherlands the South Holland Synod of 1574 declared, in reply to a question, that money-lenders should not be admitted to communion even though the business was permitted by law; and the Deventer Provincial Synod of 1598 (Art. 24) extended this to the employees of moneylenders. The Synod of Gorichem in 1606 prescribed severe and humiliating conditions under which the wives of usurers might be admitted, and the question was discussed as late as 1644 and 1657 whether Lombards should be admitted to communion (this against Brentano, who cites his own Catholic ancestors, although foreign traders and bankers have existed in the whole European and Asiatic world for thousands of years). Gisbert Voet *(Disp. Theol.,* IV, 1667, *de usuris,* p. 665) still wanted to exclude the Trapezites (Lombards, Piedmontese). The same was true of the Huguenot Synods. This type of capitalistic classes were not the typical representatives of the philosophy or the type of conduct with which we are concerned. They were also not new as compared with antiquity or the Middle Ages.

8. Developed in detail in the tenth chapter of the *Saints' Everlasting Rest.* He who should seek to rest in the shelter of possessions which God gives, God strikes even in this life. A self-satisfied enjoyment of wealth already gained is almost always a symptom of moral degradation. If we had everything which we could have in this world, would that be all we hoped for? Complete satisfaction of desires is not attainable on earth because God's will has decreed it should not be so.

9. *Christian Directory,* I, pp. 375–6. "It is for action that God maintaineth us and our activities; work is the moral as well as the natural end of power. . . . It is action that God is most served and honoured by. . . . The public welfare or the good of the many is to be valued above our own." Here is the connecting-point for the transition from the will of God to the purely utilitarian view-point of the later liberal theory. On the religious sources of Utilitarianism, see below in the text and above, chap. iv, note 145.

10. The commandment of silence has been, starting from the Biblical threat of punishment for every useless word, especially since

the Cluny monks, a favourite ascetic means of education in self-control. Baxter also speaks in detail of the sinfulness of unnecessary words. Its place in his character has been pointed out by Sanford, *op. cit.*, pp. 90 ff.

What contemporaries felt as the deep melancholy and moroseness of the Puritans was the result of breaking down the spontaneity of the *status naturalis,* and the condemnation of thoughtless speech was in the service of this end. When Washington Irving (*Bracebridge Hall,* chap. xxx) seeks the reason for it partly in the calculating spirit of capitalism and partly in the effect of political freedom, which promotes a sense of responsibility, it may be remarked that it does not apply to the Latin peoples. For England the situation was probably that: (1) Puritanism enabled its adherents to create free institutions and still become a world power; and (2) it transformed that calculating spirit (what Sombart calls *Rechenhaftigkeit*), which is in truth essential to capitalism, from a mere means to economy into a principle of general conduct.

11. *Op. cit.,* I, p. 111.

12. *Op. cit.,* I, p. 383 f.

13. Similarly on the preciousness of time, see Barclay, *op. cit.,* p. 14.

14. Baxter, *op. cit.,* I, p. 79. "Keep up a high esteem of time and be every day more careful that you lose none of your time, than you are that you lose none of your gold and silver. And if vain recreation, dressings, feastings, idle talk, unprofitable company, or sleep be any of them temptations to rob you of any of your time, accordingly heighten your watchfulness." "Those that are prodigal of their time despise their own souls" says Matthew Henry (*Worth of the Soul, Works of the Puritan Divines,* p. 315). Here also Protestant asceticism follows a well-beaten track. We are accustomed to think it characteristic of the modern man that he has no time, and for instance, like Goethe in the *Wanderjahren,* to measure the degree of capitalistic development by the fact that the clocks strike every quarter-hour. So also Sombart in his *Kapitalismus.* We ought not, however, to forget that the first people to live (in the Middle Ages) with careful measurement of time were the monks, and that the church bells were meant above all to meet their needs.

15. Compare Baxter's discussion of the calling, *op. cit.,* I, pp. 108 ff. Especially the following passage: "Question: But may I not cast off the world that I may only think of my salvation? Answer: You may cast off all such excess of worldly cares or business as unnecessarily hinder you in spiritual things. But you may not cast off all bodily employment and mental labour in which you may serve the common good. Everyone as a member of Church or Commonwealth must employ their parts to the utmost for the good of the Church and the Commonwealth. To neglect this and say: I will pray and meditate, is as if your servant should refuse his greatest work and tie himself

to some lesser, easier part. And God hath commanded you some way or other to labour for your daily bread and not to live as drones of the sweat of others only." God's commandment to Adam, "In the sweat of thy brow" and Paul's declaration, "He who will not work shall not eat" are also quoted. It has always been known of the Quakers that even the most well-to-do of them have had their sons learn a calling, for ethical and not, as Alberti recommends, for utilitarian reasons.

16. Here are points where Pietism, on account of its emotional character, takes a different view. Spener, although he emphasizes in characteristic Lutheran fashion that labour in a calling is worship of God (*Theologische Bedenken*, III, p. 445), nevertheless holds that the restlessness of business affairs distracts one from God, a most characteristic difference from Puritanism.

17. I, *op. cit.*, p. 242." It's they that are lazy in their callings that can find no time for holy duties." Hence the idea that the cities, the seat of the middle class with its rational business activities, are the seats of ascetic virtue. Thus Baxter says of his hand-loom weavers in Kidderminster: "And their constant converse and traffic with London doth much to promote civility and piety among tradesmen . . ." in his autobiography (*Works of the Puritan Divines*, p. 38). That the proximity of the capital should promote virtue would astonish modern clergymen, at least in Germany. But Pietism also inclined to similar views. Thus Spener, speaking of a young colleague, writes: "At least it appears that among the great multitudes in the cities, though the majority is quite depraved, there are nevertheless a number of good people who can accomplish much, while in villages often hardly anything good can be found in a whole community" (*Theologische Bedenken*, I, 66, p. 303). In other words, the peasant is little suited to rational ascetic conduct. Its ethical glorification is very modern. We cannot here enter into the significance of this and similar statements for the question of the relation of asceticism to social classes.

18. Take, for instance, the following passages (*op. cit.*, p. 336 f.): "Be wholly taken up in diligent business of your lawful callings when you are not exercised in the more immediate service of God." "Labour hard in your callings." "See that you have a calling which will find you employment for all the time which God's immediate service spareth."

19. That the peculiar ethical valuation of labour and its dignity was not originally a Christian idea nor even peculiar to Christianity has recently again been strongly emphasized by Harnack (*Mitt. des Ev.-Soz. Kongr.*, 14. Folge, 1905, Nos. 3, 4, p. 48).

20. Similarly in Pietism (Spener, *op. cit.*, III, pp. 429–30). The characteristic Pietist version is that loyalty to a calling which is imposed upon us by the fall serves to annihilate one's own selfish

Notes

will. Labour in the calling is, as a service of love to one's neighbour, a duty of gratitude for God's grace (a Lutheran idea), and hence it is not pleasing to God that it should be performed reluctantly (*op. cit.,* III, p. 272). The Christian should thus "prove himself as industrious in his labour as a worldly man" (III, p. 278). That is obviously less drastic than the Puritan version.

21. The significance of this important difference, which has been evident ever since the Benedictine rules, can only be shown by a much wider investigation.

22. "A sober procreation of children" is its purpose according to Baxter. Similarly Spener, at the same time with concessions to the coarse Lutheran attitude, which makes the avoidance of immorality, which is otherwise unavoidable, an accessory aim. Concupiscence as an accompaniment of sexual intercourse is sinful even in marriage. For instance, in Spener's view it is a result of the fall which transformed such a natural, divinely ordained process into something inevitably accompanied by sinful sensations, which is hence shameful. Also in the opinion of various Pietistic groups the highest form of Christian marriage is that with the preservation of virginity, the next highest that in which sexual intercourse is only indulged in for the procreation of children, and so on down to those which are contracted for purely erotic or external reasons and which are, from an ethical standpoint, concubinage. On these lower levels a marriage entered into for purely economic reasons is preferred (because after all it is inspired by rational motives) to one with erotic foundations. We may here neglect the Herrnhut theory and practice of marriage. Rationalistic philosophy (Christian Wolff) adopted the ascetic theory in the form that what was designed as a means to an end, concupiscence and its satisfaction, should not be made an end in itself.

The transition to a pure, hygienically oriented utilitarianism had already taken place in Franklin, who took approximately the ethical standpoint of modern physicians, who understand by chastity the restriction of sexual intercourse to the amount desirable for health, and who have, as is well known, even given theoretical advice as to how that should be accomplished. As soon as these matters have become the object of purely rational consideration the same development has everywhere taken place. The Puritan and the hygienic sex-rationalist generally tread very different paths, but here they understand each other perfectly. In a lecture, a zealous adherent of hygienic prostitution—it was a question of the regulation of brothels and prostitutes—defended the moral legitimacy of extra-marital intercourse (which was looked upon as hygienically useful) by referring to its poetic justification in the case of Faust and Margaret. To treat Margaret as a prostitute and to fail to distinguish the powerful sway of human passions from sexual intercourse for hygienic reasons, both are thoroughly congenial to the Puritan standpoint. Similar, for instance, is the typical specialist's view, occasionally put forward by very distinguished physicians, that a question which extends so far into the subtlest problems of personality and of culture as that of sexual abstinence should be dealt with exclusively in the forum of the physician (as an expert). For the Puritan the expert was the moral theorist, now he is the medical man; but the claim of competence to dispose of the questions which seem to us somewhat narrow-minded is, with opposite signs of course, the same in both cases.

But with all its prudery, the powerful idealism of the Puritan attitude can show positive accomplishments, even from the point of view of race conservation in a purely hygienic sense, while modern sex hygiene, on account of the appeal to unprejudicedness which it is forced to make, is in danger of destroying the basis of all its success. How, with the rationalistic interpretation of sexual relations among peoples influenced by Puritanism, a certain refinement and spiritual and ethical penetration of marital relationships, with a blossoming of matrimonial chivalry, has grown up, in contrast to the patriarchal sentimentality (*Brodem*), which is typical of Germany even in the circles of the intellectual aristocracy, must necessarily remain outside this discussion. Baptist influences have played a part in the emancipation of woman; the protection of her freedom of conscience, and the extension of the idea of the universal priesthood to her were here also the first breaches in patriarchal ideas.

23. This recurs again and again in Baxter. The Biblical basis is regularly either the passages in Proverbs, which we already know from Franklin (xxii. 29), or those in praise of labour (xxxi. i6). Cf. *op. cit.,* I, pp. 377, 382, etc.

24. Even Zinzendorf says at one point: "One does not only work in order to live, but one lives for the sake of one's work, and if there is no more work to do one suffers or goes to sleep" (Plitt, *op. cit.,* I, p. 428).

25. Also a symbol of the Mormons closes (after quotations) with the words: "But a lazy or indolent man cannot be a Christian and be saved. He is destined to be struck down and cast from the hive." But in this case it was primarily the grandiose discipline, half-way between monastery and factory, which placed the individual before the dilemma of labour or annihilation and, of course in connection with religious enthusiasm and only possible through it, brought forth the astonishing economic achievements of this sect.

26. Hence (*op. cit.,* I, p. 380) its symptoms are carefully analysed. Sloth and idleness are such deadly sins because they have a cumulative character. They are even regarded by Baxter as "destroyers of grace" (*op. cit.,* I, pp. 279–80). That is, they are the antitheses of the methodical life.

Notes

27. See above, chap. iii, note 5.

28. Baxter, *op. cit.*, I, pp. 108 ff. Especially striking are the following passages: "Question: But will not wealth excuse us? Answer: It may excuse you from some sordid sort of work by making you more serviceable to another, but you are no more excused from service of work . . . than the poorest man." Also, p. 376: "Though they [the rich] have no outward want to urge them, they have as great a necessity to obey God . . . God hath strictly commanded it [labour] to all." Chap. iv, note 47.

29. Similarly Spener (*op. cit.*, III, pp. 338, 425), who for this reason opposes the tendency to early retirement as morally objectionable, and, in refuting an objection to the taking of interest, that the enjoyment of interest leads to laziness, emphasizes that anyone who was in a position to live upon interest would still be obligated to work by God's commandment.

30. Including Pietism. Whenever a question of change of calling arises, Spener takes the attitude that after a certain calling has once been entered upon, it is a duty of obedience to Providence to remain and acquiesce in it.

31. The tremendous force, dominating the whole of conduct, with which the Indian religious teaching sanctions economic traditionalism in terms of chances of favourable rebirth, I have shown in the essays on the *Wirtschaftsethik der Weltreligionen*. It is an excellent example by which to show the difference between mere ethical theories and the creation of psychological sanctions with a religious background for certain types of conduct. The pious Hindu could advance in the scale of transmigration only by the strictly traditional fulfilment of the duties of the caste of his birth. It was the strongest conceivable religious basis for traditionalism. In fact, the Indian ethic is in this respect the most completely consistent antithesis of the Puritan, as in another respect (traditionalism of the caste structure) it is opposed to the Hebrew.

32. Baxter, *op. cit.*, I, p. 377.

33. But this does not mean that the Puritan view-point was historically derived from the latter. On the contrary, it is an expression of the genuinely Calvinistic idea that the cosmos of the world serves the glory of God. The utilitarian turn, that the economic cosmos should serve the good of the many, the common good, etc., was a consequence of the idea that any other interpretation of it would lead to aristocratic idolatry of the flesh, or at least did not serve the glory of God, but only fleshly cultural ends. But God's will, as it is expressed (chap iv, note 34) in the purposeful arrangements of the economic cosmos, can, so far as secular ends are in question at all, only be embodied in the good of the community, in impersonal usefulness. Utilitarianism is thus, as has already been pointed out, the result of the impersonal character of brotherly love and the

repudiation of all glorification of this world by the exclusiveness of the Puritan *in majorem Dei gloriam.*

How completely this idea, that all idolatry of the flesh is inconsistent with the glory of God and hence unconditionally bad, dominated ascetic Protestantism is clearly shown by the doubts and hesitation which it cost even Spener, who certainly was not infected with democracy, to maintain the use of titles as ἀδιάφορον against numerous objections. He finally comforted himself with the reflection that even in the Bible the Prætor Festus was given the title of κράτιστος by the Apostles. The political side of the question does not arise in this connection.

34. "The inconstant man is a stranger in his own house", says Thomas Adams (*Works of the Puritan Divines,* p. 77).

35. On this, see especially George Fox's remarks in the *Friends' Library* (ed. W. & T. Evans, Philadelphia, 1837), I, p. 130.

36. Above all, this sort of religious ethic cannot be regarded as a reflex of economic conditions. The specialization of occupations had, if anything, gone further in mediæval Italy than in the England of that period.

37. For, as is often pointed out in the Puritan literature, God never commanded "love thy neighbour more than thyself" but only as thyself. Hence self-regard is also it duty. For instance, a man who can make better use of his possessions, to the greater glory of God, than his neighbour, is not obliged by the duty of brotherly love to part with them.

38. Spener is also close to this view-point. But even in the case of transfer from commercial occupations (regarded as especially dangerous to virtue) to theology, he remains hesitant and on the whole opposed to it (*op. cit.,* III, pp. 435, 443; I, p. 524). The frequent occurrence of the reply to just this question (of the permissibility of changing a calling) in Spener's naturally biassed opinion shows, incidentally, how eminently practical the different ways of interpreting 1 Corinthians vii were.

39. Such ideas are not to be found, at least in the writings, of the leading Continental Pietists. Spener's attitude vacillates between the Lutheran (that of satisfaction of needs) and Mercantilist arguments for the usefulness of the prosperity of commerce, etc. (*op. cit.,* III, pp. 330, 332; I, p. 418: "the cultivation of tobacco brings money into the country and is thus useful, hence not sinful". Compare also III, pp. 426–7, 429, 434). But he does not neglect to point out that, as the example of the Quakers and the Mennonites shows, one can make profit and yet remain pious; in fact, that even especially high profits, as we shall point out later, may be the direct result of pious uprightness (*op. cit.,* p. 435).

40. These views of Baxter are not a reflection of the economic environment in which he lived. On the contrary, his autobiography

Notes

shows that the success of his home missionary work was partly due to the fact that the Kidderminster tradesmen were not rich, but only earned food and raiment, and that the master craftsmen had to live from hand to mouth just as their employees did. "It is the poor who receive the glad tidings of the Gospel." Thomas Adams remarks on the pursuit of gain: "He [the knowing man] knows . . . that money may make a man richer, not better, and thereupon chooseth rather to sleep with a good conscience than a full purse . . . therefore desires no more wealth than an honest man may bear away" (*Works of the Puritan Divines*, LI). But he does want that much, and that means that every formally honest gain is legitimate.

41. Thus Baxter, *op. cit.*, I, chap. x, 1, 9 (par. 24); I, p. 378, 2. In Prov. xxiii. 4: "Weary thyself not to be rich" means only "riches for our fleshly ends must not ultimately be intended". Possession in the feudal-seigneurial form of its use is what is odious (cf. the remark, *op. cit.*, I, p. 380, on the "debauched part of the gentry"), not possession in itself. Milton, in the first *Defensio pro populo Anglicano*, held the well-known theory that only the middle class can maintain virtue. That middle class here means bourgeoisie as against the aristocracy is shown by the statement that both luxury and necessity are unfavourable to virtue.

42. This is most important. We may again add the general remark: we are here naturally not so much concerned with what concepts the theological moralists developed in their ethical theories, but, rather, what was the effective morality in the life of believers—that is, how the religious background of economic ethics affected practice. In the casuistic literature of Catholicism, especially the Jesuit, one can occasionally read discussions which—for instance on the question of the justification of interest, into which we do not enter here—sound like those of many Protestant casuists, or even seem to go farther in permitting or tolerating things. The Puritans have since often enough been reproached that their ethic is at bottom the same as that of the Jesuits. Just as the Calvinists often cite Catholic moralists, not only Thomas Aquinas, Bernhard of Clairvaux, Bonaventura, etc., but also contemporaries, the Catholic casuists also took notice of heretical ethics. We cannot discuss all that here.

But quite apart from the decisive fact of the religious sanction of the ascetic life for the layman, there is the fundamental difference, even in theory, that these latitudinarian ideas within Catholicism were the products of peculiarly lax ethical theories, not sanctioned by the authority of the Church, but opposed by the most serious and strictest disciples of it. On the other hand, the Protestant idea of the calling in effect placed the most serious enthusiasts for asceticism in the service of capitalistic acquisition. What in the one case might under certain conditions be allowed, appeared in the other as a positive moral good. The fundamental differences of the two ethics, very important in practice, have been finally crystallized, even for modern times, by the Jansenist controversy and the Bull *Unigenitus*.

43. "You may labour in that manner as tendeth most to your success and lawful gain. You are bound to improve all your talents." There follows the passage cited above in the text. A direct parallel between the pursuit of wealth in the Kingdom of Heaven and the pursuit of success in an earthly calling is found in Janeway, *Heaven upon Earth* (*Works of the Puritan Divines*, p. 275).

44. Even in the Lutheran Confession of Duke Christopher of Württemberg, which was submitted to the Council of Trent, objection is made to the oath of poverty. He who is poor in his station should bear it, but if he swore to remain so it would be the same as if he swore to remain sick or to maintain a bad reputation.

45. Thus in Baxter and also in Duke Christopher's confession. Compare further passages like: " . . . the vagrant rogues whose lives are nothing but an exorbitant course; the main begging" etc. (Thomas Adams, *Works of the Puritan Divines*, p. 259). Even Calvin had strictly forbidden begging, and the Dutch Synods campaigned against licences to beg. During the epoch of the Stuarts, especially Laud's regime under Charles I, which had systematically developed the principle of public poor relief and provision of work for the unemployed, the Puritan battle-cry was: "Giving alms is no charity" (title of Defoe's later well-known work). Towards the end of the seventeenth century they began the deterrent system of workhouses for the unemployed (compare Leonard, *Early History of English Poor Relief*, Cambridge, 1900, and H. Levy, *Die Grundlagen des ökonomischen Liberalismus in der Geschichte der englischen Volkswirtschaft*, Jena, 1912, pp. 69 ff.).

46. The President of the Baptist Union of Great Britain and Ireland, G. White, said emphatically in his inaugural address before the assembly in London in 1903 (*Baptist Handbook*, 1904, p. 104): "The best men on the roll of our Puritan Churches were men of affairs, who believed that religion should permeate the whole of life."

47. Here also lies the characteristic difference from all feudal viewpoints. For the latter only the descendants of the parvenu (political or social) can reap the benefit of his success in a recognized station (characteristically expressed in the Spanish *Hidalgo* = *hijo d'algo* = *filius de aliquo* where the *aliquid* means an inherited property). However rapidly these differences are today fading out in the rapid change and Europeanization of the American national character, nevertheless the precisely opposite bourgeois attitude which glorifies business success and earnings as a symptom of mental achievement, but has no respect for mere inherited wealth, is still sometimes represented there. On the other hand, in Europe (as James Bryce once remarked) in effect almost every social honour is now purchasable

Notes

for money, so long as the buyer has not himself stood behind the counter, and carries out the necessary metamorphosis of his property (formation of trusts, etc.). Against the aristocracy of blood, see for instance Thomas Adams, *Works of the Puritan Divines,* p. 216.

48. That was, for instance, already true of the founder of the Familist sect, Hendrik Nicklaes, who was a merchant (Barclay, *Inner Life of the Religious Societies of the Commonwealth,* p. 34).

49. This is, for instance, definitely true for Hoornbeek, since Matt. v. 5 and 1 Tim. iv. 8 also made purely worldly promises to the saints *(op. cit.,* I, p. 193). Everything is the work of God's Providence, but in particular He takes care of His own. *Op. cit.,* p. 192: "Super alios autem summa cura et modis singularissimis versatur Dei providentia circa fideles." There follows a discussion of how one can know that a stroke of luck comes not from the *communis providentia,* but from that special care. Bailey also *(op. cit.,* p. 191) explains success in worldly labours by reference to Providence. That prosperity is often the reward of a godly life is a common expression in Quaker writings (for example see such an expression as late as 1848 in *Selection from the Christian Advices,* issued by the General Meeting of the Society of Friends, London, sixth edition, 1851, p. 209). We shall return to the connection with the Quaker ethics.

50. Thomas Adams's analysis of the quarrel of Jacob and Esau may serve as an example of this attention to the patriarchs, which is equally characteristic of the Puritan view of life *(Works of the Puritan Divines,* p. 235): "His [Esau's] folly may be argued from the base estimation of the birthright" [the passage is also important for the development of the idea of the birthright, of which more later] "that he would so lightly pass from it and on so easy condition as a pottage." But then it was perfidious that he would not recognize the sale, charging he had been cheated. He is, in other words, "a cunning hunter, a man of the fields"; a man of irrational, barbarous life; while Jacob, "a plain man, dwelling in tents" represents the "man of grace".

The sense of an inner relationship to Judaism, which is expressed even in the well-known work of Roosevelt, Köhler *(op. cit.)* found widespread among the peasants in Holland. But, on the other hand, Puritanism was fully conscious of its differences from Hebrew ethics in practical affairs, as Prynne's attack on the Jews (apropos of Cromwell's proposals for toleration) plainly shows. See below, note 58.

51. *Zur bäuerlichen Glaubens- und Sittenlehre.* Von einem thüringischen Landpfarrer, second edition, Gotha, 1890, p. 16. The peasants who are here described are characteristic products of the Lutheran Church. Again and again I wrote Lutheran in the margin when the excellent author spoke of peasant religion in general.

52. Compare for instance the passage cited in Ritschl, *Pietismus* II, p. 158. Spener also bases his objections to change of calling and

pursuit of gain partly on passages in Jesus Sirach. *Theologische Bedenken,* III, p. 426.

53. It is true that Bailey, nevertheless, recommends reading them, and references to the Apocrypha occur now and then, though naturally not often. I can remember none to Jesus Sirach just now (though perhaps by chance).

54. Where outward success comes to persons evidently damned, the Calvinist (as for instance Hoornbeek) comforts himself with the reflection, following the theory of stubbornness, that God allows it to them in order to harden them and make their doom the more certain.

55. We cannot go farther into this point in this connection. We are here interested only in the formalistic character of Puritan righteousness. On the significance of Old Testament ethics for the *lex naturæ* there is much in Troeltsch's *Soziallehren.*

56. The binding character of the ethical norms of the Scriptures goes for Baxter (*Christian Directory,* III, p. 173 f.) so far that they are (1) only a transcript of the law of nature, or (2) bear the "express character of universality and perpetuity".

57. For instance Dowden (with reference to Bunyan), *op. cit.,* p. 39.

58. More on this point in the essays on the *Wirtschaftsethik der Weltreligionen.* The enormous influence which, for instance, the second commandment ("thou shalt not make unto thee a graven image") has had on the development of the Jewish character, its rationality and abhorrence of sensuous culture, cannot be analysed here. However, it may perhaps be noted as characteristic that one of the leaders of the Educational Alliance in the United States, an organization which carries on the Americanization of Jewish immigrants on a grand scale and with astonishing success, told me that one of the first purposes aimed at in all forms of artistic and social educational work was emancipation from the second commandment. To the Israelite's prohibition of any anthropomorphic representation of God corresponds in Puritanism the somewhat different but in effect similar prohibition of idolatry of the flesh.

As far as Talmudic Judaism is concerned, some fundamental traits of Puritan morality are certainly related to it. For instance, it is stated in the Talmud (in Wünsche, *Babyl. Talmud,* II, p. 34) that it is better and will be more richly rewarded by God if one does a good deed for duty's sake than one which is not commanded by the law. In other words, loveless fulfillment of duty stands higher ethically than sentimental philanthropy. The Puritan ethics would accept that in essentials. Kant in effect also comes close to it, being partly of Scotch ancestry and strongly influenced by Pietism in his bringing up. Though we cannot discuss the subject here, many of his formulations are closely related to ideas of ascetic Protestantism.

Notes

But nevertheless the Talmudic ethic is deeply saturated with Oriental traditionalism. "R. Tanchum said to Ben Chanilai, 'Never alter a custom'" (Gemara to Mischna. VII, i, 86b, No. 93, in Wünsche. It is a question of the standard of living of day labourers). The only exception to this conformity is relation to strangers.

Moreover, the Puritan conception of lawfulness as proof evidently provided a much stronger motive to positive action than the Jewish unquestioned fulfillment of all commandments. The idea that success reveals the blessing of God is of course not unknown to Judaism. But the fundamental difference in religious and ethical significance which it took on for Judaism on account of the double ethic prevented the appearance of similar results at just the most important point. Acts toward a stranger were allowed which were forbidden toward a brother. For that reason alone it was impossible for success in this field of what was not commanded but only allowed to be a sign of religious worth and a motive to methodical conduct in the way in which it was for the Puritan. On this whole problem, which Sombart, in his book *Die Juden und das Wirtschaftsleben,* has often dealt with incorrectly, see the essays referred to above. The details have no place here.

The Jewish ethics, however strange that may at first sound, remained very strongly traditionalistic. We can likewise not enter into the tremendous change which the inner attitude toward the world underwent with the Christian form of the ideas of grace and salvation which contained in a peculiar way the seeds of new possibilities of development. On Old Testament lawfulness compare for example Ritschl, *Die christliche Lehre von der Rechtfertigung und Versöhnung,* II, p. 265.

To the English Puritans, the Jews of their time were representatives of that type of capitalism which was involved in war, Government contracts, State monopolies, speculative promotions, and the construction and financial projects of princes, which they themselves condemned. In fact the difference may, in general, with the necessary qualifications, be formulated: that Jewish capitalism was speculative pariah-capitalism, while the Puritan was bourgeois organization of labour.

59. The truth of the Holy Scriptures follows for Baxter in the last analysis from the "wonderful difference of the godly and ungodly" the absolute difference of the renewed man from others, and God's evident quite special care for His chosen people (which may of course be expressed in temptations), *Christian Directory,* I, p. 165.

60. As a characterization of this, it is only necessary to read how tortuously even Bunyan, who still occasionally approaches the atmosphere of Luther's *Freiheit eines Christenmenschen* (for example in *Of the Law and a Christian, Works of the Puritan Divines,* p. 254), reconciles himself with the parable of the Pharisee and the Publican

271

The Protestant Ethic and the Spirit of Capitalism

(see the sermon *The Pharisee and the Publican, op. cit.,* p. 100). Why is the Pharisee condemned? He does not truly keep God's commandments, for he is evidently a sectarian who is only concerned with external details and ceremonies (p. 107), but above all because he ascribes merit to himself, and at the same time, like the Quakers, thanks God for virtue by misuse of His name. In a sinful manner he exalts this virtue (p. 126), and thus implicitly contests God's predestination (p. 139). His prayer is thus idolatry of the flesh, and that is the reason it is sinful. On the other hand, the publican is, as the honesty of his confession shows, spiritually reborn, for, as it is put with a characteristic Puritan mitigation of the Lutheran sense of sin, "to a right and sincere conviction of sin there must be a conviction of the probability of mercy" (p. 209).

61. Printed in Gardiner's *Constitutional Documents.* One may compare this struggle against anti-authoritarian asceticism with Louis XIV's persecution of Port Royal and the Jansenists.

62. Calvin's own standpoint was in this respect distinctly less drastic, at least in so far as the finer aristocratic forms of the enjoyment of life were concerned. The only limitation is the Bible. Whoever adheres to it and has a good conscience, need not observe his every impulse to enjoy life with anxiety. The discussion in Chapter X of the *Instit. Christ* (for instance, "nec fugere ea quoque possumus quæ videntur oblectatione magis quam necessitate inservire") might in itself have opened the way to a very lax practice. Along with increasing anxiety over the *certitudo salutis* the most important circumstance for the later disciples was, however, as we shall point out in another place, that in the era of the *ecclesia militans* it was the small bourgeoisie who were the principal representatives of Calvinistic ethics.

63. Thomas Adams (*Works of the Puritan Divines,* p. 3) begins a sermon on the "three divine sisters" ("but love is the greatest of these") with the remark that even Paris gave the golden apple to Aphrodite!

64. Novels and the like should not be read; they are "wastetimes" (Baxter, *Christian Directory,* I, p. 51). The decline of lyric poetry and folk-music, as well as the drama, after the Elizabethan age in England is well known. In the pictorial arts Puritanism perhaps did not find very much to suppress. But very striking is the decline from what seemed to be a promising musical beginning (England's part in the history of music was by no means unimportant) to that absolute musical vacuum which we find typical of the Anglo-Saxon peoples later, and even to-day. Except for the negro churches, and the professional singers whom the Churches now engage as attractions (Trinity Church in Boston in 1904 for $8,000 annually), in America one also hears as community singing in general only a noise which is intolerable to German ears (partly analogous things in Holland also).

Notes

65. Just the same in Holland, as the reports of the Synods show. (See the resolutions on the Maypole in the Reitmaas Collection, VI, 78, 139.)

66. That the "Renaissance of the Old Testament" and the Pietistic orientation to certain Christian attitudes hostile to beauty in art, which in the last analysis go back to Isaiah and the 22nd Psalm, must have contributed to making ugliness more of a possible object for art, and that the Puritan repudiation of idolatry of the flesh played a part, seems likely. But in detail everything seems uncertain. In the Roman Church quite different demagogic motives led to outwardly similar effects, but, however, with quite different artistic results. Standing before Rembrandt's *Saul and David* (in the Mauritshuis), one seems directly to feel the powerful influence of Puritan emotions. The excellent analysis of Dutch cultural influences in Carl Neumann's *Rembrandt* probably gives everything that for the time being we can know about how far ascetic Protestantism may be credited with a positive fructifying influence on art.

67. The most complex causes, into which we cannot go here, were responsible for the relatively smaller extent to which the Calvinistic ethic penetrated practical life there. The ascetic spirit began to weaken in Holland as early as the beginning of the seventeenth century (the English Congregationalists who fled to Holland in 1608 were disturbed by the lack of respect for the Sabbath there), but especially under the Stadtholder Frederick Henry. Moreover, Dutch Puritanism had in general much less expansive power than English. The reasons for it lay in part in the political constitution (particularistic confederation of towns and provinces) and in the far smaller degree of military force (the War of Independence was soon fought principally with the money of Amsterdam and mercenary armies. English preachers illustrated the Babylonian confusion of tongues by reference to the Dutch Army). Thus the burden of the war of religion was to a large extent passed on to others, but at the same time a part of their political power was lost. On the other hand, Cromwell's army, even though it was partly conscripted, felt that it was an army of citizens. It was, to be sure, all the more characteristic that just this army adopted the abolition of conscription in its programme, because one could fight justly only for the glory of God in a cause hallowed by conscience, but not at the whim of a sovereign. The constitution of the British Army, so immoral to traditional German ideas, had its historical origin in very moral motives, and was an attainment of soldiers who had never been beaten. Only after the Restoration was it placed in the service of the interests of the Crown.

The Dutch *schutterijen,* the champions of Calvinism in the period of the Great War, only half a generation after the Synod of Dordrecht, do not look in the least ascetic in the pictures of Hals. Protests of

273

the Synods against their conduct occur frequently. The Dutch concept of *Deftigkeit* is a mixture of bourgeois-rational honesty and patrician consciousness of status. The division of church pews according to classes in the Dutch churches shows the aristocratic character of this religion even to-day. The continuance of the town economy hampered industry. It prospered almost alone through refugees, and hence only sporadically. Nevertheless, the worldly asceticism of Calvinism and Pietism was an important influence in Holland in the same direction as elsewhere. Also in the sense to be referred to presently of ascetic compulsion to save, as Groen van Prinsterer shows in the passage cited below, note 87.

Moreover, the almost complete lack of *belles lettres* in Calvinistic Holland is of course no accident (see for instance Busken-Huet, *Het Land van Rembrandt).* The significance of Dutch religion as ascetic compulsion to save appears clearly even in the eighteenth century in the writings of Albertus Haller. For the characteristic peculiarities of the Dutch attitude toward art and its motives, compare for example the autobiographical remarks of Constantine Huyghens (written in 1629–31) in *Oud Holland,* 1891. The work of Groen van Prinsterer, *La Hollande et l'influence de Calvin,* 1864, already referred to, offers nothing important for our problems. The New Netherlands colony in America was socially a half-feudal settlement of *patroons,* merchants who advanced capital, and, unlike New England, it was difficult to persuade small people to settle there.

68. We may recall that the Puritan town government closed the theatre at Stratford-on-Avon while Shakespeare was still alive and residing there in his last years. Shakespeare's hatred and contempt of the Puritans appear on every occasion. As late as 1777 the City of Birmingham refused to license a theatre because it was conducive to slothfulness, and hence unfavourable to trade (Ashley, *Birmingham Trade and Commerce,* 1913).

69. Here also it was of decisive importance that for the Puritan there was only the alternative of divine will or earthly vanity. Hence for him there could be no *adiaphora.* As we have already pointed out, Calvin's own view was different in this respect. What one eats, wears, etc., as long as there is no enslavement of the soul to earthly desire as a result, is indifferent. Freedom from the world should be expressed, as for the Jesuits, in indifference, which for Calvin meant an indifferent, uncovetous use of whatever goods the earth offered (pp. 409 ff. of the original edition of the *Instit. Christ).*

70. The Quaker attitude in this respect is well known. But as early as the beginning of the seventeenth century the heaviest storms shook the pious congregation of exiles in Amsterdam for a decade over the fashionable hats and dresses of a preacher's wife (charmingly described in Dexter's *Congregationalism of the Last Three Hundred Years).* Sanford (*op. cit.*) has pointed out that the present-day male

Notes

hair-cut is that of the ridiculous Roundheads, and the equally ridiculous (for the time) male clothing of the Puritans is at least in principle fundamentally the same as that of to-day.

71. On this point again see Veblen's *Theory of Business Enterprise*.

72. Again and again we come back to this attitude. It explains statements like the following: "Every penny which is paid upon yourselves and children and friends must be done as by God's own appointment and to serve and please Him. Watch narrowly, or else that thievish, carnal self will leave God nothing" (Baxter, *op. cit.,* I, 108). This is decisive; what is expended for personal ends is withdrawn from the service of God's glory.

73. Quite rightly it is customary to recall (Dowden, *op. cit.*) that Cromwell saved Raphael's drawings and Mantegna's *Triumph of Cæsar* from destruction, while Charles II tried to sell them. Moreover, the society of the Restoration was distinctly cool or even hostile to English national literature. In fact the influence of Versailles was all-powerful at courts everywhere. A detailed analysis of the influence of the unfavourable atmosphere for the spontaneous enjoyment of every-day life on the spirit of the higher types of Puritan, and the men who went through the schooling of Puritanism, is a task which cannot be undertaken within the limits of this sketch. Washington Irving *(Bracebridge Hall)* formulates it in the usual English terms thus: "It [he says political freedom, we should say Puritanism] evinces less play of the fancy, but more power of the imagination." It is only necessary to think of the place of the Scotch in science, literature, and technical invention, as well as in the business life of Great Britain, to be convinced that this remark approaches the truth, even though put somewhat too narrowly. We cannot speak here of its significance for the development of technique and the empirical sciences. The relation itself is always appearing in everyday life. For the Quakers, for instance, the recreations which are permissible (according to Barclay) are: visiting of friends, reading of historical works, mathematical and physical experiments, gardening, discussion of business and other occurrences in the world, etc. The reason is that pointed out above.

74. Already very finely analysed in Carl Neumann's *Rembrandt,* which should be compared with the above remarks in general.

75. Thus Baxter in the passage cited above, I, p. 108, and below.

76. Compare the well-known description of Colonel Hutchinson (often quoted, for instance, in Sanford, *op. cit.,* p. 57) in the biography written by his widow. After describing all his chivalrous virtues and his cheerful, joyous nature, it goes on: "He was wonderfully neat, cleanly, and genteel in his habit, and had a very good fancy in it; but he left off very early the wearing of anything that was costly." Quite similar is the ideal of the educated and highly civilized Puritan

The Protestant Ethic and the Spirit of Capitalism

woman who, however, is penurious of two things: (1) time, and (2) expenditure for pomp and pleasure, as drawn in Baxter's funeral oration for Mary Hammer (*Works of the Puritan Divines*, p. 533).

77. I think, among many other examples, especially of a manufacturer unusually successful in his business ventures, and in his later years very wealthy, who, when for the treatment of a troublesome digestive disorder the doctor prescribed a few oysters a day, could only be brought to comply with difficulty. Very considerable gifts for philanthropic purposes which he made during his lifetime and a certain openhandedness showed, on the other hand, that it was simply a survival of that ascetic feeling which looks upon enjoyment of wealth for oneself as morally reprehensible, but has nothing whatever to do with avarice.

78. The separation of workshop, office, of business in general and the private dwelling, of firm and name, of business capital and private wealth, the tendency to make of the business a *corpus mysticum* (at least in the case of corporate property) all lay in this direction. On this, see my *Handelsgesellschaften im Mittelalter (Gesammelte Aufsätze zur Sozial- und Wirtschaftsgeschichte*, pp. 312 ff.).

79. Sombart in his *Kapitalismus* (first edition) has already well pointed out this characteristic phenomenon. It must, however, be noted that the accumulation of wealth springs from two quite distinct psychological sources. One reaches into the dimmest antiquity and is expressed in foundations, family fortunes, and trusts, as well as much more purely and clearly in the desire to die weighted down with a great burden of material goods; above all to insure the continuation of a business even at the cost of the personal interests of the majority of one's children. In such cases it is, besides the desire to give one's own creation an ideal life beyond one's death, and thus to maintain the *splendor familiæ* and extend the personality of the founder, a question of, so to speak, fundamentally egocentric motives. That is not the case with that bourgeois motive with which we are here dealing. There the motto of asceticism is "Entsagen sollst du, sollst entsagen" in the positive capitalistic sense of "Erwerben sollst du, sollst erwerben". In its pure and simple non-rationality it is a sort of categorical imperative. Only the glory of God and one's own duty, not human vanity, is the motive for the Puritans; and to-day only the duty to one's calling. If it pleases anyone to illustrate an idea by its extreme consequences, we may recall the theory of certain American millionaires, that their millions should not be left to their children, so that they will not be deprived of the good moral effects of the necessity of working and earning for themselves. To-day that idea is certainly no more than a theoretical soap-bubble.

80. This is, as must continually be emphasized, the final decisive religious motive (along with the purely ascetic desire to mortify the flesh). It is especially clear in the Quakers.

Notes

81. Baxter (*Saints' Everlasting Rest*, p. 12) repudiates this with precisely the same reasoning as the Jesuits: the body must have what it needs, otherwise one becomes a slave to it.

82. This ideal is clearly present, especially for Quakerism, in the first period of its development, as has already been shown in important points by Weingarten in his *Englische Revolutionskirchen*. Also Barclay's thorough discussion (*op. cit*, pp. 519 ff., 533) shows it very clearly. To be avoided are: (1) Worldly vanity; thus all ostentation, frivolity, and use of things having no practical purpose, or which are valuable only for their scarcity (i.e. for vanity's sake). (2) Any unconscientious use of wealth, such as excessive expenditure for not very urgent needs above necessary provision for the real needs of life and for the future. The Quaker was, so to speak, a living law of marginal utility. "Moderate use of the creature" is definitely permissible, but in particular one might pay attention to the quality and durability of materials so long as it did not lead to vanity. On all this compare *Morgenblatt für gebildete Leser*, 1846, pp. 216 ff. Especially on comfort and solidity among the Quakers, compare Schneckenburger, *Vorlesungen*, pp. 96 f.

83. Adapted by Weber from Faust, Act I. Goethe there depicts Mephistopheles as "Die Kraft, die stets das Bödse will, und stets das Gute schafft".—TRANSLATOR'S NOTE.

84. It has already been remarked that we cannot here enter into the question of the class relations of these religious movements (see the essays on the *Wirtschaftsethik der Weltreligionen*). In order to see, however, that for example Baxter, of whom we make so much use in this study, did not see things solely as a bourgeois of his time, it will suffice to recall that even for him in the order of the religious value of callings, after the learned professions comes the husbandman, and only then mariners, clothiers, booksellers, tailors, etc. Also, under mariners (characteristically enough) he probably thinks at least as often of fishermen as of shipowners. In this regard several things in the *Talmud* are in a different class. Compare, for instance, in Wünsche, *Babyl. Talmud*, II, pp. 20, 21, the sayings of Rabbi Eleasar, which though not unchallenged, all contend in effect that business is better than agriculture. In between see II, 2, p. 68, on the wise investment of capital: one-third in land, one-third in merchandise, and one-third in cash.

For those to whom no causal explanation is adequate without an economic (or materialistic as it is unfortunately still called) interpretation, it may be remarked that I consider the influence of economic development on the fate of religious ideas to be very important and shall later attempt to show how in our case the process of mutual adaptation of the two took place. On the other hand, those religious ideas themselves simply cannot be deduced from economic circumstances. They are in themselves, that is beyond doubt, the most powerful plastic elements of national character, and contain a law of development and a compelling force entirely their own. Moreover, the most important differences, so far as non-religious factors play a part, are, as with Lutheranism and Calvinism, the result of political circumstances, not economic.

85. That is what Eduard Bernstein means to express when he says, in the essay referred to above (pp. 625, 681), "Asceticism is a bourgeois virtue." His discussion is the first which has suggested these important relationships. But the connection is a much wider one than he suspected. For not only the accumulation of capital, but the ascetic rationalization of the whole of economic life was involved.

For the American Colonies, the difference between the Puritan North, where, on account of the ascetic compulsion to save, capital in search of investment was always available, from the conditions in the South has already been clearly brought out by Doyle.

86. Doyle, *The English in America,* II, chap. 1. The existence of iron-works (1643), weaving for the market (1659), and also the high development of the handicrafts in New England in the first generation after the foundation of the colonies are, from a purely economic viewpoint, astounding. They are in striking contrast to the conditions in the South, as well as the non-Calvinistic Rhode Island with its complete freedom of conscience. There, in spite of the excellent harbour, the report of the Governor and Council of 1686 said: "The great obstruction concerning trade is the want of merchants and men of considerable estates amongst us" (Arnold, *History of the State of Rhode Island,* p. 490). It can in fact hardly be doubted that the compulsion continually to reinvest savings, which the Puritan curtailment of consumption exercised, played a part. In addition there was the part of Church discipline which cannot be discussed here.

87. That, however, these circles rapidly diminished in the Netherlands is shown by Busken-Huet's discussion (*op. cit.,* II, chaps. iii and iv). Nevertheless, Groen van Prinsterer says (*Handb. der Gesch. van het Vaderland,* third edition, par. 303, note, p. 254), "De Nederlanders verkoopen veel en verbruiken wenig" even of the time after the Peace of Westphalia.

88. For England, for instance, a petition of an aristocratic Royalist (quoted in Ranke, *Engl. Geschichte,* IV, p. 197) presented after the entry of Charles II into London, advocated a legal prohibition of the acquisition of landed estates by bourgeois capital, which should thereby be forced to find employment in trade. The class of Dutch regents was distinguished as an estate from the bourgeois patricians of the cities by the purchase of landed estates. See the complaints, cited by Fruin, *Tien jaren uit den tachtigjarigen oorlog,* of the year 1652, that the regents have become landlords and are no longer merchants. To be sure these circles had never been at bottom strictly

Notes

Calvinistic. And the notorious scramble for membership in the nobility and titles in large parts of the Dutch middle class in the second half of the seventeenth century in itself shows that at least for this period the contrast between English and Dutch conditions must be accepted with caution. In this case the power of hereditary moneyed property broke through the ascetic spirit.

89. Upon the strong movement for bourgeois capital to buy English landed estates followed the great period of prosperity of English agriculture.

90. Even down into this century Anglican landlords have often refused to accept Nonconformists as tenants. At the present time the two parties of the Church are of approximately equal numbers, while in earlier times the Nonconformists were always in the minority.

91. H. Levy (article in *Archiv für Sozialwissenschaft und Sozialpolitik*, XLVI, p. 605) rightly notes that according to the native character of the English people, as seen from numerous of its traits, they were, if anything, less disposed to welcome an ascetic ethic and the middle-class virtues than other peoples. A hearty and unrestrained enjoyment of life was, and is, one of their fundamental traits. The power of Puritan asceticism at the time of its predominance is shown most strikingly in the astonishing degree to which this trait of character was brought under discipline among its adherents.

92. This contrast recurs continually in Doyle's presentation. In the attitude of the Puritan to everything the religious motive always played an important part (not always, of course, the sole important one). The colony (under Winthrop's leadership) was inclined to permit the settlement of gentlemen in Massachusetts, even an upper house with a hereditary nobility, if only the gentlemen would adhere to the Church. The colony remained closed for the sake of Church discipline. The colonization of New Hampshire and Maine was carried out by large Anglican merchants, who laid out large stockraising plantations. Between them and the Puritans there was very little social connection. There were complaints over the strong greed for profits of the New Englanders as early as 1632 (see Weeden's *Economic and Social History of New England*, I, p. 125).

93. This is noted by Petty (*Pol. Arith.*), and all the contemporary sources without exception speak in particular of the Puritan sectarians, Baptists, Quakers, Mennonites, etc., as belonging partly to a propertyless class, partly to one of small capitalists, and contrast them both with the great merchant aristocracy and the financial adventurers. But it was from just this small capitalist class, and not from the great financial magnates, monopolists, Government contractors, lenders to the King, colonial entrepreneurs, promoters, etc., that there originated what was characteristic of Occidental capitalism: the middle-class organization of industrial labour on the basis of private

property (see Unwin, *Industrial Organization in the Sixteenth and Seventeenth Centuries,* London, 1914, pp. 196 ff.). To see that this difference was fully known even to contemporaries, compare Parker's *Discourse Concerning Puritans* of 1641, where the contrast to promoters and courtiers is also emphasized.

94. On the way in which this was expressed in the politics of Pennsylvania in the eighteenth century, especially during the War of Independence, see Sharpless, *A Quaker Experiment in Government,* Philadelphia, 1902.

95. Quoted in Southey, *Life of Wesley,* chap. xxix (second American edition, II, p. 308). For the reference, which I did not know, I am indebted to a letter from Professor Ashley (1913). Ernst Troeltsch, to whom I communicated it for the purpose, has already made use of it.

96. The reading of this passage may be recommended to all those who consider themselves to-day better informed on these matters than the leaders and contemporaries of the movements themselves. As we see, they knew very well what they were doing and what dangers they faced. It is really inexcusable to contest so lightly, as some of my critics have done, facts which are quite beyond dispute, and have hitherto never been disputed by anyone. All I have done is to investigate their underlying motives somewhat more carefully. No one in the seventeenth century doubted the existence of these relationships (compare Manley, *Usury of 6 per Cent. Examined,* 1669, p. 137). Besides the modern writers already noted, poets like Heine and Keats, as well as historians like Macaulay, Cunningham, Rogers, or an essayist such as Matthew Arnold, have assumed them as obvious. From the most recent literature see Ashley, *Birmingham Industry and Commerce* (1913). He has also expressed his complete agreement with me in correspondence. On the whole problem now compare the study by H. Levy referred to above, note 91.

97. Weber's italics.

98. That exactly the same things were obvious to the Puritans of the classical era cannot perhaps be more clearly shown than by the fact that in Bunyan Mr. Money-Love argues that one may become religious in order to get rich, for instance to attract customers. For why one has become religious makes no difference (see p. 114, Tauchnitz edition).

99. Defoe was a zealous Nonconformist.

100. Spener also (*Theologische Bedenken,* pp. 426, 429, 432 ff.), although he holds that the merchant's calling is full of temptations and pitfalls, nevertheless declares in answer to a question: "I am glad to see, so far as trade is concerned, that my dear friend knows no scruples, but takes it as an art of life, which it is, in which much good may be done for the human race, and God's will may be carried out through love." This is more fully justified in other passages by mercantilist arguments. Spener, at times in a purely Lutheran strain,

Notes

designates the desire to become rich as the main pitfall, following 1 Tim. vi, viii, and ix, and referring to Jesus Sirach (see above), and hence rigidly to be condemned. But, on the other hand, he takes some of it back by referring to the prosperous sectarians who yet live righteously (see above, note 39). As the result of industrious work wealth is not objectionable to him either. But on account of the Lutheran influence his standpoint is less consistent than that of Baxter.

101. Baxter, *op. cit.*, II, p. 16, warns against the employment of "heavy, flegmatic, sluggish, fleshly, slothful persons" as servants, and recommends preference for godly servants, not only because ungodly servants would be mere eye-servants, but above all because "a truly godly servant will do all your service in obedience to God, as if God Himself had bid him do it". Others, on the other hand, are inclined "to make no great matter of conscience of it". However, the criterion of saintliness of the workman is not for him the external confession of faith, but the "conscience to do their duty". It appears here that the interests of God and of the employers are curiously harmonious. Spener also (*Theologische Bedenken*, III, p. 272), who otherwise strongly urges taking time to think of God, assumes it to be obvious that workers must be satisfied with the extreme minimum of leisure time (even on Sundays). English writers have rightly called the Protestant immigrants the pioneers of skilled labour. See also proofs in H. Levy, *Die Grundlagen des ökonomischen Liberalimus in der Geschichte der englischen Volkswirtschaft*, p. 53.

102. The analogy between the unjust (according to human standards) predestination of only a few and the equally unjust, but equally divinely ordained, distribution of wealth, was too obvious to be escaped. See for example Hoornbeek, *op. cit.*, I, p. 153. Furthermore, as for Baxter, *op. cit.*, I, p. 380, poverty is very often a symptom of sinful slothfulness.

103. Thomas Adams (*Works of the Puritan Divines*, p. 158) thinks that God probably allows so many people to remain poor because He knows that they would not be able to withstand the temptations that go with wealth. For wealth all too often draws men away from religion.

104. See above, note 45, and the study of H. Levy referred to there. The same is noted in all the discussions (thus by Manley for the Huguenots).

105. *Charisma* is a sociological term coined by Weber himself. It refers to the quality of leadership which appeals to non-rational motives. See *Wirtschaft und Gesellschaft*, pp. 140 ff.—TRANSLATOR'S NOTE.

106. Similar things were not lacking in England. There was, for example, that Pietism which, starting from Law's *Serious Call* (1728), preached poverty, chastity, and, originally, isolation from the world.

107. Baxter's activity in Kidderminster, a community absolutely debauched when he arrived, which was almost unique in the history of the ministry for its success, is at the same time a typical example of how asceticism educated the masses to labour, or, in Marxian terms, to the production of surplus value, and thereby for the first time made their employment in the capitalistic labour relation (putting-out industry, weaving, etc.) possible at all. That is very generally the causal relationship. From Baxter's own view-point he accepted the employment of his charges in capitalistic production for the sake of his religious and ethical interests. From the standpoint of the development of capitalism these latter were brought into the service of the development of the spirit of capitalism.

108. Furthermore, one may well doubt to what extent the joy of the mediæval craftsman in his creation, which is so commonly appealed to, was effective as a psychological motive force. Nevertheless, there is undoubtedly something in that thesis. But in any case asceticism certainly deprived all labour of this worldly attractiveness, to-day for ever destroyed by capitalism, and oriented it to the beyond. Labour in a calling as such is willed by God. The impersonality of present-day labour, what, from the standpoint of the individual, is its joyless lack of meaning, still has a religious justification here. Capitalism at the time of its development needed labourers who were available for economic exploitation for conscience' sake. To-day it is in the saddle, and hence able to force people to labour without transcendental sanctions.

109. Petty, *Political Arithmetick, Works,* edited by Hull, I, p. 262.

110. On these conflicts and developments see H. Levy in the book cited above. The very powerful hostility of public opinion to monopolies, which is characteristic of England, originated historically in a combination of the political struggle for power against the Crown—the Long Parliament excluded monopolists from its membership—with the ethical motives of Puritanism; and the economic interests of the small bourgeois and moderate-scale capitalists against the financial magnates in the seventeenth century. The Declaration of the Army of August 2, 1652, as well as the Petition of the Levellers of January 28, 1653, demand, besides the abolition of excises, tariffs, and indirect taxes, and the introduction of a single tax on estates, above all free trade, i.e. the abolition of the monopolistic barriers to trade at home and abroad, as a violation of the natural rights of man.

111. Compare H. Levy, *Die Grundlagen des ökonomischen Liberalismus in der Geschichte der englischen Volkswirtschaft,* pp. 51f.

112. That those other elements, which have here not yet been traced to their religious roots, especially the idea that honesty is the best policy (Franklin's discussion of credit), are also of Puritan origin, must be proved in a somewhat different connection (see the following essay [not translated here]). Here I shall limit myself to

Notes

repeating the following remark of J. A. Rowntree (*Quakerism, Past and Present,* pp. 95–6), to which E. Bernstein has called my attention: "Is it merely a coincidence, or is it a consequence, that the lofty profession of spirituality made by the Friends has gone hand in hand with shrewdness and tact in the transaction of mundane affairs? Real piety favours the success of a trader by insuring his integrity and fostering habits of prudence and forethought, important items in obtaining that standing and credit in the commercial world, which are requisites for the steady accumulation of wealth" (see the following essay). "Honest as a Huguenot" was as proverbial in the seventeenth century as the respect for law of the Dutch which Sir W. Temple admired, and, a century later, that of the English as compared with those Continental peoples that had not been through this ethical schooling.

113. Well analysed in Bielschowsky's *Goethe,* II, chap. xviii. For the development of the scientific cosmos Windelband, at the end of his *Blütezeit der deutschen Philosophie* (Vol. II of the *Gesch. d. Neueren Philosophie*), has expressed a similar idea.

114. *Saints' Everlasting Rest,* chap. xii.

115. "Couldn't the old man be satisfied with his $75,000 a year and rest? No! The frontage of the store must be widened to 400 feet. Why? That beats everything, he says. In the evening when his wife and daughter read together, he wants to go to bed. Sundays he looks at the clock every five minutes to see when the day will be over—what a futile life!" In these terms the son-in-law (who had emigrated from Germany) of the leading dry-goods man of an Ohio city expressed his judgment of the latter, a judgment which would undoubtedly have seemed simply incomprehensible to the old man. A symptom of German lack of energy.

116. This remark alone (unchanged since his criticism) might have, shown Brentano (*op. cit.*) that I have never doubted its independent significance. That humanism was also not pure rationalism has lately again been strongly emphasized by Borinski in the *Abhandl. der Münchener Akad. der Wiss.,* 1919.

117. The academic oration of v. Below, *Die Ursachen der Reformation* (Freiburg, 1919), is not concerned with this problem, but with that of the Reformation in general, especially Luther. For the question dealt with here, especially the controversies which have grown out of this study, I may refer finally to the work of Hermelink, *Reformation und Gegenreformation,* which, however, is also primarily concerned with other problems.

118. For the above sketch has deliberately taken up only the relations in which an influence of religious ideas on the material culture is really beyond doubt. It would have been easy to proceed beyond that to a regular construction which logically deduced everything characteristic of modern culture from Protestant rational-

ism. But that sort of thing may be left to the type of dilettante who believes in the unity of the group mind and its reducibility to a single formula. Let it be remarked only that the period of capitalistic development lying before that which we have studied was everywhere in part determined by religious influences, both hindering and helping. Of what sort these were belongs in another chapter. Furthermore, whether, of the broader problems sketched above, one or another can be dealt with in the limits of this Journal [the essay first appeared in the *Archiv für Sozialwissenschaft und Sozialpolitik*—TRANSLATOR'S NOTE] is not certain in view of the problems to which it is devoted. On the other hand, to write heavy tomes, as thick as they would have to be in this case, and dependent on the work of others (theologians and historians), I have no great inclination (I have left these sentences unchanged).

For the tension between ideals and reality in early capitalistic times before the Reformation, see now Strieder, *Studien zur Geschichte der kapit. Organizationformen*, 1914, Book II. (Also as against the work of Keller, cited above, which was utilized by Sombart.)

119. I should have thought that this sentence and the remarks and notes immediately preceding it would have sufficed to prevent any misunderstanding of what this study was meant to accomplish, and I find no occasion for adding anything. Instead of following up with an immediate continuation in terms of the above programme, I have, partly for fortuitous reasons, especially the appearance of Troeltsch's *Die Soziallehren der christlichen Kirchen und Gruppen*, which disposed of many things I should have had to investigate in a way in which I, not being a theologian, could not have done it; but partly also in order to correct the isolation of this study and to place it in relation to the whole of cultural development, determined, first, to write down some comparative studies of the general historical relationship of religion and society. These follow. Before them is placed only a short essay in order to clear up the concept of sect used above, and at the same time to show the significance of the Puritan conception of the Church for the capitalistic spirit of modern times.

INDEX

absolution, sacrament of, 116, 134,
acquisition, as principle of economic action, 63
acquisition, impulse to, 16, 56
Adams, Thomas, 223, 237, 258, 259, 266, 267, 269, 272, 281
adaptation, 72
(see selection)
adiaphora, 256, 274
administration, 25
adventurers, capitalistic, 20, 24, 58, 69, 76, 166, 174, 186, 199, 279
after-life, idea of, 97, 109
Alberti, Leon Battista, 194, 202, 262
Anglican Church, 82, 99, 179
Anthony of Florence, 73, 83, 197, 201, 202
anthropology, 30
Anti-authoritarianism, 167
(see also asceticism)
architecture, in West, 15
aristocracy, antagonism to, 150
aristocracy, commerical, 37, 65, 74
Aristotle, 14, 235, 244, 249
Arminians, 200, 217
Arnold, Matthew, 191, 280
Arnold, Samuel G., 278
art in West, 14
Arte di Calimala, 203
arts, Puritan attitude to, 168, 272
asceticism, anti-authoritarian, tendency of, 167, 255
asceticism, definition of, 193–4
asceticism, monastic, 80, 121, 253–4
asceticism, sexual, 158
asceticism, tendency of capitalism to, 71
asceticism, types of, 118
asceticism, worldly, 149, 154
Ashley, W. J., 280
Augsburg Confession, 102, 206, 209

Augustine, St., 101
Aymon, Jean, 190

Bailey, R., 106, 129, 132, 222 228, 231, 233, 238, 245, 259
Baird, Henry M., 219
Bank of England, 186
baptism, 145, 222
Barclay, Robert, 148, 156, 171, 252, 257, 269
Barebones, Praisegod, 243
Bartholomew's day, St., 156
Bax, E. Belfort, 253
Baxter, Richard, 106, 155, 181, 218, 224, 226 ff., 245, 259 ff.
Becker, Bernhard, 247
begging, 177, 268
believers' church, 122, 144
(see also sect)
Below, Georg von, 283
Benedict, St., 118
Bernhard, St., 230, 236, 238, 241, 267
Bernhard of Siena, 197, 201, 202
Bernstein, Eduard, 219, 256, 258, 278, 283
Berthold of Regensburg, 208
Beruf, 79, 204 ff.
Beruf, translation of, 194
Beza, Theodore, 110, 230
bibliocracy, 123, 146
Bielachowsky, Albert, 283
Bohemian Brothers, 197
Bonaventura, St., 236, 242, 267
Bonn, M. J., 217
book-keeping, 22, 67
book-keeping, moral, 124, 238
Borinski, Karl, 283
bourgeoisie, 23, 24, 176
Brassey, Thomas, 198

285

Braune, Wilhelm, 207
Brentano, Lujo, 185, 187, 190, 192, 193, 194, 198, 205, 209, 210, 217, 259, 283
Brodnitz, Georg, 203
brotherly love, 81, 108, 163, 226
Brown, John, 219
Browne, John, 243
Bryce, James, 235, 268
Bucer, letter to, 228
Buckle, Henry Thomas, 44
Buddhism, 228
Bunyan, John, 107, 124, 176, 223, 227, 230, 234, 259, 271, 280
Busken-Huet, 274, 278
Butler, Samuel, 168

C'sarism, Puritan immunity to, 224
calling, duty in a, 54, 62
calling, idea of, 79 ff
Calvin, John, 45, 89
   and predestination, 102
   attitude to *certitudo salutis,* 110
   attitude toward wealth, 157
Calvinism, social organization of, 224
Calw, 44
Campbell, Douglas, 218
capital, definition of, 17
capital, origin of, 68
capital, ownership of, 36
capitalism, concept of, 16
Carlyle, Thomas, 37, 214, 219
Cato, 195, 201
Cavaliers, 88, 169
certitudo salutis, 110, 114–15, 129, 133, 139–40, 203, 226, 229, 272
charisma, 178, 281
Charles I, 166
Charnock, Stuart, 231, 232, 235, 238, 259
Chillingworth, William, 127
chosen people, belief in, 166
   (*see also* elect)

Christopher, Duke of Würtemburg, 268
Cicero, 205
Cistercians, 118
Cluny, Monks of, 118
Colbert, Jean Baptiste, 43
Columella, 196
comfort, idea of, 171
commenda, 17, 20, 58
Communion, admission to, 111, 155
confession, 106, 124, 134, 137, 153
confessions, Baptist, 231
   (*see also* Dordrecht, Westmunster, Augsburg, Hanserd Knolly)
Congregationalists, 217
consilia evangelica, 80, 120, 137
contemplation, 26, 112, 158, 159, 212
conventicles, 130, 131, 167, 245
conversion, 140
Corinthians, 1st Epistle to the, 84, 164, 206, 208, 214
Cornelius, Carl Adolf, 253, 255
counterpoint, 14
Court, Peter de la, 177
Cramer, S., 257
Cranmer, Thomas, 210
creation, joy of, 282
Cromwell, Oliver, 82, 156, 213, 226, 275
Cromwell, Richard, 251
Crosby, Thomas, 235
Cunningham, William, 280

Da Costa, 226
Defoe, Daniel, 180, 280
Deissmann, Adolf, 209
democracy, 224
Denifle, Heinrich, 211
Deventer, Provincial Synod of, 260
Dexter, H. M., 219, 252, 274
Dieterich, A., 205

Index

dilettantes, 29
Dionysius of Halicarnassus, 209
Dippel, Johann Conrad, 248
discipline, Church, 97, 152, 155, 178
discipline, monastic, 174
distribution of goods, unequal, 177
Divine Comedy, 87
Döllinger, Johann Joseph Iquaz von, 107
domestic industry, 21, 192
Dordrecht, Synod of, 99, 102, 226, 240
Dowden, Edward, 176, 221, 222, 258, 270, 275
Doyle, John Andrew, 172, 219, 278
Dunckards, 150

Eck Bible translation, 10
Economic interpretation of History (see Materialism, historical)
education and capitalism, 38
Eger, Karl, 211
elect, aristocracy of, 104, 121, 122, 131–8, 151, 242
elect, membership in, 110
emotion, emphasis on, 131, 135, 138–40
Enlightenment, The, 45, 70, 106, 182
Entzauberung der Welt, 221
(see also magic, elimination of)
Erastianism, 217
d'Este, Renata, 237
Ethnography, 29
experiment, method of, 13

faith, justification by, 112, 114
faith, results of, 114
(see also proof)
fatalism, 131, 232
feudal state, 16
feudalism, 185
Fieschi, 235

Firth, Charles Harding, 219, 236
Fleischütz, Bible translator, 207
formalism, as characteristic of Puritanism, 166
Fox, George, 89, 146, 148, 253, 266
Francis of Assisi, 120, 146, 254
Franciscans, 253
Franck, Sebastian, 121, 220
Francke, August Hermann, 132–3, 138, 246
Franklin, Benjamin, 48, 50, 64, 71, 82, 124, 151, 158, 180, 192, 195, 263
Frederick, Henry, Stadholder, 273
Frederick William I, 44, 250
Freytag, Gustav, 242
Froude, James Anthony, 223
Fruin, Robert, 219, 278
Fugger, Jacob, 51, 192
Fuggers, 82, 202, 213
Fuller, Thomas, 231
Funck, 201

Gardiner, Samuel Rawson, 213, 219, 272
Gerhard, Johannes, 229
Gerhard, Paul, 88
Giles, St., 146
God, Calvinistic conception of, 103
Goethe, Wolfgang, 151, 181, 261, 277
Goodwin, John, 246
Gorichem, Synod Of, 260
Gothein, Eberhard, 43
Grab, Hermann von, 222
Grubbe, Edward, 253

Haller, Albertus, 274
Hals, Frans, 273
handicrafts, 21, 38, 65
Hanna, C. A., 189

287

Hanserd Knolly, Confession of, 125, 220, 221, 225, 231, 257
harmony, 14
Harnack, Adolf, 262
Hasbach, Wilhelm, 198
Hebrews, 265
  (*see* Jews)
Heidegger, Johann Heinrich, 228
Heine, Heinrich, 280
Hellpach, W., 244
Henry, Matthew, 238, 259, 261
Heppe, Heinrich Ludwig, 221, 228, 247
heredity, influence of, 30, 279
Hermelink, Heinrich, 283
Herrnhut, 135, 248
Hertling, Georg von, 188
historical individual, 47
Hoenicke, 238
Hoffmann, 255
honesty, best policy, 282
Honigsheim, Paul, 212, 222, 226, 229
Hooker, Richard, 127
Hoops, Johannes, 207
Hoornbeek, J., 221, 223, 228, 232, 234, 259
Howe, Daniel Wait, 219
Howe, John, 237, 251, 259
Hudibras, 235
  (*see also* Butler)
Hugenots, 39, 43, 201
Humiliati, 254
Hundeshagen, Carl Bernhard, 226
Huntingdon, Lady, 125
Huss, John, 95, 198
Hutchinson, Colonel John, 275
Huyghens, Constantine, 274

ideal type, 71, 98, 200
idolatry of the flesh, 105, 146, 150, 169, 171, 224, 266, 270, 272–3
Ignatius, St., 119
Independents, 99, 122, 217, 242
India, religious teaching of, 265
individualism, 105, 222

indulgence, 120
industria, 73, 196, 197
inner light, doctrine of, 147
institution for salvation, church as, 227
interest, prohibition of, 73, 201
interests, capitalistic, influence of, 24
Irving, Washington, 261, 275
isolation of individual, 108

Jacoby, Ludwig S., 250
Jains, 191, 197, 228
James I, 99, 166
James, William, 232
Janeway, James, 259, 268
Jansenists, 221, 222, 229
Jaspers, Karl, 186
Jerome, St., 205
Jesuits, 81, 118, 124, 267, 274, 277
Jesus, 83
Jews as minorities, 39, 191
Jews as representing adventurer's capitalism, 186, 271
Jews, problem of, 187, 197
Jews, Puritans' relation to, 165, 180
Jews, rationalization of, 117, 222
Job, Book of, 164
Jones, Rufus B., 253
joy of living, 41, 42, 45
joy of living, relation of Puritanism to, 163, 166–7, 173
Judaism (*see* Jews)
Jülicher, A., 214
Jüngst, Johannes, 251

Kampschulte, F. Wilhelm, 218
Kant, Immanuel, 270
Kattenbusch, Ferdinand, 255
Kautsky, Karl, 258
Keats, John, 44, 270
Keller, F., 191, 200, 284
Keller, Gottfried, 107

Index

Kierkegaard, Soren, 109
Klages, Ludwig, 186
Knolley, Hanserd (see Hanserd Knolley)
Knox, John, 45, 219
de Kock, 226
Koehler, Walther, 211
Koester, A., 211
Köhler, August, 219, 226, 247, 269
Kolde, Theodor, 251
Kommanditgesellschaft, 20
Köstlin, Julius, 221
Kürnberger, Ferdinand, 50

Labadie, Jean de, 240, 241, 245
laboratory, modern, 13
labour, division of, 81, 160, 161
labour, rational, capitalistic organization of, 21, 22, 24, 166
labour, valuation of, 158
Lambeth Article, 220
Lamprecht, Karl, 244, 248
Lang, J. C., 252
Laud, Bishop William, 179, 213
Lavelye, Émile, 191
law, canon, 14, 73
law, mosaic, 123, 165, 271
law, natural (see lex naturæ)
law, rational structure of, 25
law, Roman, 14, 77
Lenau, Nicolaus, 192
Leonard, Ellen M., 268
Levy, Hermann, 213, 217, 268, 279, 281, 282
lex naturæ, 109, 114, 211, 256, 270
liberum arbitrium, 57, 77
Liguori, Alfonso of, 107
literature, Puritan attitude to, 168
Lobstein, Paul, 229
Lodensteyn, Jodocus van, 241
Loofs, Friedrich, 250, 252
Lorimer, G., 253
Löscher, Valentine Ernest, 246
Luthardt, Christoph Ernst, 214
Luther, use of "calling," 164, 204 ff.

Lutheranism, ethical theory of, 238
Lutheranism, moral helplessness of, 126
Lutheranism, relation to Pietism, 95
Lutheranism, relation to world, 87, 160
Lutheranism, traditionalistic tendency of, 86
Lutheranism, and Predestination, 102

Macaulay, Thomas Babington, 219, 220, 223, 280
Machiavelli, Nicolo, 14, 107
magic, elimination of, 105, 117, 149
Magna Charta, 217
Maliniak, J., 200
Manley, Thomas, 280
manors, 21
Marcks, Erich, 218
marriage, Puritan conception of, 158, 263
masserizia, 195
Masson, David, 219, 220
materialism, historical, 24, 55, 75, 90–2, 183, 266, 277
Maurenbrecher, Max, 211
Maurice of Orange, 235
Meissner, Balthasar, 229
Melancthon, Philip, 102, 227, 239, 244
Menno, Simons, 89, 145
Mennonites, 44, 144, 149, 150, 217, 255, 256, 257
mercantilism, 23, 152, 197, 242
Merx, Albrecht, 203, 204, 208
Milton, John, 87, 101, 220, 267
minorities, 39, 190
Mirbt, Carl, 242
missionary, 136, 225
monasticism, 118, 119, 158, 174

money-lenders, 20
monopolies, 65, 82, 179, 271
Montesquieu, Charles Louis de, 45
Moravians, 96, 135
Mormons, 264
Motley, John Lothrop, 219
Müller, Karl, 219, 253, 255
Münster, 149, 253
Murch, J., 253
music, 14
Muthmann, 223
mystics, German, 79, 86, 112, 132

Naber, 219
Neal, David, 235
needs, satisfaction of, 63
Neumann, Carl, 273, 275
Newman, A. H., 253
Nicklaes, Hendrik, 269
Nicolai, Philip, 229
Nietzsche, Friedrich, 232
Nuyens, W. J. F., 219, 221

Offenbacher, Martin, 188
official, 16
oikos, 22
Old Testament, 123
Oldenbarneveld, Joan van, 99
Olevianus, Kaspar, 221, 228
organization, capitalistic forms of, 64, 67
organization, Church, 128
organization, social, superiority of Calvinism in, 108
orphans, Amsterdam, 226
ostentation, avoidance of, 71
otherworldliness, 40, 41, 42, 118, 145
Owen, John, 237

Parker, 179
Parsees, 191
parvenus, 65, 71, 163, 268
Pascal, Blaise, 81, 113, 211 222, 227, 229
Paterson, William, 186

Paul, St., 84, 159, 160, 212
Petty, Sir William, 43, 179, 189, 279, 282
piece-rates, 59
Pierson, Allard, 219
Pietism, 47
Plitt, Hermann, 247
Plutarch, 236
Polenz, Gottlob van, 219
Poor relief, English, 178
poverty, glorification of, 136
Prætorius, Abdias, 229
Praxis pietatis, 129, 130
Precisians, 117
predestination, doctrine of, 98 ff., 109 ff., 121, 125, 128, 131, 143, 148, 226, 227, 232
Presbyterians, 125, 146
Price, Thomas, 219
Prinsterer, Groen van, 219, 274, 278
printing, 15
privileges, 65
profitableness, as sign of grace, 162
proletariat, 25
proof, doctrine of, 112, 115, 126, 129, 133, 137, 141, 142, 153, 203
Prynne, William, 179, 269
psychology, in sociological investigation, 31, 244
Puritanism, attitude to sensuous culture, 105
Puritanism, definition of, 96
putting-out system, 23, 66, 179

Quakers, 39, 44, 86, 144ff., 150, 217, 276, 283
(*see also* Barclay, Robert)

Rabelais, François, 190
Rachfel, Felix, 186
Ranke, Leopold von, 219
rationalism, 26, 40, 75
(*see also* rationalization)

Index

rationalization, 25, 68, 136, 147
(see also rationalism; magic, elimination of)
Rembrandt, 169, 273
Renaissance, Puritan relation to 168
Rhodes, Cecil, 42
Ritschl, Albrecht, 134, 139, 219, 221, 229, 237, 240, 245, 247, 253, 254, 271
Rogers, Thorold, 280
Roloff, Gustav, 235
romanticism, 71
romanticists, 65
Roosevelt, Theodore, 269
Roundheads, 88
Rowntree, J. A., 283

Sack, Carl Heinrich, 219
sacraments, 104
Salmasius, Claudius, 201
salvation, conditions of, 113
sanctification, 138, 140
sanctions, psychological, 97, 128, 178, 197, 267
Sanford, John Langton, 123, 217, 274
saving, ascetic compulsion to, 172, 276
Savoy Declaration, 114, 125, 231
Schäfer, Dietrich, 222
Schechter, Solomon, 204
Scheibe, Max, 221
Schell, Hermann, 188
Schmoller, Gustav, 214
Schneckenburger, Matthias, 112, 143, 214, 219, 228, 230, 232, 251, 277
Scholasticism, 83, 168
(see also Thomas Aquinas)
Schortinghuis, Wilhelinus, 229, 244
Schulze-Gaevernitz, G. von, 198
Schwenkfeld, Caspar, 146, 256
science, Puritan attitude to, 168, 249
science, Western characteristics of, 13, 15, 24

Scotists, 202
Scotus, Duns, 235
sea loans, 20
sect, distinguished from church, 145, 152, 254
(see also believers' church)
Sedgwick, Obadiah, 228, 231, 234, 259
Sée, Henri, 185
Seeberg, 211, 214, 215, 219, 235
Seiss, J. A., 253
selection, concept of, 55, 72
Seneca, 205
Septuagint, 204
Sermon on the Mount, 250
Shakespeare, William, 274
Simmel, Georg, 185, 193
Sirach, Jesus, 79, 164, 204 ff.
Skeats, Herbert S., 252
Skoptsi, 197
Sloth, 264
Smend, Rudolf, 204
Smith, Adam, 81, 161
socialism, 23
Sombart, Werner, 63, 75, 185, 187, 191, 192, 193–8, 200 ff., 214, 217, 259, 261, 271, 276
South Sea Bubble, 186
Southey, Robert, 251, 280
Spangenberg, A. G., 136, 223, 248
Spener, Philip Jacob, 95, 132–5, 138, 150, 156, 222, 245, 247, 257, 262, 266
Spinoza, Baruch de, 245
Sports, Book of, 166
St. André, Dupin de, 190
State, characteristics of, 179
State, modern, 16, 72
Sternberg, H. von, 214
Strieder, Jacob, 284
Stundists, 197

talents, parable of the, 163
Talmud, 83, 165, 207, 270, 277

Tauler, Johannes, 86, 208, 212, 216, 229, 236, 245
Taylor, Hudson, 225
Taylor, J. J., 219
Teellinck, W., 241
Teersteegen, 245
Terminism, doctrine of, 133
theodicy problem, 109
Theophylaktos, 209
Tholuck, A., 240
Thomas à Kempis, St., 242, 245
Thomas, Alton C., 253
Thomas Aquinas, St., 80, 150, 159, 160, 196, 211, 215, 267
Thucydides, 14
time is money, 48, 158
time, waste of, 157
toleration, idea of, 242
traditionalism, 36, 59 ff., 65 ff., 76, 84, 164, 191, 215, 265, 271
Troeltsch, Ernst, 188, 211, 214, 218, 219, 236, 239, 255, 270, 284
Tyerman, Luke, 251
Tyermans, 218
Tyndale, William, 210

Ullrich, F., 227, 240
uniformity, tendency toward, 169
unio mystica, 112, 113, 130
Unwin, George, 280
utilitarianism, 52, 81, 109, 126, 161, 176, 183, 196, 265
utilitarianism, hygienic, 263

value, judgments of, 29, 98, 112, 182, 236
Van Wyck, A., 227
Varro, 196
Veblen, Thorstein, 258, 275
Vedder, Henry C., 253
Vischer, F. T., 247
Voët, Gisbert, 45, 218, 234, 241, 259
Volgate, 205
Voltaire, 77

wages and productivity, 60, 198
Wagner, Richard, 107
Wahl, Adalbert, 191
waiting for Spirit, 148
Ward, Frank G., 214
Warneck, Johannes, 225
Watson, Richard, 251
Watts, Isaac, 251
wealth, temptations of, 156, 172, 174
wealth, uses approved by Puritans, 171
Weingarten, H., 219, 277
Wesley, John, 89, 125, 135, 140, 142, 175, 218, 227, 251
Westminster Confession, 99, 220, 228, 244
Westminster, Synod of, 99, 102, 156, 226
Whitaker, W., 242
White, G., 246, 268
Whitefield, George, 125, 251
William of Orange, 242
Williams, Roger, 243
Windelband, Wilhelm, 236, 249, 283
Wiskemann, Heinrich, 214
Wittich, W., 190
Wolff, Christian, 263
workers, women, 62
works, good, 115, 117, 148
works, salvation by, 115, 116, 141, 143, 150
Wupperthal, 44
Wyclif, John, 198, 203, 210

Xenophon, 196

Zeller, 226
Zinzendorf, Count Nicolaus, 95, 132, 134, 138, 143, 178, 248, 264
Zwingli, Ullrich, 87
Zwinglianism, 217